Mormons and Mormonism in U.S. Government Documents

Mormons and Mormonism in U.S. Government Documents

A BIBLIOGRAPHY

Compiled by

Susan L. Fales

and

Chad J. Flake

University of Utah Press
Salt Lake City, Utah
1989

Copyright 1989 University of Utah Press

Printed in the United States of America

Fales, Susan L., 1943-

    Mormons and Mormonism in U.S. government documents : a
bibliography / compiled by Susan L. Fales and Chad J. Flake.
        p.   cm.
    Includes indexes.
    ISBN 0-87480-312-8
    1. Mormon Church--Bibliography. 2. Mormons--Bibliography.
3. Church of Jesus Christ of Latter-Day Saints--Bibliography.
4. United States--Government publications--Bibliography.
I. Flake, Chad J. II. Title. III. Titles: Mormons and
Mormonism in United States government documents.
Z6611.M77F35   1989
[BX8635.2]
016.2893--dc19
                                                    88-39653
                                                    CIP

Contents

Introduction

"Mormonism is one of the monstrosities of the age in which
we live," wrote John Cradlebaugh of Nevada in the <u>Congressional
Globe</u> during the Civil War (see entry 245). Perhaps no other
religious group in America has found itself under such minute
scrutiny by government and political leaders as has the Mormon
Church. Yet the results of this examination, printed in the
pages of government documents, have always been difficult, at
best, to access. Recent empirical evidence by Peter Hernon in
his book <u>Use of Government Publications by Social Scientists</u> has
reinforced the perception that government documents are difficult
to access and frequently underutilized even among faculty members
whose area of expertise is American history.

Historians of the Mormon experience have, however, often
used government publications in their works. The 1986 University
of Illinois Press publication by Edward Leo Lyman entitled
<u>Political Deliverance: The Mormon Quest for Utah Statehood</u> makes
ample use of government publications as it develops the complicated
story of the politics of the Utah statehood process. Gustive
Larsen's earlier classic work on Utah statehood, <u>The Americanization
of Utah for Statehood</u>, can also be cited as a representative work
in retrieving the information buried in government publications.
Both of these fine works relied heavily on the pages of the
<u>Congressional Globe</u> and the <u>Congressional Record</u>. Government
documents also assist in revealing Utah and Mormon involvement in
the Civil War in Everett B. Long's 1981 book entitled <u>The Saints
and the Union: Utah Territory during the Civil War</u>.

Despite these excellent examples of historical studies of
the Mormon experience, strengthened by using government publications,
there are still areas of government publishing which have not
been touched by the scholar of Mormonism. The brief, but exciting,
entries in <u>The Foreign Relations of the United States</u> have never
been cited by Mormon scholars, and yet these entries have the
potential for opening up new understanding of the Mormon international
experience, missionary work, and emigration, as well as leading
the scholar to additional sources at the National Archives. The
understanding within the scholarly community of the inheritance
rights of children of polygamous families could be enhanced by
better utilization of Territorial Supreme Court reports known as
<u>The Territory of Utah Reports,</u> and of their accompanying briefs
and abstracts.

This guide to Mormon entries in printed government documents
will ease the research process for scholars of the Mormon experience
as they seek for a more complete understanding of the Mormon and
United States government relationship.

Scope

The government publishing period for the first 100 years of
the Mormon Church's existence (1830-1930) is covered in this
guide. In reality, although a full hundred years of government

publishing was searched, it was not until 1838 that an entry
regarding the Mormons was located. This chosen time period
coincides with the years found in Chad Flake's <u>A Mormon Bibliography</u>
<u>1830-1930</u>, although the cutoff date of 1930 is more than a
coincidence. The practice of polygamy, in the eyes of the
federal government, was resolved with the issuance of the Manifesto
in 1890, the granting of statehood in 1896, and the Reed Smoot
hearings of 1904-1907. Public belief and acceptance of the
Mormon Church's changed position regarding the practice of
polygamy took longer to accomplish. Numerous groups in the early
1920s were stirred up by the National Reform Association to
submit petitions and memorials to Congress requesting a constitutional
amendment to prohibit polygamy. However, by the late 1920s
government publishing regarding the Mormons slowed to an insignificant
amount.

Included within the scope of the printed publications
searched were federal documents and Utah territorial documents.
Until statehood in 1896, Utah as a territory produced a number of
publication series, most notably the governor's reports, Utah
Territorial Supreme Court reports with their accompanying briefs
and abstracts, and the Utah Commission reports.

In addition to territorial documents, a liberal view of what
constitutes a government document is used. Sometimes a privately
published work brought a government manuscript into print.
Entry 1283a, entitled <u>The Inside of Mormonism: A Judicial</u>
<u>Examination of the Endowment Oaths Administered in all the</u> Mormon
<u>Temples</u>, was published by an anti-Mormon faction to bring to
public attention the proceedings of the Third Judicial District
Court of Utah.

Other instances of what appeared to be private publishing
were in fact examples of contracted printing prior to widespread
use of the Government Printing Office. The Government Printing
Office was actually empowered to handle all government printing
in 1860, but it did not become the primary U.S. printer until an
act of 1895. For example, many of the early Serial Sets were
published by prominent government printing contractors such as
Thomas Allen, Blair & Rives, Wendell and Van Benthuysen, or A. O.
P. Nicholson, rather than the Government Printing Office.

Supreme Court briefs were often privately published by the
lawyers concerned. However, because of their intimate ties with
the officially published Territorial Supreme Court and U.S.
Supreme Court decisions, it seems important to include them.
According to the National Archives, many lawyers, especially when
it was apparent they would lose their case, had their legal
briefs printed privately. Entry 856a is an example of such a
publication--the argument of Franklin S. Richards, attorney for
the appellant in the Hans Nielsen polygamy case--printed by the
Deseret News Company in Salt Lake City.

In addition to the problem of government versus private
publisher, the question of subject content was crucial. Entries
were examined to determine if they contained direct or even
indirect references to Mormonism. The number of entries for
Brigham Young could have been significantly expanded if <u>all</u> of
his messages as governor or Indian Superintendent had been
included, rather than only those containing direct or indirect
references to Mormonism. Researchers interested solely in

Brigham Young may be disappointed to find that all of these
entries are not provided; however, the number of such reports is
significant. This same policy applied to the messages of all the
territorial governors.

The issue of Utah statehood posed another problem. Although
numerous entries under that subject appear in the index, others
are available in government publications not extracted because
nothing in the entry related to Mormonism. This may disappoint
some researchers interested primarily in Utah history as opposed
to Mormon history. The scope has been extended to include some
items that do not explicitly appear to be related to Mormonism,
but are important to Mormon history, such as the issue of
probate court jurisdiction in Utah Territory. Also included
from the Congressional Record are numerous petitions and memorials,
frequently only referred to rather than printed in full. These
are included because they provide important research leads to any
originals located at the National Archives.

Sources Examined

A number of sources were examined to ensure that all printed
works had been thoroughly searched. Chad Flake's A Mormon
Bibliography 1830-1930 was searched for government publishing
entries. Four hundred eighteen documents from that source became
the nucleus of this project. In his bibliography Flake concentrated
on government publications published as disbound Serial Set
documents or Congressional and Senatorial speeches published
separately from the Congressional Globe or the Congressional
Record.

To find more of the separately published documents, The
Monthly Catalog, the Serial Set Index, U.S. Committee Hearings
Index, U.S. Congressional Committee Prints Index, and the Unpublished
U.S. Senate Committee Hearings Index were searched. Next, all
major government documents series were scrutinized, such as the
Congressional Globe and the Congressional Record, the Serial Set,
War of the Rebellion, the Foreign Relations of the United States,
and annual reports of the War Department and other agencies such
as Interior, Education and the Bureau of Indian Affairs. A
complete listing of the document series that yielded entries can
be found in a separate index at the end of this publication.

These series provided numerous entries of their own, but
they also led to other materials. For example, the Globe and
Record listed bills ordered to be printed. Over 150 of these
bills were located only at the Law Library of the Library of
Congress.

Arrangement

A year-by-year chronological arrangement by event date,
subdivided alphabetically by author or title, dramatically
reveals the rise and fall of governmental concerns. It was for
this reason that the chronological arrangement was chosen rather
than the alphabetical.

Within the pages of government documents the concerns of
federal officials as well as Mormons are revealed. The first four
entries, spanning the years 1838 through 1841, were related to
the Mormon Church's difficulties in Missouri. Citations in the

subsequent years through 1849 concentrated primarily on government exploring expeditions that made brief mention of the Mormons. With the official announcement of polygamy in 1852, an increase in government prose might have been expected. Although 1852 included more entries than any previous year, with 16, the dominant theme was not polygamy, but Brigham Young's theocracy as portrayed through the eyes of Brandebury, Brocchus, and Harris. The first polygamy entry was in 1854 with a speech by August Caesar Dodge of Iowa printed in the <u>Congressional Globe</u> Appendix (entry 65c).

In tracing the concerns of government officials in chronological order, we found that the period 1857-58 was dominated by the Utah Expedition. Little interest was shown for Mormonism in the early 1860s except in the series known as <u>The Official Records of the War of the Rebellion</u>, where numerous letters were recorded. Patrick Edward Connor, a severe critic of Brigham Young and Mormonism, who later chose to remain in Utah to build up its mining industry, was a major contributor during this period.

In 1870, discussions on Shelby Cullom's bill (H.R. 1089) to suppress polygamy began. The consequences of both a belief in and the practice of polygamy were recorded consistently from this time onward in government reports. The first case before the Territorial Supreme Court and the U.S. Supreme Court was that of George Reynolds in 1875. Interest generated between federal officials and polygamous Mormons reached an apex in the 1880s. The highest number of entries occurred in 1882 with 88, but in 1886, 1888, and 1890 (the year of the Manifesto), there was enough interest to result in 70, 76, and 75 entries respectively. Preoccupation with polygamy continued into the twentieth century with B. H. Roberts' contested election of 1889-1900 and the pivotal Reed Smoot investigations of 1904-1907. In 1924, constitutional amendments and petitions to prohibit polygamy were still being proposed.

Use

To facilitate use of these publications, where possible, at the end of each entry, the government document classification number, known as the Superintendent of Documents classification, is provided. There may be two call numbers listed; the first is the original number assigned to that particular series of documents and the second is the subsequent classification change that may have occurred over the years from governmental reorganization. Most major academic and research libraries have these series of government publications, and many of these libraries use the Superintendent of Documents classification scheme.

For the government publications having no document call numbers, a symbol identifying the libraries owning either an original, or a photocopy, of a particular document is provided. The libraries were identified through personal research at a particular library or through the pages of the <u>National Union Catalog</u>; of course there may be other libraries that have added these publications since the printing of the <u>National Union Catalog</u>. The library symbols are included at the end of this introduction.

Most entries have been annotated. The majority of entries not annotated are the constitutional amendment bills proposed repeatedly

in the early twentieth century. A handful of other entries had
titles that were self-explanatory and did not require further
explanation. The annotations are brief but describe the richness
and variety of subject matter included. In addition to the
annotations and in an attempt to further reveal the scope and
flavor of the subjects treated in printed government reports, a
sampling of quotations is included at the beginning of each year.

Each citation is consecutively numbered throughout the
bibliography. Although the number of entries appears to be
1,440, in reality there are 1,469. This apparent discrepancy
occurred because of the insertion of entries, or the occasional
need to leave an entry number vacant, after the indexing had been
completed (see entries 65a and 520 as examples).

The Flake numbers found in A Mormon Bibliography 1830-1930
are listed in the entry when available. The use of these numbers
has become standardized among book dealers listing Mormon entries
in their catalogs. Also, many libraries with extensive Mormon
collections use this bibliography to list call numbers of the
publications held in their collections. Of the 1,467 entries,
418 have Flake numbers, indicating that approximately 28 percent
of the entries in this bibliography can also be found in A Mormon
Bibliography. In addition to the 418 Flake numbers, there are
approximately 75 entries that will be included in Flake's supplement
to A Mormon Bibliography, soon to be published. These Flake
numbers include a small letter at the end of their entry number.

The bibliographical citations in the two guides often differ
significantly. Flake provided rare book cataloging entries,
which include a physical description of the binding, size of the
publication in centimeters, and the existence of illustrative
material. A standardized bibliographical citation, based on both
The Chicago Manual of Style and the Complete Guide to Citing
Government Documents, is used in this bibliography, because its
major purposes are to provide easier access for researchers to
relatively inaccessible materials, and to assist scholars in
appropriately citing these materials in their historical works.

Finally, three indexes are provided. The first index is
arranged by subject, author, and court case names. The second
index is a title index which includes titles of separately
published documents, but not entries from the Globe or Record or
other series where, because material had often been extracted
from part of a larger section of the work, it was felt that the
title would be meaningless. The series index provides a listing
of all the specific series examined where any entry was found.

Susan L. Fales
Chad J. Flake

SAMPLE ENTRY

Entry Number

Government Document
Call Number

[357] Wheeler, George Montague. Preliminary report concerning
explorations and surveys principally Nevada and Arizona,
prosecuted in accordance with paragraph 2, Special
Order No. 109, War Department, March 18, 1871, and
letter of instructions of March 18, 1871, and letter of
instructions of March 23, 1871, from Brigadier General
A. A. Humphreys, Chief of Engineers, 1871. Washington:
Govt. Print. Off., 1872. 96p. [W8.1:871]

Field operations, primarily in Nevada and Arizona in
1871; includes side expedition of First Lieut. Daniel
W. Lockwood into southwestern Utah. References to
Mormons, Mormon roads pp. 26, 65-66, 70-72, 74-75, 85-
86, 91. Areas included are mail routes, Mormon settlements
in Nevada such as Saint Joe and Saint Thomas and the
areas of St. George and the Muddy and Virgin River.

[Flake 9720]
CU-B, DLC, UPB, US1C

Library Location Symbols

Entry Number from
Chad Flake's
A Mormon Bibliography
1830-1930

Key to Library Symbols

CLU	University of California at Los Angeles
CSmH	Henry E. Huntington Library, San Marino, Calif.
CtY	Yale University, New Haven, Conn.
CU	University of California, Berkeley, Calif.
CU-B	University of California, Bancroft Library, Berkeley, Calif.
CU-L	University of California Law Library, Berkeley, Calif.
DHC	Holy Cross College Library, Washington, D.C.
DHU	Howard University Library, Washington, D.C.
DLC	U.S. Library of Congress, Washington, D.C.
DNA	U.S. National Archives Library, Washington, D.C.
IAr	Idaho State Archives, Boise, Idaho
ICHi	Chicago Historical Society, Chicago, Ill.
ICN	Newberry Library, Chicago, Ill.
ICU	University of Chicago, Chicago, Ill.
IdB	Boise Public Library
InU	Indiana University, Bloomington, Ind.
KU	University of Kansas, Lawrence, Kansas
MB	Boston Public Library, Boston, Mass.
MH	Harvard University, Cambridge, Mass.
MiU	University of Michigan, Ann Arbor, Mich.
MnHi	Minnesota Historical Society, St. Paul, Minn.
MoInRc	Reorganized Church of Jesus Christ of Latter Day Saints, Independence, Mo.
MoK	Kansas City Public Library, Kansas City, Mo.
MoU	University of Missouri, Columbia, Mo.
MtU	University of Montana, Missoula, Mont.
NjP	Princeton University, Princeton, N.J.
NN	New York Public Library, New York, N.Y.
OclWhi	Western Reserve Historical Society, Cleveland, Ohio
OO	Oberlin College, Oberlin, Ohio
Or	Oregon State Library, Salem
PHi	Historical Society of Pennsylvania, Philadelphia, Pa.
PPL	Library Company of Philadelphia, Philadelphia, Pa.
PU	University of Pennsylvania, Philadelphia, Pa.
RPB	Brown University, Providence, R.I.
TxU	University of Texas, Austin, Tex.
UAr	Utah State Archives, Salt Lake City, Utah
UHi	Utah State Historical Society, Salt Lake City, Utah
ULA	Utah State University, Logan, Utah
UPB	Brigham Young University, Lee Library, Provo, Utah
USl	Salt Lake City Public Library, Salt Lake City, Utah

USlc	Church Historical Department, Church of Jesus Christ of Latter-day Saints, Salt Lake City, Utah
UU	University of Utah, Marriott Library, Salt Lake City, Utah
Vi	Virginia State Library, Richmond, Va.
ViU	University of Virginia, Charlottesville, Va.
ViU-L	University of Virginia Law Library, Charlottesville, Va.
WHi	State Historical Society of Wisconsin, Madison, Wis.

Bibliography

1838

"Must helpless women and children be turned
out naked in the world to beg their bread?"
Ephraim Owen
[Entry 1]

---

[1] U.S. House. 25th Congress. 3d Session. Committee on the
Judiciary. Mormons: Memorial of Ephraim Owen, Jr.,
late of Green County, Indiana, now of Davis County,
Missouri, asking of Congress to afford protection to
the people called Mormons, in the enjoyment of their
civil rights as citizens of the United States; and
complaining of loss of property, etc., December 20,
1838. (H. Doc. No. 42) Washington: Thomas Allen,
Print., 1838. 5p. [Serial Set 346]

Mormons' expulsion from Jackson and Clay Counties,
Missouri. Brief sketch of the Mormon difficulties in
the west.
[Flake 6026]

1840

". . . that in August, 1838, a riot commenced,
growing out of an attempt of a Mormon to
vote, which resulted in creating great
excitement and the preparation of many scenes
of lawless outrage."
[Entry 3]

---

[2] U.S. House. 26th Congress. 2d Session. Committee on the
Judiciary. "Latter-Day Saints," alias Mormons. The
petition of the Latter-Day Saints, commonly known as
Mormons, stating that they have purchased lands of the
General Government, lying in the State of Missouri,
from which they have been driven with force by the
constituted authorities of the State, and prevented
from occupying the same; and have suffered other
wrongs, for which they pray Congress to provide a
remedy. (H. Doc. No. 22) Washington, 1840. 13p.
[Serial Set 383]

The memorialists were Elias Higbee and Robert B.
Thompson.
[Flake 3993]

[3] U.S. Senate. 26th Congress. 1st Session. Committee on the
Judiciary. The Memorial of a delegation of the Latter

1

Day Saints, commonly called Mormons, report. (S. Doc.
No. 247) Washington: Blair and Rives, 1840. 2p.
[Serial Set 358]

Requests the discharge from further consideration of
claims for damages in destruction of property, etc. in
Missouri.

Action was presumably on the memorial signed by E.
Partridge, H. C. Kimball, J. Taylor, T. Turley, B.
Young. Far West, Mo., Dec. 10, 1838, found in History
of the Church of Jesus Christ of Latter-day Saints vol.
3, pp. 217-224.

[Flake 9187]

1841

"The covenant taken by all the Danite band
was as follows, to wit: They declared,
holding up their right hands, 'In the name of
Jesus Christ, the Son of God, I do solemnly
obligate myself ever to conceal, and never to
reveal, the secret purposes of this society
called the Daughters of Zion. Should I ever
do the same, I hold my life as the forfeiture.'"
[Entry 4]

[4] U.S. Senate. 26th Congress. 2d Session. Document showing
the testimony given before the judge of the Fifth
Judicial Circuit of the State of Missouri, on the trial
of Joseph Smith, Jr., and others, for high treason and
other crimes against that state. (S. Doc. No. 189)
[Washington: Blair & Rives, Printers, 1841]. 47p.
[Serial Set 378]

This document includes copy of the testimony given
before the Fifth Judicial Circuit, Missouri beginning
Nov. 12, 1838, regarding the Daughter's of Zion (since
called the Danites) and their work to drive non-Mormons
from Caldwell Co., Missouri.

[Flake 5428]

1844

"But, whatever, may be the name of the sect
or church, whose doctrines Mr. Page professes
to preach and inculcate, or under what
estimation they may have heretofore been held
by a prejudiced and uninquiring community, so
far as they bear, as their main characteristic,
a literal and unqualified interpretation of
Scripture, and followed by a strict belief in
Biblical doctrine, and accompanied by such an
explanation as the dictates of nature and
reason teach an impartial mind to be correct,

so far are we bound to coincide with them. We are
vulnerable to truth . . ."

[Entry 5]

---

[5] Page, John E. An address to the inhabitants and sojourners
of Washington, to his excellency the President of the
United States, the honorable Senators and Representatives
in Congress, and all the Rev. Divines, magistrates,
landlords, merchants, artists, mechanics, laborers,
soldiers, marines and the world at large. [Washington?
1844] 4p.

A short description of L.D.S. beliefs with admonitions
to call upon Mr. Page for additional information.
Testimonials concerning character included.

Notice at end. Washington, March 12, 1844, signed by
Jos. S. Potter, Franklin Little, clerk at the [Washington]
Globe Office, F. Edmonston, Printer, with testimonial
by Charles W. Feston, Printer, L. A. Edmonston.

[Flake 6065]
UPB, USlC

1845

"There is at this time, and has been for
several months past, a large number of
Mormons (supposed to be from four to eight
thousand) in the Indian country. They have
passed into the Pottawatomie country at the
Council Bluffs. A large number of them have
crossed the Missouri river, and are on their
way to Grand Island, in the Platte or Nebraska
river, where they have made arrangements to
winter. Another portion of them are desirous
to remain until next spring on the Boyer
river, in the Pottawatomie country; to which
they have obtained the consent of the Indians.
The sub-agent at that place reports that they
are conducting themselves well, and do not
seem disposed to interfere at all with the
Indians."

[Entry 6]

---

[6] Harvey, Thomas H. [Letter to the Superintendent of Indian
Affairs] pp. 282-288. In Report of the Commissioner of
Indian Affairs, 1845-1846. Washington, 1846. [I20.1:845-
846]

Reports that a group of Mormons have been granted the
right to spend the winter on Indian lands in western
Iowa.

"In conclusion, much credit is due to the
battalion for the cheerful and faithful
manner in which they have accomplished the
great labors of this march, and submitted to
its exposures and privations."

[Entry 8]

---

[7] "Officers of U.S. Volunteers in the Service of the United
States during the War with Mexico, 1846-1848," vol. 2,
pp. 43-73. In Historical Register and Dictionary of
the United States Army, from its organization September
29, 1789 to March 2, 1903. Washington: Govt. Print.
Off., 1903. [W3.11:789-903/v.2]

In this alphabetical list, the members of the Mormon
Battalion are included, and after each name the individual
is designated as an Iowa Mormon volunteer.

[8] U.S. House. 30th Congress. 1st Session. Notes of a military
reconnaissance from Fort Leavenworth in Missouri, to
San Diego, in California, including part of the Arkansas,
Del Norte, and Gila Rivers: Made in 1846-7, with the
advanced guard of the "Army of the West." By Lieut.
Col. W. H. Emory. (H. Ex. Doc. No. 41) Washington:
Wendell and Van Benthuysen, Printers, 1848. 614p.
[Serial Set 517]

Includes brief mention of the Mormon Battalion, p. 430.
Also includes the report of Lieutenant J. W. Abert, on
his examination of New Mexico, 1846-47; Report of
Lieutenant Colonel P. St. George Cooke on his march
from Santa Fe, New Mexico to San Diego; and Journal of
Captain A. R. Johnston, first Dragoons.

[Flake 3165]

[9] U.S. Senate. 30th Congress. 1st Session. Notes of a
military reconnaissance, from Fort Leavenworth in
Missouri, to San Diego, in California, including part
of the Arkansas, Del Norte, and Gila Rivers: Made in
1846-7, with the advanced guard of the "Army of the
West." By Lieut. Col. W. H. Emory. (S. Ex. Doc. No.
7) Washington: Wendell and Van Benthuysen, Printers,
1848. 416p. [Serial Set 505]

Includes material on the Mormon Battalion.

Other editions: New York, H. Long & Bro., 1848.

[Flake 3164]

"Before leaving the Del Norte valley, Lieutenant-
colonel Cooke sent a part of his baggage
train, and all the sick Mormons back to Fort
Pueblo, on the Arkansas, above Fort Bent, at

which place a large number of Mormon families
were collecting, with the view of emigrating
to California early in the spring of 1847."
[Entry 11]

---

[10] Harvey, Thomas H. [Letter to the Superintendant of Indian
Affairs] pp. 832-841. In Report of the Commissioner of
Indian Affairs, 1847-1848. Washington, 1848. [I20.1:847-
848]

Brief note of the Mormon settlement, p. 840, on Indian
lands south of the Missouri River during the winter of
1846, and of their agreement to leave in the summer.

[Flake 4126]

[11] Miller, John. Condition of Indians, No. 11, pp. 140-1. In
Annual report of the commissioner of Indian Affairs,
transmitted with the message of the President, at the
opening of the first session of the thirtieth Congress,
1847... 1848. Washington: Wendell and Van Benthuysen,
Printers, 1848. [I20.1:847-848]

Notes problems between the Mormons and the Omaha
Indians due to the Mormons remaining after the first
winter.

[Flake 9107a]

[12] U.S. Senate. 63rd Congress. 2nd Session. Doniphan's
expedition: containing an account of the conquest of
New Mexico. General Kearney's overland expedition to
California; Doniphan's campaign against the Navajos,
his unparalleled march upon Chihuahua and Durango; and
the operations of General Price at Santa Fe: With a
sketch of the life of Col. Doniphan... (S. Doc. No.
608) Washington: Govt. Print. Off., 1914. 202p.
[Serial Set 6589]

John Taylor Hughes' book originally published in 1847.
Material on the Mormon Battalion in chapters 7 and 15.

1848

"Partly arid and sparsely inhabited, the
general character of the GREAT BASIN is that
of desert, but with great exceptions, there
being many parts of it very fit for the
residence of a civilized people; and of these
parts, the Mormons have lately established
themselves in one of the largest and best."
[Entry 13]

---

[13] U.S. Senate. 30th Congress. 1st Session. Geographical
memoir upon upper California, in illustration of his

map of Oregon and California. By John Charles Fremont: Addressed to the Senate of the United States. (S. Misc. No. 148) Washington: Wendell and Van Benthuysen, Printers, 1848. 67p. [Serial Set 511]

Mention of Mormons, pp. 7-8. The map drawn by Charles Preuss, was the first published map to reflect the Mormon settlement of the Utah region.

[Flake 3451]

[14] U.S. Senate. 30th Congress. 1st Session. Message of the U.S. Communicating the proceedings of the Court Material in the trial of Lt. Col. Fremont, Apr. 7, 1848. (S. Ex. Doc. No. 33) Washington: Wendell and Van Benthuysen, 1848. 446p. [Serial Set 507]

References to the Mormons pp. 28, 33, 42, 80, 99, 122, 137, 140-43, 150, 165-66, 171, 203, 233, 234, 242-43, 259-63, 271, 273-75.

[Flake 3455]

[15] U.S. Senate. 30th Congress. 1st Session. Report of the Secretary of War, communicating, in answer to a resolution of the Senate, a report and map of the examination of New Mexico. Made by Lieutenant J. W. Abert, of the Topographical Corps. (S. Ex. Doc. No. 23) Washington, 1848. 132p. [Serial Set 506]

Page 14 tells of his encounter with the Mormon Battalion during the expedition.

[Flake 7]

1849

"Lend, lend your aid, O ye rulers of republican America! Save the helpless females of the Salt Lake territory from a life of misery, degradation, and vice; many of them have been flagrantly deceived by the false pretences of these sacerdotal hypocrites."

[Entry 20]

[16] "The Mormons," Congressional Globe 31st Congress, 1st session (31 December 1849) vol. 92, pp. 92-3. [X92]

The memorial of William Smith and Isaac Sheen representing themselves as the legitimate presidents of the Church of Jesus Christ of Latter Day Saints.

[17] Stansbury, Howard. An expedition to the valley of the Great Salt Lake of Utah: including a description of its geography, natural history, and minerals, and an analysis of its waters; with an authentic account of the Mormon settlement... Also, a reconnaissance of a new route through the Rocky mountains. And two large maps of that region. London: S. Low, Son, and Co; Philadelphia: Lippencott, Grambo, and Co., 1852. 487p. [W7.5: St2]

An expedition to the valley of the Great Salt Lake, June, 1849-September, 1850.

[Flake 8358]

[18] U.S. House. 30th Congress. 2d Session. Geographical memoir upon upper California, in illustration of his map of Oregon and California. By John Charles Fremont: Addressed to the Senate of the United States. (H. Misc. Doc. No. 5) Washington: Printed by Tippin & Streeper, 1849. 40p. [Serial Set 544]

Mentions Mormons; see entry No. 13 for annotation.

[Flake 3452]

[19] U.S. House. 31st Congress. 1st Session. California and New Mexico. Message from the President of the United States, transmitting information in answer to a resolution of the House of the 31st of December, 1849, on the subject of California and New Mexico. January 24, 1850. (H. Ex. Doc. No. 17) Washington, 1850. 976p. [Serial Set 573]

Contains Salt Lake Indian agent John Wilson's report from Great Salt Lake Valley, Sept. 4, 1847, pp. 104-112, and many documents concerning the enlistment, and experiences of the Mormon Battalion in California, 1846-1848.

Another edition: Senate version same but reads "Rep. Com." on p. 1. instead of "Ex. Doc." (U.S. 31st. Cong. 1st Sess. S. Ex. Doc. No. 18) [Serial Set 557]

[Flake 9213]

[20] U.S. House. 31st Congress. 1st Session. Deseret. Remonstrance of William Smith, et al., of Covington, Kentucky, against the admission of Deseret into the Union, Dec. 31, 1849. (H. Misc. Doc. No. 43) Washington: Wm. M. Belt, 1850. 3p. [Serial Set 581]

Petition against the formation of the Mormon State of Deseret. Indicates they have information that 1500 Salt Lake Mormons took an oath in the Nauvoo Temple.

[Flake 8140]

[21] U.S. Senate. 31st Congress. 1st Session. Memorial of the members of the legislative council of the provisional government of Deseret, praying for admission into the Union as a State, or for a Territorial Government. Dec. 27, 1849. (S. Misc. Doc. No. 10) Washington: Wm. M. Belt, 1850. 14p. [Serial Set 563]

Includes the Constitution of the proposed State of Deseret.

[Flake 2789]

[22] U.S. Senate. 31st Congress. 2d Session. A report in the form of a journal, to the Quartermaster General, of the

march of the regiment of mounted riflemen to Oregon,
from May 18 to October 5, 1849. By Major O. Cross,
Quartermaster, United State Army... (S. Doc. No. 1, Pt
II) Washington: Printed for the Senate, 1850. 490p.
[Serial Set 587]

Reference to Mormon ferry at North Platte, at Green
River, and Mormon trading on Bear River, pp. 126-244.
[Flake 2598]

[23] U.S. Senate. 31st Congress. Special Session. Report from
the Secretary of War, communicating, in compliance with
a resolution of the Senate, of the 21st February, 1849,
a copy of the official journal of Lieutenant Colonel
Philip St. George Cooke, from Sante Fe to San Diego,
etc... (S. Doc. No. 2) Washington: Printed at the
Union Office, 1849. 85p. [Serial Set 547]

The march of the Mormon Battalion.
[Flake 2500]

[24] U.S. Senate. 32d Congress. 1st Session. Memorial of Henry
O'Reilly, proposing a system of intercommunication by
mail and telegraph, along a military road through our
own Territories, between the Atlantic and Pacific
States, (being the plan approved by the St. Louis
national convention, in 1849.) (S. Misc. Doc. No. 67)
Washington: A. Boyd Hamilton, 1852. 34p. [Serial Set
629]

The increasing Mormon population in Deseret or Utah
given as one reason for the need of a telegraph.

[25] Wilson, John. [Letter to the Superintendent of Indian
Affairs]... pp. 66-68. In Annual report of the
Commissioner of Indian Affairs, 1849-1850. Washington:
Printed by Gideon & Co., 1850. [I20.1:849-850]

Describes the plight of the Indians due to the Mormon
occupation of the valleys.

1850

"Forgive a single allusion to the past. The
oppressed became the oppressor, and the
oppressed again go forth to form new communities,
new settlements, and new governments. Hence
are we here, amid these vast mountains and
solitary plains; hence are we here, assembled
in solemn council to frame laws for the
organization and rule of communities; and,
what gives zest to the picture, devise such
laws and regulations as shall perpetuate,
guarantee, and sustain, in time to come, our
free and glorious institutions to the latest
generation."
[Entry 38]

"Mr. Walker presented the memorial of James
J. Strang, George J. Adams, and William
Marks, Presidents of the Church of the
Saints, Apostles of the Lord Jesus Christ,
and witnesses of his name unto all nations,
asking that Congress will pass a law giving
the consent of the nation that the saints may
settle upon and forever occupy all the
uninhabited lands of the islands in Lake
Michigan, and asking of the people of the
United States, as they have not allowed their
brethren to remain in peace with them, they
will at least suffer them to remain there,
separate from them."

[Entry 31]

---

[26] "Contested Election - Iowa," <u>Congressional Globe</u> 31st
Congress, 1st session (27 June 1850) vol. 93, pp. 1299-
1303. [X93]

Mr. Leffler, on pp. 1301-1302, talks of the treatment
of the Mormon vote at Kanesville in 1848.

[27] "Delegate from Utah," <u>Congressional Globe</u> 31st Congress, 1st
session (13 September, 18 September 1850) vol. 93, pp.
1811, 1850. [X93]

Mr. Harris' presentation of Mr. Babbitt, to be seated
as a delegate, created a mild controversy.

[28] "The Latter-Day Saints," <u>Congressional Globe</u> 31st Congress,
1st Session (14 March 1850) vol. 92, p. 524. [X92]

Petition, by the Josephite branch of the Church against
Utah Mormon's request for entry as a territory, asking
that the banditry of mails be stopped.

[29] Leffler, Shepherd. <u>Iowa contested election! Speech of Hon.
S. Leffler, of Iowa, in the House of Representatives,
June 27, 1850, on the Report of the Committee of
Elections, in the Iowa Contested Election Case.</u>
[Washington? 1850] 8 p.

Illegality of the treatment of the Mormon vote at
Kanesville in 1848.

[Flake 4867]
MH

[30] Leffler, Shepherd (Iowa). "Iowa Contested Election,"
<u>Congressional Globe</u> 31st Congress, 1st session (27 June
1850) vol. 94, Appendix, pp. 818-823. [X94]

Mormon population in Iowa, and the illegality of the
Mormon vote in Kanesville in 1848.

[31] "The Mormons," <u>Congressional Globe</u> 31st Congress, 1st
session (15 June 1850) vol. 93, pp. 1221. [X93]

The Memorial of James J. Strang, George J. Adams, and
William Marks, Presidents of the Church of the Saints,

9

Apostles of the Lord [Strangites] petitioning lands on
the islands of Michigan for settlement.

[32] Smith, Truman. "The compromise Bill," Congressional Globe
31st Congress, 1st Session (15 August 1850) vol. 95,
Appendix, pp. 1173-1186. [X95]

Describes the Territory of Utah, pp. 1182-1184.
Letters from J. H. Bernhisel and Erastus Snow, however,
little on Mormonism.

[33] Smith, Truman. Speech of Mr. Smith, of Conn., on the bill
"to admit California into the Union - to establish
territorial governments for Utah and New Mexico..."
Delivered in the Senate of the United States, July 8,
1850. Washington: Gideon & Co., 1850. 32p.

Includes an attempt to get the State of Deseret admitted
to the Union.

[Flake 8122]
CU-B, NjP, UHi, UPB, USlc

[34] "State of Deseret," Congressional Globe 31st Congress, 1st
session (22 February 1850) vol. 92, pt. 413. [X93]

Petitions from citizens of Shelbourne, Lee County,
Illinois, praying Congress to protect the rights of
citizens when traveling through Mormon Salt Lake
Valley.

[35] U.S. House. 31st Congress. 1st Session. Committee on
Elections. Almon W. Babbitt, delegate from Deseret.
April 4, 1850... Mr. Strong, from the Committee of
Elections, made the following report: The Committee of
Elections, to whom were referred the credentials of
Almon W. Babbitt, esq., and his memorial praying to be
admitted to a seat in the House of Representatives as a
delegate from the provisional State of Deseret. (H.
Rep. No. 219) Washington: Govt. Print. Off., 1850.
16p. [Serial Set 584]

Constitution of the State of Deseret is included.

[Flake 9115]

[36] U.S. House. 31st Congress. 1st Session. Constitution of
the State of Deseret, with the journal of the convention
which formed it, and the proceedings of the legislature
consequent thereon. (H. Misc. Doc. No. 18) Washington:
Wm. M. Belt, 1850. 12p. [Serial Set 581]

[Flake 2784]

[37] "Utah (or Deseret)," Congressional Globe 31st Congress, 1st
session (18 July, 19 July 1850) vol. 93, pp. 1413-1415,
1418-1423. [X93]

Controversy over the seating of Almon W. Babbitt as a
delegate from the alleged state of Deseret. Admission
of the delegate doesn't mean acceptance of his beliefs.

The question of the principle of territorial government was discussed.

[38] Young, Brigham. <u>Governor's Message; Deseret, December 2, 1850</u>. [Great Salt Lake City, 1850] 3p.

Talk of the previous oppressions of the Mormons which brought them to Deseret.

[Flake 2791]
UPB, US1C

1851

". . . that the pursuit of bliss, and the enjoyment of life, in every capacity of public association and domestic happiness, temporal expansion, or spiritual increase upon the earth, may not legally be questioned: provided, however, that each and every act, or practice so established, or adopted for law, or custom, shall relate to solemnities, sacraments, ceremonies, consecrations, endowments, tithings, marriages, fellowship, or the religious duties of man to his Maker; inasmuch as the doctrines, principles, practices, or performances, support virtue, and increase morality, and are not inconsistent with, or repugnant to the Constitution of the United States . . ."

[Entry 42]

---

[39] "Delegate from Utah," <u>Congressional Globe</u> 31st Congress, 2d session (5 February 1851) vol. 96, pp. 431-432. [X96]

Brief debate on seating Almon W. Babbit.

[40] Holeman, J. H. [Letter to Hon. L. Lea, Commissioner Indian Affairs] pp. 182-184. In <u>Annual report of the Commissioner of Indian Affairs. 1851</u>. Washington: Gideon & Co., printers, 1851. [I20.1:851]

The worst problem of the Indians is that the Mormons take over of all the valleys.

[41] "Letter of John H. Holeman, Commissioner of Indian Affairs, September 21, 1851," pp. 444-446. In <u>Report of the Secretary of the Interior, December 2, 1851</u>. Washington: A. Boyd Hamilton, 1852. [I1.1:851]

Document No. 53 deals primarily with Indian affairs in Utah. Brief mention is made of Mormon emigrants to Utah and a meeting of Holeman with Brigham Young.

Variant ed. 32nd Cong. 1st sess. S. Ex. Doc. No. 1, Serial Set 613.

[42] "An Ordinance incorporating the Church of Jesus Christ of
     Latter Day Saints" (Chapter XVII, 8 Feb 1851) Acts,
     Resolutions and Memorials, passed at the Several Annual
     Sessions of the Legislative Assembly of the Territory
     of Utah, 1855, pp. 103-105.

     Incorporation under the General Assembly of the State
     of Deseret. Sec. 3 has an interesting anomaly regarding
     the Church's doctrines which should be practiced, as
     long as they weren't repugnant to the Constitution.

                                                 UPB, USlc

[43] "Resolution," Congressional Globe 32nd Congress, 1st session
     (15 December 1851, 6 January 1852) vol. 97, p. 100,
     211. [X97]

     Report on the actual conditions in Utah. John M.
     Bernhisel objects to the reports of returning territorial
     officers in Missouri papers and in the New York Herald
     being discussed before conditions are ascertained.

                                                      1852

          "But here three young men, of good character
          and deportment, who entered upon their duties
          with the honest purpose of discharging them,
          under the authority of the United States, and
          not under the "Latter-day Saints"--with a
          responsibility to the United States, and not
          a responsibility to a degraded fanaticism--
          because they would not enter into the common
          prostitution of others, because they would
          not stand by, defenseless as they were, and
          see the Republic and its Government abused
          and condemned, and returned to testify to the
          Government the scenes of violence and outrage
          that transpired, amounting, in all the theory
          on the subject, to treason, were dismissed by
          this Administration."
                                          [Entry 51]

          "The letter-writer states, moreover, that at
          the celebration of the 24th of July, `that
          the orator of the day spoke bitterly of the
          course of the United States towards the
          Church of Latter Day Saints, in taking a
          battalion of men from them for the war with
          Mexico, while on the banks of the Missouri
          river, in their flight from the mob at
          Nauvoo: that the government had devised the
          most wanton, cruel, and dastardly means for
          the accomplishment of their ruin, overthrow,
          and utter extermination; at which time also
          Governor Young denounced, in the most sacrilegious
          terms, President Taylor.'"
                                          [Entry 55]

12

[44] "An act in relation to marks and brands" (1 March 1852)
      Acts, Resolutions and Memorials passed by the first
      annual, and special sessions, of the Legislative
      Assembly, of the Territory of Utah, 1852, pp. 64-66.

      According to Section 13, money from the sale of impounded
      stock would be added to Emigration Fund.
                                                        UPB, US1C

[45] "Affairs in Utah," Congressional Globe 32nd Congress, 1st
      Session (14 January 1852) vol. 97 p. 274. [X97]

      Referring back to entry 43, Mr. Bernhisel objects to
      the official printed report and the New York Herald
      report on the Territory of Utah difficulties, as
      reported by three returning territorial officials
      [probably Brandebury, Brocchus, and Harris] as different
      than that given to the Department of State.

[46] "Affairs in Utah," Congressional Globe 32nd Congress, 1st
      Session (20 January 1852) vol. 97, p. 315-316. [X97]

      Includes a letter from Brigham Young denying any wrong
      doing in Utah Territory

[47] Brocchus, Perry E. Letter of Judge Brocchus, of Alabama, to
      the public, upon the difficulties in the Territory of
      Utah. Washington: Printed by L. Towers, 1852. 30p.

                                                  [Flake 871]
                                          DLC, MH, NN, PPL

[48] "The election of the delegate from Utah," Congressional
      Globe 32nd Congress, 1st session (19, 22 January 1852)
      vol. 97, pp. 306, 353-354. [X97]

      Questions the election of John M. Bernhisel to Congress.

[49] "Letters from Brigham Young, September 25 and 29, 1852," pp.
      437-445. In Report of the Secretary of the Interior
      December 4, 1852. Washington: Robert Armstrong, 1852.
      [I1.1:852]

      Documents No. 63 and 64 are an exchange of letters
      between Governor Brigham Young and Indian Agent J. H.
      Holeman. No mention made of Mormons, except the Mormon
      Station in Carson Valley.

      Variant ed. U.S. 32nd Cong. 2d sess. H. Ex. Doc. No. 1,
      Serial Set 673.

      "Resolution," Congressional Globe, 1852, see entry 43.

[50] "Salaries of Territorial Officers," Congressional Globe 32nd
      Congress, 1st session (23 March 1852) vol. 97, pp. 826-
      28. [X97]

      The departure of Brandebury, Brocchus, and Harris from
      the Territory of Utah is discussed. Material accompanies
      that found in entry 51.

[51] "Salaries of Territorial Officers," <u>Congressional Globe</u> 32nd
          Congress, 1st Session (20 May 1852) vol. 98, pp. 1409-
          1419, 1446-1450, 1531. [X98]

          Tells Why Brandebury, Brocchus, and Harris were forced
          to leave the Territory of Utah.

          The runaway justices brought debates in the spring of
          1852 on a bill to pay the officials for services.
          These were the first significant rehearsals of the
          peculiarities of the Mormons in the halls of Congress.

[52] U.S. House. 32d Congress. 1st Session. <u>Utah: Message</u>
          <u>from the President of the United States, transmitting</u>
          <u>information in reference to the condition of affairs</u> in
          <u>the Territory of Utah.</u> January 9, 1852. (H. Ex. Doc.
          No. 25) Washington, 1852. 33p. [Serial Set 640]

          The bulk of this document is the "Report of Messrs.
          Brandebury, Brocchus, and Harris, to the President of
          the United States", pp. 8-22.

          The theocratic nature of government in Utah is soundly
          criticized and specifically Brigham Young's role.
          Numerous quotes from various Church leaders are included
          to buttress their arguments.

                                                      [Flake 9214]

[53] U.S. Senate. 33d Congress. Special Session. <u>Exploration</u>
          <u>and survey of the valley of the Great Salt Lake of</u>
          <u>Utah, including a reconnaissance of a new route through</u>
          <u>the Rocky Mountains.</u> (S. Ex. Doc. No. 3) Philadelphia:
          Lippincott, Grambo & Co., 1852. 487p. [Serial Set 608]

          Wintering in Salt Lake City in 1849, the author [Howard
          Stansbury] gives detailed sketch of Mormons in Chapter
          7.

                                                      [Flake 8359]

[54] "Utah Territory," <u>Congressional Globe</u> 32d Congress, 1st
          Session (9 January 1852) vol. 97, pp. 240-241. [X97]

          Concerns the Brandebury, Brocchus, and Harris report on
          the Territory of Utah. A brief mention of the report
          on p. 211.

[55] "Utah Territory," <u>Congressional Globe</u> 32d Congress, 1st
          session (9 January 1852) vol. 100, pp. Appendix 84-93.
          [X100]

          The report of Daniel Webster, Secretary of State, to
          the President with accompanying letters from Mr.
          Bernhisel to the President, Justice Zerubbabel Snow to
          the President, Gov. Brigham Young to the President,
          reports of Brandebury, Brocchus and Harris to the
          President, Mr. Harris, Secretary of the Territory of
          Utah to the President and to the Secretary of State,
          and a memorial signed by the members of the Legislative
          Assembly to the President. These letters contain an

14

intriguing mixture of anti-Mormon and pro-Mormon
material.

[56] Young, Brigham. Annual Message of Governor Brigham Young
presented to the Legislature of Utah, December 13,
1852. [n.p., n.d.] 10p.

In eloquent "Brighamese" the need for more emphasis on
home industry, and the sentiments regarding Africa's
sons, or the descendants of Cain, are expressed.
[Flake 9348]
UPB, US1C

[57] Young, Brigham. Governor's message to the Legislative
Assembly of Utah Territory, January 5, 1852. [Great
Salt Lake City, 1852] 8p.

Comments upon God's beneficence to the Territory.
Brigham Young's feelings about the purchase of Indian
children as slaves in trade with Mexico. Mentions the
seed of Canaan [sic] carrying the curse. Also discusses
domestic manufacturing.
[Flake 9349]
CSmH, Cty, NjP, UPB, US1C

[58] Young, Brigham. "Governor's Message to the Legislative
Assembly, January 5, 1852," pp. 104-113. In the
Journals of the House of Representatives, Council and
Joint Sessions of the First Annual and Special Sessions
of the Legislative Assembly of the Territory of Utah.
Great Salt Lake City: Brigham H. Young, Printer, 1852.

See entry 57 for annotation.
UPB, US1C

[59] Young, Brigham. [Letter to the Commissioner of Indian
Affairs], pp. 147-149. In Annual Report of the Commissioner
of Indian Affairs. 1852. Washington: Robert Armstrong,
printer, 1852. [I20.1:852]

Description of his peace overtures to the Indians.

1853

"Happily for Utah, she has no party politics
for her Legislature to discuss, she can
therefore lend her energies for the benefit
of the country."
[Entry 64]

---

[60] U.S. House. 36th Congress. 1st Session. Committee on
Military Affairs. Utah - Expenses incurred in suppressing
Indian hostilities. [To accompany bill H.R. No.
435...] Report. The Committee on Military Affairs, to
whom was referred the claim of the Territory of Utah
for reimbursement of expenses incurred by said territory
in suppressing Indian hostilities in 1853. (H. Rept.
No. 201) Washington: Thomas H. Ford, 1860. 2p.
[Serial Set 1068]

A claim for service in 1853. The bill suggests that the militia be reimbursed on the same scale that the regular army in the Pacific are paid.

[61] U.S. Senate. 32d Congress. Special Session. Exploration survey of the valley of the Great Salt Lake of Utah, including a reconnaissance of a new route through the Rocky Mountains. (S. Ex. Doc. No. 3) Washington: Robert Armstrong, Public Printer, 1853. 495p. [Serial Set 608]

Wintering in Salt Lake City in 1849, the author gives a detailed sketch of Mormons and their early history. See chapter 7.

[Flake 8360]

[62] U.S. War Department. Reports of explorations and surveys, to ascertain the most practicable and economical route for a railroad from the Mississippi River to the Pacific Ocean. Made under the direction of the Secretary of War, in 1853-54 . . . vol. 3. Washington: A. O. P. Nicholson, Printer, 1856. [W7.14:3]

Includes extracts from the [preliminary] report of Lieutenant A. W. Whipple, Corps of Topographical Engineers, upon the route near the Thirty-fifth Parallel, with an explanatory note by Captain A. A. Humphreys. References to the Mormons at San Bernardino and the Mormon road to Salt Lake on pp. 113, 126-127, 129, 131.

33d Cong. 2d sess. S. Ex. Doc. No. 78, Serial Set 760.

[Flake 9255]

[63] U.S. War Department. Reports of Explorations and Surveys, to ascertain the most practicable and economical route for a railroad from the Mississippi River to the Pacific Ocean made under the direction of the Secretary of War in 1853-4 . . . vol. 5. Washington: Beverley Tucker, Printer, 1856. [W7.14:5]

Report of Lt. R. W. Williamson, Corps of Topographical Engineers, upon the routes in California to connect with the routes near the Thirty-fifth and thirty-second parallels. References to the Mormon settlement at San Bernardino, p. 64, 80; Mormon Island on the American River, p. 275.

33d Congress, 2d sess., S. Ex. Doc. no. 78, Serial Set 762.

[Flake 9255]

[64] Young, Brigham. "Governor's Message to the Legislative Assembly, Dec. 13, 1853," pp. 111-123. In the Journals of the House of Representatives, Council and Joint Sessions of the Third Annual Session, of the Legislative Assembly of the Territory of Utah. Great Salt Lake City: Printed by Arieh C. Brower, 1854.

On p. 114, Brigham Young mentions the immigration from
northern European states and the British Isles. On p.
112 the theocratic nature of politics in Utah Territory
is evident when Brigham Young says "Owing to human
frailty, we may not attain unto a perfect code until
the fullness of times shall more fully disclose heaven's
brightness."

UPB, USlC

[65] Young, Brigham. [Letter to the Commissioner of Indian
     Affairs], pp. 201-203. In Annual report of the Commissioner
     of Indian Affairs. 1853. Washington, Robert Armstrong,
     printer, 1853. [I20.1:853]

     Depredations of the Indians due to the influence of
     Chief Walker.

DLC, NN, UPB, ViU

1854

"Let us, as Christians, follow and legislate
in the doctrines of Christ, not of Joe Smith;
let us take the holy Gospel, not the Book of
Mormon."
                                        [Entry 67]

[65a] Clayton, John Middleton (Delaware). "Nebraska and Kansas,"
      Congressional Globe 33d Congress, 1st session (1 and 2
      March 1854), Appendix, pp. 383-393. [X106]

      On pages 390-391, Clayton takes exception to the Utah
      Act of 1850, part of the Compromise of 1850, which
      established Utah Territory. The result of this decision
      has been a Mormon theocracy.

[65b] Clayton, John Middleton. Speech of John M. Clayton, of
      Delaware, on the Bill to Organize Territorial governments
      in Nebraska and Kansas; discussing the Missouri Compromise
      and the Doctrine of Non-Intervention. Delivered in the
      Senate of the United States, March 1 and 2, 1854.
      Washington: Congressional Globe Office, 1854. 22p.

      Pages 17-18 includes the same information found in the
      Congressional Globe entry. See entry 65a for annotation.

MHi, RPB, UPB

[65c] Dodge, Augustus Caesar (Iowa). "Nebraska and Kansas,"
      Congressional Globe 33d Congress, 1st session (25
      February 1854), Appendix, pp. 375-393. [X106]

      On page 378, Mr. Dodge, takes exception to
      Mr. Smith's allegations that people in the
      territories should be denied self-government,
      even in the case of Utah, over their practice
      of polygamy. See entries 67c and 67d for Mr.
      Smith's speech.

[65d] Dodge, Augustus Caesar. <u>Nebraska and Kansas</u>. <u>Speech of Mr. Dodge, of Iowa, in the Senate of the United States, Feb. 25, 1854</u>. [n.p., n.d.] 15p.

Page 6 includes the same information as found in the <u>Congressional Globe</u> entry. See entry 65c for annotation.

DLC, NN, UPB, ViU

[66] "Letters from Fort Laramie, August 29, October 2, 1854," pp. 301-306. In <u>Report of the Secretary of the Interior, December 4, 1854</u>. Washington: Beverley Tucker, 1854. [I1.1:854]

The letters tell of the killing of a "Mormon cow" which resulted in a major confrontation.

Variant ed. U.S. 33d Cong. 2d sess. Senate Ex. Doc No. 1, Serial Set 746.

[67] Lyon, Caleb (New York). "No government bounty to polygamy," <u>Congressional Globe</u> 33d Congress, 1st session (10 May 1854) vol. 106, Appendix, pp. 603-604. [X106]

Speech of Mr. Lyon, of Lyonsdale, May 4, 1854, in which he admits that the Mormons are a persecuted people, but persecution does not condone polygamy.

[67a] Norris, Moses (New Hampshire). "The Nebraska and Kansas Bill--Debate," <u>Congressional Globe</u> 33d Congress, 1st session (3 March 1854), Appendix, p. 306-307. [X106]

In the midst of a lengthy debate, among several delegates, Mr. Norris, Senator from New Hampshire, takes exception to Mr. Smith's remarks which "dwelt a full hour on the institution of polygamy in Utah, and characterized it as one of the results of self-government there." Mr. Norris feels sure that the Senate knew about polygamy when Utah was granted territorial status.

[67b] Norris, Moses. <u>Speech of the Hon. M. Norris, of New Hamphire, in the United States Senate, March 3, 1854, on Nebraska and Kansas</u>. Washington: Sentinel Office, 1854. 16p.

Pages 7-8 repeat the same information found in the <u>Congressional Globe</u>. See entry 67a for annotation.

DLC, KU, MH, OC1WHi, UPB

[67c] Smith, Truman (Connecticut). "Nebraska and Kansas Bill," <u>Congressional Globe</u> 33d Congress, 1st session (10 and 11 February 1854), Appendix, pp. 168-178. [X106]

The same speech was printed separately, see entry 67d. Page 175 includes the material regarding polygamy.

[67d] Smith, Truman. <u>Speech of Truman Smith, of Connecticut, on the Nebraska Question. Delivered in the Senate of the United States, February 10 and 11, 1854</u>. Washington: John T. and Lem. Towers, 1854. 23p.

On pages 16-18, Mr. Smith, in the midst of a lengthy debate on the Kansas-Nebraska question, delivers some salient comments on the broad interpretation of the territorial bill which would leave Utah free to regulate their domestic institutions, i.e., polygamous relationships.

CU, DLC, MB, NN, OO, UPB, ViU

[68] "Surveyor General of Utah," <u>Congressional Globe</u> 33d Congress, 1st session (4, 5 May 1854) vol. 104, pp. 1091-1102, 1109-1112, 1431-1433. [X104]

House bill no. 317 is debated. The bill would donate to every white male citizen over 21 years, one quarter section of land upon condition of actual settlement and cultivation for not less than four years. The problem for Utah Territory centered around whether a man with more than one wife should be allowed to participate. Opinion was divided and heated on that issue.

[69] U.S. House. 33d Congress. 2d Session. <u>Central Railroad route to the Pacific. Letter of J. C. Fremont to the editors of the National Intelligencer, communicating some general results of a recent winter expedition across the Rocky Mountains, for the survey of a route for a railroad to the Pacific.</u> (H. Misc. Doc. No. 8) Washington: A. O. P. Nicholson, Printer, 1854. 7p. [Serial Set 807]

Relates his stay in Mormon settlements and Mormon exploration.

[Flake 3454]

[70] U.S. House. 33d Congress. 1st Session. <u>Utah-public buildings-further appropriations. Letter from the Secretary of the Treasury, transmitting communications in regard to the necessity of further appropriations for public buildings in Utah.</u> (H. Misc. Doc. No. 58) Washington: A. O. P. Nicholson, 1854. 3p. [Serial 741]

Includes material on Mormons and their treatment of the territorial judges.

[Flake 9196]

[71] U.S. Senate. 33d Congress. 1st Session. <u>Letter of J. C. Fremont to the editors of the National Intelligencer, communicating some general results of a recent winter expedition across the Rocky Mountains, for the survey of a route for a railroad to the Pacific.</u> June 15, 1854. Referred to the Select Committee on the Pacific Railroad and ordered to be printed. (S. Misc. Doc. 67) [Washington, 1854] 7p. [Serial Set 705]

Describes his winter journey of 1853-54, with an account of the Mormon settlements of Parowan and Cedar City, and mention of Mormon explorations of the Virgin River, p. 4-6.

[Flake 3454]

[72] U.S. Senate. 33d Congress. 1st Session. Report of exploration of a route for the Pacific railroad [Part I] near the 38th and 39th parallels of latitude, from the mouth of the Kansas to Sevier River, in the Great Basin. [Part 2] On the line of the forty-first parallel of north latitude. By Lt. E. G. Beckwith, third artillery. 1854. (S. Ex. Doc. No. 78) [Washington: Beverley Tucker, 1855] vol. 2 [Serial Set 759]

Includes a section on Utah and Mormonism. Chapter 5 includes Edward Beckwith's arrival in Utah and Chapter 8 his leaving. Gives a description of local Mormon settlements. He assumed command after Capt. J. W. Gunnison was killed in 1853.

[Flake 368]

[73] Walbridge, Hiram (New York). "Polygamy hostile to republican institutions," Congressional Globe 33d Congress, 1st Session (10 May 1854) v.106, Appendix, pp. 592-593. [X106]

The anti-polygamy action in the Homestead Act, also known as the Morrill act.

[74] Young, Brigham. "Governor's Message to the Legislative Assembly, Dec. 11, 1854," pp. 93-103. In the Journal of the Legislative Assembly of the Territory of Utah for the Fourth Annual Session. Great Salt Lake City: Joseph Cain, Public Printer, 1855.

Comments upon God's beneficence to the Territory. Ward school mentioned. Introduction into schools of the Deseret alphabet. Talks of the Perpetual Emigrating Company.

UPB, US1C

[75] Young, Brigham. Governor's message to the legislative Assembly of the Territory of Utah: delivered December eleventh, A. D. Eighteen hundred and fifty four. [Great Salt Lake City, 1854] 8p.

See entry 74 for annotation.

[Flake 9350]
NjP, UPB, US1C

1855

"They [the Mormons] embrace a class of rude and lawless young men, such as might be regarded as a curse to any civilized community. But I do not wish to excite prejudice and encourage feelings of hostility against these people; on the contrary, I think such a course would be unwise and impolitic. They always have, and ever will thrive by persecution. They know well the effect it has had upon them, and consequently crave to be persecuted.
[Entry 80]

[76] Armstrong, George W. [Letters to the Commissioner of Indian Affairs. 1855] pp. 201-206. In Annual report of the Commissioner of Indian Affairs. 1855. Washington: Printed by A. O. P. Nicholson, 1856. [I20.1:855]

Relations between the Ute Indians and the Mormons in the Provo area, particularly in regard to fishing in Utah Lake.

MHi, RPB, UPB

[76a] Houston, Samuel. Speeches of Sam Houston, of Texas, on the subject of an Increase of the Army, and the Indian Policy of the Government, delivered in the Senate of the United States, January 29 and 31, 1855. Washington: Congressional Globe Office, 1855. 20p.

Mr. Houston, on pages 1-2, uses the example of a Mormon emigrant company encamped by Fort Laramie whose cow was slaughtered by the Sioux, to explain the fact that it is not the Indians who have been aggressive and hostile, but the white men. Although the Indians agreed to make restitution it was not satisfactory to the commander of Fort Laramie.

Cty, DLC, TxU, UPB

[76b] Houston, Samuel (Texas). "Army Appropriation Bill," Congressional Globe. 33d Congress, 2d session (29 January 1855), pp. 436-444. [X107]

Page 437 includes the same information as found in the separately published speech of Mr. Houston. See entry 76a for annotation.

[77] "Surveyor General of Utah," Congressional Globe 33d Congress, 2d Session (1 February 1855) vol. 107, pp. 504-506. [X107]

In a discussion on the bill to appoint a Surveyor General for Utah, the subject of polygamy is briefly discussed. For a text of the bill see v. 108 of the Congressional Globe p. 381.

[78] U.S. Senate. 33d Congress. 2d Session. Letter, James Bordeaux for Samuel Smith, concerning the Mormon cow which precipitated an altercation between Lieut. John L. Grattan and the Sioux. (S. Ex. Doc. No. 1) Washington: Beverley Tucker, 1855. 629p. [Serial Set 746]

Mormon entry on pp. 301-2.

[79] U.S. Senate. 34th Congress. 1st Session. Letter to Major General Thos. S. Jesup concerning expedition through Utah with Colonel E. J. Steptoe. (S. Ex. Doc. N. 1, pt. 2) Washington: Printed by Beverley Tucker, 1855. pp. 156-168 [Serial Set 811]

Description of the Mormons.

Also published in U.S. 34th Cong. House Ex. Doc. No. 1.
1st & 2d Sess.

[Flake 4243]

[80] "Utah Superintendency, 1855," pp. 593-602. In Report of
the Secretary of the Interior, December 3, 1857.
Washington: William A. Harris, 1858. [I1.1:857]

Reports from various men. Garland Hurt accuses the
Mormons of having made a distinction between themselves
and other people. He emphasizes the need to scrutinize
the Mormon missionaries and their work with the Indians.

Variant ed. U.S. 35th Cong., 1st sess. Senate Ex. Doc.
No. 11, Serial Set 919.

[81] Young, Brigham. [Letter to the Commissioner of Indian
Affairs] pp. 195-197. In Annual report of the Commissioner
of Indian Affairs. 1855. Washington: Printed by A.
O. P. Nicholson, 1856. [I20.1:855]

Indians at peace with the Utah settlers after the war
of 1853.

1856

"If the Federal Government has the right to
dissolve the latter, [slavery] then it may
also declare, that within its territory the
marriage contract shall be considered dissolved-
-prescribe a plurality of wives--enact all
the absurdities characterizing fanaticism--
may establish Mormonism, Maine-lawism,
spiritualism, witchcraft, a religious test--
indeed all the whole code of blue laws."

[Entry 86]

[82] "An Act amending, confirming and legalizing an 'Ordinance
incorporating the Perpetual Emigrating Fund Company'"
(Chapter 90, 12 January 1856) Acts, resolutions and
memorials passed at the several annual sessions of the
Legislative Assembly of the Territory of Utah. Great
Salt Lake City: Henry McEwan, Public Printer, 1866,
pp. 111-112.

UPB, US1C

[83] "Annual Report of the Surveyor General of Utah, September
30, 1856," pp. 542-549. In Report of The Secretary of
the Interior, November 29, 1856. Washington: A. O. P.
Nicholson, 1856. [I1.1:856]

David H. Burr, Surveyor General of Utah, tells of one
valley being the exclusive right of Brigham Young and
associates and of the plight of the Shoshonee Indians
due to the Mormons having driven away deer and elk.
Favorites of the Mormon Church given land rights.

Variant ed. U.S. 34th Cong., 3d sess. Senate Ex. Doc.
No. 5, Serial Set 875.

[84] "Plurality of Wives," <u>Congressional Globe</u> 34th Congress, 1st
     session (14 April 1856) vol. 110, p. 895. [X110]

     A resolution voted on regarding an immediate preparation
     of a bill for the prohibition of polygamy in the territories.

[85] "Polygamy in the Territories," <u>Congressional Globe</u> 34th
     Congress, 1st session (26 June 1856) vol. 110, pp.
     1491, 1501. [X110]

     Mr. Justin S. Morrill of Vermont made a report from the
     Committee on Territories regarding the polygamy bill.
     He characterized the practice of polygamy and the
     bill's purpose to "prevent practices which outrage the
     moral sense of the civilized world."

[86] "Twin Relics of barbarism--polygamy and slavery," <u>Congressional
     Globe</u> 34th Congress, 1st session (23 April, 1 July, 23
     July, 29 July, 7 August, 4 August, 6 August, 2 August
     1856) vol. 112, Appendix, pp. 410-11, 713, 908, 987,
     1181, 1195, 1211, 1216-17, 1283. [X112]

     In numerous debates in 1856 on the subject of slavery,
     Kansas-Nebraska Act, Missouri Compromise, etc., the
     subject of polygamy was unearthed. On several occasions
     the 1856 Republican Party Platform was reprinted on p.
     713, 1181, and 1195 for example.

[86a] U.S. House. 34th Congress. 1st Session. H.R. 433, "A
      bill to punish and prevent the practice of polygamy in
      the Territories of the United States, and other places,
      June 26, 1856." [Washington: Govt. Print. Off., 1856]
      2p.

      Mr. Morrill, from the Committee on the Territories,
      reported the bill. Without naming the Territory, Mr.
      Morrill, proposes that the offenders of the admitted
      practice of polygamy in one of the Territories of the
      Union should pay a fine of at least $500 and be imprisoned
      for not less than two years nor more than five years.
      See entry 85 for the <u>Congressional Globe</u> debate.

                                        DLC, UPB, US1C

[87] U.S. Senate. 34th Congress. 1st Session. <u>Report of the
     Secretary of war, in compliance with a resolution of
     the Senate of the 1st instant, calling for copies of
     the correspondence respecting the massacre of Lieutenant
     Grattan and his command by Indians.</u> (S. Ex. Doc. No.
     91) Washington: A. O. P. Nicholson, 1856. 27p.
     [Serial Set 823]

     A cow which strayed from a Mormon wagon train caused
     the trouble.

[88] "Utah Superintendency, 1856," pp. 765-787. In <u>Report of the
     Secretary of the Interior, November 29, 1856</u>. Washington:
     A. O. P. Nicholson, 1856. [I1.1:856]

23

The reports of Brigham Young, Garland Hurt, and George
W. Armstrong relate the relationship between the
settlers and the Indians.

Variant ed. U.S. 34th Cong., 3d sess. Senate Ex. doc
No. 5, Serial Set 875.

[89] Young, Brigham. "Letter from Brigham Young, Great Salt Lake
City, June 30, 1856," pp. 224-7. In Report of the
Commissioner of Indian Affairs. 1856. Washington: A.
O. P. Nicholson, 1857. [I20.1:856]

The letter outlines Young's Indian farm ideas.

1857

"From the first hour they fixed themselves in
that remote and almost inaccessible region of
our Territory, from which they are now
sending defiance to the sovereign power,
their whole plan has been to prepare for a
successful secession from the authority of
the United States and a permanent establishment
of their own. They have practised an exclusiveness
unlike anything ever before known in a
Christian country, and have inculcated a
jealous distrust of all whose religious faith
differed from their own; whom they characterize
under the general denomination of GENTILES."
                                        [Entry 101]

---

[90] Buchanan, James. "First Annual message 8 December 1857,"
pp. 2985-2987. In A Compilation of the Messages and
Papers of the Presidents, by James D. Richardson, vol.
4. New York: Bureau of National Literature, 1911,
c1897. [GS4.113:4, AE2.114:1-27/v.4]

Describes the absolutism of church and state in Utah
with Brigham Young as governor, superintendent of
Indian Affairs, and head of the Mormon Church. Mentions
the withdrawal of judicial and executive officers of
the U.S. from Utah Territory for their own personal
safety. Indicates that the U.S. government ought to go
to Utah Territory "with such an imposing force as to
convince these deluded people that resistance would be
vain, and thus spare the effusion of blood."

[91] "Capitol building - Utah," Congressional Globe 34th Congress,
3rd Session (7 February 1857) vol. 113, p. 608. [X113]

Discussion on whether the people of Utah, who are
living out of the law, should be provided money for a
statehouse.

[92] "The Delegate from Utah," Congressional Globe 35th Congress,
1st session (21, 23 December 1857) vol. 115, p. 134,
pp. 165-170. [X115]

Mr. Warren of Arkansas, led a spirited discussion on the seating of John M. Bernhisel, delegate from Utah, due to the open rebellion of the territory. Brigham Young naturally takes much of the heated debate.

[93] Denver, J. W. [Letter to Brigham Young concerning his exceeding the alloted budget] pp. 314-316. In the Report of the Commissioner of Indian Affairs. 1857. Washington: William A. Harris, 1858. [I20.1:857]

Letter critizing Brigham Young for his irresponsible handling of alloted funds.

[94] Denver, J. W. Report of the Commissioner of Indian Affairs," pp. 1-12. In the Report of the Commissioner of Indian Affairs. 1857. Washington: William A. Harris, 1858. [I20.1:857]

Only scanty information out of Utah but he fears that the Mormons have been tampering with the Indians.

[95] Hurt, Garland. "Utah Superintendency," pp. 305-306. In the Report of the Commissioner of Indian Affairs. 1857. Washington: William A. Harris, 1858. [I20.1:857]

Mormon missionaries are creating a distinction between Mormons and the people of the United States. The acting Commissioner Charles E. Mix sends the letter with his comments on the subject.

[96] "Message of the President of the United States," Congressional Globe 35th Congress 1st session (8 December 1857) vol. 118, Appendix, pp. 1-7. [X118]

On page 5 and 6, President Buchanan maintains the need to quell this first rebellion which has occurred in the territories. He further concludes that such "frenzied fanaticism" requires a force large enough "to convince these deluded people that resistance would be vain."

[97] Mix, Charles E. "Memoranda for the Secretary of the Interior," pp. 307-308. In the Report of the Commissioner of Indian Affairs. 1857. Washington: William A. Harris, 1858. [I20.1:857]

Agents are warned to scrutinize the Mormon missionary activity among the Indians both within Utah, and other places, to see if the Mormons are creating a rift between the Indians and the people of the United States.

[98] Morrill, Justin Smith (Vermont) "Utah Territory and its Late laws--Polygamy and its License," Congressional Globe 34th Congress 3d session (24 February 1857) vol. 114, Appendix, pp. 284-290. [X114]

Morrill reiterates his belief that Utah and its laws, where the patriarchal institution of polygamy prevails, are "hostile to the republican form of government." Brigham Young naturally takes a great deal of heat regarding both polygamy and his alleged riches.

Morrill actually quotes a poem from the News [Deseret?]
which encourages tithes. He cites Indian slavery in
the laws of the territory, polygamy (quoting from the
Book of Mormon) and the fact that the "spiritual wives"
were in rebellion under polygamy.

[99] Morrill, Justin Smith. Speech of Hon. Justin S. Morrill, of
Vermont, on Utah Territory and its laws - Polygamy and
its license; delivered in the House of Representatives,
February 23, 1857. Washington: Office of the Congressional
Globe, 1857. 14p.

See entry 98 for annotation. Although both entry 98
and 99 are the same speech, the dates of the speech as
listed here, 24 February and 23 February, respectively,
are the dates as listed on the documents.
[Flake 5570]
CtY, CU-B, UHi, UPB, US1C

[100] "Report of the Secretary of the Interior," Congressional
Globe 35th Congress, 1st session (3 December 1857) vol.
118, Appendix, pp. 14-19. [X118]

Secretary Thompson briefly mentions, on p. 14, that the
surveys have been stopped in Utah because of the
reported hostilities of the Mormon authorities.

[101] "Reports on Utah Expedition," pp. 1-39. In Report of the
Secretary of War, December 5, 1857. Washington: A. O.
P. Nicholson, 1858. [W1.1:857]

The initial documents to appear in the War Department
annual reports regarding the Utah Expedition, including
the Report of the Secretary of War.

[102] "Resolution," (21 December 1857) Acts, resolutions and
memorials passed by the Legislative Assembly of the
Territory of Utah, 1919, pp. 18-19.

Expresses appreciation of the legislators to Governor
Brigham Young and the course he has followed as governor.
They especially decried the "bitter hostility manifested
towards a most loyal and innocent people by the present
Administration."

UPB, UU

[103] U.S. House. 34th Congress. 3d Session. Committee on the
Territories. Carson Valley, Utah - annexation to State
of California - and eastern boundary of California.
(H. Report. No. 116) Washington: Cornelius Wendell,
Printer, 1857. 2p. [Serial Set 912]

Desire of Carson Valley residents to be divided from
Utah due to Mormon discrimination.

[104] U.S. House. 35th Congress. 1st Session. In Message from
the President of the United States to the Two Houses of
Congress at the commencement of the First Session of
the Thirty-sixth Congress. (Report of the Secretary of

War) (H. Ex. Doc. No. 2) Washington: Cornelius
Wendell, Printer, 1857. 572p. [Serial Set 943]

Pages 6-9, 21-38, includes reports and letters on the
Utah Expedition, as well as a Proclamation from Brigham
Young.

[Flake 9249]

[105] U.S. House. 36th Congress. 1st Session. Report upon the
Colorado River of the West, explored in 1857 and 1858
by Lieutenant Joseph C. Ives, Corps of Topographical
Engineers, under the direction of the Office of Explorations
and Surveys, A. A. Humphreys, Captain Topographical
Engineers, in charge. By Order of the Secretary of
War. (H. Ex. Doc. No. 90, pt. 1) Washington: Govt.
Print Off., 1861. 131p. [Serial Set 1058]

References are made to Mormon road, pp. 80, 87-89;
encounter with Jacob Hamblin party, pp. 88-91; quotes
from the narrative of Olive Oatman, a Mormon, p. 75.

[Flake 4287]

[106] U.S. War Department. General Orders. Washington, New
York, 1857-58. 20 nos.

Orders dealing with the deployment of troops for the
invasion of Utah, etc.

[Flake 9246]
CtY, UPB (#1,2,3,5,6,11,12,16,17,19,20)

[107] "Utah and the expedition thither," Congressional Globe 35th
Congress, 1st Session (5 December 1857) vol. 118,
Appendix, pp. 33-34. [X118]

Report of Secretary of War, Floyd, on Utah the expedition
thither.

[108] Young, Brigham. Governor's Message to the Legislative
Assembly of the Territory of Utah: Delivered in Great
Salt Lake City, December 15, 1857. [Great Salt Lake
City, 1857] 11p.

Oblique references by Brigham Young to the Utah Expedition,
and mention of the system of Ward schools throughout
the Territory.

[Flake 9352]
CSmH, CtY, CU-B, NjP, UPB, US1C

[109] Young, Brigham. "Governor's Message to the Legislative
Assembly of the Territory of Utah, Dec. 15, 1857,"
[inserted] after p. 57. In the Journal of the Legislative
Assembly of the Territory of Utah for the Sixth Annual
session, 1856-57. Great Salt Lake City: James Macknight,
public printer, 1857.

The Wednesday, December 23, 1857, issue of the Deseret
News is inserted, which contains the Governor's message.
It includes oblique references to the Utah Expedition,
mention of the system of Ward schools throughout the
territory.

UPB, US1C

"Whereas the Territory of Utah was settled by
certain emigrants from the States and from
foreign countries, who have for several years
past, manifested a spirit of insubordination
to the constitution and laws of the United
States. The great mass of those settlers,
acting under the influence of leaders to whom
they seem to have surrendered their judgment,
refuse to be controlled by any other authority.
They have been often advised to obedience,
and these friendly counsels have been answered
with defiance."

[Entry 118]

---

[110] "Additional Volunteer regiments," Congressional Globe 35th
Congress, 1st session (24 March 1858) vol. 116 p. 1297.
[X116]

The occasion for the discussion of H.R. No. 313, to
provide for the organization of a regiment of mounted
volunteers for the defense of the frontier of Texas was
seized by Mr. Iverson of Georgia to request four
regiments to be used in quelling the Utah rebellion.

[111] "Affairs in Utah," pp. 28-223. In Report of the Secretary
of War, December 6, 1858. Washington: James B.
Steedman, printer, 1858. [W1.1:858]

One of the three major series of documents from the War
Department on the Utah Expedition. Ninety-two separate
series of documents are included.

Variant ed. U.S. 35th Congress, 2d session. Senate Ex.
Doc. No. 13. Serial Set 976.

[112] "Army Bill," Congressional Globe 35th Congress, 1st session
(1 April 1858) vol. 116, pp. 1425-1433. [X116]

Continued debate on H.R. No. 313, to provide troops for
Texas frontier fighting. The debate continued around
the need for troops in Utah to quell the rebellion.

[113] "Bill to raise volunteers," Congressional Globe 35th
Congress, 1st session (10, 17, 18 March 1858) vol. 116,
pp. 1037-1042, 1072, 1165-1175, 1177-1187. [X116]

A bill (unnamed and unnumbered) to raise troops to go
to Utah Territory to quell the open rebellion. Important
debates regarding the Utah Expedition.

[114] Bingham, John Armor. Increase of the army: Speech of Hon.
John A. Bingham, of Ohio, in the House of Representatives,
March 17, 1858. [Washington: Printed at the Congressional
Globe Office, 1858] 7p.

Related particularly to the raising of troops for use in Utah. Bingham's speech included in entry 113 above.

[Flake 521]
DLC, OClWHi

[115] Boyce, William W. (S.C.) "Kansas Affairs," Congressional Globe 35th Congress, 1st session (11 March 1858) vol. 116, pp. 1084-1086. [X116]

In the middle of the Kansas debate, Mr. Boyce made remarks concerning methods for suppressing the Mormons, then in "rebellion."

[116] Buchanan, James. "By James Buchanan, President of the United States of America: A Proclamation, 6 April 1858," pp. 3024-3026. In A Compilation of the Messages and Papers of the Presidents, by James D. Richardson, vol. 4. New York: Bureau of National Literature, 1911, c1897. [GS4.113:4, AE2.114:1-27/v.4]

The proclamation gives Buchanan's justification for his actions in sending the troops to Utah in what became known as the Utah War. The proclamation also addresses directly the "fellow-citizens of Utah" as to the error of their ways.

[117] Buchanan, James. Message of the President of the United States. [Washington: Printed at the Congressional Globe Office, 1858] 16p.

Treats trouble in Kansas and sending troops to Utah.

[Flake 9217]
CtY

[118] Buchanan, James. A proclamation. [Washington, 1858] 3p.

Signed: April 6, 1858.

Concerning the Utah Expedition and its necessity.

[Flake 9220]
CtY, NjP, ULA, UPB, USlC

[119] Buchanan, James. "Second Annual message, 6 December 1858," pp. 3034-3037. In A Compilation of the Messages and Papers of the Presidents, by James D. Richardson, Vol. 4. New York: Bureau of National Literature, 1911, c1897. [GS4.113:4, AE2.114:1-27/v.4]

Various incidents in the Utah War are described.

[120] Buchanan, James. "Transmission to Congress, 26 February 1858," p. 3013. In A Compilation of the Messages and Papers of the Presidents, by James D. Richardson, Vol. 4. New York: Bureau of National Literature, 1911, c1897. [GS4.113:4, AE2.114:1-27/v.4]

Message to the House of Representatives from Buchanan, which deals with the Utah Expedition and throws light "upon the question as to how far said Brigham Young and his followers are in a state of rebellion or resistance to the Government of the United States."

[121] Buchanan, James. "Transmission to Congress, June 10, 1858," p. 3018. In A Compilation of the Messages and Papers of the Presidents, by James. D. Richardson, Vol. 4. New York: Bureau of National Literature, 1911, c1897. [GS4.113:4, AE2.114:1-27/v.4]

Deals with a letter from Governor Cumming which describes the Utah War as over and the "reign of the Constitution and the laws" as having been restored.

[122] Cumming, Alfred A. Governor's message to the Legislative Assembly of the Territory of Utah. December 13, 1858. [Great Salt Lake City, 1858] 5p.

Notes thankfulness for not having the horrors of civil war (Utah expedition). Tells of his part in bringing about peace.

[Flake 9357]
UPB, US1C

[123] Cumming, Alfred A. "Governor's Message to the Legislative Assembly of the Territory of Utah, Dec. 13, 1858," pp. 1-5. In the Journal of the Legislative Assembly of the Territory of Utah [n.p., n.d.]

There is no title page on the BYU copy, in fact, most of the pages are simply cut and pasted into the book which contains the journals for 1852-59. Gov. Cumming's notes thankfulness for not having the horrors of civil war [Utah Expedition]. Tells of his part in bringing about peace.

UPB, US1C

[124] Curtis, Samuel Ryan. The Mormon rebellion and the bill to raise volunteers: Speech of Hon. Samuel R. Curtis, of Iowa. Delivered in the U.S. House of Representatives, March 10, 1858. [Washington, 1858] 16p.

Mr. Curtis' speech can also be found in the Congressional Globe, see entry 113.

[Flake 2624]
CU-B, DLC, MH, UPB, US1C

[125] "Deficiency Bill," Congressional Globe 35th Congress, 1st session (6, 7 April 1858) vol. 116, pp. 1493-1494, 1517-1519. [X116]

Provides information on the cost and formation of the Utah Expedition. The latter paging includes a table of rates of payment and names of posts or places from which stores are to be taken.

[126] "Delegate from Utah," Congressional Globe 35th Congress, 1st session (5 January 1858) vol. 115, pp. 134, 165-170. [X115]

Debates the right of Representative Bernhisel to his
seat during the Utah expedition.

[127] "Difficulties in Utah," <u>Congressional Globe</u> 35th Congress,
1st session (24 March 1858) vol. 116, p. 1297. [X116]

A resolution was presented to suspend the territorial
Laws of Utah while the rebellion was ensuing. The
papers were referred to the Committee on the Judiciary.

[128] Faulkner, Charles James. <u>Speech of the Hon. Charles J.</u>
<u>Faulkner of Virginia in favor of an increase of the</u>
<u>army and in opposition to the employment of volunteers</u>
<u>in Utah. Delivered in the House of Representatives,</u>
<u>March 9, 1858</u>. Washington, 1858. 18p.

A speech against the church situation in Utah, and the
folly of hiring volunteers to serve in Utah.
[Flake 3314]
NjP, Vi, ViU

[129] Faulkner, Charles James (Virginia), "Bill to Raise Volunteers,"
<u>Congressional Globe</u> 35th Congress, 1st session (9 March
1858) vol. 115, pp. 1007-1009. [X115]

See entry 128 for annotation.

[130] Forney, Jacob. "Utah Superintendency, September 6, 1858,"
pp. 209-213. In <u>Report of the Commissioner of Indian</u>
<u>Affairs, accompanying the annual report of the Secretary</u>
<u>of the Interior for the year 1858</u>. Washington: Wm. A.
Harris, 1858. [I20.1:858]

Forney refers to the visit to Great Salt Lake of Little
Soldier, chief, and Benjamin Simons, sub-chief of a
band of Shoshonees. Some merchants, "who were well
acquainted with this tribe from their proximity to the
Mormon settlement," looked upon their visit with
suspicion. The Indians wanted to know why there were
troops in the Territory.

Trouble with Spanish Fork over the Indian farm close
by. Brief mention of the Mountain Meadows Massacre.

[131] "Memorial from Utah," <u>Congressional Globe</u>, 35th Congress,
1st session (14 April 1858) vol. 116, pp. 1577-1578.
[X116]

Petition of Utah people for withdrawal of troops from
Utah. The troops were of course part of the Utah
Expedition.

[132] "Memorial of the Legislature of Utah," <u>Congressional Globe</u>
35th Congress, 1st session (16 March 1858) vol. 116,
pp. 1151-1152. [X116]

With some marvelous rhetoric, the Utah legislature,
with Heber C. Kimball as President of the Council and

John Taylor as Speaker of the House, request withdrawal of Johnston's troops.

[133] "New Regiment Bill," <u>Congressional Globe</u> 35th Congress, 1st session (5 April 1858) vol. 116, pp. 1474-1477. [X116]

Mr. Curtis of Iowa, expresses concern over the new regiment bill, because he feels the number of troops being sent to Utah was too small.

[134] Seville, William P. <u>Narrative of the march of Co. A engineers from Fort Leavenworth, Kansas, to Fort Bridger, Utah, and return, May 6 to October 3, 1858. A contribution to the history of the United States Corps of Engineers</u> by William P. Seville. Rev. under the direction of the Commandant Engineer School, U. S. Army, by First Lieut. John W. N. Schulz... Washington Barracks: Press of Engineers School, 1912. 46p. (Occasional papers. Engineer school. U.S. Army. No. 48) [W7.16/2:48]

On p. 5 the grave of Susan G. Hale, Mormon, 1852, was mentioned. Pages 30-34 contain material on the Mormon trail and the Utah Expedition.

[Flake 7623]

[135] Sinclair, Charles E. <u>Charge of Hon. Chas E. Sinclair, Judge of the Third Judicial District of the Territory of Utah; Delivered in Great Salt Lake City, Nov. 22nd, 1858.</u> Great Salt Lake City, 1858. 8p.

Problem of Judges in Utah.

[Flake 7729]
US1C

[136] "Suppression of Polygamy," <u>Congressional Record</u> 35th Congress, 1st session (4 January 1858) vol. 115, pp. 184-185. [X115]

Bill (unnumbered, but apparently H.60) introduced by Mr. Morrill to suppress polygamy in the territories. Brief debate, and a certain lack of seriousness over the issue of polygamy. It is suggested that the bill should be sent to the Committee on Naval Affairs because polygamy is practiced more generally in that profession than any other.

[137] "Telegraph to Utah," <u>Congressional Globe</u> 35th Congress, 1st session (13 April 1858) vol. 116, pp. 1296, 1542, 1559-1564. [X116]

S.211 to facilitate communications with the army in Utah. Lively debate ensued on whether there should be more troops sent to Utah, and in a little tongue in cheek, it was even suggested that we should vote in some sloops-of-war.

[138] Thompson, John B. <u>Mormonism - increase of the army. Speech of Hon. John Thompson, of New York. Delivered</u>

in the House of Representatives, January 27, 1858.
Washington: Buell & Blanchard, Printers, 1858. 8p.

See entry 139 for annotation.

[Flake 8939]

CSmH, CtY, CU-B, DLC, ICN, MH, NjP, NN, UHi, UPB

[139] Thompson, John B. (Kentucky) Congressional Globe 35th
Congress, 1st session (27 January 1858) vol. 115, pp.
448-452. [X115]

In the middle of a lengthy debate on slavery, Mr.
Thompson of Kentucky, launched into a debate on Mormonism
and its evils. He would do three basic things to
eliminate this evil: 1. Pass a law eliminating
polygamy; 2. Send an army large enough to capture
Brigham Young; and 3. Secure for the territories'
citizens a republican form of government. If all these
failed, he would turn the city into a vast military camp.

[140] U.S. House. 35th Congress. 1st Session. Carson's Valley.
Message from the President of the United States,
transmitting a memorial of citizens of Carson's Valley,
asking for the establishment of a territorial government
over them. (H. Ex. Doc. No. 102) Washington: James
B. Steedman, Printer, 1858. 3p. [Serial Set 957]

Need to be free of the Mormons' domination.

[Flake 1216]

[141] U.S. House. 35th Congress. 1st Session. Cessation of
difficulties in Utah. Message from the President of
the United States relative to the probable termination
of Mormon troubles in Utah Territory. (H. Ex. Doc. No.
138) Washington: James B. Steedman, 1858. 7p.
[Serial Set 959]

[Flake 9356]

[142] U.S. House. 35th Congress. 1st Session. Committee on the
Territories. Territory of Nevada. [To accompany Bill
H.R. No. 567] May 12, 1858. (H. Report. No. 375)
Washington: James B Steedman, Printer, 1858. 5p.
[Serial Set 966]

To accompany a petition from Carson Valley, requesting
that that part of Utah Territory be cut off to get out
from under the domination of the Mormons.

[143] U.S. House. 35th Congress. 1st Session. Committee on
Territories. The Utah Expedition. Message from the
President of the United States, transmitting reports
from the Secretaries of State, of War, of the Interior,
and of the Attorney-General, relative to the military
expedition ordered into the Territory of Utah. February
26, 1858. (H. Ex. Doc. No. 71) Washington: James B.
Steedman, 1858. 215p. [Serial Set 956]

One of the three major government reports dealing with
the Utah expedition. Includes numerous letters and
circulars which is basically a blow-by-blow account of
the Utah expedition in 1857 and 1858, with such documents

as a Proclamation by Brigham Young, and numerous letters of his, as well as Johnston, Daniel Wells, John Taylor, and numerous others. Page 63 lists all the supplies burnt by the Mormons at Green River Utah.

[Flake 9221]

[144] U.S. House. 35th Congress. 1st Session. Contracts-Utah Expedition. Letter from the Secretary of War, in answer to a Resolution of the House calling for a statement of all contracts made in connexion [sic] with the Utah Expedition. (H. Ex. Doc. No. 99) Washington: James B. Steedman, 1858. 5p. [Serial Set 958]

Reiterates the contracts made with the Army during the Utah Expedition by various contractors for supplies such as bacon, cider vinegar, salt, etc. Also includes schedule of prices per hundred pounds, per hundred miles to be paid to Russell, Majors, and Waddell.

[Flake 9244]

[145] U.S. House. 35th Congress. 1st Session. Estimate-Utah Expedition; letter from the Secretary of War, transmitting an estimate for subsistence of troops for the Utah Expedition. (H. Ex. Doc. No. 33) Washington: Govt. Print. Off., 1858. 2p. [Serial Set 955]

[Flake 9245]

[146] U.S. House. 35th Congress. 1st Session. Indian war in Oregon and Washington Territories. Letter from the Secretary of the Interior, transmitting, in compliance with the resolution of the House of the 15th instant, the report of J. Ross Browne, on the subject of the Indian war in Oregon and Washington Territories. (H. Ex. Doc. 38) Washington: James B. Steedman, 1858. 62p. [Serial Set 955]

On p. 12, allegations of Mormon interference.

[Flake 945]

[147] U.S. House. 35th Congress. 1st Session. Utah. Memorial of the members and officers of the Legislative Assembly of the Territory of Utah, setting forth their grievances, and praying Congress to give them a voice in the selection of their rulers. . . (H. Misc. Doc. No. 100) Washington: James B. Steedman, 1858. 5p. [Serial Set 963]

A memorial from the members and officers of the Territorial legislature, including Heber C. Kimball, Daniel H. Wells, Franklin D. Richards, Lorenzo Snow, Wilford Woodruff and others. They begged for troops to be withdrawn, and for a voice in choosing their leaders. Brought up Mormonism's bloody past in Missouri and Illinois.

[Flake 9389]

[148] U.S. Senate. 35th Congress. 1st Session. Committee on Military Affairs. In the Senate of the United States... Report. [To accompany Bill S. 211.] The Committee on

Military Affairs and the Militia, to whom was referred the memorial of Henry O'Rielly, John J. Speed, and Tal. P. Shaffner, proposing to establish telegraphic communication between the army of Utah and the War Department, by erecting a line from the westerly terminus of the Missouri river line to Utah, have had the same under consideration, and report. (S. Rep. No. 128) Washington: William A. Harris, 1858. 3p. [Serial Set 938]

Need of telegraphic facilities for the Mexican war, and the Mormon difficulties.

[149] U.S. Senate. 35th Congress. 1st Session. H.R. 313, "An act to provide for the organization of a regiment of mounted volunteers for the defense of the frontier of Texas, and to authorize the President to cal into the Service of the United States four additional regiments of volunteers. March 22, 1858." [Washington: Govt. Print. Off., 1858] 4p.

Referred to the Committee on Military Affairs and the Militia. Section 4 speaks of quelling disturbances in the Territory of Utah.

DLC, UPB, US1C

[150] U.S. Senate. 35th Congress. 1st Session. Letter of the delegate of the Territory of Utah in Congress, enclosing the Memorial of delegates of the convention which assembled in Great Salt Lake City, and adopted a constitution with a view to the admission of Utah into the Union as a state, together with a copy of that constitution. (S. Misc. Doc. No. 240) Washington: William A. Harris, printer, 1858. 10p. [Serial Set 936]

Includes the full text of the Constitution of Deseret.

[Flake 9340]

[151] U.S. Senate. 35th Congress. 1st Session. Memorial of the members and officers of the Legislative Assembly of the Territory of Utah, setting forth their grievances, and praying congress to reconsider the course already taken, to respect their constitutional rights, withdraw the troops, and give them a voice in the selection of their rulers. (S. Misc. Doc. No. 201) Washington: William A. Harris, 1858. 5p. [Serial Set 936]

See entry 147 for annotation.

[Flake 9389]

[152] U.S. Senate. 35th Congress. 1st Session. Message of the President of the United States, communicating a despatch form Governor Cumming, relative to the termination of the difficulties with the Territory of Utah. (S. Ex. Doc. No. 67) Washington: William A. Harris, 1858. 7p. [Serial Set 930]

Letters relative to the termination of the difficulties in the Territory of Utah; report of Governor Cumming

upon the establishment of the Territorial government
and the suppression of rebellion in the Territory.

[Flake 9358]

[153] U.S. Senate. 35th Congress. 1st Session. Message of the
President of the United States to the Two Houses of
Congress at the commencement of the First Session of
the Thirty-fifth Congress. Report of the Secretary of
War. (S. Ex. Doc. No. 11) Washington: William A.
Harris, Printer, 1858. 38p. [Serial Set 919]

Contains letters from Brigham Young, officers of the
Army, and the Secretary of War in reference to the
entrance of troops into Utah.

[Flake 9253]

[154] U.S. Senate. 35th Congress. 2d Session. Message of the
President of the United States to the two houses of
Congress... Dec. 6, 1858. (S. Ex. Doc. No. 1) Washington:
William A. Harris, 1858. 150p. [Serial Set 974]

Proclamation of James Buchanan, 6 April 1858. Need for
citizens of Utah to abide by the laws on pp. 69-72.

[155] U. S. Senate. 35th Congress. 1st Session. Resolution of
the Legislature of the State of California, in favor of
the establishment of a territorial government in Carson
Valley. (S. Misc. Doc. No. 181) Washington: William
A. Harris, Printer, 1858. 1p. [Serial Set 936]

Need to establish the territorial government, with the
coming of the Utah Expedition.

[156] U.S. Senate. 35th Congress. 1s Session. S. 14, "Joint
Resolution authorizing the appointment of commissioners
to examine into the difficulties in the affairs of the
Territory of Utah, with a view to their settlement,
June 14, 1858." [Washintgon: Govt. Print. Off., 1858]
1p.

Referred to the Committee on Military Affairs and the
Militia.

The President is authorized to appoint three commissioners
to go to Utah Territory to look into the difficulties.

DLC, UPB, US1C

[157] "Utah Affairs," Congressional Globe 35th Congress, 1st
session (10 June 1858) vol. 117, pp. 2900, 2919.
[X117]

Contains a letter from President James Buchanan to
Congress expressing his believe that there is reason to
believe that the rebellion in Utah has terminated.

1859

"There can be no reasonable doubt that the
great mass of the Mormon community are misled

into all their errors by a religious fanaticism,
while a set of heartless, hypocritical
leaders are feeding the fire and fanning the
flame of their mad infatuation."

[Entry 160]

"During the past year the inhabitants of
this Territory, for the most part, have been
peacefully and profitably employed in their
various occupations. But I regret to be
obliged to state that this city and the
village of Fairfield, near Camp Floyd, within
the military Reserve, have been the scenes of
many murders and other acts of violence, the
perpetrators of which have fled, and thus
eluded justice."

[Entry 161]

---

[158] "Affairs in the Department of Utah," pp. 121-255. In
Report of the Secretary of War, December 1, 1859.
Washington: George W. Bowman, Printer, 1860. [W1.1:859]

One of the three major reports to appear in the War
Department Annual Reports regarding the Utah Expedition.
Sixty-eight separate series of documents are included
in this volume.

A summary of the sixty-eight reports by the Secretary
of War appears on pp. 14-15.

Variant ed. U. S. Senate. 36th Congress, 1st session.
Senate Ex. Doc. No. 2. Serial Set 1024.

[159] Bates, Edward. The diary of Edward Bates, 1859-1866.
Edited by Howard K. Beale. Washington: Govt. Print.
Off., 1933. [SI4.1:930/v.4]

Note on the government's attempt to stop polygamy, pp.
5, 7. No country where polygamy was established had
even obtained a well-ordered constitution.

Volume 4 of the 1930 Annual Report of the American
Historical Association.

[160] Brocchus, Perry E. Letter of Judge Brocchus, of Alabama,
to the public, upon the difficulties in the Territory
of Utah. Washington: H. Polkinhorn, 1859. 32p.

Includes a letter to Hon. Daniel Webster, dated 1852,
pp. 15-32. Brocchus' favorable opinions of the Mormons
were erroneous. Thinks President should remove Brigham
Young from office as Governor. Discusses nomination of
Orson Hyde as his successor (later withdrawn because of
Senate disapproval). He characterized Brigham Young as

a "ring leader in the works of sedition and social abomination".

[Flake 872]

NN, US1C

[161] Cumming, Alfred. A. The Governor's Message to the Legislative Assembly, 12th December, 1859. [n.p., n.d.] 4p.

Briefly Cumming mentions the large fund acquired in the Territory by tithing and his belief that this should be taxed along with other Church Property.

UPB

[162] Forney, Jacob. "Utah Superintendency," pp. 369-372. In Report of the Commissioner of Indian Affairs. 1859. Washington: George W. Bowman, Printer, 1860. [I20.1:859]

Contains his summary of his investigation into the Mountain Meadows Massacre.

[163] Greenwood, A. B. "Report," pp.4, 21-2. In Report of the Commissioner of Indian Affairs. 1859. Washington: George W. Bowman, printer, 1860. [I20.1:859]

Brief mention of the Mountain Meadows Massacre by the Secretary of the Interior and the Commissioner of Indian Affairs. The Indian participation was instigated by lawless whites using starving Indians.

[164] "Independence, Salt Lake City, and Placerville Mails," pp. 26-27. In Post Office Department Annual Report for 1859, [Pl.1:859]

Mentions that this connection with the Pacific was formerly a monthly service but because of the "threatened rebellion of the Mormon population" it was increased to a weekly mail service.

Xerox of appropriate pages at UPB, US1C. Original in full at DLC.

[165] "Indians in Utah," pp. 155-156. In Report of the Commissioner of Indians Affairs. November 26, 1860. Washington: Govt. Print. Off., 1861. [I20.1:860]

Brief discussion of the Mountain Meadows Massacre in regard to conditions of the Indians due to their hunting grounds being taken by the Mormons.

[166] Porter, James. Memorial of J. & R. H. Porter. [n.p., 1859?] 37p.

"Brief in the case of J. C. Irwin & Co. & J. & R. Porter" pp. [3]-10. "Affidavits" pp. [11]-37. Utah Expedition claims.

UPB

[167] Simpson, James Hervey. Report of explorations across the Great Basin of the Territory of Utah for a direct wagon-route from Camp Floyd to Genoa, in Carson Valley,

in 1859, by Captain J. H. Simpson... Made by authority
of the Secretary of War and under instructions from
Bvt. Brig. Gen. A. S. Johnston... Washington: Govt.
Print. Off. 1876. 518p. [W7.5:Si5]

Published by U. S. Army, Corps of engineers.

Early descriptions of Utah with brief mention of its
people.

Pages 35-36 Mountain Meadows Massacre; pages 62, 118
mention of a wagon road in Nevada used by Mormons when
they supposedly fled troops, Steptoe Valley; page 146,
Fort Bridger where 100 Mormon handcarts passed through
on Aug. 28, 1859; pages 217-218 Mormon toll on Timpanogos
Pass; page 299 Fort Supply; pages 454-455, and 462
Mountain Meadows Massacre.

[Flake 772]

[168] U.S. District Court. Utah. (Second District). Report of
the Grand Jury of the Second District of Utah Territory,
September Term, 1859. Carson Valley: Printed at the
Office of the Territorial Enterprise, 1859. 2, 3-4p.

Discusses Mormon theology, Mormon outrages and the
creation of a Nevada Territory, to ensure independence
from the Mormons.

[Flake 9196a]
CtY

[169] U.S. House. 35th Congress. 2d Session. Pacific wagon
roads. Letter from the Secretary of the Interior,
transmitting a report upon the several wagon roads
constructed under the direction of the Interior Department.
(H. Ex. Doc. No. 108) Washington: James Steedman,
Printer, 1859. 125p. [Serial Set 1008]

Includes material on roads through Mormon territory,
Mormon ferries, Indian version of the Salmon River
Colony attack. Report prepared by A. H. Campbell,
General Superintendent.

[Flake 9192]

[170] U.S. Senate. 35th Congress. 2d Session. Report of the
Secretary of War, communicating, in compliance with a
resolution of the Senate, Captain Simpson's report and
map of wagon road routes in Utah Territory. (S. Ex.
Doc. No. 40) Washington: Govt. Print. Off., 1859.
84p. [Serial Set 984]

Brief mention of Mormons and a description of the
territory.

[Flake 7725]

[171] "Utah," Congressional Globe 36th Congress, 1st session (1
December 1859), vol. 124, Appendix, p. 12. [X124]

Continuation of the Secretary of War, Floyd, on Utah
and the expedition thither which appeared in v .118,
pp. 33-34. Decidedly anti-Mormon.

"But, sir, some thirteen years ago, one
Brigham Young, a shrewd and selfish and
unscrupulous adventurer, led certain Mormons
from Illinois, or from Missouri across what
was then called the Great American desert, by
a long and wearisome journey, to the basin of
the Great Salt Lake. Poor, deluded, ignorant
fanatics were his followers, who, from having
no religion at all, had been captivated by
the theories of Joe Smith, and had joined the
ranks of the Latter Day Saints."

[Entry 192]

"It is a curious fact, that Mormonism makes
its impression upon the countenance. Whether
owing to the practice of a purely sensual and
material religion, to the premature development
of the passions, or to isolation, there is,
nevertheless, an expression of countenance
and a style of feature, which may be styled
the Mormon expression and style; an expression
compounded of sensuality, cunning, suspicion,
and a smirking self-conceit. The yellow,
sunken, cadaverous visage; the greenish-
colored eyes; the thick, protuberant lips;
the low forehead; the light, yellowish hair;
and the lank, angular person, constitute an
appearance so characteristic of the new race,
the production of polygamy, as to distinguish
them at a glance."

[Entry 199]

---

[172] "Affairs in the Department of Utah," pp. 69-106. In Report
      of the Secretary of War, December 3, 1860. Washington:
      George W. Bowman, Printer, 1860. [W1.1:860]

      Series of letters and petitions regarding troops in
      Utah, and Mormon-Gentile, Mormon government, and
      Mormon-Indian relations. Page 111 also includes
      references to the Mormons inciting the Indians in the
      Carson Valley area.

      Variant ed. U.S. Senate 36th Congress, 2d session.
      Senate Ex. Doc. No. 1, Serial Set 1079.

[173] Buchanan, James. "Fourth annual message, 3 December 1860,"
      p. 3179. In A compilation of the Messages and Papers
      of the Presidents, by James D. Richardson. vol. 5.
      New York: Published by Bureau of National Literature,
      1911, c1897. [GS4.113:5, AE2.114:1-27/v.5]

      Restoration of peace in Utah Territory, which Buchanan
      still maintains was in open rebellion.

[174] Cradlebaugh, John.   "Utah and Mormonism," Congressional
      Globe 36th Congress, 1st session (5 April 1860) vol.
      124, Appendix, pp. 193-194.   [X124]

      An insert in Representative Nelson's speech which is a
      report of Cradlebaugh's speech at Circleville, Ohio in
      which he gives anti-Mormon report on history of Mormons,
      illiteracy, polygamy, and degradation of Mormons.

[175] Cumming, Alfred A.   "Governor's Message to the Council and
      House of Representatives of the Legislature of Utah,
      Nov. 12, 1860," pp. 12-16.   In the Journals of the
      Legislative Assembly of the Territory of Utah of the
      Tenth Annual Session, for the years 1860-61.   Great
      Salt Lake City: Elias Smith, public printer, 1861.

      Brief mention of the establishment of the College of
      Deseret by Brigham Young and the problem in Utah
      Territory of no free or common schools.   Education is
      dominated by the Mormon Church.

                                                     UPB, US1C

[176] Cumming, Alfred A.   "Governor's Message to the Legislative
      Assembly of Utah, 12th November 1860."   4p.

      See entry 175 for annotation.
                                                           UPB

[177] Etheridge, Emerson.   Speech of Emerson Etheridge, of
      Tennessee, delivered in the House of Representatives,
      April 2, 1860.   [Washington]:   Printed by L. Towers
      [1860]   16p.

      Speech given regarding a bill for prohibiting and
      punishing polygamy in the territories.
                                                   [Flake 3184]
                                        CU-B, DLC, OC1WHi, UPB

[178] Foster, Stephen Clark.   Republican land policy - homes for
      the million.   Give the public lands to the people, and
      you settle the slavery question, obliterate the frontiers,
      dispense with a standing army and extinguish Mormonism.
      Speech of Hon. Stephen C. Foster, of Maine, delivered
      in the house of Representatives, April 27, 1860.
      Washington: Buell & Blanchard, Printers, 1860.   8p.

      See entry 179 for annotation.   Appears to be a discrepancy
      on the date the speech was given between the Congressional
      Globe entry below and this entry.

                                                   [Flake 3409]
                                                           UHi

[179] Foster, Stephen Clark (Maine).   "The Republican Land
      Policy--Homes for the Million," Congressional Globe
      36th Congress, 1st session (24 April 1860) vol. 124,
      Appendix, pp. 244-246.   [X124]

      The introduction of H.R. 7 to suppress polygamy met
      with his "hearty support."   He believes that "the only

way to render the abolition of polygamy effectual is to encourage the settlement of the Territories". All in Utah, including law enforcement officials, believe in and practice polygamy.

[180] Gooch, Daniel Wheelright. <u>Polygamy in Utah. Speech of Hon. Daniel W. Gooch, of Mass., delivered in the house of Representatives, April 4, 1860</u>. [Washington, 1860] 8p.

See entry 187 for annotation.

[Flake 3612]
CSmH, CtY, CU-B, DLC, ICN, MH, NjP, UHi, ULA, UPB

[181] Humphreys, A. "Utah Agency," pp. 169-171. In <u>Report of the Commissioner of Indian Affairs</u>. 1860. Washington: George W. Bowman, printer, 1860. [I20.1:860]

Claims that the Mormon population has no sympathy with the plight of the Indians.

[182] Keitt, L. M. (South Carolina). "Polygamy in Utah," <u>Congressiona Globe</u> 36th Congress, 1st session (4 April 1860) vol. 124, Appendix, pp. 195-198. [X124]

Considers polygamy outside the field of congress and as interference with the sovereignty of the state.

[183] "Military Academy bill," <u>Congressional Globe</u> 36th Congress, 1st session (1 March 1860) vol. 121, pp. 942-944. [X121]

Need to withdraw the army from Utah as the Mormons are getting wealthy from the army's presence.

[184] Nelson, Thomas Amos Rogers (Tennessee). "Polygamy in Utah," <u>Congressional Globe</u> 36th Congress, 1st session (4 and 5 April 1860) vol. 124, Appendix, pp. 190-195. [X124]

Urges the passage of a bill (H.R. 7) to suppress polygamy in Utah.

[185] Nelson, Thomas Amos Rogers. <u>Speech of Hon. Thomas A. R. Nelson...on polygamy in Utah. Delivered in the House of Representatives, April 4 and 5, 1860</u>. [Washington]: Printed by L. Towers [1860] 16p.

See entry No. 184 for annotation.

[Flake 5780]
CU-B, DLC, MH, OClWHi, UHi, USl, USlC

[186] "An Ordinance incorporating the Church of Jesus Christ of Latter Day Saints," <u>Congressional Globe</u> 36th Congress, 1st session (4 April 1860) vol. 124, Appendix, p. 190. [X124]

Inserted as a part of Representative Nelson's speech as cited above.

[187] "Polygamy in Utah," Congressional Globe 36th Congress, 1st
      session (22, 28 March, 2, 3, 4, 5 April 1860) vol. 122,
      pp. 1319, 1409-1412, 1492-1501, 1512-1523, 1540-1546,
      1551, 1557-1560. [X122]

      Lengthy debate on polygamy bill (H.R. 7), fear expressed
      on the effect this legislation would have on women.
      The failure of the federal government to properly
      govern Utah is at the base of the Mormon problem.
      Includes, at least in part, Mr. Etheridge's, Mr.
      Gooch's, and Mr. Thayer's speeches listed as separate
      entries 177, 180, and 192 respectively.

[188] "Prohibition of Polygamy," Congressional Globe 36th Congress,
      1st session (14 March 1860) vol. 122, pp. 1150-1151. [X122]

      Bill providing for the punishment of the crime of
      polygamy in the territories was read and briefly
      discussed.

[189] Simms, William Emmett (Kentucky). "Polygamy in Utah,"
      Congressional Globe 36th Congress, 1st session (4 April
      1860) vol. 124, Appendix, pp. 198-202. [X124]

      Arguments for H.R. 7 to suppress polygamy.

[190] Simms, William Emmett. Speech of Hon. W. E. Simms, of
      Kentucky on polygamy in Utah. Delivered in the House
      of Representatives, April 4, 1860. [Washington]:
      Printed by Lemuel Towers, 1860. 16p.

      See entry 187 for annotation.

                                          [Flakt 7719]
                                 Cty, DLC, US1, US1C

[191] Taylor, Miles (Louisiana), "Polygamy in Utah," Congressional
      Globe 36th Congress, 1st session (2 April 1860) vol.
      124, Appendix, pp. 187-190. [X124]

      Author does not think Congress has the right to legislate
      against polygamy.

[192] Thayer, Eli. The polygamy question. Speech of Hon. Eli
      Thayer, of Massachusetts. Delivered in the House of
      Representatives, April 3, 1860. Washington: Buell &
      Blanchard, Printers, 1860. 8p.

      See entry 187 for annotation.
                                          [Flake 8888]
                     CtY, DLC, NjP, OClWHi, UHi, UPB, US1C

[193] U.S. Census 1860, Part 4: Statistics of the United States
      (including Mortality, Property, etc.) in 1860. Washington:
      Govt. Print. Off., 1866. [I9.5:4]

      Under Miscellaneous statistics, there is a table
      entitled "Statistics of the Churches in ..." Utah
      Territory is on p. 495. Only nine counties were
      reported and the note indicates that there were no
      returns from the following counties: Box Elder, Cache,

Cedar, Davis, Deseret, Greasewood, Green River, Shambip, Summit, Tooele, Walade. Have not been able to identify Walade County.

[194] U.S. House. 36th Congress. 1st Session. Committee on the Judiciary. Polygamy in the territories of the United States [to accompany Bill H.R. No. 7]... Report. The Committee on the Judiciary, to whom was referred "a bill to punish and prevent the practice of polygamy in the territories of the United States, and other places, and disapproving and annulling certain acts of the Legislative Assembly of the Territory of Utah," having had the same under consideration report as follows. (H. Rept. No. 83) Washington: Thomas H. Ford, 1860. 5p. [Serial Set 1067]

[Flake 9128]

[195] U.S. House. 36th Congress. 1st Session. H.R. 7, "A bill to punish and prevent the practice of polygamy in the Territories of the United States, and other places, and disapproving and annulling certain acts of the legislative assembly of the Territory of Utah, February 15, 1860." [Washington: Govt. Print. Off., 1860] 3p.

Referred to the Committee on the Judiciary. Reported by March 14, 1860 without amendment.

Against polygamy and the Utah act incorporating the Church of Jesus Christ of Latter Day Saints, also any other laws that establish, maintain, protect, or countenance the practice of polygamy.

DLC, UPB, US1C

[196] U.S. House. 36th Congress. 1st Session. Utah Territory. Message of the President of the U.S., communicating, in compliance with a resolution of the House, copies of correspondence relative to the condition of affairs in the Territory of Utah. . . (H. Ex. Doc. No. 78) Washington: Thomas H. Ford, Printer, 1860. 51p. [Serial Set 1056]

Most of the pamphlet deals with Judge Cradlebaugh and his difficulties at Provo.

[Flake 9222]

[197] U.S. Senate. 36th Congress. 1st Session. Message of the President of the U.S. communicating, in compliance with a resolution of the Senate, the correspondence between the judges of Utah and the Attorney General or President, with reference to the legal proceedings and conditions of affairs in that Territory. . . (S. Ex. Doc. No. 32) Washington: George W. Bowman, Printer, 1860. 64p. [Serial Set 1031]

Situation in Utah and Mountain Meadows Massacre.

[Flake 9219]

[198] U.S. Senate. 36th Congress. 1st Session. Message of the President of the United States, communicating, in compliance with a resolution of the Senate, information in relation to the massacre at Mountain Meadows and

other massacres in Utah Territory (S. Ex. Doc. No. 42)
Washington: George w. Bowman, 1860. 139p. [Serial Set
1033]

The major printed source on the Mountain Meadows
Massacre to appear in a government publication.

[Flake 9191]

[199] U.S. Senate. 36th Congress. 1st Session. Statistical
report on the sickness and morality in the Army of the
United States, compiled from the records of the Surgeon
General's Office; embracing a period of five years from
January 1, 1855, to January, 1860... (S. Ex. Doc. No.
52) Washington: George W. Bowman, 1860. 525p.
[Serial Set 1035]

Utah section pp. 281-328 discusses disease among the
troops in Utah. Chastises the Mormons and their belief
in faith healing. A Mormon physical type is graphically
depicted.

[Flake 2502]

1861

"Nearly all Mormons are foreigners. Among
these are Welsh, English, Norwegians, Swedes,
some Germans, and a few French. They are
evidently of the lowest and most ignorant
grade of the people in the several countries
from whence they have come. Mixed in with
these are a few low, unprincipled Americans."
[Entry 200]

---

[200] Carleton, James H. Brevet Major, J.S. Army, commanding.
"[Letter to] Maj. D. C. Buell, Assistant Adjutant-
General in San Francisco, from Headquarters Camp
Fitzgerald, near Los Angeles, Cal., July 31, 1861. . ."
pp. 548-551. In The War of the Rebellion, Series I,
Vol. L, Part I. Washington: Govt. Print. Off., 1902.
[W45.5:Ser.I/vol. 50]

Dealing with San Bernardino, where Carleton indicated
there are about 1500 souls, about 1000 being Mormons.
He claims that no matter what the Mormons profess that
they really hate us [the country the army?] at heart.
Carleton's concern is over sending a commander to this
area which is dominated by the Mormons, with a Mormon
sheriff, judge and justice of the peace. He also
appends an enclosure entitled "The Mormons as a People"
which describes ethnic backgrounds and low class
nature.

[201] Dawson, John W. Governor's message to the Legislative
Assembly of Utah, December 10, 1861. [Great Salt Lake
City, 1861] 9pp.

Gives a rundown of the Civil War and then makes a plea
for the Men of Utah to support the Union cause. Quotes

both Brigham Young and Daniel H. Well's statement regarding following the Constitution.

[Flake 9359]
CU-B, UPB, US1C

[202] Dawson, John W. "Governor's Message to the Joint Session of the Legislative Assembly, Dec. 10, 1961," pp. 12-26. In the Journals of the Legislative Assembly of the Territory of Utah, of the Eleventh Annual Session, for the years 1861-62. Great Salt Lake City: Elias Smith, public printer, 1862.

See entry 201 for annotation.

UPB, US1C

[203] Hall, Benjamin F. "[Letter to] Hon. William H. Seward, Denver, Colo. Terr., October 30, 1861. . . In The War of the Rebellion . . ." pp. 636-637. Series III, Vol. I, Washington: Govt. Print. Off., 1899. [W45.5:Ser.III/vol. 1]

Hall reiterates the problems that Gov. Gilpin of Colorado Territory is having among, what Hall calls, malcontented office-seekers and the secessionists or open rebels. In number there are about 5,000 of the border ruffians of Kansas and the destroying angels of Brigham Young. Hall indicates that they are the worst people on the face of the earth to govern.

[204] Martin, Henry. "Utah Superintendency," pp. 135-138. In Report of the Commissioner of Indian Affairs. 1861. Washington: Govt. Print. Off., 1861. [I20.1:861]

Loss of game due to the advent of white settlers.

[205] "Mountain Meadows Massacre," Congressional Globe 36th Congress, 2d session (18 January 1861) vol. 125, p. 442. [X125]

Simply the resolution presented by Mr. Latham regarding Major James Henry Carleton's report on the Mountain Meadows Massacre.

[206] "Report of the Commissioner of the General Land Office, November 30, 1861," pp. 473-474. In Message of the President of the United States to the Two-Houses of Congress at the Commencement of the Second Session of the Thirty-Seventh Congress. Washington: Govt. Print. Off., 1862. [I1.1:861]

Utah's late surveyor general advised in an earlier report that public surveys in Utah cease until a different policy be arranged through Congress to "induce other than Mormon emigration to the Territory."

Variant ed. 37th Congress, 2d session, S. Ex. Doc. No. 1, Serial Set 1117.

[207] "Reports from Committees," Congressional Globe 36th Congress, 2d session (19 February 1861) vol. 126, p. 1013. [X126]

One small paragraph, from the committee, regarding the
heirs of persons killed at Mountain Meadows Massacre.

1862

"The Federal officers are entirely powerless,
and talk in whispers for fear of being
overheard by Brigham's spies. Brigham Young
rules with despotic sway, and death by
assassination is the penalty of disobedience
to his commands. I have a difficult and
dengerous task before me, and will endeavor
to act with prudence and firmness."
                                        [Entry 212]

---

[208] "An Act to punish and prevent the Practice of Polygamy in
      the Territories of the United States and other Places"
      (Chapter CXXVI, July 1, 1862), United States Statutes
      at Large 12, pp. 501-502. [GS4.111:12, AE2.111:12]

      The first of four laws to prohibit polygamy. Known as
      the Morrill Act.

[209] "An Act to Punish and Prevent the Practice of Polygamy in
      the Territories of the United States and Other Places,
      and disapproving and annulling certain Acts of the
      Legislative Assembly of the Territory of Utah," Congressional
      Globe 37th Congress, 2d session (Approved 1, 2 July
      1862) vol. 131, Appendix, p. 385 [X131]

      Text of Chapter CXXVI of the Laws of the United States.

[210] Arny, W.F.M. "[Letter] to Hon. W. H. Seward, Secretary of
      War, Santa Fe, N. Mexico, December 13, 1862 . . .", pp.
      641-642. In The War of the Rebellion, Series I, Vol.
      XV. Washington: Govt. Print. Off., 1886. [W45.5:Ser.I/vol.
      15]

      Arny informed W. H. Seward, Secretary of the State
      Department that 5,000 troops from Texas are preparing
      to invade New Mexico and also obtain possession of
      Colorado and Utah, under Brigham Young, and establish a
      number of slave states.

[211] Connor, Patrick Edward. "[Letter to] Lieut. Col. R. C.
      Drum, Camp Douglas, Dec. 20, 1862..." pp. 256-257. In
      The War of Rebellion Series I, Vol. L, Pt. II.
      Washington: Govt. Print. Off., 1897. [W45.5:Ser.I/vol.
      50/pt. 2]

      Brigham Young's attempt to take over Connor's command.
      Mormons encourage Indian depredations.

[212] Connor, Patrick Edward. "[Letter to] Maj. R. C. Drum, Fort
      Ruby, September 14, 1862..." pp. 119-120. In The War
      of the Rebellion Series I, Vol. L, Pt. II. Washington:
      Govt. Print. Off., 1897. [W45.5:Ser.I/vol. 50/pt. 2]

Mormonism is a community of traitors, murderers, fanatics, and whores. The despotic rule of Brigham Young is decried.

[213] Craig, James. "[Letter] to Major-General Halleck, Fort Laramie, Wyo., August 25, 1862 . . ." p. 596. In The War of the Rebellion, Series I, Vol. XIII. Washington: Govt. Print. Off., 1885. [W45.5:Ser.I/vol. 13]

Mentions a correspondence form Gov. Harding of Utah Territory explaining an interview with Brigham Young regarding Mormon troops. Harding closed the dispatch as follows: "You need not expect anything for the present. Things are not right."

[214] Dole, William P. "Utah Superintendency," pp. 11-45. In Report of the Commissioner of Indian Affairs. 1862. Washington: Govt. Print. Off., 1863. [I20.1:862]

On p. 32, the restless and rebellious spirit of the Indians is in part due to the unwarrantable interference on the part of the Mormons.

[215] Harding, Stephen S. "Governor's Message to the Council and House of Representatives of the Territory of Utah, Dec. 8, 1862," pp. i-xviii. In the Journals of the Legislative Assembly of the Territory of Utah, of the Twelfth Annual Session, for the years 1862-63. Great Salt Lake City: Elias Smith, public printer, 1862.

On pages v-x, Gov. Harding refers to polygamy and its practice and the recent act of Congress passed against it, and the balancing of the liberty of conscience with law.

UPB

[216] "Morrill Act," Congressional Globe 37th Congress, 2d session (3, 1 July 1862) vol. 131, pp. 3023, 3082, 3088, Appendix, p. 385. [X131]

The notice of the passage of the Morrill Act and the complete text of the act is found in the appendix.

[217] "Polygamy," Congressional Globe 37th Congress, 2d session (8 April, 17 June 1862) vol. 129, p. 1581. [X129]

Note of Mr. Morrill's bill to punish polygamy, and also other acts of the Legislative Assembly of the Territory of Utah.

[218] "Polygamy." Congressional Globe 37th Congress, 2d session (9 May, 5 June 1862) vol. 130, pp. 2031, 2587. [X130]

Anti-polygmay bill (H.R. 391).

[219] "Polygamy," Congressional Globe 37 Congress, 2d session (24 June 1862) vol. 131, p. 2906, 3010, 3088. [X131]

Further amendments to the anti-polygamy law (H.R. 391) Morrill Act.

[220] "Polygamy in Utah," <u>Congressional Globe</u> 37th Congress, 2d
       session (3, 17 June 1862) vol. 130, pp. 2506-2507,
       2769. [X130]

       Anti-polygamy bill (H.R. 391) with some amendments.

[221] "Punishment of polygamy," <u>Congressional Globe</u> 37th Congress,
       2d session (28 April 1862) vol. 129, pp. 1847-1848. [X129]

       Talks of a polygamy bill passed by the house two years
       earlier.

[222] Thomas, L. "[Letter] to Mr. Brigham Young, Washington,
       April 28, 1862 . . ." p. 27. In <u>The War of the Rebellion</u>,
       Series III, Vol. II. Washington: Govt. Print. Off.,
       1899. [W45.5:Ser.III/vol. 2]

       L. Thomas, Adjutant-General, is telling Brigham Young
       that by the express direction of the President, Young
       is authorized to raise, arm, and equip one company of
       cavalry for 90 days service.

[223] U.S. House. 37th Congress. 2d Session. <u>Accounts of</u>
       <u>Brigham Young, Supt. of Indian Affairs in Utah Territory.</u>
       <u>Letter from the Secretary of the Interior, transmitting</u>
       <u>report of the investigation of the acts of Governor</u>
       <u>Young, ex-officio Superintendent of Indian Affairs in</u>
       <u>Utah Territory.</u> (H. Ex. Doc. No. 29) Washington,
       1862. 124p. [Serial Set 1128]

       In testimony of William H. Rogers, he reports that
       Jacob Hamblin was hired by Superintendent Forney to
       gather children from the Mountain Meadows Massacre.

                                              [Flake 9210]

[224] U.S. House. 37th Congress. 2d Session. <u>Constitution of</u>
       <u>the State of Deseret.</u> <u>Memorials of the legislature and</u>
       <u>Constitutional Convention of Utah Territory, praying</u>
       <u>the admission into the Union as the State of Deseret.</u>
       (H. Misc. Doc. No. 78) Washington: Govt. Print. Off.,
       1862. 11p. [Serial Set 1141]
                                              [Flake 2786]

[225] U.S. House. 37th Congress. 2d Session. H.R. 391, "An Act
       to punish the practice of polygamy in the Territories
       of the United States and other places, and disapproving
       and annulling certain acts of the legislative assembly
       of the Territory of Utah, April 29, 1862." [Washington:
       Govt. Print. Off., 1862] 3p.

       Referred to the Committee on the Judiciary.

       All acts passed by the Territorial Legislature which
       establish, support, maintain, shield, or countenance
       polygamy, would be disapproved and annulled.

                                           DLC, UPB, US1C

[226] U.S. House. 37th Congress. 2d Session. <u>Indian Department</u>
       <u>property in Utah Territory.</u> <u>Letter from the Secretary</u>

of the Interior in answer to resolution of the House of
24th March, furnishing the evidence called for in
relation of Indian department property in Utah Territory.
(H. Ex. Doc. No. 97) Washington: Govt. Print. Off.,
1862. 31p. [Serial Set 1135]

Includes the accounts of Brigham Young while he was
governor of the territory and ex-officio Superintendent
of Indian Affairs.

[227] "Utah Superintendency, 1862," pp. 72-73. In Report of the
Secretary of the Interior, 1862. Washington: Govt.
Print. Off., 1862. [I1.1:862]

Brief summary report of Indian affairs with special
mention of Mormon interference in official Indian
affairs causing rebellion on the part of the Indians.

Variant ed. 37th Cong., 3d sess., Senate Ex. Doc. 1,
Serial Set 1157.

[228] Young, Brigham. Governor's message to the first General
Assembly of the State of Deseret. [Great Salt Lake
City, 1862] 3p.

In this "ghost" legislature, Young mentions the Mormon
Battalion.

[Flake 2792]
CSmH, NjP, NN, UPB, USlC

1863

"The people are by order of Brigham Young
busily engaged in preparing ammunition and
cannon, and their foundry for some weeks past
has been used for casting cannon balls; they
also loudly assert that I shall not be re-
enforced, and that if the attempt is made
they will cut off the re-enforcements in
detail and attack me."

[Entry 235]

---

[229] Connor, Patrick Edward. "[Letter to] Edwin M. Stanton,
Camp Douglas, Utah Territory, February 6, 1863. . .,"
pp. 185-187. In The War of the Rebellion. . . Series
I, Vol. L., Part I. Washington: Govt. Print. Off.,
1902. [W45.5:Ser.I/vol. 50/pt.1]

Most of the letter contains a vivid description of the
problems with Indians and the troops marching from Camp
Douglas in freezing weather. Connor is quite bitter
over the fact that the Mormons would not help with
information about the Indians and that the Army was
overcharged for every article furnished.

[230] Connor, Patrick Edward. "[Letter to] Lieut. Col. R. C.
Drum, Camp Douglas, Feb. 19, 1863...," pp. 318-320. In
The War of the Rebellion Series I, Vol. L, Pt. II.

Washington: Govt. Print. Off., 1897. [W45.5:Ser.I/
vol. 50/pt. 2]

Polygamy law violated, and the seditious activities of
the Mormons are cited.

[231] Connor, Patrick Edward. "[Letter to] Lieut Col. R.C. Drum,
Camp Douglas, March 3, 1863...," p. 334. In The War of
the Rebellion Series I, Vol. L, Pt. II. Washington:
Govt. Print. Off., 1897. [W45.5:Ser.I/vol. 50/pt. 2]

Mormon meeting to demand the resignation of Governor
Harding and Judges Waite and Drake.

[232] Connor, Patrick Edward. "[Letter to] Lieut. Col. R. C.
Drum, Camp Douglas, March 6, 1863...," p. 342. In The
War of the Rebellion Series I, Vol. L, Pt. II. Washington:
Govt. Print. Off., 1897. [W45.5:Ser.I/ vol. 50/pt. 2]

Mormons are making cartridges and guarding Brigham
Young with 400 men.

[233] Connor, Patrick Edward. "[Letter to] Lieut. Col. R. C.
Drum, Camp Douglas, March 10, 1863...," p. 344. In The
War of the Rebellion Series I, Vol. L, Pt. II. Washington:
Govt. Print. Off., 1897. [W45.5:Ser.I/ vol. 50/pt. 2]

Brigham Young's attempt to provoke an incident with
Connor.

[234] Connor, Patrick Edward. "[Letter to] Lieut. Col. R. C.
Drum, Salt Lake, March 12, 1863...," p. 348. In The
War of the Rebellion Series I, Vol. L, Pt. II. Washington:
Govt. Print. Off., 1897. [W45.5:Ser.I/ vol. 50/pt. 2]

Brigham Young hoisted a signal flag and 1,500 armed men
assembled.

[235] Connor, Patrick Edward. "[Letter to] Lieut. Col. R. C.
Drum, Camp Douglas, March 15, 1863...," pp. 370-374.
In The War of the Rebellion Series I, Vol. L, Pt. II.
Washington: Govt. Print. Off., 1897. [W45.5:Ser.I/
vol. 50/pt. 2]

Summary of the rhetoric concerning the desire of the
Mormons to remove Governor Harding and Judges Waite and
Drake.

[236] Connor, Patrick Edward. "[Letter to] Lieut. Col. R. C.
Drum, Camp Douglas, April 13, 1863...," p. 391. In The
War of the Rebellion Series I, Vol, L, Pt. II. Washington,
Govt. Print. Off., 1897. [W45.5:Ser.I/ vol. 50/pt. 2]

There is a need for more troops to guard the overland
mail from the Indians, who are being urged on by the
Mormons. Mormon refusal to aid army.

[237] Connor, Patrick Edward. "[Letter to] Lieut. Col. R. C.
Drum, Camp Douglas, April 22, 1863...," pp. 410-411.
In The War of Rebellion Series I, Vol. L, Pt. II.

Washington: Govt. Print. Off., 1897. [W45.5:Ser.I/
vol. 50]

Connor to aid the Morrisites (a Mormon schism) as they
were being persecuted by the Mormons.

[238] Connor, Patrick Edward. "[Letter to] Col. R. C. Drum, Camp
Douglas, April 28, 1863...," p. 415. In The War of the
Rebellion Series I, Vol. L, Pt. II. Washington: Govt.
Print. Off., 1897, [W45.5:Ser.I/vol. 50/pt. 2]

Need of more troops, due to the Indians congregating to
disrupt the overland mail, Indians urged on by the
Mormons.

[239] Connor, Patrick Edward. "[Letter to] Lieut Col. R. C.
Drum, Camp Douglas, June 11, 1863...", p. 481. In The
War of the Rebellion Series I, Vol. L, Pt. II. Washington:
Govt. Print. Off., 1897. [W45.5:Ser.I/ vol. 50/pt. 2]

Ute Indians in Mormon settlements waiting to attack the
overland mail.

[240] Connor, Patrick Edward. "[Letter to] Lieut. Col. R. C.
Drum, Great Salt Lake City, June 24, 1863...," pp. 492-
495. In The War of the Rebellion Series I, Vol. L, Pt.
II. Washington: Govt. Print. Off., 1897. [W45.5:Ser.I/
vol. 50/pt. 2]

Hostility between the Mormons, military and the Union.
Mormon encouragement of Indian hostilities.

[241] Connor, Patrick Edward. "[Letter to] Lieut. Col. R. C.
Drum, Great Salt Lake City, June 29, 1863...," pp. 501-
502. In The War of the Rebellion Series I, Vol. L, Pt.
II. Washington: Govt. Print. Off., 1897. [W45.5:Se-
r.I/vol. 50/pt. 2]

Mormon treatment of the Indians at Salt Creek, who
raided the overland mail line.

[242] Connor, Patrick Edward. "[Letter to] Lieut. Col. R. C.
Drum, Great Salt Lake City, July 18, 1863...," pp. 527-
531. In The War of the Rebellion Series I, Vol. L. Pt.
II. Washington: Govt. Print. Off., 1897. [W45.5:Ser.I/vo
50/pt. 2]

Comments on the uselessness of the small number of
troops to control the Mormons. The troops are a source
of irritation to the Mormons causing trouble.

[243] Connor, Patrick Edward. "[Letter to] Lieut. Col. R. C.
Drum, Oct. 26, 1863...," pp. 655-657. In The War of
the Rebellion Series I. Vol. L, Pt. II. Washington:
Govt. Print. Off., 1897. [W45.5:Ser.I/vol. 50/pt. 2]

Need to either have a force in Utah large enough to
punish Mormon law breakers or to invite enough Gentiles
to live in among the Mormons. One way to do this is to
develop the Territory's mineral wealth.

[244] Connor, Patrick Edward. "Report No. 1 of Brig. Gen. P. Edward Connor, Camp Douglas, Utah Territory, April 9, 1863. . .," pp. 198-199. In The War of the Rebellion Series I, Vol. L, Part I. Washington: Govt. Print. Off., 1902, 1902. [W45.5:Ser.I/vol. 50/pt. 1]

Claims that the Goshute [sic] raid on the Overland Mail Route was instigated by the Mormons living in a settlement in Tooele Valley. Connor speculates that Brigham Young's purpose in encouraging these Indian raids was to get the troops to withdraw from the mail route.

[245] Cradlebaugh, John (Nevada). "Utah and the Mormons," Congressional Globe 37th Congress, 3d session (7 February 1863) vol. 133, Appendix, pp. 119-125. [X133]

Calls Mormons thieves, robbers, mean devils; Mormons unfit for statehood.

[246] Cradlebaugh, John. Utah and the Mormons. Speech of Hon. John Cradlebaugh, of Nevada, on the admission of Utah as a state. Delivered in the House of Representatives, February 7, 1863. [Washington: L. Towers & Co., 1863?] 67p.

Appendix: Massacre at Mountain Meadows. Murder of the Parishes and Potter, of the Aiken party, of Jones and his mother, and of Forbes.

The speech was not given due to a shortage on time, but Mr. Cradlebaugh was allowed to print it.

[Flake 2572]
CSmH, CtY, CU-B, DLC, MH, NN, UHi, ULA, UPB, USlC, WHi

[247] Doty, James Duane. "[Letter to] General [Wright], August 9, 1863. . .," pp. 583-584. In The War of the Rebellion Series I, Vol. L. Pt. II. Washington: Govt. Print. Off., 1897. [W45.5:Ser.I/vol. 50/pt. 2]

Troops have displaced the Mormon power over the Indians. Need to keep the troops in Utah due to the militance of the Mormons.

[248] Ethier, Anthony. "Report of Lieut. Anthony Ethier, 2nd Lieut, Company A, 2nd California Vol. Cavalry, Camp Douglas, Utah Territory, April 6, 1863. . .," pp. 200-201. In The War of the Rebellion Series I, Vol. L, Part I. Washington: Govt. Print. Off., 1902. [W45.5: Ser.I/vol. 50/pt. 1]

According to Ethier, the Mormons gave false reports regarding the position of the Indians. While only 100 yards from Cedar Fort, Ethier's noticed a Mormon, Mr. Savage, meeting with the Indians and, apparently, riding off to report to Brigham Young about the incident.

[249] Evans, George S., Colonel, 2nd California Volunteers Cavalry. "[Letter to] G. Wright, Brigadier-General, U.S. Army, Commanding San Francisco, Camp Douglas, Utah Territory, April 17, 1863...," pp. 205-208. In The War

of the Rebellion Series I, Vol. L., Part I. Washington:
Govt. Print. Off., 1902. [W45.5:Ser.I/ vol. 50/pt. 1]

The Expedition was from April 11-20, 1863, from Camp
Douglas to the Spanish Fork Canyon, with a skirmish on
the 12th at Pleasant Grove, and action on the 15th at
Spanish Fork Canyon. The Mormons are repeatedly cited
as instigating and aiding the Indians in their marauding
on the California Volunteers. Special mention is made
of the inhabitants of Pleasant Grove.

[250] Harding, Stephen S. "[Letter to] General G. Wright, Great
Salt Lake City, Feb. 16, 1863. . .," pp. 314-315. In
The War of the Rebellion Series I, Vol, L, Pt. II.
Washington: Govt. Print. Off., 1897. [W45.5:Ser.I/
vol. 50/pt. 2]

Non Mormons would not be safe in Utah if the troops
withdrew.

[251] Wallace, William S., Agent Overland Mail Company. "[Letter
to] Brigadier-General Connor, Fort Crittenden, Utah
Territory, April 1, 1863. . .," p. 199. In The War of
the Rebellion Series I, Vol. L., Part I. Washington:
Govt. Print. Off., 1902. [W45.5:Ser.I/ vol. 50/pt. 1]

Brief note certifying that Lt. Ethier's description of
the Indian Raid on the Overland Mail Route is correct.
Mormons definitely practiced treachery.

[252] Wright, George. "[Letter to] Brig. Gen. L. Thomas, San
Francisco, March 14, 1863. . .," pp. 350-351. In The
War of the Rebellion Series I, Vol. L, Pt. II. Washington:
Govt. Print. Off., 1897. [W45.5:Ser.I/ vol. 50/pt. 2]

Need for more troops to combat Brigham Young's forces.

[253] Wright, George. "[Letter to] Brig. Gen. L. Thomas, San
Francisco, March 30, 1863. . .," pp. 369-370. In The
War of the Rebellion Series I, Vol. L, Pt. II. Washington:
Govt. Print. Off., 1897. [W45.5:Ser.I/ vol. 50/pt. 2]

Mormons only awaiting for an opportunity to strike a
blow against the Union.

[254] Wright, George. "[Letter to] Brig. Gen. L. Thomas, Brig.
General, Commanding Headquarters of the Pacific Adjutant
General, San Francisco, May 4, 1863. . .," p. 204. In
The War of the Rebellion Series I, Vol. L., Part I.
Washington Govt. Print Off., 1902. [W45.5:Ser.I/vol.
50/pt. 1]

Briefly refers to the Geo. S. Evans report which
discusses the expedition from Camp Douglas to Spanish
Fork, Utah Territory, and the perfidious conduct of the
Mormons. Brig. General Wright trusts that "retributative
justice will be meted out to these [Mormons] worse than
open traitors to their country".

[255] Wright, George. "[Letter to] Brig. Gen. L. Thomas, San
Francisco, July 10, 1863. . .," pp. 517-518. In The

War of the Rebellion Series I, Vol. L. Pt. II. Washington: Govt. Print. Off., 1897. [W45.5:Ser.I/ vol. 50/pt. 2]

Reinforcements on the way to Utah due to the civil policy of Brigham Young.

[256] U.S. Senate. 37th Congress. 3d Session. Committee on Territories. Report. The Committee on Territories to whom was referred the resolution of the Senate of the 16th of January in Regard to the Suppression of the Publication of the Message of the Governor of the Territory of Utah. (S. Rept. No. 87) Washington: Govt. Print. Off., 1863. 3p. [Serial Set 1151]

Problem of the Mormon power in the Territory.

[Flake 9183]

[257] U.S. Senate. 37th Congress. 3d Session. Gentlemen of the Council and House of Representatives of the Territory of Utah. (S. Misc. Doc. No. 37) Washington: Govt. Print. Off., 1863. 16p. [Serial Set 1150]

Governor Harding of Utah Territory 1862-1863, gave this talk to the Utah Territorial Legislature on February 28, 1863. He briefly discusses polygamy and polygamy legislation.

[Flake 9360]

1864

"Referring to the letter . . . relative to the attempt to depreciate the national currency by inaugurating in Utah a gold and silver currency, I beg leave to state that I have had reason since that date for modifyng my opinion in relation thereto and the statements therein made. I then entertained and expressed the opinion that this unpatriotic movement had no other or deeper origin than the greed or disloyalty of certain merchants in Great Salt Lake City. It has since been rendered patent to all the world that the real origin of the movement was Brigham Young, the traitor head of the Mormon Church and people."

[Entry 261]

---

[258] Connor, Patrick Edward. "[Letter to] Col. R. C. Drum, Salt Lake City, July 16, 1864. . .," p. 910. In The War of the Rebellion Series I. Vol. L, Pt. II. Washington: Govt. Print. Off., 1897. [W45.5:Ser.I/vol. 50/pt. 2]

Mormon leaders are trying to put him in a situation that would cause his removal.

[259] Connor, Patrick Edward. "[Letter to] General Henry W. Halleck, Camp Douglas, Feb. 15, 1864. . .," pp. 748-751. In The War of the Rebellion Series I. Vol. L. Pt.

II. Washington: Govt. Print Off., 1897. [W45.5:Ser.I/vol. 50/pt. 2]

Refutation of J. F. Kinney's attempt to have the army moved from Fort Douglas. The tyranny of Mormonism, especially Brigham Young, and strong Mormon rhetoric is reiterated.

[260] Connor, Patrick Edward. "[Letter to] Lieut. Col. R. C. Drum, Camp Douglas, July 1, 1864. . .," pp. 887-888. In The War of the Rebellion Series I, Vol. L, Pt. II. Washington: Govt. Print. Off., 1897. [W45.5:Ser.I/ vol. 50/pt. 2]

Peaceful district, despite the Mormon violation of anti-polygamy legislation. Relates his peaceful solution to the problem by promoting more mineral discoveries.

[261] Connor, Patrick Edward. "[Letter to] Lieut. Col. R. C. Drum, Camp Douglas, July 9, 1864. . .," pp. 893-894. In The War of the Rebellion Series I, Vol. L, Pt. II. Washington: Govt. Print. Off., 1897. [W45.5:Ser.I/ vol. 50/pt.2]

In an earlier letter (p. 889) he had told of an attempt to use gold coins rather than national currency. This was done by greedy individuals, however, in this letter he places the blame on Brigham Young, the "traitor head of the Mormon Church".

[262] Connor, Patrick Edward. "[Letter to] Lieut. Col. R. C. Drum, Camp Douglas, July 12, 1864. . .," pp. 899-200. In The War of the Rebellion Series I, Vol. L, Pt. II. Washington: Govt. Print. Off., 1897. [W45.5:Ser.I/ vol. 50/pt. 2]

Need to establish a provost guard in Salt Lake City due to the disloyalty of the Mormons who lose no opportunity to down grade the government.

[263] Connor, Patrick Edward. "[Letter to] Lieut. Col. R. C. Drum, Camp Douglas, July 13, 1864. . .," pp. 901-902. In The War of the Rebellion Series I, Vol. L, Pt. II. Washington: Govt. Print. Off., 1897. [W45.5:Ser.I/ vol. 50/pt. 2]

The Mormons muster 1,000 men under arms after hearing unfavorable news from the east.

[264] Connor, Patrick Edward. "[Letter to] Lieut. Col. R. C. Drum, Camp Douglas, July 15, 1864. . .," p. 904. In The War of the Rebellion Series I, Vol. L, Pt. II. Washington: Govt. Print. Off., 1897. [W45.5:Ser.I/ vol. 50/pt. 2]

Knowing that the army's gun can destroy the city, the Mormons seem to be settling down.

[265] Connor, Patrick Edward. "[Letter to] Lieut. Col. R. C. Drum, Camp Douglas, July 24, 1864. . .," pp. 916-917.

In <u>The War of the Rebellion</u> Series I, Vol. L, Pt. II.
Washington: Govt. Print. Off., 1897. [W45.5:Ser.I/
vol. 50/pt. 2]

Assures Drum that neither he nor Brigham Young would
instigate hostilities.

[266] Drum, Richard Coulter. "[Letter to] Brig. Gen. P. E.
Connor, San Francisco, July 15, 1864. . .," p. 904. In
<u>The War of the Rebellion</u> Series I, Vol. L, Pt. II.
Washington: Govt. Print. Off., 1897. [W45.5:Ser.I/
vol. 50/pt. 2]

Approves of his determination to avoid conflict with
the Mormons.

[267] Drum, Richard Coulter. "[Letter to] Brig. Gen. P. E.
Connor, San Francisco, July 16, 1864. . .," pp. 909-
910. In <u>The War of the Rebellion</u> Series I, Vol. L, Pt.
II. Washington: Govt. Print. Off., 1897. [W45.5:Ser.I/vol.
50/pt. 2]

Again compliments Connor on the peaceable determination
of the Mormon problem.

[268] Irish, O. H. "[Letter to the Commissioner of Indian Affairs],"
pp. 168-171. In <u>Report of the Commissioner of Indian
Affairs. 1864.</u> Washington: Govt. Print. Off.,
1865. [I20.1:864]

Continued emigration of Mormons into the state causes
the Indians great concern.

[269] Irish, O. H. "[Letter to the Commissioner of Indian
Affairs]," pp. 179-190. In <u>Report of the Commissioner
of Indian Affairs. 1864.</u> Washington: Govt. Print.
Off., 1865. [I20.1:864]

Met with Brigham Young to get his view of how to handle
the Indians in the territory.

[270] Kinney, John Fitch (Utah) "Mormon Loyalty to the Union
and the Constitution," <u>Congressional Globe</u> 38th Congress,
1st session (27 January 1864) vol. 134, pp. 372-374. [X134]

Representative Kinney defends the people of Utah as
loyal citizens of the Union and defenders of the
Constitution in his debate with Rep. Fernando Wood of
New York and Mr. Smithers of Delaware.

[271] Kinney, John Fitch. <u>Speech of Honorable John F. Kinney of
Utah in reply to Honorable Fernando Wood, delivered in
the House of Representatives, January 27, 1864.</u>
[Washington: H. Polkinhorn, 1864] 8p.

In a response to Fernando Wood of New York, Kinney
defends the loyalty of the Mormons. The Utah War is
discussed.
                                        [Flake 4641]
          CtY, CU-B, DLC, MH, NjP, PHi, UHi, UPB, USlC

[272] Kinney, John Fitch. <u>Speech of Hon. John F. Kinney, of
Utah, upon the territories and the settlement of Utah,
delivered in the House of Representatives, March 17,
1864</u>. Washington: H. Polkinhorn, Printer, 1864. 16p.

Spends a great deal of interesting time on the unnatural
state of the parent government to a Territory before
discussing the history of the settlement of Utah.
Lastly Kinney deals with efforts of people to get Utah
admitted to the Union, including quotes from Stansbury,
and Thomas J. Kane's speech to the Historical Society
of Pennsylvania.

[Flake 4642]
CtY, CU-B, DLC, MH, NjP, PHi, UHi, UPB, USlC

[273] Kinney, John Fitch (Utah). "Public Buildings in the
Territories," <u>Congressional Globe</u> 38th Congress, 1st
session (17 March 1864) vol. 135, pp. 1170-1173.
[X135]

See entry 272 for annotation.

[274] Lewis, Micajah G. "[Letter to] Capt. David J. Berry, Camp
Douglas, May 13, 1864. . .," p. 845. In <u>The War of the
Rebellion</u> Series I, Vol. L, Pt. II. Washington: Govt.
Print. Off., 1897. [W45.5:Ser.I/vol. 50/pt. 2]

Order to send troops south to Meadow Valley to protect
the miners from the Mormons and the Indians.

[275] Lewis, Micajah G. "[Letter to] Capt. Samuel P. Smith, Camp
Douglas, May 9, 1864. . .," p. 845. In <u>The War of the
Rebellion</u> Series I, Vol. L, Pt. II. Washington: Govt.
Print. Off., 1897. [W45.5:Ser.I/vol. 50/pt. 2]

Lewis tells Captain Smith to go to Raft River, Idaho to
kill all the males of five lodges who have continued to
attack emigrants. He was also to take a woman fleeing
from Mormon persecution, and the "lady of the honorable
Judge Waite" with him.

[276] McDowell, Irvin. "[Letter to] His Excellency J. Duane
Doty, Great Salt Lake City, October 3, 1864. . .," p.
1000. In <u>The War of the Rebellion</u> Series I, Vol. L,
Pt. II. Washington: Govt. Print. Off., 1897.
[W45.5:Ser.I/vol. 50/pt. 2]

Notes that the army in Utah is for the protection of
overland communications and Indian peace keeping, and
that it has no special reference to the Mormons.

[277] Monchard, M. "[Letter to] Brigadier-General Connor,
February 5, 1864. . .," pp. 751-752. In <u>The War of the
Rebellion</u> Series I, Vol. L, Pt. II. Washington: Govt.
Print. Off., 1897. [W45.5:Ser.I/vol. 50/pt. 2]

Signed M. Monchard, M. Lebeau, Pete Luffing [and 23
others]. Animosity of the Mormons towards the army.

[278] <u>Report of G. M. Dodge, Chief Engineer, with accompanying</u>
<u>reports of chiefs of parties, for the year 1867</u>.
Washington: Govt. Print. Off., 1868. 85p.

Includes reports of reconnaissances in Utah, and
Wyoming for areas north of those examined by Samuel
Reed in 1864-1865, with occasional mention of the
Mormons and their settlements.

At head of title: Union Pacific Railroad.
[Flake 9084]
CU-B, UHi

[279] "Utah Superintendency, September 26, 1864," pp. 312-324.
In <u>Report of the Secretary of the Interior. 1864</u>.
Washington: Govt. Print. Off., 1864. [I.1.1:864]

Only peripheral mention of Mormons, with a visit of
O.H. Irish, Superintendent of Indian Affairs, Utah
Territory, with Brigham Young and a discussion of
territorial Indian affairs.

Variant ed. U.S. 38th Cong., 2d sess. Senate Ex. Doc.
1, Serial Set 1220.

[280] Wright, George. "[Letter to] Adjutant-General U.S. Army,
March 5, 1864. . .," p. 778. In <u>The War of the Rebellion</u>
Series I, Vol. L, Pt. II. Washington: Govt. Print.
Off., 1897. [W45.5:Ser.I/vol. 50/pt. 2]

Concerning the moving of troops from Camp Douglas. Has
little faith in the loyalty of the Mormons.

1865

"Brigham's power is evidently on the wane,
the scepter is leaving his hands, and he is
becoming desparate."
[Entry 283]

---

[281] Atwood, R. H. "[Letter to] General Connor, Great Salt Lake
City, Utah Territory, April 26, 1865. . .," pp. 219-
220. In <u>The War of the Rebellion</u> Series I, Vol.
XLVIII, Part II. Washington: Govt. Print. Off., 1896.
[W45.5:Ser.I/vol. 48/pt. 2]

Atwood, according to Connor, is a member of the Josephites
[Reorganized LDS] and a missionary to Utah. The letter
expresses gratitude to Connor and loyalty to the government.

[282] Comstock, Cyrus Ballou, Lt. Colonel. "[Letter to] General
Patrick Edward Connor, Washington, May 4, 1865...", p.
1221. In <u>The War of the Rebellion</u> Series I, Vol. L,
Part II. Washington: Govt. Print. Off., 1897.
[W45.5:Ser.I/vol. 50/pt. 2]

States his purpose to protect the Gentiles against the
Mormons and assure that communication will remain open
with the outside world, because Mormonism cannot exist

permanently in force and in close communication with
the civilized world.

[283] Connor, Patrick Edward. Brigadier General. "[Letter to]
Maj. Gen. G. M. Dodge, Julesburg, Colo. Ter., May 28,
1865. . .," p. 646. In The War of the Rebellion Series
I, Vol. XLVIII, Part II. Washington: Govt. Print.
Off., 1896. [W45.5:Ser.I/vol. 48/pt. 2]

Based upon communication from Utah Territory, Connor
interprets that Brigham Young's power is on the wane.
Connor mentions that he has a peculiar way of managing
Brigham.

[284] Connor, Patrick Edward, Brigadier-General. "[Letter to]
Maj. Gen. G. M. Dodge, Dept. of the Missouri, Fort
Laramie, Dak. Ter., July 21, 1865. . .," p. 1113. In
The War of the Rebellion Series I, Vol. XLVIII, Part
II. Washington: Govt. Print. Off., 1896.
[W45.5:Ser.I/vol. 48/pt. 2]

Expresses regret at being relieved of command of Utah
and expresses pity for the Gentiles who have come out
against Brigham and who will no longer have Connor's
protection.

[285] Connor, Patrick Edward. "[Letter to] Maj. J. W. Barnes,
April 6, 1865. . .," pp. 1184-1186. In The War of the
Rebellion Series I, Vol. L, Pt. II. Washington: Govt.
Print. Off., 1897. [W45.5:Ser.I/vol. 50/pt. 2]

Summary of his activities during his time at Camp
Douglas. The tyranny of the Mormon leaders, and the
unpatriotic nature of Mormonism are emphasized.

[286] Dodge, Grenville Mellen, Major-General, Headquarters Dept.
of the Missouri. "[Letter to] Maj. Gen. John Pope,
Commanding Military Division of the Missouri, Fort
Leavenworth, June 8, 1865. . .," p. 822. In The War of
the Rebellion Series I, Vol. XLVIII, Part II. Washington:
Govt. Print. Off., 1896. [W45.5:Ser.I/ vol. 48/pt. 2]

Dodge approves of Connor's methods in protecting
Gentiles and anti-polygamists. This sentiment seems to
come because the Mormons were allegedly helping the
Indians in their attacks.

[287] Dodge, Grenville Mellen. "[Letter to] Maj. Gen. John Pope,
Fort Laramie, August 29, 1865. . .," p. 1220. In The
War of the Rebellion Series I, Vol. XLVIII, Part II.
Washington: Govt. Print Off., 1896. [W45.5:Ser.I/
vol. 48/pt. 2]

A one-liner about the Salt Lake Telegraph which came
out that morning referring to polygamy.

[288] Irish, O. H. "Utah Superintendency, June 29, 1865," pp.
149-152. In Report of the Commissioner of Indian
Affairs for the year 1865. Washington: Govt. Print.
Off., 1865. [I20.1:865]

Negotiations with the Utah Indians on the Uintah
Reservation and the role Brigham Young played in these
negotiations are cited. Describes the influence
Brigham Young has on the Indians and the beneficial
results of his kind and conciliatory policy towards
them.

[289] Milo, George, Lt. Colonel First Battalion Nevada Cavalry,
Commanding. "[Letter to] Capt. George F. Price, Actg.
Asst. Adjt. Gen., District of the Plains, Camp Douglas,
Utah Terr., May 4, 1865. . .," pp. 315-316. In The War
of the Rebellion Series I, Vol. XLVIII, Part II.
Washington: Govt. Print Off,. 1896. [W45.5:Ser.I/
vol. 48/pt. 2]

Describes Mormon harassment and a system of espionage
directed at Gentiles and under the direction of Brigham
Young.

[290] "Polygamists," Congressional Globe 39th Congress, 1st
session (18 December 1865) vol. 140, p. 69. [X140]

One paragraph where M. Grinnell introduces a bill to
prohibit payment of money to polygamists working for
the Federal government. No bill No. given.

[291] Pope, John, Major-General, Commanding Headquarters of the
Missouri, "[Letter to] Lieut. Gen. U.S. Grant, General-
in-chief U.S. Army, Saint Louis, Mo., July 26, 1865. .
.," p. 1123. In The War of the Rebellion Series I,
Vol. XLVIII, Part II. Washington: Govt. Print. Off.,
1896. [W45.5:Ser.I/vol. 48/pt. 2]

Pope describes the deteriorating relationship between
the Gentiles and Mormons and their constant stirring up
of the Indians.

[292] Price, George Frederick, Acting Asst. Adj. General.
"[Letter to] Brig. Gen. P. E. Connor, Julesburg, Colo,
Ter., May 18, 1865. . .," pp. 500-501. In The War of
the Rebellion Series I, Vol. XLVIII, Part II. Washington:
Govt. Print. Off., 1896. [W45.5:Ser.I/ vol. 48/pt. 2]

Declares that the Mormons are insolent and that Brigham
is preaching violence.

[293] Price, George Frederick, Acting Asst. Adj. General.
"[Letter to] Brig. Gen. P. E. Connor, Julesburg, Colo.
Terr., May 20, 1865. . .," p. 524. In The War of the
Rebellion Series I, Vol. XLVIII, Part II. Washington:
Govt. Print. Off., 1896. [W45.5:Ser.I/vol. 48/pt. 2]

Once again the Mormons are declared to be insolent and
that Brigham is preaching violence.

[294] Price, George Frederick. "[Letter to] Major General G. M.
Dodge, Fort Laramie, Dak. Ter., August 11, 1865. . .,"
p. 1178. In The War of the Rebellion Series I, Vol.
XLVIII, Part II. Washington: Govt. Print. Off., 1896.
[W45.5:Ser.I/vol. 48/pt. 2]

Indicates that there should be 4,000 troops sent to
Utah to protect the development of the silver mines
which is the surest way to crush polygamy and the one
man power [presumably Brigham Young] now crushing the
country.

[295] Price, George Frederick, Captain and Acting Asst. Adj. Gen.
"[Letter to] Maj. Gen. G. M. Dodge, Fort Laramie, Dak.
Ter., August 15, 1865. . .," pp. 1187-1188. In The War
of The Rebellion Series I, Vol. XLVIII, Part II.
Washington: Govt. Print. Off., 1896. [W45.5:Ser.I/
vol. 48/pt. 2]

Worried about the small number of troops and possible
Indian troubles in which the Mormons would do nothing
to assist the troops. Claims that development of the
mining industry and a force large enough to protect it
is needed, because the Mormons would not provide
protection.

[296] Price, George Frederick, Captain and Acting Asst. Adj. Gen.
"[Letter to] Maj. Gen. G. M. Dodge, Fort Laramie, Dak.
Ter., August 21, 1865. . .," pp. 1199-1200. In The War
of the Rebellion Series I, Vol. XLVIII, Part II.
Washington: Govt. Print. Off., 1896. [W45.5:Ser.I/
vol. 48/pt. 2]

Mormons are becoming insolent. They tried to murder Rev.
Norman McLeod which goes along with the policy to force
every man, woman, and child, not a Mormon, to leave the
Territory.

[297] Young, Brigham. Governor's Message to the General Assembly,
of the State of Deseret. Fourth annual session.
[Great Salt Lake City, 1865] 3p.

Tells of fleeing from those who wanted to destroy their
religion.

UPB, US1C

1866

"I am confident that, if the government will
afford proper protection, there are many
witnesses now in Utah who will come forward
and prove clearly that the Mormon leaders
have both instigated and sanctioned the
taking of human life."

[Entry 300]

---

[298] Accounts of the Marshal of Utah," pp. 73-75. In Attorney
General Opinions. Official Opinions of the Attorney
General of the United States, Vol. IX. Washington: W.
H. & O. M. Morrison, 1866. [J1.5:9]

Relates to Joseph L. Heywood, late marshal of Utah,
regarding expenses claimed for conveying judges of the
Territory to and from places of the Supreme and District

courts. Numerous guards, apparently, had to be provided
for safety's sake.

DLC, UPB, US1C

[299] Hooper, William H. (Utah) "Boundaries of Nevada," Congressional
Globe 39th Congress, 1st Session (3 May 1866) vol. 152,
p. 2369. [X152]

The Mormons should be considered favorably, in as much
as they were the ones who settled the area.

[300] U.S. House. 39th Congress. 1st Session. Committee on
the Territories. The condition of Utah... Mr. James
Ashley, from the Committee on Territories made the
following report. (H. Rept. No. 96) [Washington:
Govt. Print. Off., 1866] 29p. [Serial Set 1272]

Extensive testimony was gathered, especially regarding
the practice of polygamy. He gathered testimony from
Joseph Smith, III, regarding polygamy and also leadership
succession in the Mormon Church. Patrick Edward
Connor, Norman L. Rice, Chaplain at Camp Douglas, and
E. J. Bennett, Captain in the Army, discussed polygamy
and the endowments, and several gave their perspective
on Mormonism.

[Flake 9149]

[301] U.S. House. 39th Congress. 2d Session. General Ingalls's
inspection report. Letter from the Secretary of War,
in answer to a resolution of the House of February 27,
transmitting report of General Ingalls's inspection
made in 1866... (H. Ex. Doc. No. 111) Washington:
Govt. Print. Off., 1867. 25p. [Serial Set 1293]

Condition in Utah due to poor administration.
Contends that the people of Utah have suffered from the
"bad class of men appointed to civil office by the
federal government," and although the Mormons have
"acted in a too exclusive style to suit the gentile
world... deceit, bullying, and recrimination will not
make good citizens of them."

[Flake 4242]

[302] "Utah Superintendency, September 20, 1866," pp. 122-131.
In Report of the Secretary of the Interior, 1866.
Washington: Govt. Print. Off., 1866. [I1.1:866]

Document 38, pp. 129-130 mentions the Mormons. Brigham
Young, in order to avert Indian fears of a Mormon
invasion, donated 70 head of cattle to the Uintah area
and requested that 25 people in Heber City assist with
the transportation of goods.

Variant ed. U.S. 39th Cong., 2d sess. House Ex. Doc.
No. 1, Serial Set 1284.

1867

"It afforded an opportunity of studying the
logistical relations of Camp Douglas very
fully, as directed in my memoranda instructions,

and gave me a larger knowledge of Utah, and a more thorough insight into Mormonism than had been anticipated. My conclusions were bad, unfavorable to the wholesome despotism and barbarism there, as I did not hestitate to say in my report on Camp Douglas, in recommending an increased military force there, etc."

[Entry 309]

"General Connor, who commanded there during the war, I think treated Mormonism too harshly, due probably to his zeal as a Catholic; yet he exercised a strong influence against Mormonism, and was a true man in the interests of the government, and any clamor or charges made against him for corruption there I believe to have had their origin with Mormon leaders, or their friends, to counteract his influence."

[Entry 311]

---

[303] "Land offices in the Territories," Congressional Globe 39th Congress, 2d Session (23 February, 2 March 1867) vol. 147, pp. 1803-1804. [X147]

Invitation for gentiles to settle in Utah as the best way to solve the Mormon problem.

[304] Noell, Thomas Estes (Missouri). "Equality of Suffrage," Congressional Globe 39th Congress, 2d session (11, 18 February 1867) vol. 147, Appendix, pp. 108-116. [X147]

Quotes from Artemus Ward regarding polygamy.

[305] Noell, Thomas Estes. Speech of Hon. Thomas E. Noell, of Missouri, on woman suffrage and reconstruction of Massachusetts; delivered in the House of Representatives, February 11 and 18, 1867. Washington: Printed at the Congressional Globe Office, 1867. 16p.

See entry 304 for annotation.

[Flake 5858]
UPB, US1C

[306] "Polygamy in the Territories," Congressional Globe 39th Cognress, 2d session (28 February 1867) vol. 147, p. 1651. [X147]

Mr. Cook of the Committee on the Judiciary, to whom was referred a memorial from the Utah Territorial Legislature asking for repeal of the Morrill Act which was tabled.

[307] U.S. Department of Labor. A report on marriage and divorce in the U.S. 1867-1886: including an appendix relating to marriage and divorce in certain countries in Europe, by Carroll D. Wright, Feb. 1889. Washington: Govt. Print. Off., 1889. 1074p.

Section on the Mormon practice of marriage.

Other editions. Rev. ed. 1889; DLC, 1897.

[Flake 9194]
DLC

[308] U.S. House. 40th Congress. 1st Session. Proposed State of Deseret. Memorial of the Legislative Assembly of the proposed state, for the admission of the State of Deseret into the union, and accompanying papers. (H. Misc. Doc. No. 26) Washington: Govt. Print. Off., 1867. 8p. [Serial Set 1312]

The text of the proposed Constitution takes up most of the document.

[Flake 2790]

[309] U.S. House. 40th Congress. 2d Session. Affairs in Utah and the Territories. Letter from the Secretary of War, transmitting, in compliance with House resolution of the 5th instant, the report of Brevet Brigadier General James F. Rusling, Inspector &c., for the year ending June 30, 1867. (H. Misc. Doc. No. 153) Washington: Govt. Print. Off., 1868. 36p. [Serial Set 1350]

Includes the author's impression of the Mormon community and the state of affairs in and about Salt Lake City. There are other references to Mormons.

[Flake 7455]

[310] U.S. House. 39th Congress. 2d Session. Committee on the Judiciary. Utah... Report of the Committee on the Judiciary, to whom was referred the memorial of the Legislative Assembly of the Territory of Utah, praying for the repeal of "An act to prevent and punish the practice of polygamy in the Territories of the United States." (H. Rept. No. 27) Washington: Govt. Print. Off., 1867. 4p. [Serial Set 1305]

[Flake 9136]

[311] U.S. House. 39th Congress. 2d Session. Committee on Territories. Utah Territory. Resolution of Hon. John Bidwell, relative to affairs in Utah Territory. (H. Misc. Doc. No. 75) Washington: Govt. Print. Off., 1867. 5p. [Serial Set 1302]

Instructs the Committee on Territories to inquire into the necessity of having a larger force of troops in Utah to preserve order. The basic part of the document is a letter from Bvt. Maj. Gen. H. B. Hazen.

[Flake 3930]

1868

This 'statement' concludes with a challenge to match the people of Utah in devotion to that Government of which they form a part, (these are its very words,) representing them as persecuted and driven from their homes,

misstates a certain order of the Federal
Government in regard to Mormon troops as a
call of the United States there engaged in a
foreign war, exaggerates their former sufferings
and privations, and grossly misrepresents the
present population of Utah as more than one
hundred thousand. This `statement' is not
under oath, nor is it accompanied by any
affidavit or deposition."

[Entry 313]

---

[312] "Case of the Messrs. Porter," pp. 21-28. In <u>Attorney</u>
<u>General Opinions. Official Opinions of the Attorney</u>
<u>General of the United States.</u> vol. 10. Washington:
W. H. & O. H. Morrison, 1868. [J1.5:10]

Deals with the seizure on Oct. 19, 1857, at South Pass
by General Johnston, of the Porter wagon train which
was transporting merchandise to Salt Lake City from
Missouri. Johnston allegedly declared that "no goods
or supplies of any kind would be permitted to pass the
army for Salt Lake City, or other points occupied by
the Mormons".

DLC, UPB, US1C

[313] Dawes, Henry L. (Mass.) "Election Contest--M'Grorty vs.
Hooper," <u>Congressional Globe</u> 40th congress, 2d session
(23 July 1868) vol. 153, pp. 4383-89. [X153]

A defeated candidate for U.S. Congress, Mr. McGrorty,
cites before congress all the crimes of the Mormons,
both real and imaginary, and suggests innumerable
others in an attempt to gain the seat through a contest
of election. The contest was between McGrorty and
William H. Hooper.

[314] <u>Report of G. M. Dodge, Chief Engineer, with accompanying</u>
<u>reports of chiefs of parties, for 1868-69.</u> Washington:
Govt. Print. Off., 1870. 61p.

Describes construction work east of Great Salt Lake and
survey work in western Utah and eastern Nevada, with
occasional references to the Mormons and their settlements.

At head of title: Union Pacific Railroad.

[Flake 9085]
CU-B, UHi

[315] U.S. House. 40th Congress. 2d Session. Committee of
Elections. <u>McGrorty vs. Hooper. Report of the Committee</u>
<u>of Elections upon the contested election case of</u>
<u>McGrorty vs. Hooper, sitting delegate from the Territory</u>
<u>of Utah, referred to the Committee of Elections. First</u>
<u>Session, 40th Congress, 1868.</u> (H. Rep. No. 79)
Washington: Govt. Print. Off., 1868. 81p. [Serial Set
1358]

Polygamy, the history of the Church, Mountain Meadows
Massacre as well as latter-day scripture, and sections

from the Journal of Discourses are utilized in this contested election case.

[Flake 9117]

[316] Waite, Charles Burlingame. Argument of Charles B. Waite, before the Committee of Elections of the House of Representatives, March 25th-27th, 1868. In the case of William M'Grorty vs. Wm. H. Hooper, sitting delegate from the Territory of Utah. [Washington, 1868] 32p.

As a Mormon, Hooper did not represent all the people, according to Waite.

[Flake 9512]
DLC, NN, US1C

1869

"Our return was upon a rough desert road, made by the Mormons in 1857, when they were looking for places of refuge in case that our troops molested the quietude of their mountain villages."

[Entry 327]

"They were all told not more than six hundred and forty persons who were thus lying on the river flats. But the Mormons in Nauvoo and its dependencies had been numbered the year before at over twenty thousand. Where were they? They had last been seen carrying in mournful trains their sick and wounded, halt and blind, to disappear behind the western horizon, pursuing the phantom of another home. Hardly anything else was known of them; and people asked with curiosity what had been their fate--what their fortunes?"

[Entry 317]

---

[317] Hooper, William Henry. Extension of boundaries: Speech of Hon. William H. Hooper, of Utah, delivered in the House of Representatives, February 25, 1869. Washington: F. & J. Rives & G. A. Bailey, Printers, 1869. 14p.

Utah statehood. Repeats part of a speech by Thomas Kane to the Historical Society of Philadelphia where Kane gave a poignant picture of deserted Nauvoo. Mormon Battalion & Stansbury's expedition discussed. Talks of the Mormon's well-managed system of emigration.

[Flake 4080]
Cty, CSmh, CU-B, DHC, DLC, MH, MoInRC, NN, UPB, US1, US1C

[318] Hooper, William Henry (Utah). "Extension of Boundries," Congressional Globe 40th Congress, 3d session (25 February 1869) vol. 157, Appendix, pp. 242-248. [X157]

Hooper's plea for the Mormon people when congress was considering ceding much of Utah to Nevada, Colorado, and Wyoming, with evident intent to put Utah people into the hands of other governments. History of the Mormons, their industry, etc., are cited in defense of them.

[319] Hooper, William Henry. Speech of Hon. W. H. Hooper, of Utah, delivered in the House of Representatives, February 25, 1869. [Salt Lake City] 1869. 4p.

Appears to be a reprinting of the Deseret News issue of April 7, 1869, of the speech published in the Congressional Globe and by the Washington publishers of J. Rives & G. A. Bailey.

[Flake 4081]
UPB, USlC

[320] "Polygamy in Utah," Congressional Globe 41st Congress, 1st session (15 March 1869) vol. 158, p. 72. [X158]

A bill to grant woman suffrage in Utah to combat polygamy (H.R. 64)

[321] Powell, John Wesley. Exploration of the Colorado River of the west and its tributaries: Explored in 1869, 1870, 1871, and 1872, under the direction of the Secretary of the Smithsonian Institution. Washington: Govt. Print. Off., 1875. 291p. [SI1.2:C71]

A few references to Mormons, pp. 27, 88, 98, 102, 105, and 112, but more important as an item of Utah exploration.
[Flake 6429]

[322] Raymond, Rossiter Worthington. Mineral resources of the states and territories west of the Rocky mountains. Washington: Govt. Print. Off., 1869. 256p.

The section on Utah, p. 168, mentions a talk in which Brigham Young stated that he wished the mines were opened, but not to the Mormons.

[Flake 6826]
DLC, NjP, UHi, ULA, UPB

[323] Simpson, James Hervey. The Shortest Route to California illustrated by a History of Explorations of the Great Basin of Utah with its topographical and geological character and some account of the Indian Tribes. Philadelphia: J.B. Lippincott & Co., 1869. 58p.

Chiefly concerned with the route some early explorers took, and a brief mention of Mormon participation.

[Flake 7726]
CU-B, DLC, NjP, NN, UHi, UPB, USlC, UU

[324] "Supression of Polygamy," Congressional Globe 41st Congress, 2d session (20 December 1869) vol. 159, p. 241. [X159]

Mr. Moore of N. J. submitted a resolution which would
require the Committee on the Judiciary to investigate
further legislation to supress polygamy.

[325] U.S. House. 41st Congress. 1st Session. H.R. 64, "A bill
to discourage polygamy in Utah by granting the right of
suffrage to the women of that Territory, March 15,
1869." [Washington: Govt. Print. Off., 1869] 1p.

Referred to the Committee on Territories. Known as the
Julian bill.

                                        DLC, UPB, US1C

[325a] U.S. House. 41st Congress. 2d Session. H.R. 696, "A
bill in aid of the execution of the laws in the Territory
of Utah, and for other purposes, December 21, 1869."
[Washington: Govt. Print. Off., 1869]. 17p.

Referred to the Committee on the Territories. Sections
12-16, all deal with crimes of bigamy or adultery.
Section 13 specifically states that it shall not be
necessary to prove a first or subsequent marriage with
certificates. Section 20 states that no one practicing
polygamy can be a citizen of the United States nor hold
office, or be entitled to provisions of the Homestead
Act. Sections 22-23 deal with probate judges.

                                        DLC, UPB, US1C

[326] U.S. Senate. 41st Congress. 2d Session. S. 286, "A bill
to provide for the execution of the law against the
crime of polygamy in the Territory of Utah, and for
other purposes, December 6, 1869." [Washington: Govt.
Print. Off., 1869] 20p.

Referred to the Committee on the Judiciary on December
8, Committee discharged and referred to the Committee
on Territories on December 20, reported by Mr. Cragin
with amendments, on December 21.

                                        DLC, UPB, US1C

[327] Wheeler, George Montague. Preliminary report upon a
reconnaissance through southern and southeastern
Nevada, made in 1869. By Geo. M. Wheeler, Corps of
Engineers, U.S. Army, assisted by D. W. Lockwood, Corps
of Engineers, U.S. Army. Washington: Govt. Print.
Off., 1875. 72p. [W8.1:S69]

References to Mormon settlements in Nevada, especially
Meadow Valley and Muddy settlements, pp. 11-19, 21, 28,
36-37, 41-42, 44-47, 55, 57; Mountain Meadows Massacre,
p. 37., etc.

                                        [Flake 9721]

[328] Wheeler, George Montague. Report upon United State Geographical
Survey West of the 100th Meridian. In charge of Capt.
Geo. M. Wheeler, Corps of Engineers, U. S. Army, under
the direction of the Chief of Engineers, U. S. Army.
Vol. 1. Washington: Govt. Print. Off., 1889. [W8.5:1]

Geographical Report contains references to the Mormons in Utah, Arizona, and Nevada during the field seasons of 1869 and 1872, pp. 23, 28, 46-56, and more general remarks, pp. 174-177. A number of the plates are Utah views. The atlas sheets show Mormon settlements, wagon roads, etc., of the 1870's.

[Flake 9203]

1870

"Mormonism is not a savage, nor a stranger to civilization. It was not born in the desert or nurtured in the wilderness . . . It is the offspring of ambition, bigotry, avarice, and passion. It was cradled under the full blaze of American civilization . . . What reason is there then for us to hope that this social leprosy will be healed . . . by the mere contact of increasing population."

[Entry 344]

---

[329] Cragin, Aaron Harrison. Execution of laws in Utah. Speech of Hon. Aaron H. Cragin, of New Hampshire, delivered in the Senate of the United States, May 18, 1870. Washington: F. & J. Rives & G. A. Bailey, Printers, 1870. 23p.

Political situation in Utah. Begins with the "Twin relics of barbarism," and goes on to discuss one of these relics--polygamy--at great length. Quotes a number of sources including defectors such as John Hyde, Jr. Cragin also goes into considerable background on Mountain Meadows Massacre, quoting several including Judge Cradlebaugh. Mr. Cragin's speech is included also in entry 334 below.

[Flake 2574]
CU-B, DLC, ICN, MH, MoK, NN, UHi, UPB

[330] Cullom, Shelby Moore (Illinois) "Enforcement of laws in Utah," Congressional Globe 41st Congress, 2d session (17 February 1870) vol. 160, pp. 1367-1373. [X160]

The Cullom bill, House bill 1089 (reprinted in full) to suppress polygamy by enforcing the laws already making polygamy a crime. Gives the bill and explanations of it.

[331] Cullom, Shelby Moore. Enforcement of laws in Utah. Speech of Hon. Shelby M. Cullom, of Illinois... Delivered in the House of Representatives, Feb. 17, 1870. [Washington, 1870] 15p.

The text of H. bill 1089 in aid of the execution of the laws in the Territory of Utah is included. Cullom mentions that sections 7 and 8 were designed to get rid of the problem in the Mormon statute which made it impossible to summon juries for a bigamy or polygamy trial. In the 6th section, the problem of probate judgeships, and their relationship to Mormonism as high

Church officials, is discussed. In the majority of the
rest of the sections, Cullom gives an explanation of
polygamy.

[Flake 2603]
DLC, UPB

[332] "Deseret alphabet," p. 329. In Report of the Commissioner
of Education made to the Secretary of the Interior for
the year 1870. Washington: Govt. Print. Off., 1870.
[I1.1:870]

Describes the attempted use of the Deseret Alphabet in
Utah schools.

Variant ed. U.S. 41st Cong., 3d Sess., House Ex. Doc.
1, pt. 4, Serial Set 1450.

[333] "Enforcement of Laws in Utah," Congressional Globe 41st
Congress, 2d session (3, 16, 17, 23, February 1870)
vol. 160, pp. 1009, 1338, 1367-1373, 1517-1520. [X160]

Continued debate of the Cullom bill, H.R. 1089, to
suppress polygamy. Mr. Fitch feels that passage of
this bill would reap dire consequences, such as destruction
by the Mormons of the overland railroad. Passage would
be a declaration of war, resulting in a protracted and
bloody war, exterminating the Mormons. Therefore, the
bill should not be passed.

[334] "Execution of laws in Utah," Congressional Globe 41st
Congress, 2d session (18 May 1870) vol. 162, pp. 3571-
3582. [X162]

Discussion of the Cullom bill, H.R. 1089, to suppress
polygamy in Utah. Senator Cragin's comment on the
Mormons, cites all the anti-Mormon fiction stories,
such as Mrs. Waite, and various apostates to show the
degraded state of the Mormons. Mountain Meadow Massacre
and other crimes are all cited.

[335] Fitch, Thomas. The Utah bill. Speeches of Hon. Thos.
Fitch, of Nevada, and Hon. A. A. Sergeant, of California.
Delivered in the House of Representatives, Feb. 23,
1870. [Washington?: Cunningham and McIntosh Printers]
1870. 8p.

Debate on H.R. 1089, against the practice of polygamy.
He favored letting the Mormons practice polygamy. See
entry 333 for Congressional Globe citation.

[Flake 3371]
CU-B, DLC, UPB, US1C

[336] Hague, James Duncan. Mining industry. . . with geological
contributions, by Clarence King.... Washington: Govt.
Print. Off., 1870. 447p. (U. S. Geological Exploration
of the Fortieth Parallel Report... Vol. III) [W7.10:18]

Series: Professional Papers of the Engineer Department, U. S. Army, No. 18.

Report of "The Green River Coal Basin" by Clarence King, includes remarks on the deposits near Coalville mined by the Mormons, with comment on complications in ownership introduced by the "arbitrary and peculiar" land policy of the Mormon church, pp. 455-58, 467-69.

[Flake 3778]

[337] Hooper, William Henry. The Utah bill. Plea for religious liberty. Speech of Hon. W. H. Hooper of Utah, delivered in the House of Representatives, March 23, 1870. Washington: Gibson Brothers, Printers, 1870. 31p.

Defense of the right to practice polygamy.

[Flake 4082]
CtY, DHU, DLC, MH, ULA, UPB, US1C, WHi

[338] Hooper, William Henry. The Utah bill. Plea for religious liberty. Speech of Hon. W. H. Hooper of Utah, delivered in the House of Representatives, March 23, 1870. Washington: Gibson Brothers, Printers, 1870. 32p.

Variant printing of entry above.

Defense of the right to practice polygamy.

[Flake 4083]
UPB, US1C

[339] Hooper, William Henry. The Utah bill. A plea for religious liberty. Speech of Hon. W. H. Hooper, of Utah, delivered in the House of Representatives, March 23, 1870, together with the remonstration of the Citizens of Salt Lake City, in mass meeting, held March 31, 1870, to the Senate of the United States. Washington: Gibson Brothers, Printers, 1870. 40p.

Defense of the right to practice polygamy.

[Flake 4084]
CSmH, CtY, CU-B, DLC, NjP, NN, UHi, UPB, US1, US1C, WHi

[340] Hooper, William Henry (Utah) "Polygamy in Utah," Congressional Globe 41st Congress, 2d session (22, 23 March 1870) vol. 165, Appendix, pp. 173-179. [X165]

Hooper gives the Mormon point of view towards polygamy.

Entries 337-339 include the same speech.

[341] Perry, C. A., & Co., defendants. Papers in case of C. A. Perry & Co., pending in the Treasury Department. Washington: H. Polkinhorn & Co., Printers [1870?] 90p.

Claim of C. A. Perry & Co., for losses incurred by impression of property under orders of Gen. Albert Sidney Johnston, commanding the Army of Utah in 1857.

[Flake 6315]
DLC, UPB

[342] "Polygamy in Utah," Congressional Globe, 41st Congress, 2d session (28 February 1870) vol. 160, p. 1607. [X160]

Brief discussion to hurry the Cullom bill, H.R. 1089 along its route, and to get it on the calendar as soon as possible.

[343] "Polygamy in Utah," Congressional Globe 41st Congress, 2d session (22 March 1870) vol. 161, pp. 2142-2153, 2178-2181, 2603. [X161]

A continuation in the House of the Cullom bill debate, H.R. 1089, on polygamy and Mormonism. It has a decidedly anti-Mormon trend, but due to corrections by Delegate Hooper from Utah, not such a biased discussion as in the Senate.

[344] Pomeroy, Charles. Polygamy in Utah: Speech of Chas. Pomeroy, of Iowa, delivered in the House of Representatives, March 22, 1870. [Washington: F. J. Rives and G. A. Bailey, 1870] 8p.

Debate on H.R. 1089 in aid of the execution of the laws in the Territory of Utah. A spirited debate on polygamy. Mr. Pomeroy's speech is also found in the Congressional Globe entry 343 above.

[Flake 6401]
CSmH, DLC, NN, UPB

[345] "Suppression of polygamy," Congressional Globe 41st Congress, 2d session (22 April 1870) vol. 162, p. 2896, 3136. [X162]

Anti-polygamy bill (S. 286) with amendments.

[346] U.S. District Court. Utah. (Third District). Arrest of Militia Officers in Utah. Opinion of Justice C. M. Hawley. Territory of Utah. Third District Court, The United States vs. George M. Ottinger [and others]. [Salt Lake City, 1870] 8p.

Denial of the rights of Mormons to bear arms.

[Flake 9197]
CtY, MnHi

[347] U.S. House. 41st Congress. 2d Session. Committee on the Territories. Execution of the laws in Utah [to accompany bill H.R. 1089]. (H. Rep. No. 21, Pt. 1-3) Washington: Govt. Print. Off., 1870. 8p. [Serial Set 1436]

Polygamy laws. Parts 2-3 additional text.
[Flake 9151]

[347a] U.S. House. 41st Congress. 2d Session. H.R. 696, "Amendments proposed by Mr. Ward, from the Committee on the Territories, to the bill (H.R. 696) in aid of the execution of the laws in the Territory of Utah, and for other purposes, January 24, 1870." [Washington: Govt. Print. Off., 1870] 13p.

Referred to the Committee on the Territories. Section numbers are left blank, but the first lengthy section gives details, with numerous names of Mormons some prominent such as Brigham Young and Heber C. Kimball, regarding land, water, and timber rights. Section beginning on page 6 details procedures in disposal of real property of convicted polygamists, to wives and children (whether legitimate or not). A section on p. 12 provides for relief of destitute persons who were brought to that state through enforcement of polygamy laws. See entry 325a for the original bill.

DLC, UPB, US1C

[348] U.S. House. 41st Congress. 2d Session. H.R. 1089, "A bill in aid of the execution of the laws in the Territory of Utah, and for other purposes, February 3, 1870." [Washington: Govt. Print. Off., 1870] 24p.

Referred to the Committee on the Territories.

Sec. 11 mentions that for prosecutions of bigamy, the lawful wife of the accused shall be a competent witness. Sec. 15 also refers to polygamy. Sec. 19 deals with polygamy in regard to immigration. Sec. 23 Deals with those people who are qualified to perform marriages, and it is very specific about who one can marry. Sec. 30 deals with polygamy, a lengthy section from p. 17-23.

DLC, UPB, US1C

[349] U.S. Senate. 41st Congress. 2d Session. Memorial adopted by citizens of Salt Lake City, Utah Territory, at a mass meeting held at said city March 31, 1870 remonstrating against the passage of the bill (H.R. No. 1089) "in aid of the execution of the laws in the Territory of Utah and for other purposes." (S. Misc. Doc. No. 112) Washington: Govt. Print. Off., 1870. 7p. [Serial Set 1408]

The memorialists cite the history of plural marriage as a religious tenet and claim that the Cullom bill subverts religious and civil liberty. Civil liberty is subverted by clothing the governor in despotic powers. Includes a poignant resolution which begins "Whereas the Supreme Ruler of the universe has the right to command man in the concerns of life, which it is man's duty to obey".

[Flake 7496]

1871

"In 1869 the two settlements of Saint Joe and Saint Thomas were thriving towns, as Mormon

industry is understood, while West Point,
only just settled, bade fair, in time, to
equal them in agricultural benefits and
population. These settlements are now all
deserted by their former inhabitants, they
having left owing to the establishment of the
fact that the places mentioned were in the
State of Nevada. I was informed that the
people who formerly lived here are now
settled some where in Arizona, about two
hundred miles to the east of Saint George."

[Entry 357]

---

[350] Cullom, Shelby M. (Illinois). "Polygamy," Congressional
Globe 41st Congress, 3d session (4 February 1871) vol.
167, p. 966. [X167]

Mr. Cullom reported back on two bills before the
Committee on Territories, H.R. No. 64 to discourage
polygamy in Utah by granting suffrage to its women
(which didn't pass) and H.R. No. 93 for the suppression
of polygamy in the Territory of Utah (which also came
with the recommendation to not pass).

[351] Earle, George. An Argument of the legal effect of the
award and repealing resolution in the Chorpenning case.
By George Earle, Attorney for George Chorpenning.
[Washington, 1871?] 20p.

Mail contracts from Utah to California, 1851-1857.

[Flake 3088]
CU-B

[352] Fred T. Perris, surviving partner of George Cronyn and Fred
T. Perris, as George Cronyn and Company, plaintiff in
error, vs. William G. Higley, J. F. Nounnan, and Joseph
F. Phippin. In error to the Supreme Court of the
Territory of Utah. Transcript of Record. Supreme
Court of the United States, No. 423 [Crossed out].
[n.p., 1871?] 18p.

Transcript of record in the Perris v. Higley case 137
U.S. Reports 1874, pp. 375-384.

DLC, UPB, US1C

[353] Grant, Ulysses S. "Third Annual Message, 4 December 1871,"
p. 4105. In A Compilation of the Messages and Papers
of the Presidents, by James D. Richardson. vol. 6.
New York: Published by Bureau of National Literature,
1911, c1897. [GS4.113:6, AE2.114:1-27/v.6]

Polygamy still a problem in Utah.

[354] "Legalization of polygamous marriages," <u>Congressional Globe</u>
42d Congress, 2d session (18 December 1871) vol. 171,
p. 197. [X171]

H.R. 721, introduced by Mr. Blair of Missouri. This
bill would not only legalize these marriages, but all
prosecutions would be dismissed. See entry 356 for the
bill.

[355] "Polygamy," <u>Congressional Globe</u> 41st Congress, 3rd session
(4 February 1871) vol. 167, pp. 966. [X167]

Reported that bill (H.R. 64) did not pass, which would
have discouraged polygamy by granting suffrage to
women. Joint Resolution (H.R. 93) for the suppression
of polygamy also reported not to pass.

[356] U.S. House. 42d Congress. 2d Session. H.R. 721, "A bill
to legalize polygamous marriages in the Territory of
Utah, and to dismiss prosecutions in said Territory on
account of such marriages, December 8, 1871." [Washington:
Govt. Print. Off., 1871] 2p.

Probably the only pro-polygamy legislation introduced.

DLC, UPB, US1C

[357] Wheeler, George Montague. <u>Preliminary report concerning
explorations and surveys principally Nevada and Arizona,
prosecuted in accordance with paragraph 2, Special
Order No. 109, War Department, March 18, 1871, and
letter of instructions of March 18, 1871, and letter of
instructions of March 23, 1871, from Brigadier General
A. A. Humphreys, Chief of Engineers, 1871.</u> Washington:
Govt. Print. Off., 1872. 96p. [W8.1:871]

Field operations, primarily in Nevada and Arizona in
1871; includes side expedition of First Lieut. Daniel
W. Lockwood into southwestern Utah. References to
Mormons, Mormon roads pp. 26, 65-66, 70-72, 74-75, 85-
86, 91. Areas included are mail routes, Mormon settlements
in Nevada such as Saint Joe and Saint Thomas and the
areas of St. George and the Muddy and Virgin River.
[Flake 9720]
CU-B, DLC, UPB, US1C

[358] "Wyoming and Utah Territories," <u>Congressional Globe</u> 41st
Congress, 3d session (4 February 1871) vol. 167, p.
967. [X167]

H.R. No. 2858 briefly debated before passage. The bill
removed from the territorial legislatures the power to
arrange the districts of the Federal judges with that
power placed in the hands of the judges. Mr. Cullom
mentioned that in Utah Territory the Gentiles wished
this power to be placed with the governor.

[359] <u>Zerubbabel Snow, plaintiff in error, vs. The United States,
ex. rel. Charles H. Hempstead, United States District
Attorney. In error to the Supreme Court of the Territory</u>

of Utah. Supreme Court of the United States, No. 424.
[n.p., n.d.] 10p.

This document relates to the Snow v. United States case
85 U.S. Reports 317-322, October 1873 session.

Document filed 27 Nov. 1871.

UPB, US1C, Supreme Court Library

1872

"In conclusion--the soil which the people of
Utah have won, and which they have governed
so wisely and so well when the power has been
intrusted to them, they now ask to be allowed
to govern, under the Constitution. The
pledges made to the people of the nation in
that Immortal Instrument, they ask you to
redeem. The stipulations of the treaty,
which were before them when they elected to
adhere to this Republic, they ask you to
carry out. They appeal to you to relieve
them from miseries of the territorial system;
miseries which are apparent in all the
territories, and which are intensified in
Utah."

[Entry 365]

"To say on the other hand that you will make
no compromise, that you will die rather than
surrender the practice of this one feature of
your faith, is the resolve of neither philosophers
nor philanthropists. Such a resolve means
another Nauvoo; it means that you consent to
count more of your religious leaders among
your list of martyrs; it means death to some,
exile to others, ruin to many. If such be
the well-considered, deliberate determination
of the Mormon people, there is no weapon in
the armory of logic that will prevail against
it, for you cannot reason with him who is
bent on suicide."

[Entry 363]

[360] Blair, James Gorrall. Polygamous marriages in Utah.
       Speech of Hon. James G. Blair, of Missouri, in the
       House of Representatives, February 17, 1872. [Washington:
       Printed at the Congressional Globe Office, 1872] 7p.

       See entry 371 below for annotation.
                                              [Flake 552]
                                        DLC, MH, OO, US1C

[361] Constitution of the State of Deseret and memorial to
       Congress: Adopted in Convention, March 2, 1872;

ratified by vote of the people, March 18, 1872. Salt
Lake City, 1872. 28p.

[Flake add. 2814a]
USlC

[362] Constitution of the State of Deseret, with accompanying
memorial to Congress. Adopted March 2, 1872. Salt
Lake City: Printed at the Deseret News Book and Job
Establishment, 1872. 21p.

[Flake 2787]
CLu, CSmH, CtY, UPB, USlC

[363] Fitch, Thomas. The Utah problem; Review of the course of
Judge James B. McKean, and an appeal for the surrender
of polygamy. Speech of Hon. Thomas Fitch, in the
Constitutional Convention of Utah. February 20, 1872.
[Salt Lake City]: Printed at the Salt Lake Herald,
1872. 20p.

An excellent historical treatment, albeit biased, of
the course of Mormon-U.S. government relationship. The
"twin relics," 41st Congress Cullom bill, Supreme
Court, probate courts, "Mormon Rebellion" and many
other incidents are cited in Fitch's speech, which
declares that the only judicial and governmental safety
lies in statehood.

[Flake 3372]
CtY, DLC, ICN, MnHi, NN, UPB, USlC

[364] Fred T. Perris, surviving partner of George Cronyn and Fred
T. Perris, as George Cronyn and Company, plaintiff in
error, vs. William G. Higley, J. F. Nounnan, and Joseph
F. Phippin. Brief for plaintiff in error. In the
Supreme Court of the United States, December Term,
1872. No. 188. [n.p., 1872?] 7p.

Brief in the Perris v. Higley case 87 U.S. Reports
1874, 375-384.

DLC, UPB, USlC

[365] Fuller, Frank. A state government for Utah. Speech of
Hon. Frank Fuller, (member of Congress-elect from the
State of Deseret) Before the Committee of Territories
of the House of Representatives. Tuesday, April 23,
1872. Washington [1872] 15p.

The fallacy of the reasoning that the Mormon influence
in Utah should restrict statehood.

[Flake 3487]
CtY, DLC, UPB, USlC

[366] Grant, Ulysses S. "Territories," p. 4157. In A Compilation
of the Messages and Papers of the Presidents, by James
D. Richardson. vol. 6. New York: Published by Bureau
of National Literature, 1911, c1897. [GS4.113:6,
AE2.114:1-27/v.6]

Revision needed for existing laws to prohibit polygamy
in the territories (1872).

[367] Hayden, Ferdinand V. Preliminary report of the United
States Geological survey of Wyoming, and portions of
contiguous territories being a second annual report of
progress. Washington: Govt. Print. Off., 1872.
[I18.1:870]

Contains report on geology of area from Evanston to
Ogden along line of railroad, with remarks on Mormon
interest in agriculture, coal and granite for the
temple, pp. 147, 155-160, 167; also report of Cyrus
Thomas on the valleys of Utah and their cultivation pp.
237-248.

Vol. 4 in the U.S. Geological and Geographical Survey
of the Territories.

[368] Hayden, Ferdinand V. Preliminary report of the United
States Geological Survey of Montana and portions of
adjacent territories: being a fifth annual report of
progress. Washington: Govt. Print. Off., 1872.
[I18.1:871]

Contains geological observations from Ogden to Fort
Hall, with remarks on Mormon settlement pp. 13-26.

Vol. 5 in the U.S. Geological and Geographical Survey
of the Territories.

[369] Hayden, Ferdinand V. Sixth annual report of the United
States Geological Survey of the territories, embracing
portions of Montana, Idaho, Wyoming, and Utah: being a
report of progress of the exploration for the year
1872. Washington: Govt. Print. Off., 1873. [I18.1:872]

Sixth volume in the U.S. Geological and Geographical
Survey of the Territories, which contains geological
observations by A.C. Peale on area from Ogden to Salt
Lake, with comment on Mormon towns and industries in
the Wasatch Mountains, pp. 105-108, also same by Frank
H. Bradley, Ogden to Fort Hall, pp. 192-208.

[370] "Papers accompanying the Report of the Secretary of War, 30
September 1872," p. 350. In Messages and Documents
1872-73 Abridgement. Washington: Govt. Print. Off.,
1872. [Y8.42/3:]

Mentions the problem of reservation Utes preying on the
Mormons in Utah Valley, where the Utes originated.
They returned to the valley.

[371] "Polygamous Marriages in Utah," Congressional Globe 42d
Congress, 2d session (17 February 1872), vol. 172, pp.
1096-1100. [X172]

Discussion of H.R. 721 to legalize polygamy in the
territory, and to dismiss prosecutions in said territory
on account of such marriages. The bill is given in
full and the discussion was presented by Mr. Blair of
Missouri.

[372] Progress-report upon Geographical and Geological Explorations and Surveys west of the 100th Meridian in 1872. Under the direction of Brig. Gen. A. A. Humphreys, Chief of Engineers, U. S. Army, by First Lieut. George M. Wheeler. Washington: Govt. Print. Off., 1874. 56p. [W8.1:872]

Operations in Utah, 1872. Reference to Mormons, pp. 44, 46-47, 56; mining districts and mines, pp. 13-28; irrigation, pp. 28-30; agriculture, pp. 32-33; routes of communication, pp. 33-36; Indians, pp. 37-38; Great Salt Lake and Utah Lake, pp. 52-54.

[Flake 9203]

[373] U.S. House. 42d Congress. 2d Session. Admission of Utah into the Union. Memorial of the convention to frame a constitution for the admission of Utah into the Union as a state, convened at Salt Lake City, February 19, 1872, ratified by vote of the people. March 2, 1872, ratified by vote of the people, March 18, 1872. (H. Misc. Doc. No. 165) Washington: Govt. Print. Off., 1872. 21p. [Serial Set 1526]

Praying to be admitted as a State under the name of Deseret. Includes an "Ordinance" of which the Third section would guarantee perfect toleration of religion.

[Flake 2788]

[374] U.S. House. 42d Congress. 2d Session. Against the admission of Utah as a state. Memorial of citizens of Utah, against the admission of that Territory as a state... (H. Misc. Doc. No. 208) Washington: Govt. Print. Off., 1872. 82p. [Serial Set 1527]

Objections based in part on the theocratic nature of Mormon governmental beliefs and also because Mormons believe in the ultimate replacement of political government by the priesthood. Interestingly enough the objections based on polygamy appear after the political objections.

Includes a list of signers with their occupations and residences, which occupies the bulk of the pages.

[Flake 9321]

[375] U.S. House. 42d Congress. 2d Session. Freight to Salt Lake City by the Colorado River. Letter from the Secretary of War relative to the carriage and freight to Salt Lake City by the Colorado River. (H. Ex. Doc. No. 166) Washington: Govt. Print Off., 1872. 8p. [Serial Set 1513]

A conversation with Brigham Young concerning the route.

Extract of a report by James F. Rusling, Inspector of the Quartermaster's Department, describing a favourable route to California via the Colorado River with entry at a point called Callville, 440 miles from Salt Lake. Rusling spoke with Brigham Young regarding the route

but Rusling felt Young was not truly committed to this
route as it would bring an influx of Gentiles.

[376] U.S. House. 42d Congress. 2d Session. H.R. 1164, "A bill
to suppress polygamy, and to enable the people of Utah
to form a constitution and state government, January
22, 1872." [Washington: Govt. Print. Off., 1872] 8p.

DLC, UPB, US1C

[377] U.S. House. 42d Congress. 2d Session. H.R. 2694, "A bill
to aid the execution of the laws in the Territory of
Utah, May 8, 1872." [Washington: Govt. Print. Off.,
1872] 6p.

Section 6 deals with the prosecutions for the crime of
bigamy or polygamy.

DLC, UPB, US1C

[378] U.S. House. 42d Congress. 2d Session. Letter from the
Secretary of War relative to an appropriation for a
military post near the town of Beaver, Utah. (H. Ex.
Doc. No. 285) Washington: Govt. Print. Off., 1872.
3p. [Serial Set 1520]

Some facts relative to the Mountain Meadows Massacre.

[Flake 9248]

[379] U.S. Senate. 42d Congress. 2d Session. Petition of
residents of Utah Territory praying that the protection
of the general government may not be withdrawn from
them by the admission of that territory as a state.
(S. Misc. Doc. No. 118) Washington: Govt. Print.
Off., 1872. 8p. [Serial Set 1482]

A petition of over 400 "loyal women of the Territory"
who were trying to keep Utah from becoming a state
because they felt the wrongs of polygamy would be
intensified. A list of all the women who signed the
petition is included.

[Flake 9327]

[380] U.S. Senate. 42d Congress. 2d Session. S. 325, "...bill
(S.325) to aid the execution of the law against polygamy,
and to prevent that crime in the Territory of Utah, and
for other purposes, reported it with an amendment,
April 29, 1872." [Washington: Govt. Print. Off.,
1872] 5p.

Mainly concerning the judiciary in Utah Territory.

DLC, UPB, US1C

[381] Woods, George L. Governor's message to the Legislative
Assembly of the Territory of Utah. [Salt Lake City?
1872] 12p.

"Marriage" p. 3, notes that plural marriage is against
the law.

[Flake 9361]
CU-B, UPB, US1C

[382] Woods, George L. "Governor's Message to the Legislative
Assembly of the Territory of Utah, January 9, 1872,"
pp. 18-23. In the Journals of the Legislative Assembly
of the Territory of Utah, Twentieth Session, for the
year 1872. Salt Lake City: Deseret News Book and Job
Office, Angus M. Cannon, public printer [1872]

Discusses the fact that plural marriage and polygamy
are against the law.

Variant ed.

UPB

[383] Woods, George L. "Governor's Message to the Legislative
Assembly of the Territory of Utah, January 9, 1872,"
pp. 29-37. In the Journals of the Legislative Assembly
of the Territory of Utah, Twentieth session, for the
Year 1872. Salt Lake City: Daily Tribune Job Office,
1872.

Discusses the fact that plural marriage and polygamy
are against the law.

Variant ed.

UPB, US1C

1873

**"We firmly believe . . . [that if] a free
expression by the ballot is secured to all
citizens, that the vote of the women will be
found a powerful aid in doing away with the
horrible institution of polygamy. Women are
the principal sufferers from this cruel
custom, and it is unjust to deprive them of a
voice in its suppression."**

[Entry 409]

---

[384] "Admission of Colorado," Congressional Globe 42d Congress,
3d session (9 January 1873) vol. 178, p. 446. [X178]

Mr. Hooper of Utah proposes an amendment so that Utah
could also be admitted as a state along with Colorado.
Mr. Sargent of California offers an amendment to the
amendment that all officers in Utah would have to take
an oath that they weren't practicing polygamy, and
voters, prior to voting must also take the oath.

[385] "Admission of Colorado," Congressional Globe 42nd Congress,
3d session (28 Jan 1873) vol. 179, pp. 920-23, 943-8.
[X179]

The debate on the admission of Colorado, contained considerable material on Utah, as Mr. Hooper of Utah suggested that Utah be admitted as a state at the same time as Colorado. Mr. Clagett of Montana and Mr. Hooper of Utah are the prime debaters over the issue of Mormon hierarchy, polygamy, and the judicial system in Utah.

[386] "Affairs in Utah," Congressional Globe 42 Congress, 3d session (17 February 1873) vol. 179, pp. 1426-1428. [X179]

A memorial printed in full from a group of professionals in the territory some of whose names are included, responding to a memorial from lawyers in the Territory. They defend the legislature and the probate court system.

[387] "Case of J. and R. H. Porter," p. 9. In Attorney General Opinions. Official Opinions of the Attorney General of the United States. Vol. VIII. Washington: Govt. Print. off., 1873. [J1.5:8]

Refers back to the 1868 Attorney Generals Opinions regarding the Porter wagon train.

DLC, UPB, US1C

[388] Clagett, William Horace. Speech of Hon. William H. Clagett of Montana in the House of Representatives, January 28 and 29, 1873. [Washington: Congressional Globe Office, 1873] [9]-16p.

At head of title: Colorado Territory.

Speech partially concerning Utah and its religious situation. Mr. Clagett's speech can also be found in the Congressional Globe entry 385, beginning on p. 920.

[Flake 2379]
UU

[389] "Conditions of Affairs in Utah," Congressional Globe 42d Congress, 3d session (17 February 1873) vol. 179, p. 1357. [X179]

The message of President Ulysses S. Grant to the Senate and House regarding the laws passed by the territorial legislature of Utah being an embarrassment to the federal court structure in the territory.

[390] "Execution of laws in Utah," Congressional Globe 42d Congress, 3d session (19 February 1873) vol. 179, p. 1474. [X179]

Mr. Frederick Theodore mentioned Senate bill No. 1540 to aid in the execution of the laws in the territory of Utah and indicated that the object of the bill was to enforce laws equally against the Mormons and the non-Mormons.

[391] "Execution of laws in Utah," Congressional Globe 42d
      Congress, 3d session (25, 26 February 1873) vol. 180,
      pp. 1771-1772, 1779-1785, 1786-1797, 1799-1815. [X180]

      Senate bill 1540, printed in full, is discussed (possibly
      a bill submitted by Mr. Frelinghuysen of N. J.) although
      dealing ostensibly with the court structure for Utah
      Territory, the bill gets into polygamy and the discussion
      mainly centers around the suppression of polygamy.

[392] Fitch, Thomas. Argument of Hon. Thomas Fitch. Addressed
      to the House Judiciary Committee in reply to the
      memorial of the memorial of the Salt Lake Bar, and in
      opposition to House bill, 3791, February 10, 1873.
      Washington: Gibson Brothers, Printers, 1873. 34p.

      The evils of the anti-polygamy bill as contrasted with
      the belief that the peculiarities of Utah would rapidly
      disappear.
                                              [Flake 3369]
                          DLC, MH, MnHi, NN, PHi, UHi, UPB

[393] Grant, Ulysses S. "Fifth Annual Message, 10 October 1873,"
      p. 4204. In A Compilation of the Messages and Papers
      of the Presidents, by James D. Richardson. vol. 6.
      New York: Published by Bureau of National Literature,
      1911, c1897. [GS4.113:6, AE2.114:1-27/v.6]

      The Supreme Courts' action in the case of Clinton vs.
      Englebrect have practically abolished jury trials in
      Utah Territory, so that further legislation is necessary.

[394] Grant, Ulysses S. "To the Senate and House of Representatives,"
      pp. 4162-4163. In A Compilation of the Messages and
      Papers of the Presidents, by James D. Richardson. vol.
      6. New York: Published by Bureau of National Literature,
      1911, c1897. [GS4.113:6, AE2.114:1-27/v.6]

      Need for legislation to increase the power of the
      federal government over the territorial government
      before polygamy could be suppressed. (1873)

[395] Hooper, William Henry (Utah) "Colorado Territory," Congressiona
      Globe 42d Congress, 3d session (29 January 1873) vol.
      180, Appendix, pp. 29-31. [X180]

      Representative Hooper's reply to Clagett of Montana
      about the underhanded methods of the Mormon hierarchy
      which is found in vol. 179, p. 920, 921-23, 947-8.
      Part of Hooper's statements are in vol. 179, p. 945-6.
      The discussion arose over Hooper's suggestion that Utah
      be admitted as a state at the same time as Colorado.
      Naturally much of the debate centers on polygamy and
      the unheard of jurisdiction of the probate courts.

[396] Hooper, William Henry. Vindication of the people of Utah.
      Remarks of Hon. William H. Hooper of Utah in the House
      of Representatives, January 29, 1873, in reply to the
      charges of Hon. W. H. Clagett of Montana, on the 28th
      and 29th of January, 1873. [Washington: Printed at
      the Congressional Globe Office, 1873?] 16p.

A plea for understanding. Responding to Clagett's charges that freedom of speech doesn't exist is answered by a look at the newspapers in existence at the time. Of the six, three, Salt Lake Tribune, Mining Journal [may be the Utah Mining Journal], and the Corinne Reporter, are hostile to Mormons. Gives brief history of the Mormons.

[Flake 4085]
CU-B, ICN, NN, UPB, USlC, UU

[397] "Petition," Congressional Record 43d Congress, 1st session (15 December 1873) vol. 2, pt. 1, p. 187. [X182]

A petition signed by over 3,000 citizens of Utah Territory protesting the lawlessness of the Territory, especially at the hands of a "secret organization."

[398] Snow v. United States, U.S. Reports 85 (October 1873), pp. 317-322. [Ju6.8/1:85]

An error to the Supreme Court for the Territory of Utah although it deals with the seating of Zerubbabel Snow as territorial Attorney General, it also relates in its writing of the opinion, to the sovereignty of the territory. Territories are mere dependencies and this has, of course, tremendous implications for Mormonism and the relations of church and state.

[399] U.S. House. 42d Congress. 3d Session. H.R. 3791, "A bill in aid of the execution of the laws in the Territory of Utah, and for other purposes, February 3, 1873." [Washington: Govt. Print. Off., 1873] 12p.

Referred to the Committee on the Judiciary.

Section 10 deals with prosecutions for bigamy, polygamy, or adultery.
DLC, UPB, USlC

[400] U.S. House. 43d Congress. 1st Session. George R. Maxwell vs. George Q. Cannon. Papers in the case of Maxwell vs. Cannon, for a seat as delegate from Utah Territory in the Forty-third Congress. Evidence of contestant. (H. Misc. Doc. No. 49) [Washington: Govt. Print. Off., 1873] 151p. [Serial Set 1617]

[Flake 5315a]

[401] U.S. House. 43d Congress. 1st Session. H.R. 303, "A bill concerning the execution of the laws in the Territory of Utah and for other purposes, December 8, 1873." [Washington: Govt. Print. Off., 1873] 16p.

Referred to the Committee on the Territories.

Almost identical bill to S. 58, see entry 407.
DLC, UPB, USlC

[402] U.S. House. 43d Congress. 1st Session. H.R. 652, "A bill in aid of the execution of the laws in the Territory of

Utah, and for other purposes, December 15, 1873."
[Washington: Govt. Print. Off., 1873] 12p.

Referred to the Committee on the Judiciary.

Some of the sections deal with punishment for bigamy
and polygamy, and for the fact that no alien practicing
polygamy shall be granted citizenship.

DLC, UPB, US1C

[403] U.S. Senate. 42d Congress. 3d Session. Memorial of
citizens of Utah Territory remonstrating against
legislation asked for in a recent memorial of members
of the legal profession, and asking the appointment of
a commission to investigate all matters of complaint
relating to that Territory. (S. Misc. Doc. No. 73)
Washington: Franklin Telegraph Co., 1873. 12p.
[Serial Set 1546]

Protest against polygamy legislation.

[Flake 9323]

[404] U.S. Senate. 42d Congress. 3d Session. Message from the
President of the United States in relation to the
condition of affairs in the Territory of Utah, February
14, 1873. (S. Ex. Doc. No. 44) Washington: Govt.
Print. Off., 1873. 3p. [Serial Set 1545]

President Grant contends that the Federal Government
has been greatly embarrassed by the powers conferred on
the probate courts by the territorial legislature.
Grant wants legislation passed immediately which will
allow Utah's district courts to administer the law with
"independence and efficiency".

[405] U.S. Senate. 42d Congress. 3d Session. Suffrage in Utah.
Memorial of the New York Woman Suffrage Society,
protesting against the sixth section of the bill
regarding Utah. (H. Misc. Doc. No. 95) Washington:
Govt. Print. Off., 1873. 1p. [Serial Set 1572]

Letting women have the right to vote would defeat
polygamy. The bill No. is not given.

[406] U.S. Senate. 42d Congress. 3d Session. S. 1540, "A bill
in aid of the execution of the laws in the Territory of
Utah, and for other purposes, February 6, 1873."
[Washington: Govt. Print. Off., 1873] 16p.

Referred to the Committee on the Judiciary.

Section 10 deals with polygamy and other marital
offenses.

DLC, UPB, US1C

[406a] U.S. Senate. 43d Congress. 1st Session. S. 47, "A bill
in aid of the execution of the laws in the Territory of
Utah, and for other purposes, December 3, 1873."
[Washington: Govt. Print. Off., 1873] 16p.

Sections 10 and 11 deal with prosecution for polygamy, bigamy or adultery. Section 20 states that probate courts will have jurisdiction in civil but not criminal cases. Section 24 would not allow the Mormon Church to be an owner of property over six million dollars nor to solemnize marriages contrary to the existing provisions of polygamy or bigamy statutes. A whole host of acts would be repealed under the provisions of this bill.

DLC, UPB, US1C

[407] U.S. Senate. 43d Congress. 1st Session. S. 58, "A bill in aid of the execution of the laws in the Territory of Utah, and for other purposes, December 4, 1873." [Washington: Govt. Print. Off., 1873] 16p.

Referred to the Committee on the Judiciary.

Section 10 refers to the fact that no marriage ceremony and recording is required by the laws of the Territory, that it shall not be necessary to prove the first or subsequent marriages by registration. Section 11 also deals with marriages and polygamy. Section 26 annulled several Territorial acts, including an ordinance incorporating the Church of Jesus Christ of Latter-day Saints, and an act conferring the elective franchise on women.

DLC, UPB, US1C

[408] "Utah," Congressional Globe 42d Congress, 3rd session (4 February 1873) vol. 179, pp. 1092-1094. [X179]

Memorial from members of the legal profession concerning its subversive legislature, the near open rebellion of the territory, and the problems with the judicial system in Utah.

[409] "Woman Suffrage," Congressional Globe 42 Congress, 3d session (17 February 1873) vol. 179, p. 1428. [X179]

A memorial from the New York Woman Suffrage Association who believe that woman suffrage in Utah will do away with polygamy.

1874

"We, the undersigned committee . . . respectfully represent: That the political status of the Territory of Utah is anomalous in this, that five-sixths or more of the entire population are members of an organization, the adherents of which claim that it is religious in its character, while in fact it enjoins, both as to faith and practice, the commission of the highest crimes."

[Entry 424]

---

[410] "An Act in relation to courts and judicial officers in the Territory of Utah" (Chapter 469, June 23, 1874) 18,

part 3, <u>United States Statutes at Large</u>, pp. 253-256.
[GS4.111:18, AE2.111:18/3]

Specific reference is made to a writ of error from the
Supreme Court of the United States to the Supreme Court
of the Territory which shall occur in cases where the
accused have been sentenced to capital punishment for
bigamy or polygamy. This act also restricted the
jurisdiction of probate courts.

[411] "Affairs in Utah," <u>Congressional Record</u> 43rd Congress, 1st
session (16 February 1874) vol. 2, Pt. 2, pp. 1527-
1528. [X183]

The Legislative Assembly of Utah sent a memorial
requesting a commission to come to Utah to see that
many of the accusations of disloyalty and insubordination
are not true.

[412] "Courts in Utah," <u>Congressional Record</u> 43d Congress, 1st
session (2 June 1874) vol. 2, Pt. 5, pp. 4468-4475.
[X186]

The debate centers around H.R. 3097 which deals with
the courts and judicial officers in the Territory of
Utah, but which also contains a section on polygamy
charges being brought to the court system. The bill
was given in full in v. 2 pt. 4 [entry 414 below], pp.
3599-3600. Further discussion takes place in v. 2, pt.
6 [entry 413 below], pp. 5417-5419, 5443-5444.

[413] "Courts in Utah," <u>Congressional Record</u> 43rd Congress, 1st
session (23 June 1874) vol. 2, Pt. 6, pp. 5417-5419,
5443-5444. [X187]

Continues the debate over H.R. 3097 on the courts and
judicial officers in the Territory of Utah. Some of
the discussion centers around polygamy. The bill was
given in full in v. 2 pt. 4 [see entry 414 below] pp.
3599-3600. Additional discussion takes place in v. 2,
pt. 5 [entry 412 above], pp. 4468-75.

[414] "Judicial Proceedings in Utah," <u>Congressional Record</u> 43d
Congress, 1st session (5 May 1874) vol. 2, Pt. 4, pp.
3599-3600. [X185]

Presents H.R. 3097 in full regarding the courts and
judicial officers of Utah Territory. There is a
section of the bill which deals with polygamy. Discussion
on this bill takes place later and is found in v. 2,
pt. 5 [see entry 412 above] pp. 4468-4475, and v. 2,
pt. 6 [see entry 413 above], pp. 5417-5419, 5443-5444.

[415] Perris v. Higley, <u>U.S. Reports</u> 87 (Oct. 1874 session) pp.
375-384. [Ju6.8/1:87]

An error to the Supreme Court of the Territory of Utah
to the Supreme Court of the United States regarding the
granting of original jurisdiction to the Probate Courts
by the Territorial Legislature. Supreme Court voided

the legislatures decision. Had to do with the problem
of church and state.

[416] Robinson, J. W. (Ohio). "Charges of Bigamy against the
Delegate from Utah," Congressional Record 43d Congress,
1st session (19 June 1874) vol. 2, pt. 6, Appendix, pp.
481-482. [X187]

The claim that Mr. Hooper of Utah, as a polygamist,
should be allowed a seat in Congress in order not to
violate his right to worship, is denied by Mr. Robinson.

[417] U.S. House. 43d Congress. 1st Session. Committee on
Elections. George R. Maxwell vs. George Q. Cannon -
contested election, Territory of Utah. (H. Rep. No.
484) Washington: Govt. Print. Off., 1874. 15p.
[Serial Set 1625]

Accusations that Cannon couldn't represent the people
because he had to follow the Church authorities. Also
mentions voter fraud, which is answered by Cannon.

[Flake 9116a]

[418] U.S. House. 43d Congress. 1st Session. H.R. 853, "A bill
in relation to courts and judicial officers in the
Territory of Utah, January 5, 1874." [Washington:
Govt. Print. Off., 1874] 9p.

Referred to the Committee on the Judiciary.

Punishment for polygamy is briefly cited.

DLC, UPB, US1C

[419] U.S. House. 43d Congress. 1st Session. H.R. 1608, "A
bill to secure minority-representation in the Territory
of Utah, February 2, 1874." [Washington: Govt. Print.
Off., 1874] 1p.

Referred to the Committee on the Territories.

Proposes to change the Territory of Utah from its
legislative district approach so that all future
elections to the most numerous branch of the territorial
legislature would be open to every person who receives
five hundred or more votes.

DLC, UPB, US1C

[420] U.S. House. 43d Congress. 1st Session. H.R. 2204,
"Amendment in the nature of a substitute proposed to be
submitted by Mr. Crouse to the bill (H.R. 2204) concerning
the execution of laws in the Territory of Utah, and for
other purposes, March 4, 1874." [Washington: Govt.
Print. Off., 1874] 7p.

Probate courts shall have jurisdiction only in the
matter of settlement of estates for descendents and no
longer in criminal cases.

DLC, UPB, US1C

[421] U.S. House. 43d Congress. 1st Session. H.R. 3089, "A
      bill in relation to courts and judicial officers in the
      Territory of Utah, April 21, 1874." [Washington:
      Govt. Print. Off., 1874] 10p.

      Referred to the Committee on the Judiciary.

      One section deals with polygamous marriages.

                                          DLC, UPB, US1C

[422] U.S. House. 43d Congress. 1st Session. H.R. 3097, "A
      bill in relation to courts and judicial officers in the
      Territory of Utah, April 25, 1874." [Washington:
      Govt. Print. Off., 1874] 10p.

      Referred to the Committee on the Judiciary.

      A section of the bill deals with polygamy, and occasioned
      some debate within Congress.

                                          DLC, UPB, US1C

[423] U.S. House. 43d Congress. 1st Session. Memorial of the
      Legislative Assembly of Utah, asking for a commission
      of investigation to be sent to Utah to inquire into all
      alleged abuses in affairs there. (H. Misc. Doc. No.
      139) Washington: Govt. Print. Off., 1874. 2p.
      [Serial Set 1619]

      Appears to be the same memorial printed in the Congressional
      Globe, See entry 408.

                                          [Flake 9387]

[424] U.S. House. 43d Congress. 1st Session. Non-Mormon
      citizens of Utah. Memorial of a committee of forty-
      five gentlemen, selected at a public meeting of non-
      Mormon residents and voters of Salt Lake City, in the
      Territory of Utah, held on the 19th of January 1874, to
      prepare a memorial to Congress, setting forth the
      grievances of the non-Mormon people of said Territory,
      and for such legislation by Congress as is needed for
      the full protection of all classes of people residing
      in said Territory. (H. Misc. Doc. No. 120) Washington:
      Govt. Print. Off., 1874. 8p. [Serial Set 1618]

      Discusses the continued practice of polygamy in defiance
      of the law. Probably the same memorial (not printed)
      which Mr. Frelinghuysen presented in March 17, 1874 in
      Congress, Congressional Globe 43d Congress, 1st session,
      v. 2, pt. 3, p. 2183, which was referred to the Committee
      on the Judiciary.

                                          [Flake 9325]

[425] U.S. Senate. 43d Congress. 1st Session. S. 266, "A bill
      for the protection of society in the Territory of Utah,
      and for other purposes, January 9, 1874." [Washington:
      Govt. Print. Off., 1874] 5p.

      Referred to the Committee on the Judiciary.

Various sections dealing with polygamous marriages, including that no alien living in or practicing polygamy shall be admitted to U.S. citizenship.

DLC, UPB, US1C

[426] Woods, George L. <u>Governor's Message to the Legislative Assembly of the Territory of Utah, Salt Lake City, Utah Territory, January 13, 1874</u>. 16p.

George L. Woods refers to the Perpetual Emigration Fund and its need to be used for emigrants who are of other denominations. Pushes the need for a law regarding marriage licenses and a Probate Practice Act to systematize the practice in probates.

[Flake add. 6361a]
UPB

[427] Woods, George L. "Governor's Message to the Legislative Assembly of Utah Territory, January 13, 1874," pp. 19-34. In the <u>Journals of the Legislative Assembly of the Territory of Utah, Twenty-first session, for the year 1874</u>. Salt Lake City: Tribune Printing and Publishing Co., 1874.

See entry 426 for annotation.

UPB, US1C

1875

"During last summer the Mormon priesthood in Saint George, gathered together at that place some two or three hundred Indians of the surrounding tribes whom they proceeded to baptize with all the pomp, ceremony, and display calculated to make an impression on the Indian. They even had an artist on hand who produced a very fine, and no doubt, a faithful picture of the scene. The Mormon bishop in the center, up to his waist in water; hundreds of dusky forms all around him, while a vast concourse of saints looked approvingly on."

[Entry 429]

"It is alleged as error that the Court below, sustained the challenge of the prosecution to the several jurors who appeared to be otherwise qualified, but who refused to answer a question to criminate themselves. The question was asked as follows: `Are you living in polygamy?' The Court cautioned the jurors that they need not answer, if the answer would tend to criminate them. They declined, upon that ground, to answer. The inevitable conclusion is that these jurors were guilty of the crime of polygamy."

[Entry 437]

---

[428] "Bannacks, 1875," p. 45, 258. In <u>Annual Report of the Commissioner of Indian Affairs to the Secretary of the Interior for the year 1875</u>. Washington: Govt. Print. Off., 1875. [I20.1:875]

Describes the evil influence of the Mormons upon approximately 120 of the Bannacks on the Fort Hall Reservation in Idaho. At the Fort Hall Reservation the agent discusses the bad influence of the Mormon missionaries on the Indians and the "lies" which were told to convince the Indians to be baptized into Mormonism.

[429] Barnes, A. J. "Reports of Agents in Nevada, September 11, 1875," pp. 336-338. In <u>Annual Report of the Commissioner of Indian Affairs to the Secretary of the Interior for the year 1875</u>. Washington: Govt. Print. Off., 1875. [I20:1:875]

Discusses the Southeast Nevada, Moapa River Reserve Agency, and the Indian Agent uses the Mormons as an example of playing on the ignorance of the Indians. Describes a baptism and portrait painting ceremony.

[430] Grant, Ulysses S. "Message of the President of the United States, 7 December 1875," p. 25. In <u>Messages and Documents 1875-76 Abridgement</u>. Washington: Govt. Print. Off., 1875. [Y8.44/1:]

Refers again to the scandalous condition of polygamy existing in the territory of Utah.

[431] Grant, Ulysses S. "President's Annual Message," <u>Congressional Record</u> 44th Congress, 1st session (7 December 1875) vol. 4, pt. 1, pp. 174-181. [X193]

On page 180, President Grant reiterates the need to pass a law to punish polygamy.

[432] Grant, Ulysses S. "Seventh Annual Message, December 7, 1875," p. 36. In <u>Messages and Documents, 1876-'77 Abridgement</u>. Washington: Govt. Print. Off., 1876. [Y8.44/2:]

Reiterates the need to pass a law which will punish polygamy as a crime.

[433] Grant, Ulysses S. "Seventh Annual Message, 7 December 1875," pp. 4309-4310. In <u>A Compilation of the Messages and Papers of the Presidents</u>, by James D. Richardson. v. 6. New York: Published by Bureau of National Literature, 1911, c1897. [GS4.113:6, AE2.114:1-27/v.6]

The need to crush polygamy "so flagrant a crime against decency and morality".

[434] Green, Levi A. "Pyramid Lake Reserve, September 10, 1875,"
p. 342. In <u>Annual Report of the Commissioner of Indian
Affairs to the Secretary of the Interior for the year
1875</u>. Washington: Govt. Print. Off., 1875. [I20.1:875]

The Indian agent at Pyramid Lake Reserve discusses the
corruption among the Indians, perhaps due to the
Mountain Meadows Massacre.

[435] "United States Courts in Utah Territory," <u>Congressional
Record</u> 43d Congress, 2d session (17 February 1875) vol.
3, Pt. 2, p. 1417. [X190]

Need for federal courts in Utah due to the way the
Mormons ran the probate courts.

[436] The United States, respondents, v. George Reynolds, appellant,
<u>Territory of Utah Reports</u> 1 (June 1875) pp. 226-232.

Defendant, George Reynolds, who was on trial for
polygamy, offered evidence to show that polygamous
marriage was part of his religion; the decision was
made that such evidence was inadmissable. Also held
that a person who has conscientious scruples against
indicting a person for polygamy is incompetent to sit
on a Grand Jury.
                    CU-L, DLC, ICU, MH, MiU, UAr, UPB, UU, ViU-L

[437] The United States, respondent, v. George Reynolds, appellant,
<u>Territory of Utah Reports</u> 1 (June 1875) pp. 319-323.

It was held by the court that a juror who declined to
answer the question "Are you living in polygamy"
virtually admitted the fact, and he could, therefore,
be disqualified as a juror; extrinsic evidence did not
need to be shown.
                    CU-L, DLC, ICU, MH, MU, UAr, UPB, VV, ViU-L

[438] "Utah," pp. 510-514. In <u>Commissioner of Education Report,
1875</u>, vol. 2. Washington: Govt. Print. Off., 1875.
[I1.1:875]

The Utah portion contains a brief mention of the
University of Deseret, Salt Lake and Brigham Young
Academy, Provo.

Variant ed. U.S. 44th Congress, 1st session, House Ex.
Doc. 1, Part 5, Serial Set 1750.

[439] Utah Territory. Third Judicial District...<u>The United
States vs. George Reynolds. Indictment for Bigamy</u>.
[Salt Lake City?] 1875. 49p.

At head of title: United States of America, Territory
of Utah, Third Judicial District of the October Term.
A.D. 1875, of the District Court, in and for said
district, held in Salt Lake County. No title page on
UPB copy.
                                        [Flake 7120]
                                        UPB, US1C

"We also ask that each married woman in Utah
be granted the right to homestead or pre-empt
one hundred and sixty acres of land in her
own name; also, that the citizens of Utah
have the right to use for their own benefit
the timber growing on Government land in
Utah, which has been forbidden by the Government
officials, to our great detriment, thereby
depriving us of necessary material for
building habitations and otherwise improving
our homes."

[Entry 448]

---

[440] Cannon, George Quayle. Argument of Hon. George Q. Cannon,
delegate from Utah, before the Committee on Territories
of the House of Representatives, March 21, 1876, in
favor of H. B. 178, a bill to enable the people of Utah
to form a constitution and state government and for the
admission of the said state into the Union on an equal
footing with the original states. Philadelphia: J. B.
Lippincott & Co., 1876. 20p.

Mentions the earliest Mormon pioneers and the Mormon
Battalion. Mentions polygamy, and the fact that the
Mormon religion will gain sympathy if statehood is
denied because of it.

[Flake 1147]
DLC, NN, UPB, US1C

[441] Emery, George W. "Governor's Message to the Legislative
Assembly of the Territory of Utah, Jan. 11, 1876," pp.
27-34. In the Journals of the Legislative Assembly of
the Territory of Utah, Twenty-second session for the
year 1876. Salt Lake City: Printed at the Deseret
News Steam Printing Establishment, 1876.

Gov. Emery refers to current voting laws in Utah which
required voters to show for whom they voted, supposedly
enabling the Church to control the vote. He refers to
the fact that no one is authorized by the laws of Utah
to perform marriages, and finally he refers to the
peculiar social situation in Utah regarding polygamy.

UPB, US1C

[442] George Reynolds, plaintiff in error, vs. the United States,
defendant in error, October Sessions, 1876, No. 180.
Brief of plaintiff in error. [Attorneys] for plaintiff
in error, Ben Sheeks, George W. Biddle. In the Supreme
Court of the United States. [n.p., 1876?] 63p.

This brief of plaintiff in error was filed regarding
the Reynolds v. United States case 98 U.S. Reports 145-
168, October 1878. It gives a detailed history of the
case.

[Flake add. 7098a]
DLC, UPB, US1C

[443] George Reynolds, plaintiff in error vs. the United States, In error to the Supreme Court of the Territory of Utah. Transcript of record. Supreme court of the United States, No. 455 [crossed out and handwritten 180]. [n.p., 1876?] 30p.

This transcript was filed, October 4, 1876, regarding the Reynolds v. United States case 98 U.S. Reports 145-168, October 1878.

[Flake add. 7098b]
DLC, UPB, US1C

[444] "Memorial of the women of Utah to the Congress of the United States," Congressional Record 44th Congress, 1st session (10 January 1876) vol. 4, Pt. 1, p. 308. [X193]

The memorial prays that the anti-polygamy law of 1862 be repealed, that unjust imported officials be suppressed, that their religion be left alone, etc. Signed by 22,626 women.

[445] "Regulating elections in Utah," Congressional Record 44th Congress, 1st Session (28 January 1876) vol. 4, Pt. 1, p. 721. [X193]

Includes a letter from R. N. Baskin showing that a new law passed by the Utah legislature would enable the church to know how its members had voted and would disfellowship those who did not vote as they were told.

[446] Robert N. Baskin, contestant, v. George Q. Cannon, contestee. Brief and argument of Chas. A. Eldredge. [Washington: Gibson Brothers, Printers, 1876] 31p.

[Flake add. 3127a]
DLC, US1C

[447] U.S. House. 44th Congress. 1st Session. Papers in the case of Baskin vs. Cannon, as delegate from Utah Territory. April 10, 1876 - Ordered to be printed. Papers for contestant. (H. Misc. Doc. No. 166) Washington: Govt. Print. Off., 1876. 21p. [Serial Set 1702]

"Papers for contestee [George Q. Cannon]," p. 17-21.

[Flake add. 329a]

[448] U.S. House. 44th Congress. 1st Session. A petition of 22,626 women of Utah asking for the repeal of certain laws, the enactment of others, and the admission of the Territory of Utah as a state. (H. Misc. Doc. No. 42) Washington: Govt. Print. Off., 1876. 2p. [Serial Set 1698]

Praying for the repeal of the anti-polygamy law of 1862, and the enactment of a law granting to each married woman in Utah the right to homestead or preempt

one hundred and sixty acres of land in her own name.
Prays for admission of Utah as a State as well.

[Flake 9400]

[449] U.S. Senate. 44th Congress. 1st Session. S. 315, "A bill
to provide for challenges to jurors in trials for
bigamy and polygamy in the Territory of Utah, and to
amend section four of the act entitled 'An act in
relation to the courts and judicial officers in the
Territory of Utah,' approved June twenty-fourth eighteen
hundred and seventy-four, January 20, 1876." [Washington:
Govt. Print. Off., 1876] 3p.

Referred to the Committee on Territories.

DLC, UPB, US1C

[450] "Utah," pp. 458-461. In Report of the Commissioner of
Education for the year 1876. v. 2. Washington: Govt.
Print. Off., 1878. [FS5.1:876]

Summary of the history of education in Utah.

Variant ed. U.S. 44th Congress, 2d Sess. House Ex.
Doc. 1, pt. 5. Serial Set 1750.

1877

"The court erred in using the following
language to the jury in said charge: 'John
D. Lee stands before you charged with being a
participant and leader in a most atrocious
and unprovoked massacre of human beings.'"
[Entry 454]

---

[451] Critchlow, J. J. "Uintah Valley Agency, Utah, August 25,
1877," p. 182. In Annual Report of the Commissioner of
Indian Affairs to the Secretary of the Interior for the
year 1877. Washington: Govt. Print. Off., 1877.
[I20.1:877]

Feels that the Mormon leadership have tried to keep the
Indians under their control and that they have been
somewhat successful.

[452] Hayden, Ferdinand V. Eleventh Annual report of the United
States Geological and Geographical Survey of the
territories, embracing Idaho and Wyoming, being a
report on progress of the exploration for the year
1877. Washington: Govt. Print. Off., 1879. [I18.1:877]

Vol. 11 in the U.S. Geological and Geographic Survey of
the Territories. Comments on Bear River area with
mention of Mormon settlements in Cache Valley, pp. 697-
701.

[453] Irvine, Alex. G. "Navajo Indian Agency, September 4, 1877," pp. 158-159. In <u>Annual Report of the Commissioner of Indian Affairs to the Secretary of the Interior for the year 1877</u>. Washington: Govt. Print. Off., 1877. [I20.1:877]

Tells of Mormons settling among the Moquis (Hopi) Indians.

[454] The people, etc., respondents, v. John D. Lee, impleaded with eight others, appellants, <u>Territory of Utah Reports</u> 2 (1877) pp. 441-456.

Appeal of the Mountain Meadows Massacre conviction.

CU-L, DLC, ICU, MH, MiU, UAr, UPB, UU, ViU-L

[455] U.S. House. 45 Congress. 2d Session. H.R. 2078, "A bill to regulate elections and the elective franchise in the Territory of Utah, December 10, 1877." [Washington: Government Printing Office, 1877] 16p.

Referred to the Committee on the Territories.

Excludes polygamists from voting.

DLC, UPB, US1C

[456] U.S. House. 45th Congress. 2d Session. H.R. 2079, "A bill to provide for challenges to jurors in trials for bigamy and polygamy in the Territory of Utah, and to amend section four of the act entitled 'an act in relation to courts and judicial officers in the Territory of Utah,' approved June twenty-fourth, eighteen hundred and seventy-four, December 10, 1877." [Washington: Govt. Print. Off., 1877] 3p.

Referred to the Committee on the Territories.

DLC, UPB, US1C

[457] United States, respondent, v. John H. Miles, appellant, <u>Territory of Utah Reports</u> 2 (1877) pp. 19-30.

A member of the Mormon church believing in polygamy should not sit on a jury. Testimony of Caroline Owen a plural wife.

CU-L, DLC, ICU, MH, MiU, UAr, UPB, UU, ViU-L

[458] U.S. Senate. 45th Congress. 2d Session. S. 410, "A bill to provide for challenges to jurors in trials for bigamy and polygamy in the Territory of Utah, and to amend section four of the act entitled 'An act in relation to courts and judicial officers in the Territory of Utah,' approved June twenty-fourth, eighteen hundred and seventy-four, December 10, 1877." [Washington: Govt. Print. Off., 1877] 3p.

Referred to the Committee on the Judiciary.

DLC, UPB, US1C

[459] U.S. Senate. 45th Congress. 2d Session. S. 411, "A bill to regulate elections and the elective franchise in the Territory of Utah, December 10, 1877." [Washington: Government Printing Office, 1877] 16p.

Referred to the Committee on the Judiciary.

Bill disfranchising polygamists among others.

DLC, UPB, US1C

[460] "Uintah Valley Agency, Utah, August 25, 1877," pp. 577-582. In Annual report of the Secretary of the Interior on the Operations of the Department for the Fiscal Year ended June 30, 1877. Washington Govt. Print. Off., 1877. [I1.1:877]

Briefly mentions the direct influence of the Mormon Church leader on the Indians and the baptisms of Captain Joe and Kenosh.

Variant ed. U.S. House, 45 Congress, 2d session, H. Ex. Doc. No. 1, Serial Set 1800.

1878

"The history of the Mormon people shows, beyond question, that they are the subjects of the Priesthood, yielding an implicit obedience, amounting to the most abject slavery of soul and body. All their published writings, all their oral teachings, are replete with this doctrine, which is a prime tenet of their so-called religion."

[Entry 466]

"That the irreligious in the States and Territories . . . should be compelled to suffer the disgrace and punishment of dungeon-darkness, while the religionists, so called, of Utah, with the protective shield of the Constitution thrown around them, can openly violate it with impunity is a view or doctrine too monstrous to be seriously considered."

[Entry 473]

---

[461] Annual report upon the Geographical Surveys of the Territory of the United States west of the 100th Meridian, in the States and Territories of California...[Etc.] By George M. Wheeler, First Lieutenant Corps of Engineers, U. S. Army; being Appendix NN of the Annual Report of the Chief of Engineers for 1878. Washington: Govt. Print. Off., 1878. 234p. [W8.1:878]

Report of 2nd Lieutenant Willard Young (son of Brigham Young) in charge of Party No. 1 of the Utah Section,

February 22, 1878, pp. 120-122, and report of 1st
Lieutenant R. Birney, Jr., in charge of Party No. 2,
June 14, 1878, pp. 122-131, for operations in northern
Utah and southern Idaho, 1877. Primarily a detailed
geographic description of Utah and southern Idaho
territories, and Mormon settlements.

[Flake 9200]

[462] Cannon v. Pratt, U.S. Reports 99 (October 1878) pp. 619-
624. [Ju6.8/1:99]

A land dispute, which relates back to the doctrine of
the Stringfellow v. Cain case. Brigham Young, Sen. and
Brigham Young, Jr., apparently gave testimony and were
directly involved in the land dispute. Brigham Young
senior's testimony was declared immaterial or incompetent
by the Supreme Court. Unfortunately the various briefs
and abstracts are missing in this case, at least at the
Library of Congress.

[463] Emery, George W. "Governor's Message to the Legislative
Assembly of the Territory of Utah, Jan 15, 1878," pp.
31-50. In the Journals of the Legislative Assembly of
the Territory of Utah, Twenty-third session, for the
year 1878. Salt Lake City: W. C. Dunbar, public
printer, Salt Lake Herald Office, 1878.

Gov. Emery discusses both polygamy and the Mountain
Meadows Massacre.

UPB, US1C

[463a] Emery, George W. Message of Governor Emery to the Legislative
Assembly of Utah Territory convened at Salt Lake City,
January 14th, 1878. Salt Lake City: John W. Pike,
Public Printer, 1878. 34p.

See entry 463 for Journal entry.

[Flake 9363]
NjP, US1, US1C

[464] Emery, George W. "Report of the Governor of Utah Territory,
Salt Lake City, Utah Ter., October 26, 1878," pp. 1115-
1117. In Report of the Secretary of the Interior, vol.
1. Washington: Govt. Print. Off., 1878. [I1.1:878]

Mentions that agriculture is a Mormon endeavor and
mining is anti-Mormon. The Governor doesn't believe in
woman suffrage and thinks it should be abolished in
Utah. Bigamy, that is "cohabitation and living together"
should be the offense and not the marriage ceremony.

Variant ed. 45th Congress, 3d session, H. Ex. Doc. No.
1, Part 5, Serial Set 1850.

[465] George Reynolds, plaintiff in error, vs. the United States,
No. 180. In error to the Supreme Court of the Territory
of Utah. Brief for the United States. In the Supreme
Court of the United States, October Term, 1878. [n.p.,
1878?] 8p.

This brief was filed regarding the Reynolds v. United States case 98 <u>U.S. Reports</u> 145-168, October 1878.

[Flake add. 6372e]
DLC, UPB, US1C

[466] Hemingray, J. C. <u>Mormonism. Argument of Hon. J. C. Hemingray, delegate of the Liberal Party of Utah, before the House Subcommittee on Territories, on the bill "to regulate elections and elective franchise in the Territory of Utah," January 22, 1878.</u> Washington: W. H. Moore, Printer, 1878. 30p.

Reiterates the argument that Mormons are subject to the Priesthood. This of course goes beyond obedience to theocratic government. Mountain Meadows Massacre is used as an example to show obedience to the hierarchy.

[Flake 3953]
CSmH, CtY, DLC, ICHi, OClWHi, NN, ULA, UPB

[467] "Petitions," <u>Congressional Record</u> 45th Congress, 2d session (11 February 1878) vol. 7, pt. 1, p. 916. [X207]

A petition, not printed in full in the Record, signed by Emmeline B. Wells, Eliza R. Snow and 6,979 persons praying for a Constitutional amendment prohibiting states from disfranchising citizens on account of sex.

[468] "Petitions," <u>Congressional Record</u> 45th Congress, 2d session (4 March 1878) vol. 7, pt. 2, p. 1466. [X208]

Same kind of petition as the above, although a few other names are mentioned.

[469] <u>Reynolds vs. the United States, No. 180. Brief for the United States. In the Supreme Court of the United States. Appendix.</u> [n.p., 1878?] 3p.

This appendix to the brief for the United states was filed regarding the Reynolds v. United States case 98 <u>U.S. Reports</u> 145-168, October 1878.

DLC, UPB, US1C

[470] Reynolds v. United States, <u>U.S. Reports</u>, 98 (October 1878) pp. 145-168. [Ju6.8/1:98]

A person's religious belief cannot be justification for his committing an overt act, made criminal by the law of the land.

[471] Stringfellow v. Cain, <u>U.S. Reports</u> 99 (October 1878) pp. 610-619. [Ju6.8/1:99]

Although this case revolves around a land dispute in Salt Lake City, the various briefs and transcript of records bring out the Mormons early approach to land settlement. The case revolves around Joseph Cain, who died in 1857, and his widow Elizabeth Cain, and two minor children, Elizabeth and Joseph. Brigham Young was involved in the land claim because after Cain's

death, Brigham Young occupied the whole of the east
half of the lot in question. Later the Stringfellow
brothers, in 1869, became possessors of that part of
the premises. The case is extremely complicated
legally, due to inheritance and sale problems. The
presence of Brigham Young in the case provides some
lively interest.

[472] U.S. District Court, Utah. (Third District). Exposures of
a rotten priesthood by the Grand Jury of the Third
District Court of Utah. February, 1878. [Salt Lake
City, 1878?] 22p.

Includes a description of Utah penal institutions.

[Flake 9199]
UPB

[473] U.S. House. 45th Congress. 2d Session. Committee on the
Territories. Elective Franchise in Utah... Report: [To
accompany bill H.R. 2078]. (H. Rept. No. 949) Washington:
Govt. Print. Off., 1878. 2p. [Serial Set 1826]

Bill designed to abolish polygamy.

[474] U.S. House. 45th Congress. 2d Session. Report on the
lands of the arid region of the United States, with a
more detailed account of the lands of Utah. With maps.
By J. W. Powell. (H. Ex. Doc. No. 73) Washington:
Govt. Print. Off., 1878. 195p. [Serial Set 1805]

A description of land and water availability with
material concerning location of settlements; land
utilization, etc. Powell on p. 89 and 127 briefly
mentions Mormon land settlement and church government,
especially in regard to irrigation disputes.

2d ed., 1879.

[Flake 6431]

[475] "Utah," pp. 289-291. In Report of the Secretary of the
Interior. Part II Education for the year 1878.
Washington: Govt. Print. Off., 1880. [I1.1:878]

Brief mention of the inferiority of Mormon schools.

Variant ed. U.S. Congress. 3d Sess. House Ex. Doc 1,
Pt. 5. Serial Set 1851.

1879

"Inasmuch as the practice of polygamy is
based on a form of marriage, by which additional
wives are `sealed' to the men of that community,
these so-called `marriages' are pronounced by
the laws of the United States to be crimes
against the statutes of the country, and
punishable as such . . . Under whatever
specious guise the subject may be presented
by those engaged in instigating the European
movement to swell the numbers of the law-

defying Mormons of Utah, the bands and
organizations which are got together in
foreign lands as recruits cannot be regarded
as otherwise than a deliberate and systematic
attempt to bring persons to the United States
with the intent of violating their laws and
committing crimes expressly punishable under
the statute as penitentiary offenses."

[Entry 477]

---

[476] Annual report upon the Geographical Surveys of the Territory
of the United States and Territories of California...[Etc.]
By George M. Wheeler, Captain Corps of Engineers, U.S.
Army; being Appendix OO of the Annual Report of the
Chief of Engineers for 1879. Washington: Govt. Print.
Off., 1879. 340p. [W8.1:879]

Includes reports by 2nd Lieutenant Willard Young (son
of Brigham Young) on Southern California mining districts,
pp. 188-192; and report of March 17, 1879, on survey of
Great Salt Lake, pp. 228-232, 235-237, and Southern
California, pp. 232-235.

[Flake 9201]

[477] "Circular," pp. 11-12. In Foreign Relations of the United
States, 1879. Washington: Govt. Print. Off., 1879.
[S1.1:879]

Circular to be sent to all legations to halt Mormon
proselyting and emigration due to polygamy. Signed:
Wm. M. Evarts, August 9, 1879. Important circular
referred to many times in future immigration concerns.

[478] "France," pp. 349-350. In Foreign Relations of the United
States, 1879. Washington: Govt. Print. Off., 1879.
[S1.1:879]

Letter from R. R. Hitt explaining that there were no
Mormon missionary activities in France at the present
time. Confirmation of the missionary activity was made
by McKnight, nephew of Brigham Young, and a correspondent
of the St. Louis Globe-Democrat and Alfales [sic]
Young, son of Brigham Young, who was studying law in Paris.

[479] "Great Britain," pp. 450-451, 465. In Foreign Relations of
the United States, 1879. Washington: Govt. Print.
Off., 1879. [S1.1:879]

Description of Mormon missionary activities and emigration
to United States, and polygamy.

[480] Hayes, Rutherford B. "Third annual message, 1 December
1879," pp. 4511-4512. In A Compilation of the Messages
and Papers of the Presidents, by James D. Richardson.
vol. 6. New York: Published by Bureau of National
Literature, 1911, c1897. [GS4.113:6, AE2.114:1-27/v.6]

Continued deliberate violation of anti-polygamy legislation.

[481] How, John. "Western Shoshone Agency, Elko, Nevada, August
      19, 1879," p. 111. In Annual Report of the Commissioner
      for Indian Affairs to the Secretary of the Interior of
      the year 1879. Washington: Govt. Print. Off., 1879.
      [I20.1:879]

      The agent mentions that there was Mormon interference
      in regard to moving the Carlin Indians to the Duck
      Valley reserve and away from their farms.

[482] "Italy," pp. 601-604. In Foreign Relations of the United
      States, 1879. Washington: Govt. Print. Off., 1879.
      [S1.1:879]

      Mormonism not known in Italy, at the present time. A
      sect, founded by Davide Lazzaretti, is used as an
      example of how some Italians might be "led astray... by
      the spirit of religious exaltation which would blind
      them to every sense of reason and right."

[483] John Miles, plaintiff in error, vs. the United States in
      error to the Supreme Court of Utah Territory. Transcript
      of Record. Supreme Court of the United States, No.
      592. Filed October 13, 1879. [n.p.: Govt. Print.
      Off.?, 1879?] 115p.

      Transcript of record regarding Miles v. United States,
      103 U.S. Reports 304-316, October 1880 session.

                                          [Flake add. 5389a]
                                          DLC, UPB, US1C

[484] "Netherlands," pp. 852-854. In Foreign Relations of the
      United States, 1879. Washington: Govt. Print. Off.,
      1879. [S1.1:879]

      Emigration of Mormons through Netherland ports.
      Concerns of State Dept. and Netherland officials are
      expressed concerning polygamy.

[485] Paine, Halbert Eleazer. Contested election. Territory of
      Utah. George R. Maxwell vs. George Q. Cannon. Argument
      of Halbert E. Paine, counsel for sitting member. [Salt
      Lake City? 1879?] 59p.

      Defends the right of George Q. Cannon to hold his seat
      in Congress.
                                          [Flake 6073]
                                    MH, NjP, UPB, US1C, UU

[486] Patten, James I. "Shoshone and Bannack Agency, Wyoming,
      August 11, 1879," p. 168. In Annual report of the
      Commissioner of Indian Affairs to the Secretary of the
      Interior for the year 1879. Washington: Govt. Print.
      Off., 1879. [I20.1:879]

      Describes the practice of this agency's Shoshones who
      folded their tents and slipped away once a year to Salt
      Lake to renew their covenants as Mormons.

[487] "Polygamy," <u>Congressional record</u> 46th Congress, 2d session (10 December 1879) vol. 10, Pt. 1, p. 59. [X220]

Amendments to J.R. No. 2779 concerning polygamy in the territories.

[488] <u>Samuel Stringfellow, et al., appellants vs. Joseph M. Cain, et al., and Samuel Stringfellow, et al., Plaintiffs in errors, vs. Joseph M. Cain, et al. Error and appeal from the Supreme Court of Utah Territory. Brief of appellees and defendants. In the Supreme Court of the United States, No. 181 and No. 182.</u> [Salt Lake: Salt Lake Tribune Print, ca 1879] 76p.

This brief was filed in regard to the Stringfellow v. Cain case 99 <u>U.S. Reports</u> (October 1878) 610-619. Much detail is provided about the Cain family, and their history. Brigham Young also testified in this case.

DLC

[489] <u>Samuel Stringfellow, George Stringfellow, William Jennings, and Brigham Young, appellants, vs. Joseph M. Cain, Elizabeth Cain, Charles Crismon, and Elizabeth T. Crismon, and Samuel Stringfellow, George Stringfellow, William Jennings, and Brigham Young, plaintiffs in error, vs. Joseph M. Cain, Elizabeth Cain, Charles Crismon, and Elizabeth T. Crismon. Error and appeal from the Supreme court of the Territory of Utah. Brief of the plaintiffs in error and appellants, No. 181 and No. 182.</u> Philadelphia: Allen, Lane & Scott, Printers [ca 1879] 135p.

This brief was filed in the Stringfellow v. Cain case 99 <u>U.S. Reports</u> (October 1878) 610-619. It provides a history of the case.

DLC

[490] <u>Samuel Stringfellow, George Stringfellow, William Jennings, and Brigham Young, appellants, vs. Joseph M. Cain, Elizabeth Cain, Charles Crismon, and Elizabeth S. Crismon, and Samuel Stringfellow, George Stringfellow, William Jennings, and Brigham Young, plaintiffs in error, Joseph M. Cain, Elizabeth M. Cain, Elizabeth Cain, Charles Crismon, and Elizabeth S. Crismon. Transcript of Record. Error and appeal from the Supreme Court of the Territory of Utah. Supreme Court of the United States, No. 181 and No. 182.</u> [n.p., 1879] 304p.

Transcript of record filed in the Stringfellow v. Cain case 99 <u>U.S. Reports</u> (October 1878) 610-619. In this transcript John Taylor gave testimony, and discussed the laying out of the city by Brigham Young; Thomas Bullock also gave testimony. Various other people gave testimony, such as William Allen, Sophia Taylor, William H. Hockings, Joseph Taylor, John Whitney, William Taylor, and Henry Hinman.

DLC

[491] Snow, Eliza R. <u>Decision of the Supreme Court of the United States in the Reynolds Case</u>. Salt Lake City, 1879.

"From the <u>Deseret News</u>," January 21, 1879.

Broadside.
[Flake 7836]
UHi, UPB, US1C

[492] "Switzerland," pp. 964-965. In <u>Foreign Relations of the United States, 1879</u>. Washington: Govt. Print. Off., 1879. [S1.1:879]

Suppression of Mormon emigration to the U.S. from Switzerland discussed and the use of pastors in the various parishes to help in this suppression.

[493] U. S. House. 46th Congress. 2d Session. H.R. 2444, "A bill relating to bigamy, December 2, 1879." [Washington: Govt. Print. Off., 1879] 1p.

No statute of limitations to bar any prosecution for the crime of bigamy.
DLC, UPB, US1C

[494] U.S. House. 46th Congress. 2d Session. H.R. 2960, "A bill relating to the crime of bigamy, and proof thereof, December 15, 1879." [Washington: Govt. Print. Off., 1879] 2p.

Referred to the Committee on the Judiciary.
No statute of limitations on bigamy, and no proof of an actual marriage rite will be required to prove bigamy.

DLC, UPB, US1C

[495] U.S. House. 46th Congress. 2d Session. H.R. 2779, "A bill proposing an amendment to the Federal Constitution, prohibiting polygamy in the United States, December 10, 1879." [Washington: Govt. Print. Off., 1879] 1p.

Referred to the Committee on the Judiciary.

DLC, UPB, US1C

[496] "Utah," pp. 285-286. In <u>Annual Report of the Secretary of the Interior on the Operations of the Department for the year ended June 30, 1879</u>, vol. III. Washington: Govt. Print. Off., 1881. [I1.1:879]

Brief mention of the Mormon Church's Young Men's and Young Ladies' Organization and the University of Deseret.

Variant ed. U.S. 46th Congress, 2d session. House Ex. Doc. 1, part 5, Serial Set 1912, p. 285-6.

[497] Wells, Emmeline B. <u>Memorial of Emmeline B. Wells and Zina Young Williams of Salt Lake City, Utah Territory, to the Senate and House of Representatives of the United States in Congress assembled: asking for a repeal of</u>

the anti-polygamy law of 1862, and for legislation to
protect the women and children of Utah Territory.
Washington, 1879. 4p.

[Flake 9682]
DLC, UHi, ULA, UPB, USlC, UU

1880

"Mr. Campbell asserts that it `must be taken
for granted' that all votes cast by females
were cast for me. On this point also Mr.
Campbell is mistaken. If this is not shown
by the returns, the canvassers can neither
presume it nor permit Mr. Campbell to attempt
to prove it before them by extrinsic evidence,
nor can they consider the fact when so proven."
[Entry 500]

---

[498] "Austria-Hungary," pp. 49-50. In Foreign Relations of the
United States, 1880. Washington: Govt. Print. Off.,
1880. [S1.1:880]

A dispatch to the American Legation in Vienna, from the
Austrian-Hungarian Foreign Office which expresses the
willingness of the Austrian government to prosecute
Mormon missionaries.

[499] "Belgium," p. 69. In Foreign Relations of the United
States, 1880. Washington: Govt. Print. Off., 1880.
[S1.1:880]

Referring again to the State Dept. Circular dated Aug.
9, 1879, the head of the U.S. Legation in Brussels
immediately acted to contact the Belgium minister of
foreign affairs and enlist their aid in stopping
unlawful Mormon proselyting.

[500] Cannon, George Quayle. Before Territorial canvassers, Utah
Territory, Allen G. Campbell vs. George Q. Cannon.
Reply of George Q. Cannon to protest filed by Allen G.
Campbell. Washington: Thomas McGill & Co., Printers,
[1881] 18p.

Signed: Dec. 20, 1880. Cannon's views regarding
Campbell's allegations of polygamy and his citizenship
status make the 18,568 votes cast for Cannon void.

[Flake 1148]
DLC, NjP, UHi, UPB, USlC

[501] Curtis, George Ticknor. A letter to the N.Y. Evening Post
on the admission of Utah as a state, with editorial
comments thereon and a reply by Geo. Ticknor Curtis.
[Washington? 188-] 13p.

Polygamy and the admission of Utah statehood.
[Flake 2615]
NjP, USlC

[502] "Denmark," pp. 345-347.   In Foreign Relations of the United States, 1880. Washington: Govt. Print. Off., 1880. [S1.1:880]

The important Circular of the 9th of August 1879 is used as a vehicle to work with the Danish government in prohibiting Mormon missionary work.

[503] Emeline A. Young, Dora L. Young, Louisa Young Ferguson ... plaintiffs v. George Q. Cannon, Brigham Young, and Albert Carrington executors of the last will of Brigham Young Territory of Utah Reports 2 (1880) pp. 560-595.

Suit to dismiss the executors of the Brigham Young estate due to irregularities. They were discharged.

CU-L, DLC, ICU, MH, MiU, UAr, UPB, UU, ViU-L

[504] "Great Britain," pp. 465-468, 474, 476.   In Foreign Relations of the United States, 1880. Washington: Govt. Print. Off., 1880. [S1.1:880]

Mormon emigration from Great Britain is tracked during this time. Mention of William Bramall, head Elder of the Nottingham Branch is made in one of the letters. Polygamy is of course the great concern.

[505] Hatton, Charles. "Shoshone and Bannock Agency, Wyoming, August 25, 1880," p. 177. In Annual Report of the Commissioner of the Indian affairs to the Secretary of the Interior for the year 1880. Washington: Govt. Print. Off., 1880. [I20.1:880]

Mormon baptism among the Shoshones in Wyoming.

[506] Hayes, Rutherford B. Annual message of the President of the United States, to the Two Houses of Congress at the commencement of the Third Session of the Forty-sixth Congress. [Washington: Govt. Print. Off., 1880] 34p.

Need to suppress polygamy.

[Flake 9223]
DLC, UPB, US1C

[507] Hayes, Rutherford B. "Fourth annual message, 6 December 1880," pp. 4557-4558. In A Compilation of the Messages and Papers of the Presidents, by James D. Richardson. vol. 6. New York: Published by Bureau of National Literature, 1911, c1897. [GS4.113:6, AE2.114:1-27/v.6]

The continued evils of polygamy. Local government in Utah Territory should be abolished.

[508] "Italy," pp. 644-645. In Foreign Relations of the United States, 1880. Washington: Govt. Print. Off., 1880. [S1.1:880]

The U.S. Consul to Italy relates that after visiting several cities within his jurisdiction he has heard little positive regarding this "spurious" religion of Mormonism.

[509] John Miles, plaintiff in error, vs. United States, defendant
in error. Error to Supreme Court of Utah. Brief for
plaintiff in error. [Attorneys] for plaintiff in
error, E. D. Hoge, W. N. Dusenberry, Arthur Brown.
Supreme Court of the United States. [n.p., 1880?] 18p.

This brief for plaintiff in error was filed in regard
to the Miles v. United States case 102 U.S. Reports,
304-316, October 1880 session.

DLC, UPB, US1C

[510] John Miles v. United States, no. 592. Error to Supreme
Court of Utah. Government Brief. In the Supreme Court
of the United States, October term, 1880. [n.p.,
1880?] 13p.

This government brief was filed in regard to the Miles
v. United States case 103 U.S. Reports, 304-316,
October 1880 session.

DLC, UPB, US1C

[511] McBride, John R. Cannon vs. Campbell: Forty-seventh
Congress. Supplemental brief on behalf of Allen G.
Campbell. Washington: Thomas McGill & Co., Law
Printers [1880?] 30p.

At head of text: Part III.

In a reply to contestants arguments, McGill contends
that Cannon does not fit all qualifications as a
legislator and admits of his polygamy which is in
defiance of the rules of Congress.

UPB

[512] "Mexico," p. 729. In Foreign Relations of the United
States, 1880. Washington: Govt. Print. Off., 1880.
[S1.1:880]

A letter from the Legation in Mexico City mentions the
arrival of Moses Thatcher and two associates who were
attempting to proselyte.

[513] Miles v. United States, U.S. Reports 103 (October 1880
session) pp. 304-316. [Ju6.8/1:103]

A polygamy trial of John Miles based upon his illegal
marriage to Caroline Owen, after he was already married
to Emily Spencer. Decision based upon the Poland Act.
Cannot take in evidence the testimony of the second
wife. Discusses the difficulty of the proof of polygamy.

[514] Murray, Eli H. Report of the Governor of Utah made to the
Secretary of the Interior for the year 1880. Washington:
Govt. Print. Off., 1880. 9p.

See entry 515 for annotation.

[Flake 9367]
UPB

[515] Murray, Eli H. "Report of the Governor of Utah to the
      Secretary of the Interior, 1880," pp. 517-523. In
      Annual Report of the Department of the Interior, 1880,
      vol. 2. Washington: Govt. Print. Off., 1880. [I1.1:880]

      The governor expresses his opinion that polygamy laws
      are too loosely enforced. It is an injustice to the
      illegitimate children born of these unions and to the
      first wife "when lustful or religiously fanatical
      husbands thrust them aside for new and fresher companions".

      Summary of the Territorial Governor's report appears in
      vol. 1 of the Dept. of the Interior Annual Report, pp.
      73-74.

      Variant ed. U.S. 46th Congress 3d session. H. Ex. Doc.
      No. 1, Serial Set 1960.

[516] Neil, John B. Biennial message of John B. Neil, governor
      of Idaho, to the eleventh session of the Legislature of
      Idaho Territory. Boise City: Printed at the Statesman
      Office, 1880. 19p.

      On pp. 16-18, Governor Neil expresses his concern that
      Idaho is "in danger of becoming a second edition of
      Utah," because of the practice of polygamy in its
      borders. He expresses concern that polygamy sinks
      women to the level of the beast. The practice cannot
      be tolerated.
                                          [Flake add. 9179a]
                                                    UPB, UU

[517] Paine, Halbert Eleazer. G. Q. Cannon vs. A. G. Campbell.
      Contested election. Argument for contestant. [n.p.,
      1880] 62p.

      Signed: H. E. Paine, att'y for G. Q. Cannon.

                                               [Flake 6074]
                                                       CU-B

[518] Paine, Halbert Eleazer. G. Q. Cannon vs. A. G. Campbell.
      Contested election. Contestant's argument and reply.
      H. E. Paine, Council for contestants. Washington:
      Thomas McGill & Co., Law Printers [1880] 16p.

      Shows basis of Cannon's election was on the county
      returns, and rightfully so. There was no illegality
      according to Cannon's attorney.
                                          [Flake add. 6074a]
                                                        UPB

[519] "Petitions," Congressional Record 46th Congress, 3d session
      (14, 20 December 1880) vol. 11, pt. 1, pp. 143, 284.
      [X226]

      Two petitions, neither printed in full, supporting the
      enactment of the law to punish and prohibit polygamy.

[520] [Vacant]

[521] "Statistics and technology of the precious metals," pp. 407-489. In <u>Tenth Census of the United States, 1880</u>, vol. XIII. Washington: Govt. Print. Off., 1885. [I11.5:13]

> Although the majority of the report deals with mining activities in Utah, there is brief mention, on p. 422, of the over 5,000 tons of granite brought down from the Little Cottonwood Mining district for the Salt Lake Temple.

> Variant ed. U.S. 47th Cong., 2d session, House Misc. Doc. No. 42, Pt. 13, Serial Set 2143.

[522] "Sweden and Norway," pp. 933-934, 939. In <u>Foreign Relations of the United States, 1880</u>. Washington: Govt. Print. Off., 1880. [S1.1:880]

> U.S. Legation and the Swedish government express their belief that the Circular of Aug. 9, 1879 from the State Department, which set in motion foreign governments suppression of Mormon proselyting, is beneficial to the Swedish and Norwegian population who were "liable to fall victims to Mormon propaganda."

> Also includes the measures taken to prevent Mormon conversions and immigration.

[523] "Switzerland," pp. 951-954. In <u>Foreign Relations of the United States, 1880</u>. Washington: Govt. Print. Off., 1880. [S1.1:880]

> Concerns emigration of Mormon converts to the United States from Switzerland. Once again the authorities are worried over polygamy and they mention a Marie Wyss of Zaziwyl (Berne) who was seduced by the Mormons and is now living in Bear Lake County. She is now "demanded" by her parents.

[524] <u>U.S. Census, 1880, vol. VIII: The Newspaper and Periodical Press</u>, by S. N. D. North. Washington: Govt. print. Off., 1884. [I11.5:8]

> Part of this report consists of statistical tables by state and territory of a Catalogue of Periodical Publications. Page 343 includes Utah Territory which lists the periodicals (primarily newspapers) in existence including their "Character" as Religious (Mormon) or the Anti-Polygamy Standard whose character is Miscellaneous.

[525] U.S. Department of the Interior. Census Office. <u>Report on cattle, sheep, and swine: supplementary to enumeration of live stock on farms in 1880</u>. Clarence Gordon, special agent in charge. Washington: Govt. Print. Off., 1884. 162p. [I11.5:3]

> This report is bound as a part of the <u>Report on the Productions of Agriculture as Returned at the Tenth Census (June 1, 1880). Embracing General Statistics...</u>

Washington: Govt. Print Off., 1883. Utah Territory,
pp. 117-124. Other Mormon references to Arizona, and
the Mormon role in raising cattle and sheep: p. 93,
herds brought to the San Pedro and Gila by Mormons; p.
98, opening of grazing lands of the little Colorado due
largely to mining prospectors and Mormon immigrants; p.
99, small numbers of sheep were brought by Mormon
immigrants primarily to Apache County; p. 102, Mormons
for past four years have driven sheep breeding flocks
accompanying their emigration to Arizona where they
have settled primarily in the Little Colorado and
ranches in Yavapai County.

Variant ed. U. S. 47th Cong., 2d session, House Misc.
Doc No. 42 Pt. 3, Serial Set 213.

[526] The United States, ex relations, Thomas McBride, plaintiff
in error, versus Carl Schurz, Secretary of the Department
of the Interior, No. 707... In the Supreme Court of
the United States, October 12, 1880. Remarks by James
M. Mandeville Counsel for the Plaintiff in Error.
Washington City: E. Beresford, printer, 1880. 61p.

The document includes three parts: 1. Are we drifting
into Monarchy; 2. Mormon disloyalty; and 3. McBride's
Trials in Washington. The entire document revolves
around the cancellation of the Homestead Patent of
Thomas McBride in Grantsville, Utah. Schurz is accussed
of strengthening Mormonism at the expense of one lone
farmer. In the section on "Mormon Disloyalty" pp. 19-
49, a history of Mormonism's violence, polygamy,
theocracy, and its "war" are included.
                                        [Flake 5256]
                                            NN, UPB

[527] U.S. Senate. 46th Congress. 2d Session. Letter from the
Secretary of the Interior, transmitting, in response to
Senate resolution of 23d March, the report of the
Commissioner of the General Land Office upon the
subjects embraced therein. (S. Ex. Doc. No. 181)
Washington: Govt. Print. Off., 1880. 138p. [Serial
Set 1886]

Discrimination of land use by the Mormons.
                                   [Flake add. 9199a]

                                                1881

"Two Mormon preachers who, during the last
few weeks have wandered about in Holland
trying to gain proselytes for their sect,
arranged Sunday evening a meeting at a house
on Golga Hill, where they probably thought to
draw some of the simple people into their net
and persuade them to join that respectable
company who call themselves `Latter-day
Saints.' But this time their acquisition was
little or nothing, says the Holland newspaper,
for Pastor G. Gadd, who learned what the two
Utah prophets had arranged for Sunday evening,
applied to Police Commissioner Otterman, who

with Mr. Gadd went to the place of meeting
accompanied by two constables."

[Entry 536]

---

[528] "Anti-Mormon schools," p. 302. In Report of the Commissioner
of Education for the year 1881. Washington: Govt.
Print. Off., 1883. [FS5.1:881]

More properly a report of non-Mormon schools.

[529] Arthur, Chester A. "First annual message, 6 December
1881," p. 4644. In A Compilation of the Messages and
Papers of the Presidents, by James D. Richardson vol.
6. New York: Published by Bureau of National Literature,
1911, c1897. [GS4.113:6, AE2.114:1-27/v.6]

Existing anti-polygamy legislation largely ignored by
the Mormon church.

[530] Arthur, Chester A. "President's Annual Message," Congressional
Record 47th Congress, 1st session (6 December 1881)
vol. 13, pt. 1, pp. 23-30. [X231]

Reiterates need for stringent legislation against
polygamy, especially as Mormons are fast peopling many
of our western states, including Idaho and Arizona.

[531] Garfield, James A. "Inaugural Address, 4 March 1881," p.
4601. In A Compilation of the Messages and Papers of
the Presidents, by James D. Richardson. vol. 6. New
York: Published by Bureau of National Literature,
1911, c1897. [GS4.113:6, AE2.114:1-27/v.6]

The Mormon Church not only offends the moral sense, but
prevents the administration of justice.

[532] McBride, John R. In the matter of the contested election
from Utah Territory. George Q. Cannon, Contestant, vs.
Allen G. Campbell, Contestee. Brief on behalf of A. G.
Campbell, Contestee. Before Committee on Elections and
Qualifications. House of Representatives. Washington:
T. McGill & Co., 1881. 30p.

At head of title: Forty-seventh Congress, First
session.

[Flake 5101]
NN, UHi

"Memorials Against Seating of George Q. Cannon," Congressional
Record 1881, see entry 572.

[533] Miles, Jonathan D. "Office Cheyenne and Arapaho Agency,
September 1, 1881," p. 67. In Report of the Commissioner
of Indian Affairs, October 24, 1881. Washington:
Govt. Print. Off., 1881. [I20.1:881]

A report from the San Carlos Agency, Arizona, mentions
the problems of Mormons entering the area for farms and
ranches.

[534] "Petitions," Congressional Record 47th Congress, 1st
    session (6, 16, 19, 21 December 1881, 11, 12, 16, 17,
    19, 20, 23, 24, 27, 30 January 1, 2, 3, 4, 6, 8 February
    1882) vol. 13, pt. 1, pp. 45, 181, 222, 231, 368, 399,
    435, 436, 438, 468, 516, 547, 574, 607, 673, 742, 817,
    818, 892, 909, 936, 1003. [X231]

    Petitions, not printed in full, for the suppression and
    punishment of polygamy.

[535] Stone, E. A. "Fort Hall Agency, Idaho, September 3, 1881,"
    pp. 63-64. In Report of the Commissioner of Indian
    Affairs, October 24, 1881. Washington: Govt. Print.
    Off., 1881. [I20.1:881]

    Their fellow polygamists, the Mormons, have quite a
    following among the Indians of the agency.

[536] "Sweden and Norway," pp. 1067-1068. In Foreign Relations
    of the United States, 1881. Washington: Govt. Print.
    Off., 1882. [S1.1:881]

    Mormon missionary work in Sweden and Norway is discussed,
    with the problems of proselyting and recruiting,
    especially in light of polygamy. A meeting held in one
    of the Swedish provinces is described in Dagblad, a
    newspaper of Stockholm. Two Mormons, Ola Nilsson Stal
    and Peter Nilsson were involved in this meeting and
    were expelled from the city.

[537] Thomas, Arthur L. Governor's message, with accompanying
    documents. [Salt Lake City? 1881] 27p.

    Hopes that the legislature will represent the people
    rather than the Mormon church. Tithing and polygamy
    discussed.
                                            [Flake add. 9369a]
                                                          UPB

[538] U.S. House. 47th Congress. 1st Session. H.R. 756, "A
    bill to further regulate suffrage in the Territories of
    the United States, and to fix certain qualifications
    for office, December 16, 1881." [Washington: Govt.
    Print. Off., 1881] 3p.

    Referred to the Committee on the Judiciary. Prohibition
    on voting and holding office if a polygamist. Also
    includes the oath which was required in order to vote.
                                            DLC, UPB, US1C

[539] U.S. House. 47th Congress. 1st Session. H.R. 757, "A
    bill to provide for challenges and oaths to jurors in
    trials for bigamy and polygamy in the Territories of
    the United States, December 16, 1881." [Washington:
    Govt. Print. Off., 1881] 2p.

Referred to the Committee on the Judiciary. An amendment
to the Morrill Act, which would challenge a juror on
his unlawful cohabitation habits.

DLC, UPB, US1C

[540] U.S. House. 47th Congress. 1st Session. H.R. 758, "A
bill relating to the crime of bigamy, and proof thereof,
December 16, 1881." [Washington: Govt. Print. Off.,
1881] 2p.

Referred to the Committee on the Judiciary. Provides
that no statute of limitations shall prevail in the
crime of bigamy, until 2 years after the last cohabitation.
Proof of the marriage ceremony or marriage is not
required in trial, and a sealing or spiritual marriage,
however disguised by ecclesiastical solemnities, is not
valid.

DLC, UPB, US1C

[541] U.S. House. 47th Congress. 1st Session. H.R. 759, "A
bill to further regulate suffrage in the Territories of
the United States, and to fix certain qualifications
for office, and to provide for the registration of
voters in the Territory of Utah, December 16, 1881."
[Washington: Govt. Print. Off., 1881] 10p.

Referred to the Committee on the Judiciary.

Deals with the polygamists' rights to hold office,
includes the oath regarding polygamy which is required
of all prospective voters, and a separate office
holders' oath.

DLC, UPB, US1C

[541a] U.S. House. 47th Congress. 1st Session. H.R. 1423, "A
bill to define the qualifications of Territorial
Delegates in the House of Representatives, 16 December
1881." [Washington: Govt. Print. Off., 1881] 1p.

Referred to the Committee on the Judiciary. It declares
that no person who is guilty of bigamy or polygamy
shall be eligible to a seat as a congressional delegate.

DLC, UPB, US1C

[542] U.S. House. 47th Congress. 1st Session. H.R. 1465, "A
bill to prevent persons living in bigamy or polygamy
from holding any office of trust or profit in any of
the Territories of the United States, December 16,
1881." [Washington: Govt. Print. Off., 1881] 3p.

Referred to the Committee on the Judiciary. An oath is
included in Sec. 2 of all elected or appointed territorial
officials, a part of which includes a foreswearing of
polygamy.

DLC, UPB, US1C

[543] U.S. House. 47th Congress. 1st Session. H.R. 1466, "A
bill to facilitate convictions for the crime of bigamy
or adultery and to regulate marriages in the several

Territories of the United States, December 16, 1881."
[Washington: Govt. Print. Off., 1881] 3p.

Referred to the Committee on the Judiciary. Not
necessary to prove the first or subsequent marriages by
certificate or record, and no statute of limitations
will bar prosecution on bigamy.

DLC, UPB, US1C

[544] U.S. Senate. 47th Congress. 1st Session. S. 309, "A bill
to provide for the recording of marriages in the
Territories of the United States, December 8, 1881."
[Washington: Govt. Print. Off., 1881] 2p.

Referred to the Committee on the Territories. Concerned
not only with the performance of marriages but the
recording of them.

DLC, UPB, US1C

[545] U.S. Senate. 47th Congress. 1st Session. S. 310, "A bill
to make the wife a competent witness in the trials for
bigamy in the Territories of the United States, December
8, 1881." [Washington: Govt. Print. Off., 1881] 1p.

Referred to the Committee on the Judiciary.

DLC, UPB, US1C

[546] "Utah Contested Election," Congressional Record 47th
Congress, 1st session (6, 19 December 1881, 10, 11
January 1882) vol. 13, Pt. 1, pp. 33-44, 209, 322-40,
359-362. [X231]

Unseating of George Q. Cannon as delegate from Utah
because his polygamous habits made him obnoxious to the
representatives. The attempt to unseat Cannon and
place A. G. Campbell in his place was made by Gov.
Murray, despite the fact that Campbell received 1357
votes and Cannon received 18,568 votes. Neither was
granted the seat, but Cannon was paid by Congress
during the time he held the seat (see v. 13, pt. 5,
1882) 47th Congress, 1st session, pp. 4913-4914 for his
pay)

1882

"In addition to the people of Utah we have a
population amounting to over 300,000 people
in the United States subject to our jurisdiction
who have grown up under the system of polygamous
marriages, and in whose social organization
polygamy is considered one of the essential
features. I refer to the Indian tribes. We
do not hold these people to the moral account-
ability to which we hold the people of Utah
or the people of the other Territories or
States of this union, for the reason that we
do not regard them as a Christian people. We
have forborne to enact any laws for the
punishment of polygamy among the Indian

tribes; we have wisely done so, in fact, as a
matter of necessity, because we found those tribes
living under a system of social organization
and social government which tolerated polygamy
and which has attended their methods of
government from the earliest history that we
have of these races on this continent, and I
believe elsewhere throughout this hemisphere.
In the progress of our civilization, we shall
be compelled to bring the Indians as well as
the Mormons within reach of that system of
law which is considered to lie at the foundation
of our social institutions, and we shall be a
great many years in executing our purposes."
[Entry 557]

---

[547] "An act to amend section fifty-three hundred and fifty-two
of the Revised statutes of the United States, in
reference to bigamy, and for other purposes," (Chap.
47, March 22, 1882) United States Statutes at Large,
22, pp. 30-32. [GS4.111:22, AE2.111:22]

Known as the Edmunds Act, it is the third of the laws
designed to eliminate Mormon polygamy also known as the
"Mormon Control Act".

Variant. Supplement to the Revised Statutes at Large,
1874-1891, p. 331-33.

[548] Arthur, Chester A. "Second annual message, 4 December
1882," p. 4731. In A compilation of the Messages and
Papers of the Presidents, by James D. Richardson. vol.
6. New York: Published by Bureau of National Literature,
1911, c1897. [GS4.113:6, AE2.114:1-27/v.6]

Brief statement on the success of the Edmunds Act, and
a note that no additional legislation should be passed
until it has been evaluated.

[549] Arthur, Chester A. "To the Senate and House of Representatives
3 April 1882," p. 4678. In A Compilation of the
Messages and Papers of the Presidents, by James D.
Richardson. vol. 6. New York: Published by Bureau of
National Literature, 1911, C1897. [GS4.113:6, AE2.114:1-
27/v.6]

Need for funds for the Utah Commission.

[550] Belmont, Perry (New York). "Polygamy," Congressional
Record 47th Congress, 1st session (14 March 1882) vol.
13, pt. 7, Appendix, p. 58. [X237]

He will not vote for S. Bill No. 353 (Edmunds) because
it is a "crude and ill-considered" piece of legislation.

[551] Blanchard, Newton C. (Louisiana). "Polygamy," Congressional
Record 47th Congress, 1st session (14 March 1882) vol.
13, pt. 7, Appendix, p. 27. [X237]

Further debate on the Edmunds bill, in which Blanchard categorically states his opposition to polygamy and to this bill. He feels that the bill does away with polygamy and, unfortunately, the Constitution.

[552] Burrows, Joseph H. (Missouri). "Polygamy," Congressional Record 47th Congress, 1st session (14 March 1882) vol. 13, pt. 7, Appendix, pp. 37-38. [X237]

Mr. Burrows indicates that he is not going to say anything for or against S. Bill No. 353 (Edmunds) but that he does have something to say, having been raised within twelve miles of the first Mormon Temple at Nauvoo, Illinois. He refers to the Danites and subsequently to Utah as a "plague-spot".

[553] Burrows, Julius C. (Michigan). "Utah Contested-Election Case," Congressional Record 47th Congress, 1st session (20 April 1882) vol.13, pt. 7, Appendix, pp. 154-155. [X237]

Avows that Congress should not have "seated in their high council a man who offends public decency, disturbs social order, defies national authority, and outrages the moral sense of all Christendom."

[554] Cannon, George Quayle. Utah contested-election case: Speech of George Q. Cannon, of Utah, in the House of Representatives, Wednesday, April 19, 1882. Washington, 1882. 15p.

Cannon defends himself and the Mormon church, especially in regard to polygamy and his own polygamous marriages. He also gives a little of the history of the Church, its persecutions, and migration to Utah.

[Flake 1173]
CU-B, UPB, USlC

[555] "Citizens of Utah," Congressional Record 47th Congress, 1st session (10 March 1882) vol. 13, pt. 2, p. 1822. [X232]

Three brief paragraphs mentioning petitions which aren't printed here. One of the petitions makes reference for a need to investigate the "true condition of the Mormon people of Utah."

[556] Cravens, Jordan E. (Arkansas). "Polygamy," Congressional Record 47th Congress, 1st session (14 March 1882) vol. 13, Pt. 7, Appendix, pp. 40-41. [X237]

Unless S. Bill No. 353 is altered he cannot vote for it, although he believes that polygamy is a crime. He prefers the language of a bill introduced in the 45th Congress, H.R. No. 2078, which disenfranchises women.

[557] Defense of the Constitutional and Religious Rights of the People of Utah: Speeches of Senators Vest, Morgan, Call, Brown, Pendleton and LaMar. [n.p., 1882] 40p.

February 1882 speeches on the Edmunds Bill. Sen. Brown
of Georgia, who does not believe in polygamy, defends
those who do earnestly believe in it. Does not want to
place a whole community under a ban because a few
practice polygamy.

[Flake 2749]
Cty, MH, UHi, UPB, US1C

[558] "Election Contest--Campbell vs. Cannon," Congressional
Record 47th Congress, 1st session (28 February 1882)
vol. 13, pt. 2, p. 1492. [X232]

Continuation of the debate regarding the George Q.
Cannon and A. G. Campbell contested election.

[559] "Executive Communication," Congressional Record 47th
Congress, 1st Session (3 April 1882) vol. 13, pt. 3,
pp. 2528, 2546. [X233]

Letter from Chester A. Arthur asking for funding for
the Utah Commission in its campaign against bigamy in
Utah.

[560] "The General Assembly of the Presbyterian Church of the
United States," Congressional Record 47th Congress, 1st
session (11 January 1882) vol. 13, pt. 1, p. 343.
[X231]

Brief paragraph condemning the practice of polygamy as
both anti-Christian and anti-republican.

[561] Gurley, Zenos Hovey and Kelley, E. L. The Utah problem and
the solution. Washington: Printed by J. M. Burnett,
1882. 5p.

The RLDS attempt, in a conference statement of 9
September 1881, to make sure that their doctrinal
tenets are not confused with the polygamous doctrines
of the Utah body of Mormonism.

[Flake 3765]
MOInRC, US1C

[562] Hazelton, George Cochrane. Speech of G. C. Hazelton, of
Wisconsin, against permitting polygamy to be represented
in... Congress. Delivered in the house, April 18,
1882. Washington, 1882. 15p.

See entry 629 for annotation.

[Flake 3929]
NN

[563] House, John Ford. Utah contested election case - Cannon
vs. Campbell; speech of Hon. John F. House, of Tennessee,
in the House of Representatives, April 18, 1882.
Washington, 1882. 15p.

See entry 629 for annotation.

[Flake 4096]
CSmH, CU-B, UHi, UPB, US1C

1882

[564] Hewitt, Abram S. (New York). "Polygamy," Congressional
       Record 47th Congress, 1st session (14 March 1882) vol.
       13, pt. 7, Appendix, p. 42. [X237]

       He is constrained to vote against S. Bill No. 353
       (Edmunds) even though he believes polygamy is a "blot
       on our civilization", but the bill denies civil liberties
       and he cannot countenance that.

[564a] James N. Kimball, respondent vs. Franklin D. Richards,
       appellant. Mandamus, Franklin. Brief and Argument of
       R. K. Williams and F. S. Richards, attorneys for
       appellants. [Salt Lake City, 1882?] 14p.

       At head of title: In the Supreme Court of Utah Territory.

       This writ concerns charges of polygamy against James N.
       Kimball, a Probate Judge. Apparently the case never
       received a final judgment in the Territorial Supreme
       Court as it isn't printed in their reports.

                                          [Flake add. 9881a]
                                                  UPB, US1C

[565] Jones, George Washington. Utah contested election case.
       Speech of Hon. George W. Jones, of Texas, in the House
       of Representatives, Wednesday, April 19, 1882. Washington,
       1882. 16p.

       Church and politics.
                                              [Flake 4485]
                                                 CSmH, UU

[566] "Memorial Against Admission of Utah as a State," Congressional
       Record 47th Congress, 1st session (16 January 1882)
       vol. 13, pt. 1, p. 436. [X231]

       The memorial is not printed in full and it focuses on
       polygamy.

[567] "Memorial against Seating of George Q. Cannon," Congressional
       Record 47th Congress, 1st session (10 February 1882)
       vol. 13, pt. 2, p. 1076. [X232]

       Memorial is not printed in full.

[568] "Memorial from Utah," Congressional Record 47th Congress,
       1st session (18 February 1882) vol. 13, pt. 2, pp.
       1258-1259. [X232]

       A memorial, from the Legislative Assembly of Utah, is
       printed in full regarding legislation which would
       affect the disfranchisement of some citizens.

[569] "Memorial of a Convention to admit Utah as a State,"
       Congressional Record 47th Congress, 1st session (23
       June 1882) vol. 13, pt. 6, p. 5282. [X236]

       The memorial from the Legislative Assembly of Utah
       Territory is not printed in full.

[570] "Memorial of a Convention to admit Utah as a State,"
Congressional Record 47th Congress, 1st session (22
June 1882) vol. 13, pt. 5, p. 5203. [X235]

Petition from Joseph F. Smith as president of a convention
is not printed in full.

[571] Memorial to Congress, by the Legislative Assembly of the
Territory of Utah, 1882. [Salt Lake City, 1882] 8p.

Signed at end: Francis M. Lyman, Joseph F. Smith.

Memorial against polygamy legislation.
[Flake 9390]
CtY, CU-B, DLC, MH, NjP, UHi, UPB, USlC

[572] "Memorials Against Seating of George Q. Cannon," Congressional
Record 47th Congress, 1st session (19 December 1881,
10, 23, 24 January, 1, 4 February 1882) vol. 13, pt. 1,
pp. 222, 342, 575, 607, 817, 909. [X231]

None of these memorials are printed in full, but they
are all in common in their desire not to seat a polygamist.

[573] Miller, Samuel H. (Pennsylvania). "Polygamy," Congressional
Record 47th Congress, 1st session (14 March 1882)
vol. 13, pt. 7, Appendix, p. 28. [X237]

Miller comes out in support of S. Bill No. 353 (Edmunds
Bill), and states that passage of this bill is not only
a wise step but a necessary one.

[574] "Ministers of the Methodist Episcopal Church of Philadelphia,"
Congressional Record 47th Congress, 1st session (18
February 1882) vol. 13, pt. 2, p. 1258. [X232]

Although the memorial is not printed, mention is made
of the Methodist Episcopal Church declaring polygamy a
violation of the laws of the United States.

[575] Morey, Henry L. (Ohio). "Polygamy," Congressional Record
47th Congress, 1st session (14 March 1882) vol. 13, pt.
7, Appendix, p. 38. [X237]

He declares his intention to vote for the Edmunds Bill
and in addition declares that the sentiment of the
country demands it and the Republican Party is committed
to it.

[576] "Mormons," Congressional Record 47th Congress, 1st session
(20 February 1882) vol. 13, pt. 2, p. 1342. [X232]

The Utah Democratic Territorial Committee submitted a
petition to Congress which states the politico-religious
nature of the Mormon Church by claiming that its church
is the government of God on earth.

[577] Moulton, Samuel W. (Illinois). "Polygamy," Congressional
Record 47th Congress, 1st session (14 March 1882) vol.
13, pt. 7, Appendix, p. 48. [X237]

He will vote in favor of S. Bill No. 353 (Edmunds) and
he hopes that the younger generation of Mormons will
learn from the hard experiences of their past.

[578] Neil, John B. Second biennial message of John B. Neil,
governor to the Twelfth session of the Legislative
Assembly of Idaho Territory. Boise City: Printed by
Milton Kelly, 1882. 24p.

Once again Neil hits hard on the practice of polygamy,
pp. 20-23. He refers to his first message in 1880 and
notes that his recommendations in regards to polygamy's
suppression were not heeded.
[Flake add. 4180a]
UPB, UU

[579] Oates, William C. (Alabama). "Utah Contested-Election
Case," Congressional Record 47th Congress, 1st session
(19 April 1882) vol. 13, pt. 7, Appendix, p. 156.
[X237]

He argues that the recently enacted Edmunds Act cannot
be used against Cannon because laws are not to be
retroactive, but operate from the passage of that law.
Therefore, George Q. Cannon, duly elected by the voters
of Utah, must be seated.

[580] Peelle, Stanton J. (Indiana). "Polygamy," Congressional
Record 47th Congress, 1st session (14 March 1882) vol.
13, pt. 7, Appendix, p. 28. [X237]

"All the teachings of civilization . . . demand that
crime of polygamy should be wiped out." An obvious
vote for S. bill no. 353 (Edmunds Bill).

[581] Petition," Congressional Record 47th Congress, 1st session
(27 April 1882) vol. 13, pt. 4, p. 3395. [X234]

A petition, not printed in full, requesting legislation
to suppress polygamy.

[582] "Petitions," Congressional Record 47th Congress, 1st
session (20 May, 5, 19 June 1882) vol. 13, pt. 5, pp.
4144, 4556, 5123. [X235]

Petitions, not printed in full, for the suppression and
punishment of polygamy.

[583] "Petitions," Congressional Record 47th Congress, 1st
session (17, 20, 21, 22, 27, 30 March, 3, 10 April
1882) vol. 13, pt. 3, pp. 2026, 2045, 2096, 2140, 2189,
2190, 2274, 2445, 2547, 2724. [X233]

Petitions, not printed in full, for the suppression and
punishment of polygamy.

[584] "Petitions for the Suppression of Polygamy," Congressional
Record 47th Congress, 1st session (9, 10, 13, 14, 15,
16, 17, 18, 20, 21, 23, 24, 25, 28 February 1, 2, 3, 4,
6, 7, 9, 13, 15, 16 March 1882) vol. 13, pt. 2, pp.
1040, 1076, 1107, 1109, 1144, 1193, 1238, 1239, 1258,

1281, 1282, 1324, 1325, 1326, 1368, 1411, 1446, 1463,
1464, 1471, 1503, 1504, 1505, 1539, 1571, 1572, 1607,
1628, 1629, 1660, 1661, 1732-1733, 1734, 1775, 1823,
1824, 1840, 1878, 1879, 1944, 1988, 1989. [X232]

None of the petitions are printed in full, and there
are many more petitions than it would appear from the
pages, as more than one often appears on a page.

"Petitions," Congressional Record 1882, see entry 534.

[585] "Plymouth Church of Portland, Maine," Congressional Record
47th Congress, 1st session (30 January 1882) vol. 13,
pt. 1, p. 707. [X231]

Resolutions of this group against polygamy, its practice
by the Mormons, and against the history of Utah, with
its treasons and massacres.

[586] "Polygamy," Congressional Record 47th Congress, 1st session
(11 January 1882) vol. 13, pt. 1, p. 367 [X231]

A memorial from the General Assembly of the Presbyterian
Church of the United States, printed in full. They
heartily express protest against polygamy and support
Governor Murray of Utah in his hostility to polygamous
marriages.

[587] "Polygamy," Congressional Record 47th Congress, 1st session
(18 February 1882) vol. 13, pt. 2, p. 1259. [X232]

The memorial of the American Baptist Home Missionary
Society, which represents 1,000,000 people, was read
and inserted in the record. They are asking the usual,
that polygamy be prohibited.

[588] "Polygamy," Congressional Record 47th Congress, 1st session
(8 March 1882) vol. 13, pt. 2, p. 1732. [X232]

S. bill 353 to amend section 5352 of the Revised
Statutes in reference to bigamy. Interesting reference
to Mormon marriages performed prior to 1 January 1883
being legitimized and not subject to prosecution.

[589] "Polygamy," Congressional Record 47th Congress, 1st session
(13 March 1182) vol. 13, pt. 2, p. 1836. [X232]

At the same time as a memorial of the Legislative
Assembly of the Territory of Utah was mentioned,
whereby the legislature wished an investigation of the
facts, a memorial from the Michigan legislature was
read regarding polygamy and the need for congress to
take action against such.

[590] "Polygamy," Congressional Record 47th Congress, 1st session
(13 March 1882) vol. 13, pt. 2, p. 1843. [X232]

A memorial of the citizens of Syracuse, New York
regarding polygamy is printed in full. They are
concerned about the spread of polygamy and urge congress
to take some action against it.

[591] "Polygamy," Congressional Record 47th Congress, 1st session
(13, 14 March 1882) vol. 13, pt. 2, pp. 1845-1877.
[X232]

The extended debate on Senate bill 353, to amend
section 5352 of the Revised Statutes in reference to
bigamy. Numerous roll call votes were taken on various
amendments. Mr. Cassidy of Nevada gives an interesting
account of the origins of Mormonism and the fact that
polygamy was not a part of these beginnings.

[592] "Polygamy," Congressional Record 47th Congress, 1st session
(15 March 1882) vol. 13, pt. 2, p. 1926. [X232]

The Wilmington annual conference of the Methodist
Episcopal Church passed a resolution favoring passage
by Congress of a law prohibiting polygamy.

[593] "Polygamy," Congressional Record 47th Congress, 1st session
(16 March 1882) vol. 13, pt. 2, p. 1973. [X232]

The citizens of Massachusetts presented a memorial to
congress asking that they pass a law prohibiting
polygamy. In their petition they ask that such laws
enacted would "destroy it [Mormonism] from our Christian
civilization."

[594] "Polygamy," Congressional Record 47 Congress, 1st session
(10 April 1882) vol. 13, pt. 3, p. 2733. [X233]

Entry includes a telegram from Joseph Smith, III, of
the Reorganized Church thanking them for passing the
Edmunds Act prohibiting polygamy.

[595] "Punishment of Bigamy," Congressional Record 47th Congress,
1st session (15 February 1882) vol. 13, pt. 2, pp.
1152-1163, 1195-1217, 1732, 1845-1877. [X232]

Punishment of Bigamy (Edmunds bill). Most of the
speeches are anti-Mormon in nature. Cassidy in the
House, is especially so. Petitions from almost every
state in the Union being received urging laws to
suppress polygamy. See index to vols. for these in
vol. 13, Pt. 8, p. 328 [X238]

[595a] "Qualifications of Delegates," Congressional Record 47th
Congress, 1st session (11 January 1882) vol. 13, pt. 1,
pp. 359-362. [X231]

Mr. Haskell of Kansas had a resolution read into the
Record [printed in full] regarding the seating of
George Q. Cannon in the House of Representatives in the
Campbell vs. Cannon contested election case. The
question of polygamy is of course the main issue. Mr.
Haskell's resolution was defeated.

[596] Ranney, Ambrose A. (Massachusetts). "Utah Contested-
Election Case," Congressional Record 47th Congress, 1st
session (19 April 1882) vol. 13, pt. 7, Appendix, pp.
128-130. [X237]

Based upon the passage of the Edmunds Act, Mr. Ranney argues that George Q. Cannon, as a polygamist, is not eligible to hold a seat in Congress.

[597] Registration. Order of the Commissioners. [Salt Lake City? 1882]

Broadside. 21 x 14 cm.

The Commissioners of the Utah Commission.

[Flake 9238]
UPB, US1C

[598] "Report of the Utah Commission, 1882," pp. 1003-1009. In Annual Report of the Dept. of the Interior, 1882, vol. 2. Washington: Govt. Print. Off., 1883. [I1.1:882/v.2]

Report deals with polygamy in regards to the oath that voters had to take. The voter had to declare that they were not polygamous or were not living with a polygamous person. Summary of the report by the Commission is found in vol. I [Serial Set 2099] p. XL-XLI.

Variant ed. U.S. 47th Congress, 2nd session. House Exec. Doc. 1, pt. 5, vol. 2. Serial Set 2100.

[599] Resolution in relation to a constitutional convention. [Salt Lake City, 1882] 2p.

A resolution of the Utah Territorial legislative assembly regarding qualifications for statehood.

Dated: March 4, 1882. Signed F. M. Lyman, Speaker House of Representatives, Jos. F. Smith, President of the Council.

[Flake add. 9391b]
UPB

[600] Rules and regulations for the revision of the registration lists, and the conduct of the election, Nov. 7, 1882. Salt Lake City: Tribune Printing and Publishing Company, 1882. 8p.

Includes the polygamy oath.

[Flake 9240]

DLC, UHi

[601] Skinner, Charles Rufus. Polygamy. Speech of Hon. Charles R. Skinner, of New York, in the House of Representatives, Monday, March 13, 1882. Washington, 1882. 4p.

See entry 591 for annotation.

[Flake 7750a]
US1C

[602] Speech of V. Bierbower, assistant United States District Attorney in the case of the United States vs. Lorenzo Snow. [n.p., 1882?] 11p.

1882

The polygamy trial of Lorenzo Snow.

[Flake 511]
MH, UPB

[602a] "Suppression of polygamy," Congressional Record 47th
Congress, 1st session (9 January 1882) vol. 13, pt. 1,
p. 280. [X231]

Moses Ayers McCoid, representative from Iowa, introduced
a brief resolution [printed in full] resolving that the
House would select a committee of eleven called "Committee
on Suppression of the Crime of Polygamy" who would be
responsible for devising means to enforce laws against
polygamy in the Territory of Utah.

[603] Tucker, John Randolph. Polygamy. Speech of Hon. John
Randolph Tucker of Virginia, in the House of Representatives,
Tuesday, March 14, 1882. [Washington? 1882] 8p.

See entry 591 for annotation.

[Flake 9034]
ULA, UPB, US1C

[604] U.S. House. 47th Congress. 1st Session. Committee on
Claims. Richard H. Porter and James Porter... Report:
[To accompany bill H.R. 4540.] (H. Rept. No. 1181)
Washington: Govt. Print. Off., 1882. 3p. [Serial Set
2068]

Claims for property impressed by the Utah Expedition
and lost.

[Flake add. 9110c]

[605] U.S. House. 47th Congress. 1st Session. Committee on
Elections. Cannon vs. Campbell. Testimony and papers
in the contested election case of Geo. Q. Cannon vs.
Allen G. Campbell, from the Territory of Utah. (H.
Misc. Doc. No. 25, Pt. 1, 2) Washington: Govt. Print.
Off., 1882. 74, 10p. [Serial Set 2042]

Testimony in case of George Q. Cannon vs. Allen G.
Campbell, with references to polygamy and conditions in
Utah.

[Flake 9116]

[606] U.S. House. 47th Congress. 1st Session. Committee on
Elections. Pay and mileage allowed George Q. Cannon...
Report. (H. Rept. No. 1411) Washington: Govt. Print.
Off., 1882. 4p. [Serial Set 2069]

Allowance as delegate from Utah. Majority and minority
report. George Q. Cannon in his petition letter
indicates that he was unseated because he was a polygamist.

[Flake 9118]

[607] U.S. House. 47th Congress. 1st Session. Committee on
Elections. Report: In the matter of the contest of
George Q. Cannon against Allen G. Campbell, Territory
of Utah. (H. Rept. No. 559) Washington: Govt. Print.
Off., 1882. 66p. [Serial Set 2066]

Majority and minority reports. Much material on the
Mormons and polygamy.

[Flake 9119]

[608] U.S. House. 47th Congress. 1st Session. Committee on the
Judiciary. J. and R. H. Porter... Report: [To accompany
bill S. 905.] The committee on the Judiciary, to whom
was referred the bill (S. 905) for the relief of J. and
R. H. Porter, having had the same under consideration,
would respectfully report. (H. Rept. No. 1637)
Washington: Govt. Print. Off., 1882. 22p. [Serial Set
2070]

Redress for wagons destroyed during the Utah Expedition.
[Flake 9126]

[609] U.S. House. 47th Congress. 1st Session. Committee on the
Judiciary. To prevent persons living in bigamy or
polygamy from holding any civil office of trust or
profit in any of the Territories of the United States,
and from being delegates in Congress... Report: [To
accompany bill H.R. 4436. (H. Rept. No. 386) Washington:
Govt. Print. Off., 1882. 1p. [Serial Set 2065]

[Flake 9135]

[610] U.S. House. 47th Congress. 1st Session. Compensation of
Commissioners under the act for the suppression of
bigamy, &c. Message from the President of the United
States. (H. Ex. Doc. No. 152) Washington: Govt.
Print. Off., 1882. 2p. [Serial Set 2030]

Payment for the Utah Commission.
[Flake add. 9189a]

[611] U.S. House. 47th Congress. 1st Session. H. Res. 87,
"Joint Resolution proposing an amendment to the Constitution
of the United States, January 9, 1882." [Washington:
Govt. Print. Off., 1882] 2p.

Constitutional amendment regarding bigamy and polygamy.
Referred to the Committee on the Judiciary.

DLC, UPB, US1C

[612] U.S. House. 47th Congress. 1st Session. H.R. 2240, "A
bill to amend section eighteen hundred and sixty of the
Revised Statutes, to further regulate suffrage in the
Territories, and making polygamy a disability and
disqualification for office, and so forth, January 9,
1882." [Washington: Govt. Print. Off., 1882] 7p.

Referred to the Committee on the Judiciary. Once again
deals with the issue of a polygamist holding office or
voting. The oath for a man and a separate one for a
woman are included.

DLC, UPB, US1C

[613] U.S. House. 47th Congress. 1st Session. H.R. 2869, "A
bill to define the crime of bigamy and to provide for
the trial and punishment of offenders thereunder,

January 16, 1882." [Washington: Govt. Print. Off.,
1882] 4p.

Referred to the Committee on the Judiciary.

DLC, UPB, US1C

[614] U.S. House. 47th Congress. 1st Session. H.R. 2959, "A
bill to make the wife a competent witness in trials for
bigamy in the Territories of the United States, January
16, 1882." [Washington: Govt. Print. Off., 1882] 1p.

DLC, UPB, US1C

[615] U.S. House. 47th Congress. 1st Session. H.R. 2960, "A
bill to amend section fifty-three hundred and fifty-two
of the Revised Statutes of the United States, in
reference to bigamy, and for other purposes, January
16, 1882." [Washington: Govt. Print. Off., 1882] 4p.

DLC, UPB, US1C

[616] U.S. House. 47th Congress. 1st Session. H.R. 3128, "A
bill to reorganize the legislative power of Utah
Territory, and for the suppression of polygamy within
the Territories of the United States, January 16,
1882." [Washington: Govt. Print. Off., 1882] 14p.

Referred to the Committee on the Territories.

DLC, UPB, US1C

[617] U.S. House. 47th Congress. 1st Session. H.R. 4263, "A
bill to amend section eighteen hundred and sixty of the
Revised Statutes, relating to suffrage, and so forth,
February 13, 1882." [Washington: Govt. Print. Off.,
1882] 10p.

Referred to the Committee on the Judiciary. Although
the title of the bill ostensibly relates to suffrage,
it's primary focus is polygamy. Once again an oath is
included as a voter test.

DLC, UPB, US1C

[618] U.S. House. 47th Congress. 1st Session. H.R. 4436, "A
bill to prevent persons living in bigamy or polygamy
from holding any civil office of trust or profit in any
of the Territories of the United States, and from being
delegates in Congress, February 14, 1882." [Washington:
Govt. Print. Off., 1882] 3p.

Referred to the Committee on the Judiciary. An oath or
affirmation is printed as part of the bill.

DLC, UPB, US1C

[619] U.S. House. 47th Congress. 1st Session. H.R. 6036, "A
bill supplementary to an act entitled 'An Act to amend
section fifty-three hundred and fifty-two of the
Revised Statutes of the United States, in reference to

bigamy, and for other purposes,' May 1, 1882." [Washington: Govt. Print. Off., 1882] 2p.

Referred to the Committee on the Judiciary. Sections 3 and 4 deal with prosecutions for bigamy, and polygamy and the disincorporation of the church respectively.

DLC, UPB, USlC

[620] U.S. House. 47th Congress. 2d Session. H.R. 7102, "A bill to amend an act entitled 'An act to amend section fifty-three hundred and fifty-two of the Revised Statutes of the United States, in reference to bigamy, and for other purposes,' approved March twenty-second, eighteen hundred and eighty-two, December 19, 1882." [Washington: Govt. Print. Off., 1882] 3p.

Referred to the Committee on the Judiciary.

Same as S. 2238 regarding polygamous marriages. See entry 627.

DLC, UPB, USlC

[621] U.S. House. 47th Congress. 2d Session. H.R. 7127, "A bill to disapprove and repeal an act of the Governor and Legislative Assembly of the Territory of Utah entitled 'An act conferring upon women the elective franchise,' and for other purposes, December 2, 1882." [Washington: Govt. Print. Off., 1882] 1p.

Referred to the Committee on the Judiciary.

DLC, UPB, USlC

[622] U.S. House. 47th Congress. 1st Session. Letter from the Secretary of the Interior in response to resolution of the House of Representatives relative to the alleged action of certain Mormons in inciting the Piute and Navajo Indians to outbreak. (H. Ex. Doc. No. 65) Washington: Govt. Print. Off., 1882. 2p. [Serial Set 2027]

[Flake 9190]

[623] U.S. Senate. 47th Congress. 1st Session. Committee on Claims. In the Senate of the United States... Report: [To accompany bill S. 905.] The Committee on Claims, to whom was referred the bill (S. 905) for the relief of Richard H. and James Porter, having carefully considered the same, make the following report. (S. Rept. No. 154) Washington: Govt. Print. Off., 1882. 4p. [Serial Set 2004]

Compensation to the Porters for property taken during the Utah Expedition.

[Flake add. 9167a]

[624] U.S. Senate. 47th Congress. 1st Session. Memorial of the General Assembly of the Presbyterian Church of the United States, on the subject of Polygamy. (S. Misc.

Doc. No. 30) Washington: Govt. Print. Off,. 1882. 2p. [Serial Set 1993]

In opposition to polygamy.

[Flake 6728]

[625] U.S. Senate. 47th Congress. 1st Session. S. 353, "A bill to amend section fifty-three hundred and fifty-two of the Revised Statutes of the United States, in reference to bigamy, and for other purposes, January 24, 1882." [Washington: Govt. Print. Off., 1882] 7p.

Polygamy substituted for bigamy.

DLC, UPB, US1C

[626] U.S. Senate. 47th Congress. 1st Session. S. 1662, "An act to amend an act entitled, 'An Act to amend section fifty-three hundred and fifty-two of the Revised Statutes of the United States, in reference to bigamy, and for other purposes,' approved March twenty-second, eighteen hundred and eighty-two, April 27, 1882." [Washington: Govt. Print. Off., 1882] 1p.

DLC, UPB, US1C

[627] U.S. Senate. 47th Congress. 2d Session. S. 2238, "A bill to amend an act entitled 'An act to amend section fifty-three hundred and fifty-two of the Revised Statutes of the United States in reference to bigamy, and for other purposes,' approved March twenty-second, eighteen hundred and eighty-two, December 13, 1882." [Washington: Govt. Print. Off., 1882] 3p.

Referred to the Committee on the Judiciary.

Legislation which would make it easier to prosecute polygamous marriages.

DLC, UPB, US1C

[628] "Utah," Congressional Record 47th Congress, 2d session (7 December 1882) vol. 14, Pt. 1, pp. 89-90. [X239]

Petition of the Liberal Party of Utah to Congress to restrict the solidity of the Mormon vote. Returns of Utah elections by counties, and Mormon and Liberal votes are given for the years 1870-1882.

[629] "Utah Contested-Election Case," Congressional Record 47th Congress, 1st session (18 April 1882) vol. 13, Pt. 3, pp. 3001-3011. [X233]

Continuation of the debate regarding the unseating of George Q. Cannon as delegate from Utah, because his polygamous habits made him obnoxious to the representatives. Some speeches record strong feelings against polygamy.

[630] "Utah Contested-Election Case," Congressional Record 47th Congress, 1st session (19 April 1882) vol. 13, pt. 4, pp. 3045-3095. [X234]

Lengthy debate regarding the unseating of George Q.
Cannon as delegate from Utah, because his polygamous
habits made him obnoxious to the representatives. This
entry, at the end, includes the roll call vote taken on
the issue.

"Utah Contested Election Case," Congressional Record, 1882,
see entry 546.

[631] "Woman's Suffrage Association of the State of Missouri,"
Congressional Record 47th Congress, 1st session (1
February 1882) vol. 13, pt. 1, p. 780. [X231]

The memorial is quoted in part, and the women of
Missouri were protesting against the disenfranchisement
of the women of Utah, but also felt that polygamy was
subversive to morals and government.

1883

"The church then, as the church now, and here
in Utah, needs no protection against the
Government of the United States, for the
reason that the government then was and now
is the fortress of civil and religious
liberty. That man or that set of men, be
they what they may, who assert and teach a
doctrine so infamous deserve the condemnation
of all men, and must and will receive the
condemnation of a Government that protects
all men in the right `to worship God according
to the dictates of conscience.'"

[Entry 641]

---

[632] Arthur, Chester A. Message of the President of the United
States communicated to the Two Houses of Congress at
the beginning of the First Session of the Forty-eighth
Congress. Washington: Govt. Print. Off., 1883. 19p.

Results of the Utah Commission on Utah elections.

[Flake 9224]
DLC, UPB, US1C

[633] Arthur, Chester A. "Third Annual Message, 4 December
1883," p. 4771. In A Compilation of the Messages and
Papers of the Presidents, by James D. Richardson, Vol.
7. New York: Bureau of National Literature, 1911,
c1897. [GS4.113:7, AE2.114:1-27/v.7]

Referring to the second annual report of the Utah
Commission, President Arthur does not feel encouraged
that polygamy is being checked. In fact, he is convinced
that it is firmly entrenched in Utah society.

[634] Black, Jeremiah Sullivan. Federal jurisdiction in the
territories: Right of local self-government. Judge
Black's argument for Utah. Before the Judiciary
Committee of the House of Representatives, February 1,

1883. Washington: Gibson Brothers, printers, 1883.
31p.

A legal argument, based upon the concept of constitutional
morality, which should not, because of a people's
religious beliefs, deprive them of self-government.
Finally he contends that Congress has no right to
"legislate about marriage in a territory," only "God
Himself".

[Flake 544]
CtY, DLC, MH, NjP, NN, UHi, ULA, UPB

[635] Cook, A. L. "Fort Hall Agency, August 20, 1883," p. 54.
In Annual Report of the Commissioner of Indian Affairs
to the Secretary of the Interior for the year 1883.
Washington: Govt. Print. Off., 1883. [I20.1:883]

Cook mentions the problem of Mormon baptism at the Fort
Hall reservation in Idaho. The agent especially
comments on the problem of polygamy, along with other
vile doctrines (not specified) which make the Indians
discontented.

[636] Davis, Elisha W. "Uintah Valley Agency, Utah, August 14,
1883," p. 141. In Annual report of the Commissioner of
Indian Affairs to the Secretary of the Interior for the
year 1883. Washington: Govt. Print. Off., 1883.
[I20.1:883]

Agent says that nearly half the Indians on the reservation
are Mormons, but this does not signify piety on the
part of the Indians only that the Mormons have always
curried favor with them.

[637] Lord, Eliot. Comstock mining and miners. Washington:
Govt. Print. Off., 1883. 451p. [I19.9:4]

(U.S. Geological Survey. Monographs. Vol. 4)

Mormon participation in Nevada gold discoveries and the
Mormons' recall from Nevada.

[Flake 4987]

Emigrant train of Mormons, first settlers of Carson
Valley, pp. 11, 15, and 18.

[638] Mayhugh, John S. "Western Shoshone Agency, Nevada, August
20, 1883," p. 114. In Annual report of the Commissioner
of Indian Affairs to the Secretary of the Interior for
the year 1883. Washington: Govt. Print. Off., 1883.
[I20.1:883]

The bad influence of Mormon polygamy on the eradication
of polygamy among the Indians is mentioned.

[639] "Memorial of Delegates from the Constitutional Convention
of Utah," Congressional Record 47th Congress, 2d
session (23 February 1883) vol. 14, pt. 4, p. 3149.
[X242]

Petition by delegates from Utah to have Congress strike
out certain sections of the Punishment of Bigamy
(Edmunds Bill) which were claimed to disenfranchise
innocent people of Utah.

[640] Minniss, J. F. "Ouray Indian Agency, Utah, August 13,
1883," pp. 137-138. In Annual Report of the Commissioner
of Indian Affairs to the Secretary of the Interior for
the year 1883. Washington: Govt. Print. Off., 1883.
[I20.1:883]

The agent describes the Indians as good-natured and
friendly to whites and Mormons. The Indians do not
consider Mormons white men because "they know too much
about them". Also mentions two Mormons A. C. Hatch and
P. Dodds who claim ranches on this reservation.

[641] Murray, Eli H. Report of the Governor of Utah, made to the
Secretary of the Interior, for the year 1883. Washington:
Govt. Print. Off., 1883. 13p.

Material on polygamy and church-state relations.

[Flake 9368]
UPB, US1C

[642] Murray, Eli H. "Report of the Governor of Utah to the
Secretary of the Interior, 1883," pp. 627-637. In
Annual Report of the Department of the Interior, 1883,
vol. 2. Washington: Govt. Print. Off., 1883. [I1-
.1:885/v.2]

Deals with the problem of church and state in Utah
Territory, and the Mormon's defiance of federal law.

Variant ed. U.S. 48th Congress, 1st session. H. Ex.
Doc. No. 1, Serial Set 2191.

[643] "Report of the Utah Commission, 1883," pp. [499]-504. In
Annual Report of the Department of the Interior, 1883,
vol. 2. Washington: Govt. Print. Off., 1883.
[I.1.1:883/v.2]

Defines the duties of the Commission to matters of the
election and eligibility to hold office, rather than
prosecution of polygamy. A summary of the commission
report by the secretary of the interior in Vol. I. p.
XLVIII-XLIV. [Serial Set 2192]

Variant ed. 48th cong., 1st session. House Ex. Doc.
No. 1. Serial Set 2191.

[644] U.S. House. 47th Congress. 2d Session. Committee on
Elections. Delegate from the Territory of Utah....
Report: The Committee on Elections, to whom was
referred the application and accompanying papers of
John T. Caine, asking to be admitted to a seat in the
Forty-seventh Congress as a delegate from the Territory
of Utah, having had the same under consideration, beg
leave to report as follows. (H. Rept. No. 1865)

Washington: Govt. Print. Off., 1883. 4p. [Serial Set 2159]

Special election after the disputed Cannon vs. Campbell election. The committee recommends that John T. Caine be seated as delegate from Utah.

[Flake add. 9116b]

[645] [Vacant]

[646] U.S. House. 47th Congress. 2d Session. H.R. 7379, "A bill to provide for the further suppression of the crimes of bigamy, polygamy, and unlawful cohabitation in the Territories of the United States, and to provide for the better government of the Territory of Utah, and for other purposes, January 22, 1883." [Washington: Govt. Print. Off., 1883] 5p.

Referred to the Committee on the Judiciary. Similar bill to the 48th Congress S. 1283 and S. 18 as amending the Edmunds Act. Sections once again on punishment of polygamous marriages, recording of marriages, and disenfranchisement of women.

DLC, UPB, US1C

[647] U.S. House. 47th Congress. 2d Session. H.R. 7467, "A bill to authorize the Court of Claims to hear and determine certain claims, January 29, 1883." [Washington: Govt. Print. Off., 1883] 1p.

Referred to the Committee on the Judiciary. Regarding claims of Joseph C. Irwin and Company and others for property impressed into service in 1857 by Colonel Albert Sidney Johnston.

DLC, UPB, US1C

[648] U.S. House. 47th Congress. 2d Session. Report on the social statistics of cities, Pt. II. The Southern and Western States. Compiled by George E. Waring, Jr., expert and special agent. (H. Misc. Doc. No. 42. V. 19, Pt. 2) Washington: Govt. Print. Off., 1883. 915p. [Serial Set 2148]

Historical sketch of Salt Lake City, pp. 829-835.

[Flake 9104]

[649] U.S. House. 48th Congress. 1st Session. H. Res. 12, "Joint Resolution proposing an amendment to the Constitution, December 10, 1883." [Washington: Govt. Print. Off., 1883] 2p.

Referred to the Committee on the Judiciary. Constitutional amendment regarding polygamy.

DLC, UPB, US1C

[650] U.S. House. 48th Congress. 1st Session. H. Res. 50, "Joint Resolution proposing an amendment to the Constitution

of the United States, prohibiting polygamy, December
11, 1883." [Washington: Govt. Print. Off., 1883] 2p.

Referred to the Committee on the Judiciary.

DLC, UPB, USlC

[651] U.S. Senate. 48th Congress. 1st Session. S. 18, "A bill
to amend an act entitled 'An act to amend section
fifty-three hundred and fifty-two of the Revised
Statutes of the United States, in reference to bigamy,
and for other purposes,' approved March twenty-second,
eighteen hundred and eighty-two, December 4, 1883."
[Washington: Govt. Print. Off., 1883] 7p.

Referred to the Committee on the Judiciary. Another
bill to amend the Edmunds Act, which refers to unlawful
cohabitation and its prosecution, the recording of
marriages, disenfranchisement of women, and the registration
and election of territorial officers, among other things.
DLC, UPB, USlC

[652] U.S. Senate. 48th Congress. 1st Session. S. 68, "A
bill to amend the act establishing a Territorial
government for Utah, and to change the name to Altamont."
[Washington, 1883] 12p.

Includes a discussion of polygamy.

[Flake 9166b]
USlC

[653] "Utah Commission," Congressional Record 47th Congress, 2d
session (3 March 1883) vol. 14, pt. 4, pp. 3688-3689.
[X242]

Mr. Brown of Georgia proposed a resolution that the
Utah Commission should report to the Senate on the
first Monday in December in regard to their accomplishments
in denying anyone the right to vote or hold office
because of the practice of polygamy.

1884

"Then, Mr. President, the Constitution of the
United States guarantees to every citizen of
the United Sttes the free exercise of his
religion, whether he be Christian, Turk,
Hindoo, or Mormon, and the Congress of the
United States not only has no right by any
act to restrict the free exercise of religion,
or of religious opinion, but such restriction
is absolutely forbidden. But this free
exercise of religion which is guaranteed by
the Constitution of the United States does
not authorize the practice of gross immorality
under the cloak or in the name of religion."
[Entry 658]

[654] Arthur, Chester A. "Fourth Annual Message, 1 December 1884," p. 4837. In A Compilation of the Messages and Papers of the Presidents, by James D. Richardson, vol. 7. New York: Bureau of National Literature, 1911, c1897. [GS4.113:7, AE2.114:1-27/v.7]

A couple of paragraphs which refer to the Utah Commission reports and the problem of polygamy in Utah Territory. Arthur "again recommends that Congress assume absolute political control of the Territory."

[655] Arthur, Chester A. Message of the President of the United States communicated to the Two Houses of Congress at the beginning of the Second Session of the Forty-eight Congress. Washington: Govt. Print. Off., 1884. 21p.

Brief mention of the prevention and punishment of polygamy in Utah.

[Flake 9225]
DLC, UPB, US1C

[656] "Austria-Hungary," pp. 10-13. In Foreign Relations of the United States, 1884. Washington: Govt. Print. Off., 1885. [S1.1:884]

Relates measures adopted by Austrian government to ward off Mormon missionary activity, because of Mormon polygamy. U.S. Government is accepting of the restrictions placed on missionary work in Austria. A Mormon missionary, Thomas Biesinger from Lehi, Utah, is cited as an example. Interview with Count Kalnoky who remarked that he did not believe "many persons in this Empire ... were led away by the Mormon superstition."

[657] Brown, Joseph Emerson. The Mormon question. Speech of Hon. Joseph E. Brown, of Georgia, in the Senate of the United States, Friday, January 11, 1884. [Washington: Govt. Print. Off., 1884] 24p.

See entry 707 for annotation.

[Flake 907]
CSmH, CtY, CU-B, DLC, MH, NjP, NN, UHi, UPB, US1C, UU

[658] Brown, Joseph Emerson. Polygamy in Utah and New England contrasted. Speech of Hon. Joseph E. Brown, of Georgia, delivered in the Senate of the United States, Tuesday, May 27, 1884. Washington: [Govt. Print. Off.,] 1884. 32p.

States that all men who marry after divorce are polygamists.

See entry 686.

[Flake 908]
CtY, CU-B, DLC, UHi, UPB, US1C, UU

[659] Bunn, William M. Biennial message of William M. Bunn, Governor of Idaho, to the Thirteenth session of the Legislative Assembly of Idaho Territory. Boise City: Milton Kelly, printer, 1884. 22p.

In his message, Governor Bunn refers to the polygamous and treasonous Mormons on pp. 21-22.

[Flake add. 4180b]
UPB, UU

[660] Clawson v. The United States, Appendix to Brief for the United States. In the Supreme Court of the United States, October Term, 1884, No. 1263. [n.p., 1884?] 13p.

This appendix to the United States brief was filed in the Clawson v. United States case 114 U.S. Reports 477-488.

[Flake add. 6372d]
DLC, UPB, US1C

[661] Clawson v. The United States. Brief for the United States. In the Supreme court of the United States, October Term, 1884, No. 1263. [n.p., 1884?] 5p.

This brief was filed in regard to the Clawson v. United States case 114 U.S. Reports (October 1884) 477-488.

[Flake add. 6372c]
DLC, UPB, US1C

[662] Clawson v. The United States, no. 1235. Brief for the United States. In the Supreme Court of the United States, October term, 1884. [n.p., 1884?] 3p.

This brief was filed in regard to the Clawson v. United States case 113 U.S. Reports (October 1884) 143-149, October 1884 session.

[Flake add. 6372b]
DLC, UPB, US1C

[663] Clawson v. United States, U.S. Reports 113 (October 1884 session) pp. 143-149. [Ju6.8/1:113]

The Supreme court upheld the decision of the District Court for the Third Judicial District of Utah and the Utah Territorial Supreme Court, of Rudger Clawson's unlawful cohabitation conviction.

[664] Clawson v. United States, U.S. Reports 114 (October 1884 session) pp. 477-488. [Ju6.8/1:114]

The judgement of the Supreme court of the Territory of Utah is affirmed by the Supreme Court on April 30, 1885 in the polygamy case of Rudger Clawson. The case was brought before the court under section 5 of the Edmunds Act.

[665] Cullom, Shelby Moore. (Illinois) "Petition adopted by the Grand Army of the Republic of the Department of Utah," Congressional Record 48th Congress, 1st session (10 April 1884) vol. 15, pt. 3, p. 2827. [X246]

An abbreviated version, one paragraph only, which prays Congress to take away all legislative powers from the people of Utah until they prove worthy of the trust.

[666] Cullom, Shelby Moore. The Mormon problem. Address of Hon.
Shelby M. Cullom, in support of his bill to reorganize
the legislative power of the Territory of Utah.
Delivered in the United States Senate, Friday, January
11, 1884. Washington: Govt. Print. Off., 1884. 11p.

See entry 707 for annotation.

[Flake 2605]
DLC

[667] Ellen C. Clawson and Hiram B. Clawson, appellants, vs.
Alexander Ramsey, A. S. Paddock, G.L. Godfrey, A. B.
Carleton, J. R. Pettigrew, E. D. Hoge, and James T.
Little, appellees. Appeal from Judgment of the Supreme
Court of Utah. Brief and argument for appellants.
[Attorneys] for appellants George G. Vest, Wayne
MacVeagh, Franklin S. Richards, Charles W. Bennett.
Supreme Court of the United States, October Term, 1884.
Washington: Gibson Bros., Printers and Bookbinders,
1885. 12p.

This brief was filed regarding the Murphy v. Ramsey
case 114 U.S. Reports 15-47, 23 March 1885.

[Flake add. 2404a]
DLC, UPB, US1C

[668] Frederick Hopt, plaintiff in error, vs. The people of the
Territory of Utah. Certiori and Return. Filed March
25, 1885. Supreme Court of the United States. October
term, 1884. No. 1141. [n.p.] 1885? 11p.

Hopt v. Utah 114 U.S. Reports 488-491, April 20, 1885.

Juror refused to answer whether he was a polygamist.

DLC, UPB, US1C

[669] Frederick Hopt, plaintiff in error, vs. The people of the
Territory of Utah. Brief for plaintiff in error. R.
N. Baskin, S. H. Snider, W. G. Van Horne, attorneys for
plaintiff in error. Supreme Court of the United
States, October term, 1884. [n.p.] 1884? 18p.

Brief for plaintiff in error in Hopt v. Utah 114 U.S.
Reports 488-491, April 20, 1885.

It was an error that the jurors were not asked if they
were polygamists. Justice Twiss held that the practice
of polygamy did not disqualify a juror.

DLC, UPB, US1C

[670] Frederick Hopt, plaintiff in error vs. The People of the
Territory of Utah. In error to the Supreme Court of
the Territory of Utah. Transcript of record. Supreme
Court of the United States. October term, 1884.
[n.p.] 1884? 24p.

Transcript of record in Hopt v. Utah 114 U.S. Reports
488-491, April 20, 1885.

1884

Questions whether a polygamist could be a juror.

DLC, UPB, USlC

[671] "Germany," p. 198. In Foreign Relations of the United States, 1884. Washington: Govt. Print. Off., 1885. [S1.1:884]

Problems of Mormon missionary work in Bavaria. Concern expressed about the increase of Mormons, especially in regard to their working outside the pale of U.S. law because of polygamy.

[672] "Germany," pp. 202-206. In Foreign Relations of the United States, 1884. Washington: Govt. Print. Off., 1885. [S1.1:884]

Describes the reason for expulsion, from Munich and Nuremberg, of Mormon missionaries, James E. Jennings, William A. Smoot, Jr., Lyman and Johann George Hafen (all of Utah). Expulsion is related to polygamy laws.

[673] "Great Britain," pp. 223-224. In Foreign Relations of the United States, 1884. Washington: Govt. Print. Off., 1885. [S1.1:884]

The Consulate-General of the U.S. describes the arrival of three Mormon missionaries in Calcutta, Willis, McCann [McCune], and Pratt. Mr. Frelinghuysen is bringing this matter to the attention of the British government, inasmuch as the Mormons, who exercise polygamy, recruit converts for purpose of increasing their numbers.

[674] James M. Barlow, appellant, vs. Alexander Ramsey, A. S. Paddock, G. L. Godfrey, A. B. Carleton, J. R. Pettigrew, E. D. Hoge and Harmel Pratt. Appeal from the Supreme Court of the Territory of Utah. Transcript of Record. Supreme Court of the United States, October Term, 1884. No. 1031. [Washington: Judd & Detweiler, Printers, 1884?] 12p.

This transcript of record was filed regarding the Murphy v. Ramsey case 114 U.S. Reports 15-47, 23 March 1885.

[Flake add. 3031a]
DLC, UPB, USlC

[674a] James M. Barlow, appellant vs. Alexander Ramsey, A. S. Paddock, G. L. Godfrey, A. B. Carleton, J. R. Pettigrew, E. D. Hoge, and Harmel Pratt, appellees. Appeal from Judgment of the Supreme Court of Utah. Brief and Argument for Appellants. Washington: Gibson Bros., Printers and Bookbinders, 1885. 1p.

At head of title: Supreme Court of the United States. October term, 1884. No. 1031.

138

This appeal was filed in the Murphy vs. Ramsey case 114 U. S. Reports 15-47, 23 March 1885.

[Flake add. 9466d]
DLC, UPB, US1C

[675] Jesse J. Murphy, appellant, vs. Alexander Ramsey, A. S. Paddock, G. L. Godfrey, A. B. Carelton, J. R. Pettigrew, E. D. Hoge and Arthur Pratt. Appeal from the Supreme Court of the Territory of Utah. Transcript of Record. Supreme Court of the United States, October term, 1884, No. 1027. [Washington: Judd & Detweiler, Printers, 1884?] 12p.

This transcript was filed, October 9, 1884, regarding the Murphy v. Ramsey case 114 U.S. Reports 15-47, 23 March 1885.

DLC, UPB, US1C

[676] Jesse J. Murphy, appellant, vs. Alexander Ramsey, A. S. Paddock, G. L. Godfrey, A. B. Carelton, J. R. Pettigrew, E. D. Hoge, and Arthur Pratt, appellees, No. 1027. Appeal from Judgment of the Supreme Court of Utah. Brief and argument for appellant. [Attorneys] for appellant George G. Vest, Wayne MacVeagh, Franklin S. Richards, Charles W. Bennett. Supreme Court of the United States, October term, 1884. Washington: Gibson Bros., printers and bookbinders, 1885. 3p.

This brief was filed October 9, 1884, regarding the Murphy v. Ramsey case 114 U.S. Reports 15-47, 23 March 1885.

[Flake add. 9466e]
DLC, UPB, US1C

[676a] Mary Ann M. Pratt, appellant, vs. Alexander Ramsey, A. S. Paddock, G. L. Godfrey, A. B. Carleton, J. R. Pettigrew, E. D. Hoge and John S. Lindsay. Appeal from the Supreme Court of the Territory of Utah. [Washington: Judd & Detweiller, 1884?] 11p.

At head of title: Transcript of Record, Supreme Court of the United States. October term, 1884. No. 1028.

Appeal in the Murphy vs. Ramsey case 114 U. S. Reports 15-47, 23 March 1885.

[Flake add. 6441a]
DLC, UPB, US1C

[677] Mary Ann M. Pratt, appellant, vs. Alexander Ramsey, A. S. Paddock, G. L. Godfrey, A. B. Carleton, J. R. Pettigrew, E. D. Hoge, and John S. Lindsay, appellees, No. 1028. Appeal from judgment of the Supreme Court of Utah. Brief and argument for appellant. [Attorneys] for appellant, George G. Vest, Wayne MacVeigh, Franklin S. Richards, Charles W. Bennett. Supreme Court of the United States, October Term, 1884. Washington: Gibson Bros., Printers and bookbinders, 1885. 42p.

This brief was filed regarding the Murphy v. Ramsey case 114 U.S. Reports 15-47, 23 March 1885.

[Flake add. 9467a]
DLC, UPB, US1C

[678] "Memorial of the Legislative Assembly of the Territory of Utah," Congressional Record 48th Congress, 1st session (27 March 1884) vol. 15, pt. 3, pp. 2318-2321. [X246]

The Memorial is addressed to the Senate and House of Representatives and expresses deep concern over certain provisions of the Edmunds Act, especially the oath (printed in full) which had to be taken prior to registering to vote or hold office, and which had direct questions regarding polygamy.

The memorialists give a rundown of the political situation in Utah.

[679] Mildred E. Randall and Alfred Randall, appellants, vs. Alexander Ramsey, A. S. Paddock, G. L. Godfrey, A. B. Carleton, J. R. Pettigrew, E. D. Hoge and Harmel Pratt. Appeal from the Supreme Court of the Territory of Utah. Transcript of Record. Supreme Court of the United States, October Term, 1884. No. 1029. [Washington: Judd & Detweiler, Printers, 1884?] 12p.

This Transcript of Record was filed regarding the Murphy v. Ramsey case 114 U.S. Reports 15-47, 23 March 1885.

[Flake add. 6815a]
DLC, UPB, US1C

[680] Mildred E. Randall and Alfred Randall, appellants, vs. Alexander Ramsey, A. S. Paddock, G. L. Godfrey, A. B. Carleton, J. R. Pettigrew, E. D. Hoge, and Harmel Pratt, appellees, No. 1029. Appeal from Judgment of the Supreme Court of Utah. Brief and Argument for appellants. [Attorneys] for appellants, George G. Vest, Wayne MacVeagh Franklin S. Richards, Charles W. Bennett. Supreme Court of the United States, October term, 1884. Washington: Gibson Bros., Printers and Bookbinders, 1885. 3p.

This brief was filed regarding the Murphy v. Ramsey case 114 U.S. Reports 15-47, 23 March 1885.

[Flake add. 9467b]
DLC, UPB, US1C

[681] Murphy v. The United States, No. 1027, Pratt v. Same, No. 1028, Randall and Husband v. Same, No. 1029, Clawson and husband v. Same, No. 1030, [and] Barlow v. Same, No. 1031. Brief for the United States. [n.p., 1884?] 33p.

This Brief for the United States relates to the Murphy
v. Ramsey case 114 U.S. Reports 15-47, 23 March 1885.

[Flake add. 6372f]
DLC, UPB, US1C

[682] Murray, Eli H.   "Governor's Message to the Joint Session,
January 15, 1884," pp. 24-37. In the Council Journal
of the Twenty-sixth session of the Legislative Assembly
of the Territory of Utah. Salt Lake City: Tribune
Printing and Publishing Co., 1884.

Gov. Murray discusses the pioneers of Utah, polygamy,
immigration, the Perpetual Emigrating Fund and the
Church Corporation.

UPB, US1C

[683] Murray, Eli H.   Message of His excellency Gov. Eli H.
Murray, to the Twenty-sixth session of the Legislative
Assembly of Utah Territory, 1884, with accompanying
documents. [Salt Lake City]: T. E. Taylor, 1884.
23p.

Problems of ecclesiastical domination over the legislature,
the courts, and polygamy are discussed.

[Flake 9366]
CSmH, CU-B, MH, NjP, UHi, UPB, US1C

[684] People v. Hopt, Territory of Utah Reports 3 (June 1884) pp.
396-404.

The concern is that disqualification of a jurist
because of bigamy, does not hold true in jury trial
for other than bigamy or polygamy.

CU-L, DLC, ICU, MH, MiU, UAr, UPB, UU, ViU-L

[685] "Petition," Congressional Record 48th Congress, 1st session
(28 February 1884) vol. 15, pt. 2, p. 1443. [X245]

Petition, unprinted, from the Boston preachers' meeting
of the Methodist Episcopal Church, supporting the last
annual Presidential address to Congress regarding
Mormonism and polygamy.

[686] "Polygamy in Utah," Congressional Record 48th Congress, 1st
session (23, 26, 27 May, 16, 17, 18 June 1884) vol. 15,
pt. 5, pp. 4431, 4503-4504, 4513-4515, 4553-4565, 5182-
5191, 5234-5250, 5281-5298. [X248]

Discussions of polygamy as an institution; rights of
polygamous children; legal rights of man and wife;
divorce as a form of polygamy; confiscation of L.D.S.
church property; and the Immigration fund, etc.

[687] "Report of the Utah Commission, 1884," pp. 517-522.   In
Annual Report of the Department of the Interior, 1884,
vol. 2. Washington: Govt. Print. Off., 1884.
[I1.1:884/V.2]

Tells of the election of 1884 and the number of Mormons elected, relates a polygamy trial, and details needed for further legislation. No summary.

Variant ed. U.S. 48th Cong. 2nd session. House Ex. Doc. No. 1, Serial Set 2287.

[688] Report of the Utah Commission to the Secretary of the Interior. 1884. Washington: Govt. Print. Off., 1884. 8p.

Status of polygamy after the Edmunds Act. Increase of polygamy due to the opening of the Logan Temple.
[Flake 9239]
CtY, DLC, ICN, NN, UPB, USlC

[689] "Resolution," Congressional Record 48th Congress, 1st session (16 January 1884) vol. 15, pt. 1, p. 459. [X244]

A resolution, not printed in full, adopted at a mass meeting in Salt Lake City, regarding polygamy.

[690] Rudger Clawson, appellant, vs. The United States. Appeal from the Supreme Court of the Territory of Utah. Transcript of Record. Supreme Court of the United States, October term, 1884. No. 1235. [Washington: Judd & Detweiler, printers, 1884?] 7p.

This transcript was filed, December 3, 1884, in regard to the Clawson v. United States case 113 U.S. Reports 143-149, October 1884 session.
[Flake add. 2411a]
DLC, UPB, USlC

[691] Rudger Clawson, appellant, vs. The United States, appellee. Appeal from the judgment on a writ of habeas corpus of the Supreme Court of the Territory of Utah. Brief of argument for appellant. [Attorneys] for appellant. Franklin S. Richards, Wayne MacVeagh. Supreme Court of the United States, October term, 1884. No. 1235. Philadelphia: Allen, Lane & Scott, Printers, [1884?] 14p.

This brief was filed in regard to the Clawson v. United States case 113 U.S. Reports 143-149, October 1884 session.
[Flake add. 7232a]
DLC, UPB, USlC

[692] Rudger Clawson, plaintiff in error, vs. The United States. An error to the Supreme Court of the Territory of Utah. Transcript of Record. Supreme Court of the United States. October Term, 1884, No. 1263. [Washington: Judd & Detweiler, printers, 1885?] 23p.

This transcript was filed February 5, 1885 in the
Clawson v. United States case 114 U.S. Reports, (October
1884) 477-488.

> [Flake add. 2411b]
> DLC, UPB, US1C

[693] Rudger Clawson, plaintiff in error, vs. The United States,
defendant in error. Brief for plaintiff in error.
[Attorneys] for plaintiff in error, Franklin S. Richards,
Wayne MacVeagh. Supreme Court of the United States,
October Term, 1884, No. 1263. Washington: Gibson
Bros., Printers and Bookbinders, 1885. 25p.

This brief was filed in the Clawson v. United States
case 114 U.S. Reports (October 1884) 477-488.

> DLC, UPB, US1C

[694] Rudger Clawson, plaintiff in error, vs. The United States.
Brief for the Plaintiff in Error. [Washington, 1885]
26p.

At head of title: Supreme Court of the United States.
October Term, 1884. No. 1263.

This brief was filed in regard to the Clawson v. United
States case 114 U.S. Reports 477-488, October 1884
session.

> [Flake 7233]
> UPB, US1C

[695] Rudger Clawson, plaintiff in error, vs. The United States,
Defendant in Error. From supreme Court of Utah, Brief
for Plaintiff in Error. Washington, 1885. 26p.

Signed: Franklin S. Richards, Wayne MacVeagh.

Variant printing.

This brief was filed in regard to the Clawson v. United
States case 114 U.S. Reports 477-488, October 1884
session.

> [Flake add. 9234a]
> US1C

[696] U.S. House. 48th Congress. 1st Session. Committee on the
Territories. Marriages in Territory of Utah. Report:
[To accompany bill H.R. 6765.] The Committee on the
Territories, to whom was referred the bill (H.R. 946)
to provide for the governing of the Territory of Utah
by a commission, submit the following. (H. Rept. No.
1351, pt. 1) Washington: Govt. Print. Off., 1884.
4p. [Serial Set 2257]

Provisions for solemnizing marriages in Utah recommended.
Extensive coverage on marriages and polygamy in Utah.
> [Flake 9155]

[697] U.S. House. 48th Congress. 1st Session. Committee on the
Territories. Reorganization of the legislative power
of Utah Territory. Views of the minority [To accompany

bill H.R. 6765.] The minority of the Committee on the
Territories, to whom was referred the bill (H.R. 946)
to reorganize the legislative power of Utah Territory,
having leave from the House to express its views,
respectfully submit the following. (H. Rept. No. 1351,
pt. 2) Washington: Govt. Print. Off., 1884. 57p.
[Serial Set 2257]

Bill to fight polygamy and the power of the Mormon
Church in Utah. The minority are against this bill.
It includes numerous statements, and reprints of
articles regarding church government, Mountain Meadows,
etc.

[Flake 9159]

[698] U.S. House. 48th Congress. 1st Session. H.R. 2042, "A
bill supplementary to an act entitled 'An act to amend
section fifty-three hundred and fifty two of the
Revised Statutes of the United States, in reference to
bigamy, and for other purposes,' January 7, 1884."
[Washington: Govt. Print. Off., 1884] 2p.

Referred to the Committee on the Judiciary. Amendment
to the Edmunds Act regarding elections, Sec. 3 and 4
specifically deal with witnesses at polygamy trials and
the disincorporation of the Mormon Church.

DLC, UPB, US1C

[699] U.S. House. 48th Congress. 1st Session. H.R. 4931, "A
bill relating to the qualification of voters in the
Territories of Utah and Idaho, and for other purposes,
February 11, 1884." [Washington: Govt. Print. Off.,
1884] 3p.

Referred to the Committee on the Judiciary. No person
who is a member of the Mormon Church can vote or hold
office.

DLC, UPB, US1C

[700] U.S. House. 48th Congress. 1st Session. H.R. 6395, "A
bill prescribing a certain oath to be taken by persons
offering to file upon or enter any public lands of the
United States situated in the Territories of Idaho and
Utah, March 31, 1884." [Washington: Government
Printing Office, 1884] 2p.

Referred to the Committee on the Judiciary. Bill
requiring anyone registering for land to declare that
they are polygamists.

DLC, UPB, US1C

[701] U.S. House. 48th Congress. 1st Session. H.R. 6765, "A
bill to provide for the manner of solemnizing marriages
in the Territory of Utah and to provide for the recording
of certificates of marriages therein, and for other
purposes, April 24, 1884." [Washington: Govt. Print.
Off., 1884] 2p.

Referred to the Committee on the Territories as a
substitute for H.R. 946. Section 2 refers to the

penalty for not recording marriages, apparently a
veiled threat regarding polygamous marriages.

DLC, UPB, US1C

[702] U.S. House. 48th Congress. 1st Session. Polygamy in
Utah. Message from the President of the United States,
transmitting a communication from the Secretary of the
Interior relative to polygamy in Utah. (H. Ex. Doc.
No. 153) Washington: Govt. Print. Off, 1884. 6p.
[Serial Set 2207]

Political situation and status of polygamy as a result
of the Edmunds Act.

[Flake 9193]

[703] U.S. House. 48th Congress. 1st Session. Protest of
Legislative Assembly of Utah. Memorial of the Legislative
Assembly of the Territory of Utah, protesting against
the passage of the bills now pending in Congress or any
other measures inimical to the people of said Territory,
until after a full investigation by a Congressional
committee. (H. Misc. Doc. No. 45) Washington: Govt.
Print. Off., 1884. 13p. [Serial Set 2231]

Protest of further legislation against polygamy. They
point to the governor's false statements and note that
married women in polygamy are excluded from voting
while those who commit the most flagrant sex crimes are
permitted to exercise the franchise.

[Flake add. 9391a]

[704] U.S. Senate. 48th Congress. 1st Session. Committee on
Claims. In the Senate of the United States... Report:
[To accompany bills S. 1391 and 2166.] (S. Rept. No.
517) Washington: Govt. Print. Off., 1884. 3p.
[Serial Set 2176]

Claim of Richard H. and James Porter for horses and
other property lost during the Utah expedition.

[705] U.S. Senate. 48th Congress. 1st Session. S. 1283, "A
bill to amend an act entitled 'An act to amend section
fifty-three hundred and fifty-two of the Revised
Statutes of the United States, in reference to bigamy,
and for other purposes,' approved March twenty-second,
eighteen hundred and eighty-two, January 28 1884."
[Washington: Govt. Print. Off., 1884] 11p.

Referred to the Committee on the Judiciary. Apparently
a predecessor bill to the Edmunds-Tucker, this bill
would of course prosecute polygamous marriages disenfranchise
women, and disincorporate the church.

DLC, UPB, US1C

[706] Utah Commission. Special report of the Utah Commission
made to the Secretary of the Interior, 1884. (H. Ex.
Doc. No. 153) Washington: Govt. Print. Off., 1884.
15p. [Serial Set 2207]

Cover title. This is an expanded version of entry 702, in which the Utah Commission had added material pp. 6-15.

[Flake 9242]

[707] "Utah Territorial Government," Congressional Record 48th Congress, 1st session (11 January 1884) vol. 15, pt. 1, pp. 354-365. [X244]

Arguments on constitutionality of Edmunds Laws. Brief history of the Church (anti-Mormon).

1885

"Before the bar of this court that degradation has been shown in the painful lack of manhood upon the part of those arraigned for polygamy or unlawful cohabitation, in permitting their plural wives to be sent into imprisonment for contempt in vain endeavors to shield themselves from the penalty of the law, and women under oath have denied a knowledge of the paternity of their children in attempts to shield the offenders. Men otherwise good have abandoned their families by going to the penitentiary rather than disobey the cruel edict of polygamous leaders in their defense of the infamous system. A few others, more manly and less fanatical, have had the courage to recognize the fact that the law is above us all, and these have received the lighter inflictions of the law, and are devoting themselves to the care of their families and education of all their children and pursuing the different paths of duty and business."

[Entry 720]

---

[708] Angus M. Cannon, plaintiff in error, vs. the United States. Brief for Defendant in error, No. 1169. Franklin S. Richards, attorney for plaintiff in error. [n.p., 1885] 45p.

Brief for the defendant in error relates to the Cannon v. United States case 116 U.S. Report 55-80, October 1885. This brief contains considerable family information and relationships.

[Flake add. 1139a]
UPB, USlC, Supreme Court Library

[709] Angus M. Cannon, plaintiff in error, vs. The United States, defendant in error, from Supreme Court of Utah. Brief for Plaintiff in error. Attorney for Plaintiff in Error, Franklin S. Richards. Supreme Court of the United States, October term 1885. No. 1169. Washington: Gibson Bros., Printers and Bookbinders, 1885. 24p.

Brief for plaintiff in error relates to the Cannon v.
United States case 116 U.S. Reports 55-80, October
1885.

UPB, US1C, Supreme Court Library

[710] Angus M. Cannon, plaintiff in error, vs. The United States.
In error to the Supreme Court of the Territory of Utah.
Supreme Court of the United States, October Term, 1885.
No. 1169. Washington: Judd & Detweiler, Printers,
1885. 41p.

This document relates to the Cannon v. United States
case 116 U.S. Reports 55-80, October 1885 term. The
document was filed October 21, 1885.

[Flake add. 1139b]
UPB, US1C, Supreme Court Library

[711] Cannon v. United States U.S. Reports 116 (October 1885) 55-
80. [JU6.8/1:116]

The polygamy case of Angus M. Cannon and his wives
Clara, Sarah, and Amanda Cannon. Various children of
the Cannon marriages testified such as George M., and
Angus M., Jr. The changes and provisions between the
Morrill Act and the Edmunds Act are cited in this
important case.

[712] Circular for the information of registration officers,
Salt Lake City, April 21, 1885. [Salt Lake City, 1885]
4p.

At head of title: Office of the Utah Commission.

Polygamy oath.

[Flake 9231]
UHi, US1C

[713] Cleveland, Grover. "First Annual Message, 8 December
1885," pp. 4946-4947. In A Compilation of the Messages
and Papers of the Presidents, by James D. Richardson,
vol. 7. New York: Bureau of National Literature,
1911, c1897. [GS4.113:7, AE2.114:1-27/v.7]

Polygamy is discussed in relationship to the strengths
of its homes. Extols the virtue of monogamy as opposed
to polygamy. Describes polygamous wives and mothers as
"cheerless, crushed, and unwomanly mothers of polygamy."

[714] Cleveland, Grover. "Message of the President, 8 December
1885," pp. 41-42. In Messages and Documents 1885-1886
Abridgement. Washington: Govt. Print. Off., 1885.
[Y8.49/1:]

See entry 713 for annotation.

[715] Gardner, J. F. "Missionary Work, Ouray Agency, Utah,
August 12, 1885," p. 179. In Report of the Commissioner
of Indian Affairs. Washington: Govt. Print. Off.,
1885. [I20.1:885]

Reports Mormon clandestine missionary work on the Ute
Indian Reservation.

[716] Gibson, Albert M. The rights of citizenship. Brief in Re
H.R. Bills Nos. 1478, 6153, and the petition of the
citizens of Bear Lake County, Idaho Territory. [n.p.,
1885?] 27p.

Concerning the effect of polygamy legislation in Idaho.

[Flake 3557a]
UPB, US1C

[717] "Great Britain," pp. 444-445, 448-449. In Foreign Relations
of the United States, 1885. Washington: Govt. Print.
Off., 1886. [S1.1:885]

The problems of Mormon recruitment in India are aired.
Special concern for the Mormon missionaries' illegal
status, due to polygamy, was expressed.

[718] Vacant

[719] Murphy v. Ramsey, U.S. Reports 114 (23 March 1885) 15-47.
[Ju6.8/1:114]

Plaintiffs are seeking voter registration rights denied
them in the Edmunds Act.

[720] Murray, Eli H. Report of the Governor of Utah to the
Secretary of the Interior... 1885. Washington: Govt.
Print. Off., 1885. 31p.

Reports the Mormon leaders' control of the people.

[Flake 9369]
UPB

[721] "Petition," Congressional Record 48th Congress, 2d session
(30 January 1885) vol. 16, pt. 2, p. 1072. [X252]

Petition of Amos A. Lawrence and 15 other citizens of
Boston, not printed in full, asking to be made a
corporation for the purpose of promoting immigration to
Utah to develop its agricultural and mineral resources.

[722] "Petition for the Suppression of Polygamy," Congressional
Record 49th Congress, 1st session (14 December 1885)
vol. 17, pt. 1, p. 177. [X255]

Petition of 300 ladies of Cincinnati, not printed in
full.

[723] "Petitions," Congressional Record 48th Congress, 2d session
(31 January 2, 3, 4, 5, 6, 7, 10, 11, 12, 13, 16, 17
February 1885) vol. 16, pt. 2, pp. 1143, 1191, 1243,
1278, 1313, 1364, 1447, 1448, 1511, 1546, 1547, 1612,
1703, 1704, 1770, 1771, 1826, 1827. [X252]

Petitions, not printed in full, regarding the passage
of the bill (bill no. not given) relating to the Mormon

1885

question or polygamy. As usual there are many more
petitions than it would appear from the pages as there
is often more than one petition to a page.

[724] "Petitions," Congressional Record 48th Congress, 2d session
(18, 19, 20, 23, 24, 26, 27, 28 February 2, 3, March
1885) vol. 16, pt. 3, pp. 1869, 1928, 1929, 1987, 2060,
2115, 2174, 2224, 2276, 2326, 2435, 2436, 2573. [X253]

Petitions, not printed in full, regarding suppression
of polygamy. As usual there are many more petitions
than it would appear from the pages as there is often
more than one petition to a page.

[725] "Report of the Governor of Utah to the Secretary of the
Interior, 1885," pp. 1015-1043. In Annual Report of
the Department of the Interior, 1885, vol. 2. Washington:
Govt. Print. Off., 1885. [I1.1:885]

Almost all of the report deals with polygamy, the
enforcement of the Edmunds Law of 1882, including a ten
page letter from the First Presidency which urges its
members to continue the practice of polygamy.

A summary of the Governor's report appears on p. 84-5
of vol. I of the Secretary of the Interior's Report for
1885.

[726] "Report of the Utah Commission, 1885," pp. [885]-891. In
Annual Report of the Department of the Interior, 1885,
vol. 2. Washington: Govt. Print. Off., 1885.
[I1.1:885/v.2]

Summary of the commission's work during the last two
months, on the prosecutions of polygamists and further
recommendations.

Variant ed. U.S. 49th Cong., 1s session. House Ex.
Doc. No. 1, Vol. II, Serial Set 2379.

[727] "School Meetings in Utah, January 5, 1885," pp. 94-95. In
Official Opinions of the Attorneys- General United
States, Vol. XVIII. Washington: Govt. Print. Off.,
1890. [J1.5:18]

Polygamists may vote in school meetings in Utah because
they are not elections within the meaning of the March
22, 1882 Act. (Edmunds Act)

[728] "Sweden and Norway," pp. 788-789. In Foreign Relations of
the United States, 1885. Washington: Govt. Print.
Off., 1886. [S1.1:885]

Correspondence between the U.S. Legation in Stockholm
and the Dept. of State in Washington, regarding the
Legation's refusal to issue a passport to a Mormon to
enter Finland. The State Dept. reiterates the government
policy, issued through a circular in August 1879, which
requested all governments to suppress Mormon proselyting.

149

[729] "Switzerland," p. 803. In Foreign Relations of the United States, 1885. Washington: Govt. Print. Off., 1886. [S1.1:885]

Concern is expressed in this letter from the Legation in Berne regarding a shipload of 75 Mormons leaving on May 9, 1885 from Basle to New York via Antwerp.

[730] "Territorial Officers in Utah, June 5, 1885," pp. 193-195. In Official Opinions of the Attorneys-General of the United States. Vol. XVIII. Washington: Govt. Print. Off., 1890. [J1.5:18]

The superintendent of district schools, auditor of public accounts and treasurer of Utah Territory should be appointed by the governor and not elected. Utah Commission requested an opinion.

[731] U.S. House. 48th Congress. 2d Session. Committee on Claims. Utah Expedition... Report: [To accompany bill H.R. 8283.] The Committee on Claims, to whom was referred the bill (H.R. 4507) referring to the Court of Claims in the claims for property seized by General Johnston on the Utah Expedition, having carefully considered the same, make the following report. (H. Rept. No. 2650) [Washington: Govt. Print. Off.] 1885. 2p. [Serial Set 2329]

Payment for property seized from Richard H. and James Porter during the Utah Expedition.

[Flake add. 9110d]

[732] The United States, respondent, v. A. Milton Musser, appellant, Territory of Utah Reports 4 (June 1885) pp. 153-177.

The polygamy case of A. Milton Musser and his wives Belinda Pratt Musser, May Musser and Annie Segmiller McCullough Musser.

CU-L, DLC, ICU, MH, MiU, UAr, UPB, UU, ViU-L

[733] The United States, respondent, v. Angus M. Cannon, appellant, Territory of Utah Reports 4 (June 1885) pp. 122-152.

Unlawful cohabitation case regarding Angus M. Cannon and his wives Amanda, and Clara C. Mason. The defendant was guilty as charged.

CU-L, DLC, ICU, MH, MiU, UAr, UPB, UU, ViU-L

[734] The United States, respondent, v. Thomas Simpson, appellant, Territory of Utah Reports 4 (June 1885) pp. 227-230.

Affirmed the lower court indictment of Thomas Simpson for polygamy with Emma Everett at the same time as his lawful wife, Hannah Powell Simpson, was living.

CU-L, DLC, ICU, MH, MiU, UAr, UPB, UU, ViU-L

[735] U.S. Senate. 49th Congress. 1st Session. S. 10, "A bill to amend an act entitled 'An act to amend section fifty-three hundred and fifty-two of the Revised

Statutes of the United States, in reference to bigamy,
and for other purposes,' approved March twenty-second,
eighteen hundred and eighty-two, December 8, 1885."
[Washington: Govt. Print. Off., 1885]. 15p.

Referred to the Committee on the Judiciary.

The bill introduced by Mr. Edmunds as an amendment to
the Edmunds Act of 1882. Various provisions of this
bill later became the law known as the Edmunds-Tucker.

DLC, UPB, US1C

1886

"I beg, Mr. Secretary, to be explicitly
understood, that, in making this suggestion
of a better policy towards the Mormons of
Utah, I express my own opinions only, without
any prompting from any quarter. My voice may
be the voice of one crying in the wilderness.
I am conscious that I have very little power
of any kind; still less have I any political
influence. But while I have strength to
utter my protest against the policy that has
been for some time pursued I shall not cease
to utter it. I look upon that policy, and
the further measures that are proposed in the
same direction, as a huge mistake. To me it
seems very plain that we are preparing to
have on our hands a problem quite as formidable
as that which has long troubled the British
government in Ireland, but for different
reasons and on a smaller scale."

[Entry 738]

---

[736] Anti-polygamy bill: [Opinion] in re bill, recommended the
Committees of Conference on the Disagreeing Votes of
the Two Houses of Congress on the Amendments of the
House to Senate Bill No. 10..." [n.p., 1886?] 7p.

Reaction to S. 10 (the Edmunds-Tucker Act). Britton
and Gray's opinion focuses on fundamental rights of
personal liberty, private property and individual
liberty, private property and individual conscience.
Legally, and constitutionally all of these rights are
violated in this bill, including escheating of Church
property and the voter's test oath.

[Flake 859]
DLC, NN, UPB, US1C

[737] Blair, Henry W. (N. H.) "Memorial of a Mass Meeting of the
Women of Utah," Congressional Record 49th Congress, 1st
session (6 April 1886) vol. 17, pt. 3, pp. 3137-3138.
[X257]

The petition is presented in full and contains considerable
material on polygamy regarding what they characterize
as the "cruel and inhuman proceedings in the Utah

courts," and the movement to "deprive women voters in
Utah of the elective franchise."

[738] Curtis, George Ticknor. <u>Letter to the Secretary of the
Interior on the affairs of Utah. Polygamy, "cohabitation,"
etc</u>. Washington: Printed for the author by Gibson
Bros., 1886. 32p.

Curtis quotes at length from a letter which President
John Taylor sent him, in answer to Curtis' questions.
Taylor firmly states the Churches position to hold fast
to their religious convictions and at the same time
contending that the Mormons could not surrender their
rights as American citizens. Curtis recommends a
change of policy towards the Mormons so that the U.S.
does not create its own Ireland.

[Flake 2616]
CSmH, CU-B, DLC, ICN, MH, NjP, UHi, UPB, US1C, WHi

[739] <u>Ex Parte: In the matter of Lorenzo Snow, petitioner,
appellant. Appeal from Order of Third District Court
of Utah Territory, refusing application for writ of
Habeas Corpus. Brief for Appellant, No. 1282. Supreme
Court of the United States, October Term, 1886</u>.
[Attorneys] for Petitioner, George Ticknor Curtis,
Franklin S. Richards. Washington: Gibson Bros.,
Printers and Bookbinders, 1887. 34p.

This brief for appellant was filed in regard to the In
re Snow case 120 <u>U.S. Reports</u> 274-287, 7 February 1887.

DLC, UPB, US1C

[740] <u>Ex Parte: In the matter of Lorenzo Snow, Petitioner,
appellant. Appeal from the 3d Judicial District Court,
Salt Lake County, Territory of Utah. Supreme Court of
the United States, October Term, 1886, No. 1282</u>.
[n.p., 1886] 2p.

This appeal is in regard to the In re Snow case 120
<u>U.S. Reports</u> 274-287, 7 February 1887.

[Flake add. 2614a]
DLC, UPB, US1C

[741] <u>Ex Parte: In the matter of Lorenzo Snow, petitioner,
appellant. Appeal from the Third Judicial District
Court, Salt Lake County, Territory of Utah. Supreme
Court of the United States, October Term, 1886., No.
1282</u>. Washington: Judd & Detweiler, Printers [1886?]
20p.

This appeal was filed November 10, 1886 in the Snow
case 120 <u>U.S. Reports</u> 274-287, 7 February 1887.

[Flake add. 8248b]
DLC, UPB, US1C

[742] <u>Ex Parte: In the matter of Lorenzo Snow, Petitioner,
appellant, No. 1282. Appeal from the Third Judicial
District Court, Salt Lake City County, Territory of
Utah. Supreme court of the United States, October</u>

Term, 1886. [Counsel for Petitioner George Ticknor Curtis, Franklin S. Richards n.p., 1887?] 12p.

Appeal in regard to In re Snow case 120 U.S. Reports, 274-287, 7 February 1887.

DLC, UPB, US1C

[743] Gibson, Albert M. Brief in re Senate bill No. 10. A bill to amend an act entitled "An act to amend section fifty-three hundred and fifty-two of the revised statutes of the United States in reference to bigamy and for other purposes," approved March 22, 1882. [n.p., 1886] 87p.

Cover title: Have Mormons any Rights. Positive Towards the Mormons. Includes in the Appendix, organized by date, the "Polygamy and Unlawful Cohabitation Cases--Trials."

[Flake 3556, 3557]
CSmH, CtY, CU-B, DLC, ICN, MH, NjP, NN, UHi, UPB, US1, US1C

[744] Goodwin, Charles Carroll. That brief. [Washington, 1886] 22p.

Related to A. M. Gibson's "Brief in re Senate Bill No. 10," or his "Have the Mormons any rights?"

[Flake 3621]
CtY, ICN, NN, UPB, US1C, WHi

[745] "Habits and condition of Indians, Ouray Agency, Utah Territory, August 14, 1886," p. 228. In Annual Report of the Commissioner of Indian Affairs to the Secretary of the Interior for the year 1886. Washington: Govt. Print. Off., 1886. [I20.1:886]

The vice of polygamy practiced among the Indians was borrowed from the Mormon Church because it suits the Indian's inclinations, but not for religious reasons.

[746] Hunton & Chandler, law firm. In the matter of Senate bill 10, Report No. 2735, In the House of Representatives, January 12, 1886. [Salt Lake City? 1886] 15p.

Polygamy legislation, on the Edmunds-Tucker.

[Flake 4147]
UPB, US1C

[747] James Jack, appellant, vs. the people of the Territory of Utah, ex. rel, William H. Dickson, U.S. Attorney. Appeal from the Supreme Court of the Territory of Utah. Transcript of Record. Supreme court of the United States, October term, 1886 [the 6 has been crossed off and a handwritten 8 placed over it] No. 1108 [crossed off and No. 721, then 418 were written in the subsequently crossed off and finally 144 was handwritten in.] [Washington: Judd & Detweiler, Printers, 1886?] 21p.

This transcript was filed, October 11, 1886, regarding the Clayton v. Utah Territory case 132 U.S. Reports 632-643, 6 January 1890.

DLC, UPB, US1C

[748] James Jack, plaintiff in error vs. The people of the Territory of Utah, [and] Nephi W. Clayton, plaintiff in error vs. The People of the Territory of Utah. Brief for Appellants on the Motion to Dismiss the appeals for want of jurisdiction. Attorneys for appellants, Eppa Hunton, and Jeff Chandler. Supreme Court of the United States, October Term, 1886. No. 1108 and No. 1107. [Washington]: Judd & Detweiler, Printers, 1886? 15p.

Brief for Appellants regarding Clayton v. Utah Territory case, 132 U.S. Reports 632-643, 6 January 1890.

DLC, UPB, US1C

[749] James Jack, plaintiff in error, vs. The People of the Territory of Utah [and] Nephi W. Clayton, plaintiff in error, vs. the people of the Territory of Utah. Brief for appellants on the motion to dismiss the appeals for want of jurisdiction. Attorneys for appellants, J. G. Sutherland, J. R. McBridge, Arthur Brown. Supreme Court of the United States, October Term 1886. Salt Lake: Star Print [1886?] 11p.

This brief for appellants was filed regarding the Clayton v. Utah Territory case 132 U.S. Reports 632-643, 6 January 1890.

DLC, UPB, US1C

[750] Lorenzo Snow, plaintiff in error v. The United States, Defendant in Error. No. 1278. Lorenzo Snow, Plaintiff in Error v. The United States, Defendant in Error No. 1,277. Brief for Plaintiff in Error. [Washington: Gibson Bros., Printers and Bookbinders, 1886] 39p.

Signed: George Ticknor Curtis, Franklin S. Richards.

At head of title: Supreme Court of the United States, October term, 1885.

This brief was filed in the In re Snow case 120 U.S. Reports 274-287, 7 February 1887.

[Flake 2617]
US1C

[751] Memorial of the Mormon women of Utah to the President and the Congress of the United States: the outrages of which they complain - The justice they demand, April 6, 1886. Washington, 1886. 8p.

Signed: Mrs. Sarah M. Kimball, Mrs. M. Isabella Horne, Mrs. Elmina S. Taylor [and others]

Unfair results of the Edmunds Act.

Reprinted from the Congressional Record, April 6, 1886.
See entry 737.

[Flake 9396]
CSmH, CtY, CU-B, ICN, NjP, PU, UPB, USlC

[752] "The Mormon counties," p. 128. In Report of the Commissioner
of Education for the year 1886-87. Washington: Govt.
Print. Off., 1888. [FS5.1:886-87]

Problems of public education in Idaho in the predominantly
Mormon counties.

Variant ed. in Serial Set 1888.

[753] Nephi W. Clayton, appellant, vs. The People of the Territory
of Utah Ex Rel, William H. Dickson, U.S. Attorney.
Appeal from the Supreme Court of the Territory of Utah.
Transcript of Record. Supreme Court of the United
States, October Term, 1886. [Washington: Judd &
Detweiler] 1886. 29p.

Appeal regarding Clayton v. Utah Territory case, 132
U.S. Reports 632-643, 6 January 1890. The No. on the
title page started out as printed No. 1107, but it has
been crossed out and three different numbers supplied
finally ending with No. 143.

DLC, UPB, USlC

[754] "Papers Accompanying the Report of the Secretary of the
Interior, 28 September 1886," pp. 576-578. In Message
and Documents 1886-1987 Abridgement. Washington:
Govt. Print. Off., 1886. [Y8.49/2:]

In 1886, the late Indian agent of the Uintah and
Uncompaghre Reservation of the Utes indicated that he
had been told that the Indians and the Mormons combined
could successfully resist government troops.

[755] The People of the Territory of Utah, on the relation of Wm.
H. Dickson, U.S. District Attorney for said Territory,
Respondent, vs. Nephi W. Clayton, appellant . . . and
James Jack, appellant. Brief of Respondent on Motion
to Dismiss Appeals. Attorneys for respondent, Wm. H.
Dickson, U.S. Dist. Atty. for Utah, P. L. Williams.
[n.p., 1886?] 4p.

Respondents Brief regarding Clayton v. Utah Territory
case, 132 U.S. Reports 632-643, 6 January 1890.

DLC, UPB, USlC

[756] The People of Utah Territory, respondent, v. B.Y. Hampton,
appellant, Territory of Utah Reports 4 (January 1886)
pp. 258-266.

Brigham Y. Hampton, a member of the Mormon Church, was
convicted of keeping a house of ill-fame. His attorney's
decision to exclude members of the Mormon Church from
the jury because he thought they would not be impartial
was upheld.

CU-L, DLC, ICU, MH, MiU, UAr, UPB, UU, ViU-L

[757] "Petition," <u>Congressional Record</u> 49th Congress, 1st session
(24 May 1886) vol. 17, pt. 5, p. 4873. [X259]

Petition, not printed, of Thomas E. Bassett and 728
other citizens of Bingham County, Idaho against passage
of H. No. 6153, which would have prohibited polygamist
from voting or holding office.

[758] "Petitions," <u>Congressional Record</u> 49th Congress, 1st
session (8, 10 May 1886) vol. 17, pt. 4, pp. 4300,
4343. [X258]

Petitions, not printed, against any legislation which
would disenfranchise voters by requiring test oaths on
account of their religious beliefs.

[759] "Petitions," <u>Congressional Record</u> 49th Congress, 1st
session (11, 12, 14, 15, 17 May, 7 June 1886) vol. 17,
pt. 5, 4394, 4444, 4540, 4566, 4609, 5389. [X259]

Petitions, not printed, against any legislation which
would disenfranchise voters by requiring test oaths on
account of their religious beliefs.

[760] "Petitions and Memorials," <u>Congressional Record</u> 49th
Congress, 1st session (20, 29 April 1886) vol. 17, pt.
4, pp. 3657, 3999. [X258]

Petitions, not printed, on behalf of the Industrial
Christian Home for "dependent and helpless women and
children."

[761] "Petitions and Memorials," <u>Congressional Record</u> 49th
Congress, 1st session (14, 16 June 1886) vol. 17, pt.
6, pp. 5642, 5796. [X260]

Petitions of Industrial Christian Home Society, not
printed to provide support for the "dependent classes"
in suppressing polygamy.

[762] "Petitions and Memorials," <u>Congressional Record</u> 49th
Congress, 1st session (29 July 1886) vol. 17, pt. 8, p.
7668. [X262]

President of the Senate presented the proclamation of
the governor, not printed, relative to marriage violations
by Mormons.

[763] "Petitions for the Suppression of Polygamy," <u>Congressional
Record</u> 49th Congress, 1st session (15, 24 April 1886)
vol. 17, pt. 4, pp. 3536, 3811. [X258]

Petitions in support of Mr. Woodburn's bill to suppress
polygamy.

[764] <u>A plea for religious liberty and the rights of conscience.
An argument delivered in the Supreme Court of the
United States, April 28, 1886, in three cases of
Lorenzo Snow, Plaintiff in Error, v. The United States,
on writs of error to the Supreme Court of Utah Territory</u>.

By George Ticknor Curtis. Washington: Printed for the
author by Gibson Bros., Printers and Booksellers, 1886.
64p.

Cover-title: Pleas for religious liberty and the
rights of conscience...

Second section (pp. 43-64) has title: Extracts from an
argument delivered in the Supreme Court of the United
States, April 28, 1886...

This argument was presented in regard to the In re Snow
case 120 U.S. Reports 274-287, 7 February 1887.

[Flake 2619]
CU-B, UHi, UPB

[765] A plea for religious liberty and the rights of conscience.
An argument delivered in the Supreme Court of the
United States, April 28, 1886, in three cases of
Lorenzo Snow, Plaintiff in Error, v. The United States,
on writs of error to the Supreme Court of Utah Territory.
Washington: Printed for the author by Gibson Brothers
Printers and Bookbinders, 1886. 80p.

"Plea for religious liberty" (title page) pp. 1-42.

"An argument delivered in the Supreme Court of the
United States," by Franklin S. Richards," pp. 43-80.

Cover-title: Pleas for religious liberty and the
rights of conscience. Arguments delivered in the
Supreme Court of the United States, April 28, 1886, in
three cases of Lorenzo Snow, Plaintiff in Error, v. The
United States on writ of error to the Supreme Court of
Utah Territory by George Ticknor Curtis and Franklin S.
Richards.

This appeal is in regard to the In re Snow case 120
U.S. Reports 274-287, 7 February 1887.

[Flake 2618]
CSmH, CtY, DLC, MH, NjP, NN, UHi, ULA, UPB

[766] "Polygamy and Affairs in Utah," Congressional Record 49th
Congress, 1st session (5 January, 6 January, 7 January
and 8 January 1886) vol. 17, pt. 1, pp. 405-408 457-
462, 503-520, 549-567. [X255]

Debates on disenfranchising women voters; confiscation
of L.D.S. Church property in excess of $50,000; antagonism
of government authorities and the Mormons; polygamy;
etc. Arguments relating to what eventually became the
Edmunds-Tucker act.

[767] "Report of the Utah Commission, 1886," pp. 1063-1066. In
Annual Report of the Department of the Interior, 1886,
vol. 2. Washington: Govt. Print. Off., 1886.
[I1.1:886/v.2]

Discusses a recommendation that a constitutional
amendment be passed which would prohibit polygamy and

silence the Mormon Church's claim that laws against
polygamy are unconstitutional. Summary of the commissions
report by Secretary of the Interior is in vol. I, pp.
70-71. [Serial Set 2467]

Variant ed. U.S. 49th Congress. 2nd session. House
Ex. Doc. No. 1, pt. 5, vol. II. [Serial Set 2468]

[768] Report of the Utah Commission to the Secretary of the
Interior. 1886. Washington: Govt. Print. Off., 1886.
6p.

See entry 767 for a description.

[Flake 9239]
CtY, ICN, NN, UHi, UPB

[769] Stevenson, Edward A. Biennial message of Edward A. Stevenson,
governor of Idaho to the Fourteenth session of the
Legislature of Idaho Territory. Boise City, 1886. 21p.

On pp. 20-21 Governor Stevenson refers to the Mormon
question. He is referring to the Idaho Mormons refusal
to obey the law of the land regarding polygamy and he
declares that theocracy is at war with free institutions.

[Flake add. 4180c]
UPB, UU

[769a] Stevenson, Edward A. Report of the Governor of Idaho to
the Secretary of the Interior, 1886. Washington:
Govt. Print. Off., 1886. 22p.

"The Mormon question" or polygamy should be abolished
on p. 18.

DLC, IdB, InU, MtU, NjP, Or, UPB

[770] "Switzerland," pp. 846-847. In Foreign Relations of the
United States, 1886. Washington: Govt. Print. Off.,
1887. [S1.1:886]

Two brief letters, by State Department officials,
express concern over issuing passports to Mormons to
proselyte in foreign countries. Their concern centers
on polygamy.

Pages 850-851 contain another letter referring back to
p. 847 and the problem of issuing passports to Mormons
suspected of being emissaries, especially as to emigration
and polygamy.

[771] To the Senate and House of Representatives in Congress
assembled: With profound respect we represent:...
[Washington? 1886?] 12p.

A printed letter with space for a signature, concerning
the Mormon problem and the Edmunds-Tucker bill.

[Flake 8966]
NjP, US1C

[772] U.S. House. Committee on the Judiciary. <u>Proposed legislation</u>
<u>for Utah: Arguments against the new Edmunds Bill,</u>
<u>being Senate Bill No. 10</u>... made by Hon. George S.
Boutwell, Hon. Jeff. Chandler, Hon. F. S. Richards, A.
M. Gibson, Hon. Joseph A. West, and Hon. John T. Caine,
before the Committee on the Judiciary of the U.S. House
of Representatives, First Session, Forty-ninth Congress.
Washington: Govt. Print. Off., 1886. 255p.

A very good compilation of some of the typical arguments
in defence of the Mormon Church and its religious
practices, especially polygamy.

[Flake 9130a]
UPB

[773] U.S. House. Committee on the Judiciary. <u>Proposed legislation</u>
<u>for Utah Territory</u>. [Washington, 1886] 282p.

An excellent compilation of various old arguments
regarding Utah from Mountain Meadows to polygamy.

[Flake 9130]
CU-B, MH, UPB, US1C

[774] U.S. House. 49th Congress. 1st Session. Committee on
Claims. <u>Richard H. Porter and James Porter</u>. (H.
Report. No. 2696) Washington: Govt. Print. Off.,
1886. 3p. [Serial Set 2443]

Compensation for cattle lost during the Utah Expedition.
[Flake add. 9110b]

[775] U.S. House. 49th Congress. 1st Session. Committee on the
Judiciary. <u>Bigamy...views of the minority</u>. (H. Rept.
No. 2735, Pt. 2) Washington: Govt. Print. Off., 1886.
7p. [Serial Set 2443]

To accompany S. Bill 10 which became the Edmunds-Tucker
Act, this document sets forth the opinion that "it is
puerile to insist that this little community could have
at any time seriously menaced our Republic." It is
signed by Representatives R. T. Bennett and Patrick A.
Collins of North Carolina and Massachusetts respectively.
[Flake 9122]

[776] U.S. House. 49th Congress. 1st Session. Committee on the
Judiciary. <u>Polygamy</u>. (H. Rept. No. 2568) Washington:
Govt. Print. Off., 1886. 12p. [Serial Set 2442]

Report to accompany H. Res. 176. Recommends caution in
altering a Constitution. Provides an excellent discussion
of polygamy, constitutionality, and religious freedom.
[Flake 9132]

[777] [Vacant]

[778] U.S. House. 49th Congress. 1st Session. Committee on the
Judiciary. <u>Suppression of polygamy in Utah....Report</u>.
(H. Rept. No. 2735) Washington: Govt. Print. Off.,
1886. 10p. [Serial Set 2443]

To accompany S. bill 10, Edmunds Tucker.

[Flake 9134]

[779] U.S. House. 49th Congress. 1st Session. H.R. 1478, "A bill to prevent certain persons from voting at election, or holding office in the Territories of the United States, January 5, 1886." [Washington: Govt. Print. Off., 1886] 2p.

Referred to the Committee on the Territories.

Restricts polygamists' vote.

DLC, UPB, US1C

[780] U.S. House. 49th Congress. 1st Session. H. Res. 140, "Joint resolution proposing an amendment to the Constitution of the United States prohibiting polygamy, March 16, 1886." [Washington: Govt. Print. Off., 1886] 2p.

Referred to the Committee on the Judiciary.

DLC, UPB, US1C

[781] U.S. House. 49th Congress. 1st Session. H. Res. 176, "Joint resolution for the amendment of the Constitution of the United States in regard to polygamy and polygamous association or cohabitation between the sexes, May 24, 1886." [Washington: Govt. Print. Off., 1886] 2p.

Referred to the Committee on the Judiciary.

DLC, UPB, US1C

[782] U.S. House. 49th Congress. 1st Session. H.R. 6153, "A bill to provide for the qualification of voters in the Territories of the United States, and for other purposes, March 1, 1886." [Washington: Govt. Print. Off., 1886] 5p.

Referred to the Committee on the Territories.

Prohibiting people counseling or giving them the right to vote, hold office, etc.

DLC, UPB, US1C

[783] U.S. House. 49th Congress. 1st Session. J. Res. 143, "Joint resolution proposing an amendment to the Constitution of the United States prohibiting polygamy, March 22, 1886." Washington: Govt. Print. Off., 1886. 2p.

That polygamy be forever prohibited in the United States.

DLC, UPB, US1C

[784] U.S. House. 49th Congress. 1st Session. Veto power in Utah. Memorial of the Legislative Assembly of Utah, setting forth the evils arising from the sweeping exercise of the absolute veto power of the governor.

(H. Misc. Doc. No. 238) Washington: Govt. Print.
Off., 1886. 20p. [Serial Set 2418]

Veto power exercised by the governor due to the political
and religious situation.

[Flake 9392]

[785] United States of America, respondent vs. Lorenzo Snow,
Appellant. Transcript on Appeal. F. S. Richards and
Bennett, Harkness & Kirkpatrick, Attorneys for Appellant.
Salt Lake City: Deseret News Co., 1886. 31p.

At head of title: Supreme court of Utah Territory.
January Term, 1886. No. 742.

This transcript was filed in the United States v.
Lorenzo Snow case Territory of Utah Reports 4 (January
1886) pp. 280-294.

[Flake 7239]
US1C

[786] United States of America, respondent, vs. Lorenzo Snow,
Appellant. Transcript. Indictment. [Salt Lake City,
1886?] 19p.

At head of title: Supreme Court of Utah Territory.
January Term, 1886.

Second of three indictments. This transcript was filed
in the United States v. Lorenzo Snow case Territory of
Utah Reports 4 (January 1886) pp. 280-294.

[Flake 8250]
US1C

[787] United States of America, respondent, vs. Lorenzo Snow,
Appellant. Transcript. Indictment. [Salt Lake City,
1886?] 36p.

At head of title: Supreme Court of Utah Territory.
January Term. 1886.

Third of three indictments. This transcript was filed
in the United States v. Lorenzo Snow case Territory of
Utah Reports 4 (January 1886) pp. 280-294.

[Flake 8251]
US1C

[788] United States of America, respondent vs. Lorenzo Snow,
Appellant. Transcript on Appeal. F. S. Richards and
Bennett, Harkness & Kirkpatrick, Attorneys for Appellant.
[Salt Lake City, 1886] No. 741. 19p.

Third of three indictments. This transcript was filed
in the United States v. Lorenzo Snow case Territory of
Utah Reports 4 (January 1886) pp. 280-294.

[Flake 7239]
US1C

[789] The United States, respondent, v. Barnard White, appellant.
Territory of Utah Reports 4 (January 1886) pp. 499-502.

Dealing with marriage of wife, Jane Fyfe White, to declare her incompetent in an unlawful cohabitation case.
CU-L, DLC, ICU, MH, MiU, UAr, UPB, UU, ViU-L

[790] The United States, respondent, v. Lorenzo Snow, appellant, Territory of Utah Reports 4 (January 1886) pp. 280-294.

Lorenzo Snow was held guilty of the offense of polygamy with his wives under the Edmunds Act. His wives were listed as Sarah, Harriet, Eleanor, Mary, Phoebe, Minnie, and Caroline, now deceased.
CU-L, DLC, ICU, MH, MiU, UAr, UPB, UU, ViU-L

[791] The United States, respondent, v. Lorenzo Snow, appellant. Territory of Utah Reports 4 (January 1886) pp. 295-312.

Three suits in 1883, 1884, 1885, were brought against Lorenzo Snow and were upheld. Discuses the family relationships of Lorenzo Snow and his wives, Adeline, Phebe, Mary, Harriet, Eleanor, and Minnie. Interesting family histories.
CU-L, DLC, ICU, MH, MiU, UAr, UPB, UU, ViU-L

[792] The United States, respondent, v. Lorenzo Snow, appellant. Territory of Utah Report 4 (January 1886) pp. 313-326.

History of anti-polygamy and legal justification for prosecution, particularly in the case of Lorenzo Snow.

CU-L, DLC, ICU, MH, MiU, UAr, UPB, UU, ViU-L

[793] The United States, respondent, v. Nicholas H. Groesbeck, appellant. Territory of Utah Reports 4 (January 1886) pp. 487-496.

A unlawful cohabition trial in which one of the jurors, Philip Grill, was challenged.
CU-L, DLC, ICU, MH, MiU, UAr, UPB, UU, ViU-L

[794] The United States, respondent, v. William H. Bromley, appellant. Territory of Utah Reports 4 (January 1886) p. 498.

Unlawful cohabition trial which had the same results as the earlier trial of United States v. Nicolas H. Groesbeck.
CU-L, DLC, ICU, MH, MiU, UAr, UPB, UU, ViU-L

[795] U.S. Senate. Committee on Education and Labor. Notes of a hearing before the Committee on Education and labor, United States Senate, May 7, 1886, on the proposed establishment of a school under the direction of the Industrial Christian Home Association of Utah. [Washington, 1886] 44p.

Caption-title: Industrial school in Utah.

Largely written by Angie F. Newman, as an advocate for Mormon women and children.

[Flake 9168]
CU, CU-B, NjP, ULA, UPB

[796] U.S. Senate. 49th Congress. 1st Session. Committee on Claims. In the Senate of the United States... Report: [To accompany bill S. 1368.] The Committee on Claims, to whom was referred the bill (S. 1368) for the relief of Richard H. Porter and James Porter, having had the same under consideration, beg respectfully to submit the following report. (S. Rept. No. 209) Washington: Govt. Print. Off., 1886. 3p. [Serial Set 2358]

Reimbursement for property lost during the Utah Expedition.

[797] U.S. Senate. 49th Congress. 1st Session. Committee on Education and Labor. Report: [To accompany amendment by Mr. Blair to the sundry civil appropriation bill] June 5, 1886. (S. Rept. No. 1279) Washington: Govt. Print. Off., 1886. 46p. [Serial Set 2361]

Appropriation in aid of the Industrial Christian Home Association of Utah, recommended with notes of hearing before committee, including material on the polygamy situation in Utah.

[Flake 9169]

[798] U.S. Senate. 49th Congress. 1st Session. Message from the President of the United States, recommending the immediate enactment of such legislation as will authorize the assembling of the Legislature of Utah Territory in special session to make the necessary appropriations for the expenses of that Territory. (S. Ex. Doc. No. 139) Washington: Govt. Print. Off., 1886. 2p. [Serial Set 2340]

Such legislation recommended in response to a memorial from the Utah Legislature protesting against the absolute veto power exercised by the governor. Although the central government was attempting to halt certain illegal practices (polygamy), this did not include the right to suspend the operation of local government and necessary services in the territory.

[Flake 9226]

[799] U.S. Senate. 49th Congress. 1st Session. S. 10, "An act to amend an act entitled 'An act to amend section fifty-three hundred and fifty-two of the Revised Statutes of the United States, in reference to bigamy, and for other purposes,' approved March twenty-second, Eighteen hundred and eighty-two, January 12, 1886." [Washington: Govt. Print. Off., 1886] 50p.

Referred to the Committee on the Judiciary and report with an amendment June 10, 1886. A very marked up and amended version from the S. 10 introduced by Mr. Edmunds in 1885. Starting with pp. 33-50 is the

Substitute for S. Bill No. 10, from the conference
committee.

DLC, UPB, USlC

[800] U.S. Senate. 49th Congress. 1st Session. S. 10, "Amendments
proposed by Mr. Morgan to the bill (S. 10) . . .
January 6, 1886." [Washington: Govt. Print. Off.,
1886] 1p.

Additional amendments to Mr. Edmunds S. 10 amending the
Edmunds Act.

DLC, UPB, USlC

[801] U.S. Senate. 49th Congress. 1st Session. S. 10, "Amendment
proposed by Mr. Blair to the bill (S. 10) . . . January
7, 1886." [Washington: Govt. Print. Off., 1886] 2p.

Additional amendments to Mr. Edmunds S. 10 amending the
Edmunds Act.

DLC, UPB, USlC

[802] U.S. Senate. 49th Congress. 1st Session. S. R. 68,
"Joint resolution for the amendment of the Constitution
of the United States in regard to polygamy, June 2,
1886." [Washington: Govt. Print. Off., 1886] 2p.

DLC, UPB, USlC

[803] U.S. Senate. 49th Congress. 1st Session. Woman suffrage
in Utah. (S. Misc. Doc. No. 122) Washington: Govt.
Print. Off., 1886. 9p. [Serial Set 2346]

Petition of Mrs. Angie F. Newman relative to woman
suffrage in Utah, with much information on Mormonism.

[Flake 5806]

[804] West, Caleb W. Report of the Governor of Utah to the
Secretary of the Interior. 1886. Washington: Govt.
Print. off., 1886. 17p.

"Polygamy in Legislation," p. 12.

[Flake 9372]
NjP, UHi, UPB, USlC

[805] West, Caleb W. "Report of the Governor of Utah to the
Secretary of the Interior, 1886," pp. 989-1003. In
Annual Report of the Dept. of the Interior, 1886, vol.
2. Washington: Govt. Print. Off., 1886. [I1.1:886]

Briefly treats polygamy and legislation and the Industrial
Home.

Variant ed. U.S. 49th Congress, 2d session. H. Ex.
Doc. 1, Serial Set 2468.

1887

**"It is true, however, that a large majority
of the people stoutly and stubbornly affirm
publicly and privately, that the enforcement**

of certain laws is destructive of their
rights as freemen, an assault upon their
religion, and an invasion of the sanctity of
their homes. The minority with equal vigor
and openness proclaim that the practices of
those people are immoral; that they are
disloyal to the Government, and that their
attitude of defiance to the laws interferes
with the advancement and prosperity of the
Territory, and inflicts injury upon all of
its interests."

[Entry 848]

"In the church government obedience is
extracted from every member. In removing
from one ward to another they must secure a
recommendation from their bishop, which
certifies to their standing in the church.
Persons desiring to be married, or to enter
into polygamy, must also secure a recommendation
from the bishop of their ward. Every member
must hold himself ready, irrespective of
personal considerations, to leave his home to
go as a missionary to other lands, and he
must also be ready to remove his family and
effects to such place as the heads of the
church may direct him to go. The Mormon
settlements in Arizona and other places
outside Utah, were made in obedience to such
a command."

[Entry 828]

---

[806] "An act to amend an act entitled 'An Act to amend section
fifty-three hundred and fifty-two of the Revised
Statutes of the United States, in reference to bigamy
and for other purposes'" (Chapter 397, March 3, 1887)
United States Statutes at Large 24, pp. 635-641.
[GS4.11:24, AE2.111:24, AE2.111:24]

The fourth major law designed to prohibit the practice
of polygamy, generally known as the Edmunds-Tucker Act.
Also known as "Mormon Control Act."

Variant ed. in Supplement to the Revised Statutes at
Large, 1874-1891, pp. 568-574.

[807] Bennett, Risden Tyler (N.C.) "Polygamy," Congressional
Record 49th Congress, 2d session (12 January 1887) vol.
18, pt. 3, Appendix, pp. 143-146. [X266]

Speech in opposition to the Edmunds-Tucker bill.

[808] Bennett, Risden Tyler. Speeches of Hon. Risden T. Bennett
of North Carolina, in the House of Representatives,
Wednesday, January 12, and Thursday, February 17, 1887,
against the Edmunds-Tucker Anti-Mormon bill. Washington,
1887. 18p.

See entry 823 and 825 for annotation.
[Flake 405]
CSmH, CU-B, NjP, UHi, ULA, UPB, US1C, UU

[809] Caine, John Thomas. The Mormon problem. Speech of Hon. John T. Caine, of Utah, in the House of Representatives, Wednesday, January 12, 1887, in opposition to the so-called Edmunds-Tucker anti-polygamy bill. Washington: [Govt. Print. Off.,] 1887. 31p.

See entry 823 for annotation.
[Flake 1078]
CSmH, CtY, CU-B, DLC, ICN, NN, UHi, ULA, UPB, US1C, UU

[810] Call, Wilkinson. On the amendment to the bill to suppress polygamy in Utah. Speech of Hon. Wilkinson Call, of Florida, in the Senate of the United States, February 18, 1887. Washington, 1887. 13p.

In opposition to the bill. See entry 825.
[Flake 1098]
UHi

[811] Constitution of the State of Utah and memorial to Congress asking admission into the Union. [Salt Lake City, 1887] 53p.

Signed: John T. Caine, President; Heber M. Wells, Secretary.

Ratification and memorial to Congress asking for admission as a state. Abstract of vote.
[Flake 9339]
CU, NjP, UHi, UPB, US1C

[812] "Election laws of Utah, March 22, 1887," p. 314. In Official opinions of the Attorneys-General of the United States. vol. XVII. Washington: Govt. Print. Off., 1890. [J1.5:17]

Benjamin Harris Brewster of the Dept. of Justice, on March 22, 1882, states that upon examination of the Edmunds act in relation to polygamy and election laws of Utah Territory, he entertains no doubt that those appointed to perform registration and election offices will have authority to administer all oaths.

[813] "Emigration from Switzerland," pp. 158-159. In Reports from the Consuls of the United States, Vol. XXII, No. 76. April-June 1887. Washington: Govt. Print. Off., 1887. [S4.7:22/No.76]

George C. Catlin, the Consul in Zurich, briefly mentions the problems of emigration from Switzerland relative to Mormon proselyting.

[813a] In re Rudger Clawson, Territory of Utah Reports 5 (June 1887) pp.358-360.

Rudger Clawson, in prison on two polygamy charges, is petitioning for discharge based on good conduct.

CU-L, DLC, ICU, MH, MiU, UAr, UPB, UU, ViU-L

[814] In re Snow. Appeal from the Third Judicial District Court, Salt Lake County, Utah, U.S. Reports, 120 (7 February 1887) pp. 274-287. [Ju6.8/1:120]

Decision upholding the fact that polygamy was a continuous offense and that the defendant could only be tried once.

[815] The Late Corporation of the Church of Jesus Christ of Latter-day Saints et al., appellants v. The United States, appellees. No. 1423. Appeal from Supreme Court of the Territory of Utah. [Washington? 1887] 11p.

At head of title: Supreme Court of the United States, October Term, 1888.

Signed: James O. Broadhead, Joseph E. McDonald, John M. Butler, Franklin S. Richards, Solicitors for the appellants.

This appeal was filed in the Case of the Late Corporation of the Church of Jesus Christ of Latter-day Saints v. The United States 136 U.S. Reports 1-68, May 19, 1890.
[Flake 867]
US1C

[816] McDonald, Joseph E. The United States vs. The Corporation of the Church of Jesus Christ of Latter-day Saints. Argument of Senator Joseph E. McDonald, delivered October 21, 1887. [Salt Lake City, 1887?]

Broadside.
[Flake add. 5142a]
UPB, US1C

[817] Minority report of the Utah Commission. Existing laws declared sufficient. No more legislation needed. Some facts ignored by the majority report. [Salt Lake City?] 1887. 18p.

Cover title. With passage of the Edmunds-Tucker Act, no future legislation deemed necessary.
[Flake 9236]
CU-B, DLC, MH, NjP, NN, UPB, US1C, UU

[818] "The perpetual emigrating fund company and the Church of Jesus Christ of Latter-day Saints," p. xvii. In Annual report of the Attorney-General of the United States for the year 1887. Washington: Govt. Print. Off., 1887. [J1.1:887]

Litigation of Mormon church property as well as the Perpetual Emigrating Fund.

[818a] "Persons excluded from holding land, etc," <u>Congressional
Record</u> 49th Congress, 2d session (10 January 1887),
vol. 18, pt. 1, p. 502. [X264]

John Hailey, delegate from Idaho, introduced H.R. 10641
to prevent certain persons from voting or holding land
in the territories which was referred to the Committee
on the Territories. Text of the law is not included in
the entry. See entry 833 for the bill.

[819] "Petitions," <u>Congressional Record</u> 50th Congress, 1st
session (8, 12, 13, 16, 19, 20, 22 December 1887, 4, 5,
9, 10, 11, 12, 16, 17, 18, 19, 20, 23, 24, 25, 26, 27,
30, 31 January 1888, 1, 2, 4, 6, 7 February 1888) vol.
19, pt. 1, pp. 15, 17, 18, 42, 43, 52, 83, 84, 85, 86,
111, 114, 124, 182, 183, 184, 251, 253, 256, 283, 284,
286, 287, 334, 335, 338, 339, 367, 398, 433, 470, 471,
501, 532, 533, 564, 584, 608, 643, 644, 645, 688, 689,
724, 726, 765, 766, 781, 784, 822, 823, 855, 857, 925,
926, 961, 964, 1003, 1004, 1005. [X268]

Numerous petitions, not printed in full and many more
than it would appear from the dates and pages, all
remonstrating against the admission of Utah as a state.
Most of these petitions centered around polygamy as an
issue, but a few also mentioned their concern for the
territory as long as it was under the control of the
Mormon Church. Pennsylvania seemed to be especially
strong against the admission of Utah.

[820] "Petitions of Grand Army Posts relative to Polygamy,"
<u>Congressional Record</u> 49th Congress, 2d session (5, 6,
7, 15, 17, 20, 21, 22, 24, 25 January 1887) vol. 18,
pt. 1, pp. 350, 385, 386, 420, 709, 745, 824, 825, 870,
909, 925, 926, 968, 970, 971. [X264]

Petitions, not printed in full, for passage of the
Edmunds-Tucker bill.

[821] "Petitions of Grand Army Posts relative to Polygamy,"
<u>Congressional Record</u> 49th Congress, 2d session (25, 26,
27, 28, 29, 31 January 1, 2, 3, 4, 5, 7, 8, 9, 10, 11,
12, 14, 16, 17, 18 February 1887) vol. 18, pt. 2, pp.
1029, 1030, 1062, 1118, 1119, 1120, 1141, 1172, 1173,
1175, 1218, 1219, 1220, 1265, 1304, 1305, 1333, 1391,
1425, 1469, 1470, 1471, 1532, 1563, 1564, 1601, 1656,
1657, 1701, 1755, 1756, 1802, 1852, 1854, 1892, 1939.
[X265]

Petitions, not printed in full, for passage of the
Edmunds-Tucker bill.

[822] "Petitions of Grand Army Posts relative to Polygamy,"
<u>Congressional Record</u> 49th Congress, 2d session (22
February, 3 March 1887) vol. 18, pt. 3, pp. 2098, 2099,
2756. [X266]

Petitions, not printed in full, for passage of the
Edmunds-Tucker bill.

[823] "Polygamy," <u>Congressional Record</u> 49th Congress, 2nd session (12 January 1887) vol. 18, pt. 1, pp. 581-596. [X264]

Beginning debate on the Edmunds-Tucker bill, together with speeches by John T. Caine, Pomeroy Tucker and others both pro and con. Confiscation of Church property emphasized.

[824] "Polygamy," <u>Congressional record</u> 49th Congress, 2d session (15 February 1887) vol. 18, pt. 1, pp. 1785-1887. [X264]

Continued debate on the Edmunds-Tucker bill.

[825] "Polygamy and affairs in Utah," <u>Congressional Record</u> 49th Congress, 2d session (17, 18 February 1887) vol. 18, pt. 2, pp. 1855, 1877-1883, 1896-1904. [X265]

The Edmunds-Tucker bill, from the conference committee was read, discussed, and voted upon.

[826] Reed, Thomas Brackett. <u>Foundation of the right of Congress to deal with the Mormon question. Remarks of Thomas B. Reed, of Maine, on the Edmunds bill, in the House of Representatives, Wednesday, January 12, 1887.</u> [Washington, 1887] 4p.

Remarks on S. 10 (Edmunds-Tucker) in support of the bill. Throwing Thomas Caine's words back in his face, Reed feels that the Mormons went to Utah as a "government" and that is the problem. It isn't an assault on a religion, but on a people who took control of a territory which belonged to the U.S. Polygamy is only one of the problems. See entry 823.

[Flake 6836]
UHi

[827] "Report of the Utah Commission, 1887," pp. 1317-1357. In <u>Annual Report of the Department of the Interior, 1887</u>, vol. 2. Washintgon: Govt. Print. Off., 1887. [I1.1:887/v.2]

This report includes a majority and a minority report from the Commission. Various issues of Mormon doctrine and practices are discussed, including polygamy and the minority report discusses the requirement of the various anti-polygamy laws, voter's oaths and enforcement of voting laws. No summary.

Variant ed. U.S. 50th Congress, 1st session, House Exec. Doc. No. 1, pt. 5, vol. I, Serial Set 2542.

[828] <u>Report of the Utah Commission to the Secretary of the Interior. 1887.</u> Washington: Govt. Print. Off., 1887. 44p.

See entry 827 for annotation.

[Flake 9239]
CtY, CU-B, ICN, MH, NN, UHi, UPB, USlC

[829] <u>Report of the Utah Commission to the Secretary of the</u>
<u>Interior, for the year 1887</u>. Salt Lake City: Tribune
Print, 1887. 71p.

See entry 827 for annotation.

[Flake 9239]
UPB

[830] Scott, William Lawrence. <u>Anti-polygamy bill</u>. Mr. Scott's
<u>proposed amendment to the Edmunds-Tucker anti-polygamy</u>
<u>bill (Sen. 10)</u> [n.p., 1887?]

Broadside.

[Flake 7597]
NjP, UPB, USlC

[830a] Stevenson, Edward A. <u>Report of the Governor of Idaho to</u>
<u>the Secretary of the Interior, 1887</u>. Washington:
Govt. Print Off., 1887. 53p.

Concerned over schools of southern Idaho being controlled
by the Mormon priesthood, and mentions test oath, pp.
32-3.

DLC, IdB, InU, MtU, NjP, Or, UPB

[831] Tucker, John Randolph. <u>Polygamy</u>. <u>Speech of Hon. John</u>
<u>Randolph Tucker of Virginia, in the House of Representatives.</u>
<u>Wednesday, January 12, 1887</u>. Washington: Franklin
Printing House, 1887. 12p.

See entry 823 for annotation.

[Flake 9035]
CSmH, CU-B, USlC, UU

[832] U.S. House. 49th Congress. 2d Session. <u>Emigration and</u>
<u>immigration</u>. <u>Reports of the consular officers of the</u>
<u>United States</u>. (H. Ex. Doc. No. 157) Washington:
Govt. Print. Off., 1887. 748p. [Serial Set 2483]

Pages 387-389 provides the report of Consul Russell
from Liverpool. The agent writes glowingly about the
clean, orderly, respectable and industrious lot of
people called the Mormons. Page 620, which is part of
Consul General Porch's report from Mexico, contains a
brief paragraph about the Mormon colony of Juarez.

[833] U.S. House. 49th Congress. 2d Session. H.R. 10641, "A
bill to prevent persons voting or holding land in the
Territories, and for other purposes, January 10, 1887."
[Washington: Govt. Print. Off., 1887] 3p.

Referred to the Committee on the Territories.

Prohibits polygamists to own land or to vote.

DLC, UPB, USlC

[834] The United States of America, plaintiff vs. Horace S. Eldredge and Francis Armstrong, defendants, No. 6,600. Transcript of record. Appeal from the Third District Court. F. S. Richards, LeGrand Young, Sheeks & Rawlins, Attorneys for appellants. Dickson & Varian, Attorneys for Respondent. [Salt Lake City?] Parker, Printer [1887] 28p.

At head of title: In the Supreme Court of Utah Territory, January term 1887. Appeal in the United States, respondent, vs. Horace S. Eldredge Territory of Utah 5 (January 1887).

See entries 837 and 838.

[Flake add. 3128a]
US1C

[835] United States of America vs. The late Corporation of the Church of Jesus Christ of Latter-day Saints, et al. Brief of W. H. Dickson, of Counsel for defendants. [Salt Lake City]: Star Print, [1887?] 28p.

Concerning the dissolution of property ownership during the polygamy period.

[Flake 2836]
UHi, US1C, UU

[836] United States, respondent, v. George T. Peay, appellant, Territory of Utah Reports 5 (June 1887) pp. 263-271.

The polygamy case of George T. Peay of Provo and his wives Hannah Paasch, Mary Sorenson, as well as his first wife who appears to be unnamed.

CU-L, DLC, ICU, MH, MiU, UAr, UPB, UU, ViU-L

[837] United States, respondent, v. Horace S. Eldredge, and another, appellant, Territory of Utah Reports 5 (January 1887) pp. 161-176.

Unlawful cohabitation case of George Q. Cannon regarding his wives Sarah Jane Cannon, Martha Tolly Cannon, Eliza T. Cannon, and Emily Little between the first of April 1882 and first day of January 1885.

CU-L, DLC, ICU, MH, MiU, UAr, UPB, UU, ViU-L

[838] United States, respondent, v. Horace S. Eldredge and another, appellants, Territory of Utah Reports 5 (June 1887) pp. 189-196.

Unlawful cohabitation, probably referring back to the January 1887 term case of the same name.

CU-L, DLC, ICU, MH, MiU, UAr, UPB, UU, ViU-L

[839] United States, respondent, v. James Smith, appellant, Territory of Utah Reports 5 (June 1887) pp. 232-237.

The polygamy case of James Smith and his wives Sarah Jane, and Christina.

CU-L, DLC, ICU, MH, MiU, UAr, UPB, UU, ViU-L

[840] United States, respondent, v. Joseph Clark, appellant, Territory of Utah Reports 5 (June 1887) pp. 226-232.

Polygamy case of Joseph Clark and his wives, Sarah, Hannah S., and Frances Carter Clark.

CU-L, DLC, ICU, MH, MiU, UAr, UPB, UU, ViU-L

[841] United States, respondent, v. William E. Bassett, appellant, Territory of Utah Reports 5 (January 1887) pp. 131-139.

The Andrew Larsen polygamy case regarding his wives Kate Smith, and Sarah Ann Bassett and use of the wife as a competent witness, as well as the admissability of the defendant's testimony.

CU-L, DLC, ICU, MH, MiU, UAr, UPB, UU, ViU-L

[842] U.S. Senate. 50th Congress. 1st Session. S.R. 3, "Joint Resolution for the amendment of the Constitution of the United States in regard to bigamy and polygamy, December 12, 1887." [Washington: Govt. Print. Off., 1887] 2p.

Referred to the Committee on the Judiciary.

DLC, UPB, US1C

[843] U.S. Senate. 50th Congress. 1st Session. S. R. 2, "Joint resolution proposing an amendment to the Constitution of the United States empowering Congress to legislate upon the subjects of marriage and divorce, and prohibiting bigamy and polygamy, December 12, 1887." [Washington: Govt. Print. Off., 1887] 1p.

Introduced before the effects of the Edmunds-Tucker law was known.

DLC, UPB, US1C

[844] The United States vs. The Corporation of the Church of Jesus Christ of Latter-day Saints. Argument of Hon. James O. Broadhead delivered October 21, 1887. [Salt Lake City? 1887?] 11p.

At head of title: Supreme Court of Utah.

Brief filed in the United States v. The Late Corporation of the Church of Jesus Christ of Latter-day Saints and other appellants, Territory of Utah Reports 8 (June 1892) pp. 310-352.

[Flake add. 870a]
UPB, US1C

[845] "Utah," pp. 148-150. In Report of the Commissioner of Education for the year 1887-88. Washington: Govt. Print. Off., 1889. [FS5.1:887-888, HE5.1:887-888]

Forty percent of Mormon children attended the district schools in Utah, and there has been great interest in the establishment of private Mormon schools.

[846] "Utah Territory, March 31, 1887," pp. 595-597. In Official Opinions of the Attorneys-General of the United States... vol. XVIII, Washington: Govt. Print. Off., 1890. [J1.5:18]

Opinion requested by Utah Commission and the Governor regarding whether officers in the territory are required to take the oath prescribed in the 24th section of the Edmunds-Tucker Act.

[847] Vest, George Graham. Undemocratic-unAmerican-unconstitutional. Speeches of Hon. George G. Vest, of Missouri, and Hon. Wilkinson Call, of Florida, in the United States Senate, Friday, February 18, 1887, against the anti-Mormon bill. Washington, 1887. 18p.

See entry 825 for annotation.

[Flake 9469]
CSmH, MH, UHi, US1C, UU

[848] West, Caleb W. Report of the Governor of Utah to the Secretary of the Interior. 1887. Washington: Govt. Print. Off., 1887. 40p.

Statehood issue as it relates to the Mormon problem.

[Flake 9373]
UPB, US1

[849] West, Caleb W. "Report of the Governor of Utah to the Secretary of the Interior, 1887," pp. 889-926. In Annual Report of the Department of the Interior, 1887, vol. 1. Washington: Govt. Print. Off., 1887. [I1.1:887]

Deals with Mormon-Gentile relations, political problems based on Mormon Church majority and control, polygamy and the Kingdom of God on Earth.

Variant ed. U.S. 50th Congress, 1st session. H. Ex. Doc. No. 1, vol. 10, Serial Set 2541.

1888

"The Industrial Christian Home Association, incorporated under the laws of the Territory, composed of charitable and Christian women and men of high character, conceived the idea of the establishment of an industrial home here as an aid to the suppression of polygamy and as an instrument to ameliorate the sufferings incidental to a growing out of it."

[Entry 916]

[850] "An act making appropriations to supply deficiencies in the
appropriations for the fiscal year ending June thirtieth,
eighteen hundred and eighty-eight, and for other
purposes" (Chapter 1210, October 19, 1888) United
States Statutes at Large 25, pp. 565-607. [GS4.111:25,
AE2.111:25]

On pp. 584-5 in this large act, the funding for the
Industrial Christian Home in Utah Territory is listed.
The group of people that are eligible to use this home
are discussed. These include: (1) first or legal
wives; (2) women or girls in polygamous surroundings
who might succumb to polygamy; (3) girls from polygamous
parentage who wish to escape from it; and (4) women or
girls who were proselyted from outside Utah Territory
in ignorance of the existence of polygamy.

[851] Baskin, Robert Newton. Argument against the admission of
Utah. And the recent message of Governor West to the
Utah legislature. Washington: Judd & Detweiler, 1888.
22p.

Caption-title: Utah statehood.

The author was chief justice of the Supreme Court of
Utah. Theocratic nature of Mormon church is as great,
or a greater, evil than polygamy.
[Flake 328]
ICN, MH, NN, US1, US1C

[852] Caine, John Thomas (Utah). "Industrial Christian Home."
Congressional Record 50th Congress, 1st session (4
October 1888) vol. 19, pt. 10, Appendix, pp. 583-591.
[X277]

Caine expostulates that this "magnificent charity"
proposed to come to the Territory of Utah for the
Industrial Christian Home, for the benefit of women and
children of Utah's polygamous families, is a monstrous
thing attacking freedom of religion.

[853] Caine, John Thomas. Mormon facts vs. anti-Mormon fictions.
Speech of Hon. John T. Caine, of Utah, in the House of
Representatives, Thursday, October 4, 1888, on aid to
Industrial Christian Home of Utah. Washington, 1888.
30p.

See entry 852 for annotation.
[Flake 1077]
UPB, US1C

[854] Caine, John Thomas. Polygamy in Utah - a dead issue.
Speech of Hon. J. T. Caine of Utah in the House of
Representatives, August 25, 1888. Washington, 1888.
16p.

See entry 882 for annotation.
[Flake 1079]
CU-B, DLC, ICN, MH, UHi, UPB, US1, US1C, UU

[855] Cleveland, Grover. "Fourth Annual Message, December 3, 1888," p. 5379. In A Compilation of the Messages and Papers of the Presidents, by James D. Richardson, Vol. 7. New York: Bureau of National Literature, 1911, c. 1897. [GS4.113:7, AE2.114:1-27/v.7]

Polygamy convictions are cited and the suits by the government for the termination of the Perpetual Emigrating Fund Company and the Church of Jesus Christ of Latter-day Saints are both mentioned as decreed in favor of the government.

[856] Cleveland, Grover. Message of the President of the United States communicated to the two Houses of Congress at the beginning of the Second Session of the Fiftieth Congress. Washington: Govt. Print. Off., 1888. 32p.

Mormons, p. 25.

US1C

[856a] Ex Parte: In the matter of Hans Nielsen, appellant. Argument of Franklin S. Richards. For the appellant. Delivered April 22, 1889. [Salt Lake City] The Deseret News Co., Printers and Publishers, 1889. 23p.

At head of title: Supreme Court of the United States, October Term, 1888. No. 1527.

Argument for the appellant in the Hans Nielsen 131 U. S. Reports 176-191, October 1888.

[Flake add. 7231a]
DLC, UPB, US1C

[857] Ex Parte: In the matter of Hans Nielsen, appellant, No. 1527. Appeal from the First Judicial District Court of the Territory of Utah. Brief for Respondent. Supreme Court of the United States, October Term, 1888. [n.p., 1888?] 9p.

Brief for the respondent in the case of Hans Nielsen 131 U.S. Reports 176-191, October 1888.

DLC, UPB, US1C

[858] Ex Parte: in the matter of Hans Nielsen, appellant. Appeal from the first Judicial District court of the Territory of Utah. Transcipt of Record. Supreme court of the United States, October term, 1888 No. 1527. [Washington: Judd & Detweiler, Printers, 1889] 12p.

This appeal relates to the case of Hans Nielsen 131 U.S. Reports (October 1888) 176-191, filed March 24, 1889.

[Flake add. 584a]
DLC, UPB, US1C

[859] Ex Parte: In the matter of Hans Nielsen, appellant. Brief for Appellant. [Attorneys] for appellant Jeremiah M. Wilson, Franklin S. Richards, Samuel Shellabarger. Supreme Court of the United States, October Term, 1888.

No. 1527. Washington: Gibson Bros, Printers and
Bookbinders, 1889. 45p.

Brief for the appellant in the Hans Nielsen case 131
U.S. Reports 176-191, October 1888 session.

[Flake 9924]
CU-B, DLC, UPB, US1C

[860] Hale, Eugene. Polygamy. The work of the Industrial
Christian Home Association of Utah Territory. Speech
of Hon. Eugene Hale... in the Senate of the United
States, October 2, 1888. Washington, 1888. 16p.

See entry 864 for annotation.

[Flake 3785]
CtY, MH, NjP

[861] Hans Nielsen, petitioner, U.S. Reports 131 (October 1888
session) pp. 176-191. [Ju6.8/1:131]

The polygamy case on appeal from the First Judicial
District Court of the Territory of Utah of Hans Nielsen
and his wives Anna Lavinia Nielsen and Caroline Nielsen.
His petition was decided on May 13, 1889.

[862] "Idaho," p. 709. In Report of the Commissioner of Education
for the year 1888-89, vol. II. WAshington: Govt.
Print. Off., 1891. [FS5.1:888-889]

Question arose recently whether Mormons were legally
qualified to be public school teachers in Idaho.

[863] In Equity. The United States of America, plaintiff vs. The
Perpetual Emigrating Fund Company, Albert Carrington
[etc.] [Salt Lake City, 1888?] 2p.

Signed: James O. Broadhead, J. E. McDonald, Franklin
S. Richards, LeGrand Young.

Litigation caused by the Edmunds-Tucker Act.

[Flake 865]
US1C

[864] "Industrial Christian Home" Congressional Record 50th
Congress, 1st session, (2 October 1888) vol. 19, Pt. 9,
pp. 9089-9097. [X276]

Mr. Hale mentions the women of the National Home
Missionary Society who have been concerned about the
women of Utah, who wanted to leave polygamy, but who
could not because of poverty. A number of insertions
are made in the record.

[865] Innis v. Bolton, et al. Idaho Reports 2 (6 March 1888) 407-
417.

Refers and reprints the 1885 "Test Oath Statute"
Section 16, 13th Sess. Laws 106 which refers to the

oath of not being a polygamist. This case tested the
constitutional law of that test oath.

DLC, UPB, US1C

[866] "Judicial Proceedings in Utah," Congressional Record 50th
Congress, 2d session (10 December 1888) vol. 20, pt. 1,
pp. 106-107, 271. [X279]

Provides a brief insight into the escheating of the
property of the Mormon Church to the Marshall of the
Territory as the receiver of this property. Mr.
Edmunds provides the commentary.

[867] The Late Corporation of the Church of Jesus Christ of
Latter-day Saints, et al. appellants, v. The United
States, appellees. Motion to advance cause. [Attorneys]
James O. Broadhead, Joseph E. McDonald, John M. Butler,
Franklin S. Richards, for appellants. Supreme Court of
the United States. October term, 1888. No. 1423.
Washington: Gibson Bros., 1888. 11p.

Motion to advance cause. The late Corporation of the
Church of Jesus Christ of Latter-day Saints v. The
United States. 136 U.S. Reports (May 19, 1890) 1-68.

[Flake add. 867a]
DLC, UPB, US1C

[868] The Late Corporation of the Church of Jesus Christ of
Latter-day Saints and others, Appellants, vs. The
United States. No. 1423. Brief for the United States.
[Washington, 1888?] 73p.

At head of title: In the Supreme Court of the United
States. October Term, 1888.

Signed: A. H. Garland, Attorney-General, G. A. Jenks,
Solicitor-General.

This brief was filed in The Late Corporation of the
Church of Jesus Christ of Latter-day Saints v. The
United States 136 U.S. Reports 1-68, May 19, 1890.

[Flake 9098]
DLC, UPB, ULA, US1C

[869] The Late Corporation of the Church of Jesus Christ of
Latter-day Saints, et al., appellants vs. The United
States No. 1423. Brief of Joseph McDonald and John M.
Butler in behalf of Appellants. By James M. Butler.
Indianapolis: Frank H. Smith, 1888. 109p.

At head of title: Supreme Court of the United States,
October Term, 1888.

This brief was filed in The Late Corporation of the
Church of Jesus Christ of Latter-day Saints v. The
United States 136 U.S. Reports 1-68, May 19, 1890.

[Flake 1050]
DLC, UPB

[870] The Late Corporation of the Church of Jesus Christ of
       Latter-day Saints, et. al., appellants, v. The United
       States. No. 1423. George Romney, Henry Dinwoody,
       James Watson and John Clark, appellants v. The United
       States. No. 1457. Appeals from the Supreme Court of
       Utah Territory. Brief and argument for appellants.
       [Washington: Gibson Bros., Printers and Bookbinders,
       1889] 120p.

       At head of title: In the Supreme Court of the United
       States. October Term, 1888.

       This brief was filed in The Late Corporation of the
       Church of Jesus Christ of Latter-day Saints v. The
       United States 136 U.S. Reports 1-68, May 19, 1890.

                                                [Flake 868]
              CSmH, Cty, CU-B, ICN, MH, NjP, NN, UHi, UPB, US1C, UU

[871] Montgomery, Marcus Whitman. Admission of Utah: Statement
       of Rev. M. W. Montgomery, before the Committee on
       Territories, United States Senate, Monday, March 26,
       1888. [Washington, 1888] pp. 163-177.

       Rev. Montgomery, a representative of the American Home
       Missionary Society, gives testimony, based on a 3 week
       visit to Utah. His testimony relates to the practice
       of polygamy since the passage of the Edmunds Act, and
       he states that the Gentiles claim that prostitution in
       Salt Lake makes it one of the worst cities. Reiterates
       the claim that the Mormon Church is a theocracy and a
       hierarchy. "The trouble is we have dealt with Mormonism
       as a religion when we ought to have been dealing with
       it as a crime." Wants to remove civil power from the
       Mormon Church.

                                               [Flake 5453]
                                                   CtY, US1C

[872] Mormon legislation against polygamy. [Salt Lake City,
       1888] 4p.

       From the Utah Territorial Legislature. Signed: W. W.
       Riter, Speaker of the House of Representatives. Elias
       A. Smith, President of the Council. Caleb W. West,
       Governor of Utah Territory. Approved March 8th, 1888.

                                               [Flake 9391]
                                         CU-B, MH, UPB, US1C

[873] "Mormons", pp. 575-576. In Reports from the Consuls of the
       United States, vol. 23, No. 97, September 1888.
       Washington: Govt. Print. Off., 1888. [S4.7:23/No.97]

       Concern of the U.S. Consul, Warner P. Sutton, that a
       mass exodus of Mormons from Utah to Mexico are again
       contemplated. An article from Mexican Financier, is
       included, and expresses this concern. Henry Eyring
       responded with a letter to the editor of the Mexican
       Financier stating the church's position not to send
       more members to Mexico.

[874] "Pardons in Utah and Idaho," <u>Congressional Record</u> 50th
        Congress, 1st session (13 August 1888) vol. 19, pt. 8,
        p. 7494. [X275]

   Mr. Dubois of Idaho presented a resolution that the
   Attorney-General be requested to furnish a list of
   pardons granted by the President to persons convicted
   of polygamy.

[875] "The Perpetual Emigrating Fund Company and the Church of
        Jesus Christ of Latter-day Saints," p. xvi. In <u>Annual</u>
        <u>report of the Attorney-general of the United States for</u>
        <u>the year 1888</u>. Washington: Govt. Print. Off., 1888.
        [J1.1:888]

   Prosecution against Mormon church property.

[876] "Petition," <u>Congressional Record</u> 50th Congress, 1st session
        (2 June 1888) vol. 19, pt. 5, p. 4871. [X272]

   Petition, not printed in full, from citizens of Pennsylvania
   against admission of Utah as a state as long as Mormonism
   is in the Territory.

[877] "Petition," <u>Congressional Record</u> 50th Congress, 1st session
        (5 September 1888) vol. 19, pt. 9, p. 8320. [X276]

   Petition, not printed in full, from citizens of Pennsylvania
   against admission of Utah as a state with polygamy.

   "Petitions," <u>Congressional Record</u>, 1888, **see entry 819.**

[878] Petitions," <u>Congressional Record</u> 50th Congress, 1st session
        (7, 9, 13, 23, 27, 28, 29 February, 1, 6, 8, 10, 12
        March 1888) vol. 19, pt. 2, pp. 1038, 1068, 1112, 1170,
        1430, 1488, 1576, 1615, 1616, 1764, 1844, 1937, 1939,
        1940, 1991. [X269]

   Petitions, only the one on p. 1844 is printed in full,
   which are remonstrating against the admission of Utah
   as a state, primarily because of polygamy, and mention
   is also made of the Mormon priesthood.

[879] "Petitions," <u>Congressional Record</u> 50th Congress, 1st
        session (15, 17, 19, 27 March 1888, 4, 10 April 1888)
        vol. 19, pt. 3, pp. 2088, 2089, 2133, 2199, 2241, 2426,
        2464, 2725, 2871. [X270]

   Petitions, none printed in full, remonstrating against
   the admission of Utah as a state, primarily because of
   polygamy.

[880] "Petitions," <u>Congressional Record</u> 50th Congress, 1st
        session (17 April, 5 May 1888) vol. 19, pt. 4, pp.
        3030, 3767. [X271]

   Petitions, not printed, remonstrating against the
   admission of Utah as a state, primarily because of
   polygamy.

[881] "Petitions," <u>Congressional Record</u> 50th Congress, 1 session
(20, 21, <u>26</u>, 29 June 1888) vol. 19, pt. 6, pp. 5452,
5478, 5608, 5775. [X273]

Petitions, not printed in full, from citizens of
Pennsylvania against admission of Utah as a state as
long as Mormons are in control of the civil government
and as long as polygamy is practiced.

[882] "Polygamy laws," <u>Congressional Record</u> 50th Congress, 1st
session (25 August 1888) vol. 19, pt. 8, pp. 7949-7953.
[X275]

Debate regarding a resolution requiring the Attorney-
General to supply the number of convictions for polygamy
in the Territories of Idaho and Utah. Mr. DuBois of
Idaho welcomes the expansion from the original resolution
because he believes that the numbers involved in
polygamy are at least one-half. Interesting discussion
on incidence of polygamy.

[883] "Religious instruction," pp. 123-24. In <u>Fifty-seventh</u>
<u>annual report of the Commissioner of Indian Affairs,</u>
<u>December 3, 1888</u>. Washington: Govt. Print. Off.,
1888. [I20.1:888]

Brief mention of Mormon proselyting among the Five
Civilized Tribes in Oklahoma.

[884] "Religious Instruction in Public Schools," p. 437. In
<u>Report of the Commissioner of Education for the year</u>
<u>1888-89</u>, vol. I. Washington: Govt. Print. Off., 1891.
[FS5.1:888-889, HE5.1:888-889]

Brief paragraph from the Utah State Commissioner of
Schools which mentions the common practice, until
recently, of conducting public schools as Mormon Church
schools.

[885] "Report of the Utah Commission, 1888," pp. 661-675. In
<u>Annual Report of the Department of the Interior, 1888</u>,
vol. 3. Washington: Govt. Print. Off., 1888.
[I1.1:888/v.3]

Once again there is a majority and a minority report.
The majority report consists of a discussion of parochial
schools in Utah and Mormons' feelings about the purpose
of public schools. The status of polygamy takes up the
majority of the report. The minority report indicates
their feelings that polygamy was on the decline.
Summary of the commission's report by the Secretary of
the Interior is in vol. I, p. CXXXII. [Serial Set 2636]

Variant ed. U.S. 50th Congress, 2nd session, House Ex.
Doc. No. 1, pt. 5, vol. III, Serial Set 2638.

[886] <u>Report of the Utah Commission to the Secretary of the</u>
<u>Interior, 1888</u>. Washington: Govt. Print. Off., 1888.
26p.

See entry 885 for annotation.

[Flake 9239]
CtY, NN, UHi, UPB, USlC

[887] Richards, Franklin Snyder. The admission of Utah. Replies
of Hon. F. S. Richards to statements in opposition to
the admission of Utah as a state, made before the
Committee on Territories of the United States Senate,
Saturday, March 10, 1888. Washington: Gibson Brothers,
Printers and Bookbinders, 1888. 16p.

Reply to F. T. Dubois and R. N. Baskin. In his refutation,
Richards gives a detailed discussion of polygamy,
including its incidence in numbers.

[Flake 7230]
NjP, UHi, UPB, USlC, UU

[888] Stevenson, Edward A. Biennial message of Edward A. Stevenson,
governor of Idaho, to the Fifteenth session of the
Legislature of Idaho Territory, 1888-89. [n.p., 1888?]
32p.

On p. 17, Governor Stevenson again refers to the Mormon
question, by which he means the practice of polygamy
against the government of the United States. This
practice is abhorrent to him and certainly goes against
the principles of a free republic. He declares Mormonism
to be a theocracy.

[Flake add. 4180d]
UPB, UU

[889] Struble, Isaac S. (Iowa). "Aid to the Industrial Christian
Home Association of Utah," Congressional Record 50th
Congress, 1st session (4 October 1888) vol. 19, pt. 10,
Appendix, pp. 555-564. [X277]

Supports the legislation for the Industrial Christian
Home, and he includes many insertions from Utah women
which support the need for a home to break up polygamous
marriages and families.

[890] "Switzerland," pp. 1500-1507. In Foreign Relations of the
United States, 1888. Washington: Govt. Print. Off.,
1889. [S1.1:888]

Mormon activity in Berne, Switzerland, with a memorial
from the director of police concerning measures to be
taken against the sect of Mormons.

An interesting brief history of Mormons in 7 Swiss
communities is given along with the members personal
desires to emigrate. A number of members are named.

[891] "Switzerland," pp. 1532-1533, 1534. In Foreign Relations
of the United States, 1888. Washington: Govt. Print.
Off., 1889. [S1.1:888]

Ways to discourage Mormon activities in Switzerland,
particularly emigration to the United States.

[892] "Teachers," pp. 108-109. In Report of the Commissioner of Education, August 31, 1888. Washington: Govt. Print. Off., 1889. [FS5.1:888, HE5.1:888]

Demand in Idaho that Mormon children be taught by Mormons.

Variant ed. U.S. 50th Cong., 2d sess., H. Ex. Doc. 1, pt. 5, Serial Set 2640.

[893] "Territory of Utah," Congressional Record 50th Congress, 1st Session (26 March 1888) vol. 19, pt. 3, p. 2391. [X270]

Statehood should not be granted until it is proven that polygamy no longer is practiced.

[894] "Turkey," p. 1547-1549. In Foreign Relations of the United States, 1888. Washington: Govt. Print. Off., 1889. [S1.1:888]

An attempt to seize certain copies of The Book of Mormon. A book or pamphlet [probably An Invitation to the City of God, as no copy has survived] on Mormonism is in the possession of a Mr. Handji or Hintze, an American citizen.

[895] United States, complainant, v. Church of Jesus Christ of Latter-day Saints and others, respondents, Territory of Utah Reports 5 (January 1888) pp. 361-381.

Case against the Mormon Church based upon the Morrill Act of 1862, whereby the Church was not to hold property in excess of $50,000. The motion to appoint a receiver for this property in excess of the stipulated amount, and which was not used for burial ground or places of worship, was granted.

CU-L, DLC, ICU, MH, MiU, UAr, UPB, UU, ViU-L

[896] United States, complainant, v. Church of Jesus Christ of Latter-day Saints, and other, respondents, Territory of Utah Reports 5 (January 1888) pp. 538-552.

Case regarding the transfer of property from the Church to a receiver under the earlier cases adjudged and under the Morrill and Edmunds-Tucker Acts.
CU-L, DLC, ICU, MH, MiU, UAr, UPB, UU, ViU-L

[897] U.S. House. 50th Congress. 1st Session. Committee on the Judiciary. Prohibiting polygamy... Report: [To accompany H. Report 116]. (H. Rept. No. 553) Washington: Govt. Print. Off., 1888. 2p. [Serial Set 2599]

Recommending an amendment to the constitution of the United States prohibiting polygamy.
[Flake 9129]

[898] U.S. House. 50th Congress. 1st Session. Convictions for polygamy in Utah and Idaho. Letter from the acting

Attorney-General. In reply to the resolutions of the
House in relation to convictions for polygamy in Utah
and Idaho. Sept. 13, 1888. (H. Ex. Doc. No. 447)
Washington: Govt. Print. Off., 1888. 11p. [Serial Set
2561]

List of those convicted and those pardoned.

[Flake 9097]

[899] U.S. House. 50th Congress. 1st Session. H. Res. 45,
"Joint resolution for the amendment of the Constitution
of the United States in regard to polygamy and polygamous
association or cohabitation between the sexes, January
5, 1888." [Washington: Govt. Print. Off., 1888] 1p.

Referred to the Committee on the Judiciary.

DLC, UPB, US1C

[900] U.S. House. 50th Congress. 1st Session. H. Res. 49,
"Joint resolution proposing an amendment to the Constitution
of the United States prohibiting polygamy, January 9,
1888." [Washington: Govt. Print. Off., 1888] 2p.

Referred to the Committee on the Judiciary.

DLC, UPB, US1C

[901] U.S. House. 50th Congress. 1st Session. H. Res. 64,
"Joint Resolution for the amendment of the Constitution
of the United States in regard to polygamy and polygamous
association or cohabitation between the sexes, January
10, 1888." [Washington: Govt. Print. Off., 1888] 2p.

Referred to the Committee on the Judiciary.

DLC, UPB, US1C

[902] U.S. House. 50th Congress. 1st Session. H. Res. 67,
"Joint Resolution proposing an amendment to the Constitution
of the United States prohibiting polygamy, January 10,
1888." [Washington: Govt. Print. Off., 1888] 2p.

Referred to the Committee on the Judiciary.

DLC, UPB, US1C

[903] U.S. House. 50th Congress. 1st Session. H. Res. 116,
"Joint Resolution Proposing an amendment to the Constitution
of the United States prohibiting polygamy, February 21,
1888." [Washington: Govt. Print. Off., 1888] 2p.

Referred to the Committee on the Judiciary.

DLC, UPB, US1C

[904] U.S. House. 50th Congress. 2d Session. H. Res. 242,
"Joint Resolution for the amendment of the Constitution
of the United States in regard to polygamy and polygamous
association or cohabitation between the sexes, December
17, 1888." [Washington: Govt. Print. Off., 1888] 2p.

Referred to the Committee on the Judiciary.
                                    DLC, UPB, US1C

[905] U.S. House. 50th Congress. 1st Session. Reports from the
      Consuls of the United States. Vol. XXVII. July -
      September, 1888. (H. Misc. Doc. No. 609) Washington:
      Govt. Print. Off., 1888. 584p. [Serial Set 2592]

      Mormons, pp. 575-576. Settlements made by the Mormons
      in Mexico.
                                              [Flake 9188]

[906] United States, respondent, v. Andrew J. Kershaw, appellant
      Territory of Utah Reports 5 (June 1888) pp. 618-620.

      Andrew Kershaw was indicted for adultery, based upon
      the testimony of the first wife, Rose W. Kershaw,
      against the polygamous wife, Mary E. Ramsden.

                  CU-L, DLC, ICU, MH, MiU, UAr, UPB, UU, ViU-L

[907] United States, respondent v. John Harris, appellant,
      Territory of Utah Reports 5 (January 1888) pp. 436-443.

      The polygamous case of John Harris and his first wife
      of 40 years whom he married in England (unnamed) and
      his second wife, Emma, whom he married some 12 years
      ago.
                  CU-L, DLC, ICU, MH, MiU, UAr, UPB, UU, ViU-L

[908] United States, respondent v. Thomas F. Harris, appellant,
      Territory of Utah Reports 5 (June 1888) pp. 621-623.

      The polygamous trial of Thomas F. Harris, wives were
      not named. The conviction was upheld.

                  CU-L, DLC, ICU, MH, MiU, UAr, UPB, UU, ViU-L

[909] United States, respondent, v. Thomas R. Cutler, appellant,
      Territory of Utah Reports 5 (June 1888) pp. 608-611.

      The polygamous case of Thomas R. Cutler (wives unnamed).
      The point of law reiterated is the competency of a wife
      to testify against her husband, who was indicted for
      polygamy.

                  CU-L, DLC, ICU, MH, MiU, UAr, UPB, UU, ViU-L

[910] U.S. Senate. Committee on Territories. Admission of Utah:
      Report of a hearing before the Committee on Territories
      of the United States Senate in regard to the proposed
      admission of the Territory of Utah as a state in the
      federal union. 2 parts. 162p. [Washington: Govt.
      Print. Off.? 1888]

      Arguments of February 18, March 10, 1888.

      Part 1 includes arguments of Franklin S. Richards,
      Joseph E. McDonald, John T. Caine, Jeremiah M. Wilson,
      and F. T. Dubois. Arguments of R. N. Baskin and

Franklin S. Richards in part 2, pages 81-162 deal with
Mormonism and polygamy. The debate continues over
which is the greatest evil, polygamy or the theocratic
tenets of the Mormon Church. Includes numerous insertions
and quotes from sources such as the Deseret News,
Doctrine and Covenants, and Supreme Court cases dealing
with polygamy. Senators Cullom, Manderson, Stewart,
Butler, Payne, and Turpie were present, along with
Robert N. Baskin, John T. Caine, Joseph E. McDonald,
Jeremiah M. Wilson and Franklin S. Richards.

[Flake 9178]
UHi, UPB, USlC

[911] U.S. Senate. Committee on Territories. The Admission of
Utah: Arguments in favor of the admission of Utah as a
state. Made before the Committee on Territories of the
United States Senate, First Session, Fiftieth Congress.
Saturday, February 18, 1888. Washington: Govt. Print.
Off., 1888. 44p.

See entry 910 for complete hearing.
[Flake 9176a]
DLC, NN, UHi, USlC, UU

[912] U.S. Senate. Committee on Territories. The Admission of
Utah: Arguments in favor of the admission of Utah as a
state. Made before the Committee on Territories of the
United States, First Session, Fiftieth Congress,
Saturday, February 18, 1888. Washington: Govt. Print.
Off., 1888. 71p. [Y4.T27/2:Ut1]

Includes arguments of Franklin S. Richards and John T.
Caine.

The subject of polygamy and Church and state were
inevitable.

See entry 910 for complete hearing.
[Flake 9177]
CU-B, DLC, ICN, UHi, WHi

[913] U.S. Senate. 50th Congress. 1st Session. Memorial of
Mrs. Angie F. Newman, demonstrating against the admission
of Utah Territory into the Union as a state so long as
the administration of the affairs of that territory
continues in the hands of the Mormon Priesthood. (S.
Misc. Doc. No. 201) Washington: Govt. Print. Off.,
1888. 16p. [Serial Set 2517]

Memorial on several grounds, including an assortment of
evils perpetrated by the Mormon Church. An answer to
"the speech made in the House of Representatives,
August 25, 1888, by Hon. John T. Caine of Utah."

[Flake 5803]

[914] U.S. Senate. 50th Congress. 2d Session. Letter from the
Attorney-General, transmitting, in response to Senate
resolution of December 10, 1888, a statement relative
to the execution of the law against bigamy. (S. Ex.

185

Doc. No. 21) Washington: Govt. Print. Off., 1888.
65p. [Serial Set 2610]

Exceptionally detailed report regarding compliance of
Section 17 of the Edmunds-Tucker Act, in relation to
escheating of Church property and the Supreme Court
case of "The Late Corporation of the Church of Jesus
Christ of Latter-Day Saints."

[Flake 9099]

[915] U.S. Senate. 50th Congress. 1st Session. Committee on
Territories. In the Senate of the United States...
Resolutions. (S. Misc. Doc. No. 89) Washington:
Govt. Print. off., 1888. 1p. [Serial Set 2516]

Utah should not be admitted as a state until the
practice of plural marriage is stopped.

[Flake add. 9184a]

[916] U.S. Senate. 50th Congress. 1st Session. Message from
the President of the United States, transmitting report
of the Board of Control of the Industrial Home of Utah.
(S. Ex. Doc. No. 57) Washington: Govt. Print. Off.,
1888. 4p. [Serial Set 2510]

The Industrial Christian Home in Utah Territory was
built to provide employment and home for polygamist
wives. It was a failure.

[Flake 4241]

[917] United States v. Church of Jesus Christ of Latter-day
Saints, and others, Territory of Utah Reports 5 (January
1888) pp. 394-399.

Referring to the decision in United States v. Church of
Jesus Christ of Latter-day Saints in the January 1888
session which appointed a receiver for church property.
It was ruled that this was not appealable from the Utah
Supreme Court to the United States Supreme Court.

CU-L, DLC, ICU, MH, MiU, UAr, UPB, UU, ViU-Li

[918] "Utah," pp. 148-150. In Report of the Commissioner of
Education, August 31, 1888. Washington: Govt. Print.
Off., 1889. [FS5.1:888, HE5.1:888]

Teaching of polygamy in Utah schools and the need for
new legislation.

Variant ed. U.S. 50th Cong., 2d sess, H. Ex. Doc. 1,
pt. 5, Serial Set 2640.

[919] "Utah," p. 747. In Report of the Commissioner of Education
for the year 1888-89, vol. II. Washington: Govt.
Print. Off., 1891. [FS5.1:888-889, HE5.1:888-889]

The establishment of various denominational schools and
common schools in the Territory of Utah is discussed.
If common schools were established, Mormon schools
would have to give way to them.

[920] West, Caleb W. Message of His Excellency Governor Caleb W.
West and Accompany Documents. Twenty-eighth Session of
the Legislative Assembly of the Territory of Utah.
Salt Lake City: Geo. C. Lambert, Public Printer, 1888.
24p.

Tells the Territorial Legislature that they must change
their traditions and methods (meaning Mormon teachings)
and acquire new methods in order to attain statehood.
Especially refers to priesthood control and unanimity
of thinking of the people because of the Mormon background.
Renounces polygamy and the lack of free schools.
[Flake 9371]
CU-B, UPB, US1, US1C

[921] West, Caleb W. "Report of the Governor of Utah to the
Secretary of the Interior, 1888," pp. 851-872. In
Annual Report of the Department of the Interior, 1888,
vol. 3. Washington: Govt. Print. Off., 1888. [I1.1:888]

Deals with the issue of statehood and the power of the
Mormon Church, but also expresses the belief that there
has been a "bridging of the chasm" between Mormons and
Non-Mormons, at least in part.

Summary of the Territorial Governor's report appears in
vol. 1 of the Annual Report of the Dept. of the Interior,
p. cxxxix-cxxxii.

Variant ed. U.S. 50th Congress, 2d session, H. Ex. Doc.
No. 1, Pt. 12, Serial Set 2638.

[922] West, Caleb W. Report of the Governor of Utah to the
Secretary of the Interior. 1888. Washington: Govt.
Print. Off., 1888. 24p.

Gives foreign population increase since 1880, chiefly
to show that the chasm between Mormons and non-Mormons
has been bridged to an extent. Problems of polygamy
discussed, non-Mormon opposition to statehood.
[Flake 9374]
UPB, US1

[923] Wilson, Jeremiah Morrow. Admission of Utah. Argument of
Hon. Jeremiah M. Wilson. on the admission of Utah as a
state, made before the Committee on Territories of the
United States Senate, First Session, Fiftieth Congress.
Saturday, February 18, 1888. Washington: Govt. Print.
Off., 1888. 14p.

See entry 910 for complete hearing.
[Flake 9922]
UPB, US1C

1889

"The people of Utah, in very large part, are
descendants of the best stock of New England,
New York, Pennsylvania, Ohio, and other
Middle Eastern States. They are typical
Americans. The people who have builded so

187

marvelously in Utah, who found naught but
desolation reigning in the desert valley of
Great Salt lake, and who have converted the
wastes of aridness into smiling fields, were
Americans to the heart's core. They made the
most remarkable pilgrimage recorded in human
annals, and when, eighteen months after they
set out on their long journey from the banks
of the Upper Mississippi, their pioneer band
rested on the ground where Salt Lake City now
stands, their first act was to scale a lofty
peak of the Wahsatch and plant there the
American flag."

[Entry 926]

---

[924] "Admission of Utah," Congressional Record 50th Congress,
1st session (14 January 1889) vol. 20, pt. 1, pp. 760-
761. [X279]

The Memorial of the Legislative Assembly of the Territory
of Idaho against admission of Utah as a state was
presented in full. They were concerned because they
felt that admission would place the government of Utah
solely in the hands of the Mormon Church, and that all
pretenses of abandonment of polygamy would cease.

[925] "Annual report of the Utah Commission, 1889," pp. 175-213.
In Annual Report of the Department of the Interior,
1889, vol. 3. Washington: Govt. Print. Off., 1890.
[I1.1:889/v.3]

Explains the means used to carry out the provisions of
the Edmunds-Tucker Act and records the number of
Polygamy convictions in Utah for that year. Summary of
the Commission's report by the Secretary of the Interior
is in vol. I pp. CXXIV-CXXVI. [Serial Set 2724]

Variant ed. U.S. 51st Congress, 1st Session, House Ex.
Doc. No. 1, pt. 5, Vol. III. Serial Set 2726.

[926] Caine, John T. Admission of Utah. Argument of Hon. John
T. Caine of Utah, in favor of the admission of Utah as
a state, made before the House Committee on Territories.
Second Session Fiftieth Congress, January 16-17, 1889.
Washington: Govt. Print. Off., 1889. 29p.

Answers questions about polygamy and states that the
majority do not practice polygamy. Defines difference
between celestial and plural marriage. Reiterates that
the Church is a democracy.

[Flake 1071]
UPB, US1C

[926a] "Constitutional amendment," Congressional Record 51st
Congress, Special Session of the Senate (4 December
1889) vol. 21, pt. 1, p. 107. [X283]

Joseph Norton Dolph, Senator from Oregon, introduced S.
R. 5 proposing an amendment to the constitution prohibiting

bigamy and polygamy. The text of the amendment is not included.

[927] Davis v. Beason, U.S. Reports 133 (October 1889) pp. 333–348. [Ju6.8/1:133]

An appeal on behalf of Samuel D. Davis, from the Third Judicial District court of the Territory of Idaho, regarding Davis' polygamy indictment. The Supreme Court affirmed the lower courts decision. The decision revolved around an oath to vote, which Davis took, which contains a polygamy clause, and through his membership in the Mormon Church and Idaho statutes he was convicted on polygamy charges.

[928] H.S. Woolley, appellant, vs. C. N. Watkins and H. M. Bennett, respondents. Brief of Sheeks & Rawlins Attorneys for appellant. In The Supreme Court of Idaho Territory. [n.p., 1889] 23p.

This brief was filed in regard to the Woolley v. Watkins case 2 Idaho Reports (July 22, 1889) 555–578. The case dealt with polygamy and election laws of Idaho Territory.

IAr, UPB

[929] H.S. Woolley, plaintiff and appellant, versus C. N. Watkins and H. M. Bennett, defendants and respondents. In The Supreme Court of Idaho Territory, January 1889, [n.p., 1889?] 4p.

This brief was filed in regard to the Woolley v. Watkins case 2 Idaho Reports (July 22, 1889) 555–578, dealing with polygamy and election laws of Idaho Territory. Application for a writ of mandate.

[Flake add. 8147b]
IAr, UPB

[930] Hester Henderson, ex parte, Territory of Utah Reports 6 (January 1889) pp. 3–9.

Hester Henderson, called to testify at her husband, John Hendrickson, polygamy trial. She was subsequently arrested when she refused to testify regarding her husband's marriage, on the same day, to Mary Lloyd.

CU-L, DLC, ICU, MH, MiU, UAr, UPB, UU, ViU-L

[931] In Equity. The United States of America, plaintiff vs. The Late Church of Jesus Christ of Latter-day Saints and John Taylor [etc.] [Salt Lake City? 1889] 4p.

The undersigned defend the Church against its dissolution as a corporation, under the Edmunds-Tucker Act.

Signed: James O. Broadhead, J. E. McDonald, Franklin S. Richards, LeGrand Young.

[Flake 866]
UPB, US1C

[932] James Jack, plaintiff in error vs. The People of the
        Territory of Utah, No. 144 [and] Nephi W. Clayton,
        plaintiff in error vs. The People of the Territory of
        Utah, No. 143. Brief for Appellants. Attorneys for
        appellants, Eppa Hunton, Jeff. Chandler. [Washington:
        Judd & Detweiler, Printers, 1889?] 15p.

        Brief for appellants regarding Clayton v. Utah Territory
        case, 132 U.S. Reports 632-643, 6 January 1890.
                                        DLC, UPB, US1C

[933] "Journal of the Eighteenth Annual Conference with Representative
        of Missionary boards and Indian Rights Associations,
        January 17, 1889," p. 113. In Twentieth Annual report
        of the Board of Indian Commissioners, 1888. Washington:
        Govt. Print. Off., 1889. [I20.5:888]

        Mormon squatters on the lands under discussion were
        briefly mentioned and it was indicated that they were
        willing to move to make room for the Southern Utes
        removal to Utah.

[934] The Late Corporation of the Church of Jesus Christ of
        Latter-day Saints; No. 1031. George Romney et al. vs.
        the United States. No. 1054. [Washington? 1889]
        80p.

        At head of title: In the Supreme Court of the United
        States. October term, 1889. The late Corporation of
        the Church of Jesus Christ of Latter-day Saints. v.
        The United States 136 U.S. Reports 1-68 (May 19, 1890)

                                        [Flake 1457]
                                            US1C

[935] The Late Corporation of the Church of Jesus Christ of
        Latter-day Saints et al., appellants, vs. The United
        States. Argument of Hon. James O. Broadhead, for the
        appellants. Delivered January 16, and 17, 1889.
        Supreme Court of the United States. Washington:
        Gibson Bros., 1889. 80p.

        The late Corporation of the Church of Jesus Christ of
        Latter-day Saints. v. The United States 136 U.S.
        Reports 1-68 (May 19, 1890)

        "This suit was instituted in the Supreme Court of the
        Territory of Utah, and final judgment rendered by that
        court, escheating all the personal property belonging
        to this Corporation at the time of the institution of
        the suit, to the United States, and turning over the
        real property to the District Court of the Third
        Judicial District of Utah, for the purpose of instituting
        proceedings to forfeit that property, under the provisions
        of the acts of July, 1862," p. 7.

                                        [Flake 869]
                            DLC, MH, NjP, UHi, UPB, US1C

[936] The Late Corporation of the Church of Jesus Christ of
        Latter-day Saints, Appellants, vs. The United States.

Argument of Hon. Joseph E. McDonald for the Appellant, delivered January 18, 1889. Washington: Gibson Bros., Printers and Bookbinders, 1889. 23p.

At head of title: Supreme Court of the United states.

This argument was presented in the Late Corporation of the Church of Jesus Christ of Latter-day Saints v. The United States 136 U.S. Reports 1-68, May 19, 1890.

[Flake 5141]
CtY, MH, NjP, UPB, US1C

[937] The Late Corporation of the Church of Jesus Christ of Latter-day Saints vs. The United States. No. 1031. George Romney et al., vs. The United States. No. 1054. Petitions for rehearing. J. E. McDonald, Attorney for Appellants. [Washington, 1889] 9p.

At head of title: In the Supreme Court of the United States, October term, 1889.

This petition for a rehearing was in the Late Corporation of the Church of Jesus Christ of Latter-day Saints v. The United States Case 136 U.S. Reports 1-68, May 19, 1890.
[Flake 5142]
UPB, US1C

[938] McClernand, John A. Reprint of the separate report of Hon. J. A. McClernand as a member of the Utah Commission on the Mormon question, Sept. 23, 1889. Washington, 1890. 20p.

Discusses polygamy at length. McClernand states "Polygamy is contrary to the divine economy .... It breeds caprice cruelty, and license. It enervates the man and debauches the woman." Good discussion about Utah and its "peaceful and prosperous" nature.

[Flake 5118]
MoU, NjP, NN,MUHi, UPB, US1C, WHi

[939] "Mormon church receivership," p. xvi. In Annual report of the Attorney-general of the United States for the year 1889. Washington: Govt. Print. Off., 1889. [J1.1:889]

Note concerning Mormon property being illegally held, and the breakup of the Perpetual Emigration Fund Company.

[940] "Mormonism," pp. 427-428. In Report of the Secretary of the Interior, 1889, vol. 3. Washington: Govt. Print. Off, 1889. [I1.1:889/Vol.3]

Polygamy in Idaho is practiced secretly, according to the Governor. Quotes Article 1, Section 4 of the late Constitutional Convention of Idaho Territory. It states that liberty of conscience cannot justify polygamy.

A summary of the Idaho report is found in vol. 1, p. CXX, U.S. 51st Congress, 1st session, House Ex. Doc. 1, part 2, Serial Set 2840.

[941] "The Mormons," pp. 249-251. In Report of the Secretary of the Interior, 1889, vol. 3. Washington: Govt. Print. Off., 1890. [I1.1:889/Vol.3]

Mormonism is a problem in Arizona because the Mormons hold the balance of power and vote as a block.

Summary of the report is found in Vol. 1, p. cxxvii. U.S. 51st Congress, 1st session, House Ex. Doc 1, part 2, Serial Set 2840.

[942] Nephi W. Clayton, appellant, . . . James Jack, appellant, vs. The People of the Territory of Utah, ex rel. William H. Dickson, U.S. Attorney, No. 143, 144, Appeals from the Supreme Court of the Territory of Utah. Brief for Appellee. Supreme Court of the United States, October Term, 1889. [n.p., n.d.] 22p.

Brief for appellee regarding Clayton v. Utah Territory case, 132 U.S. Reports 632-643, January 6, 1890.

DLC, UPB, US1C

[943] "Petitions, etc.," Congressional Record 56th Congress, 2d session (29 January 1889) vol. 20, pt. 2, p. 1324. [X280]

Protest, not printed, of 13,000 citizens of Utah Territory against its admission as a state.

[944] "Petitions and Memorials," Congressional Record 56th Congress, 2d session (2, 3, 11, 14 January 1889) vol. 20, pt. 1, pp. 450, 513, 688, 724. [X279]

Various petitions, not printed, remonstrating against admission of Utah as a state.

[945] "Report of the Governor of Idaho, October 15, 1889," pp. 329-434. In Report of the Secretary of the Interior. . vol. III. Washington: Govt. Print. Off., 1890. [I1.1:889]

On pp. 387-8, there is a brief report on the southern counties, commonly called the Mormon counties, where there is considerable problem with Mormons who refuse to send their children to school unless the teacher is Mormon. And on pp. 427-8, there is a section entitled "Mormonism" which refers to the approximately 25,000 Mormons in Idaho and the practice of polygamy. A section of the recently adopted Idaho Constitution is cited, which refers to polygamists.

[946] Report of the Utah Commission to the Secretary of the Interior. 1889. Washington: Govt. Print. Off., 1889. 41p.

See entry 925 for annotation.

[Flake 9239]

CtY, MH, NN, UHi, UPB, US1C

[947] "Representative-elect from Utah," Congressional Record 56th
Congress, 1st session (4, 5, 19 December 1889) vol. 33,
pt. 1, pp. 5, 38-53, 583-584. [X362]

Move not to allow B. H. Roberts his seat in congress.

[948] Richards, Franklin Snyder. Admission of Utah. Argument of
Hon. F. S. Richards in favor of the admission of Utah
as a state made before the House Committee on Territories,
2d Session, 50th Congress, January 12, 1889. Washington:
Govt. Print. Off., 1889. 14p.

Gives resources of Utah, population, law abidance,
freedom from polygamy. Contends that unfavorable
reports are false.

[Flake 7229]
UHi, UPB

[949] Samuel D. Davis, appellant, vs. H. G. Beason, sheriff of
Oneida County, Idaho, appellee. Brief for Appellee.
Attorneys for Appellant, F. S. Richards, J. M. Wilson,
Samuel Shellabarger. Attorney for Appellee, H. W.
Smith. Supreme Court of the United States, October
Term, 1889. [Washington]: Judd & Detweiler, Printers,
1889? 26p.

The appellee brief in the Davis v. Beason case, 133
U.S. Reports 333-348, October 1889 session. Points of
Idaho, federal and other state laws regarding polygamy.
The case itself decided the constitutionality of an
Idaho statute which prohibited voting and the holding
of office because of polygamous activities.

DLC, UPB, US1C

[950] Samuel D. Davis, Appellant, v. H. G. Beason, Sheriff of
Oneida County, Idaho Territory. No. 1261. Brief for
Appellant. [By Franklin S. Richards, Jeremiah M.
Wilson, Samuel Shellabarger. Washington: Gibson
Bors., Printers and Bookbinders, 1889] 66p.

Mormon suffrage in Idaho.

This brief was filed in the Davis v. Beason case 133
U.S. Reports 333-348, October 1889 session.

[Flake 7235]
UHi, UPB, US1C

[951] Shoup, George Laird. Report of the Governor of Idaho to
the Secretary of the Interior. 1889. Washington:
Govt. Print. Off., 1889. 108p.

"Mormonism," pp. 101-102. Statehood implications.
Reports for the years 1887 and 1888 also mention
Mormonism.

[Flake 4181]
MH, ULA, US1C

[952] Thomas, Arthur L. Report of the Governor of Utah to the Secretary of Interior. 1889. Washington: Govt. Print. Off., 1889. 32p.

"The situation," pp. 23-31. Mormons and polygamy.

[Flake 9375]
MH, UHi, UPB

[953] Thomas, Arthur L. "Report of the Governor of Utah to the Secretary of the Interior, 1889," pp. 473-502. In Annual Report of the Department of the Interior, 1889, vol. 3. Washington: Govt. Print. Off., 1890. [I1.1:889]

Discusses Mormon-Gentile numerical and political strengths. It is his opinion that political power should be wrested from the Mormon Church. The governor's recommendation is based in part on the criminal nature of polygamy, which the Mormon Church calls religion. Summary of the Utah governors and Utah Commission reports appear in vol. 1 pp. cxxiii-cxxvi.

Variant ed. U.S. 51st Congress, 1st session. H. Ex. Doc. No. 1, Pt. 13, Serial Set 2726.

[954] United States, complainant, v. Church of Jesus Christ of Latter-day Saints and others, respondents, Territory of Utah Reports 6 (January 1889) pp. 9-83.

Due to the disincorporation of the Church, certain real estate was directed by law to be applied to the use and benefit of the common schools of the Territory of Utah.

CU-L, DLC, ICU, MH, MiU, UAr, UPB, UU, ViU-L

[955] U.S. House. Committee on the Territories. Admission of Utah: Report of the Committee on Territories on the admission of Utah as a state, to the House of Representatives, Second Session, Fiftieth Congress. Washington: Govt. Print. Off., 1889. 12p.

See entry 959 for annotation.

Published separately but is actually a reprint of the 50th Cong. 2d sess. H. Report No. 4156, Serial Set 2675.

[Flake 9144]
MH, NjP, UHi, UPB, USlC

[956] U.S. House. Committee on the Territories. Admission of Utah. Arguments in favor of the admission of Utah as a state, made before the House Committee on Territories, Second Session, Fiftieth Congress, January 12-22, 1889. Washington: Govt. Print. Off., 1889. 92p.

Arguments of Franklin S. Richards, C. C. Bean, John T. Caine, M. A. Smith, and John T. Wilson, especially regarding polygamy and Mormon history.

[Flake 9143]
CU-B, NjP, ULA, UPB, USlC

[957] U.S. House. Committee on the Territories. Admission of Utah. Argument of Hon. Jeremiah M. Wilson, in favor of the admission of Utah as a state made before the House Committee on Territories, Second Session, Fiftieth Congress, January 19-22, 1889. Undisputed facts - decadence of polygamy - no union of church and state - power of Congress to make and enforce compacts. Washington: Govt. Print. Off., 1889. 42p.

Gives statistics, opinions of observers, etc. to show good character of Mormons and to prove that polygamy is not an obstruction to statehood.

[Flake 9921]
CtY, NjP, UPB, US1C

[958] U.S. House. Committee on the Territories. Hearings before the Committee on Territories in regard to the admission of Utah as a state. Washington: Govt. Print. Off., 1889. 215p.

Debate over the use of school buildings for religious purposes by the Mormons. Polygamy is of course discussed and the Utah Penitentiary 1888 report is reprinted with the names of the prisoners their crimes, sentence and date confined. Testimony of Franklin S. Richards, Thomas Caine, Caleb West, C. C. Bean, and many others are included in this document.

[Flake 9152]
CU-B, DLC, ICN, UHi, UPB, US1C

[959] U.S. House. 50th Congress. 2d Session. Committee on the Territories. Admission of the State of Utah... Report: [To accompany bill H.R. 4428.] The Committee on Territories, to whom was referred the bill (H.R. 4428) for the admission of the State of Utah, into the Union on an equal footing with the original States. (H. Rept. No. 4156) Washington: Govt. Print. Off., 1889. 295p. [Serial Set 2675]

Objections of statehood still remain as they have been for years. "View of the minority" pp. 13-295.

[Flake 9191]

[960] U.S. House. 50th Congress. 2d Session. Report of the Select Committee of the House of Representatives to Inquire into the Alleged Violation of the Laws Prohibiting the Importation of Contract Laborers, Paupers, convicts, and other classes. (H. Rept. No. 3792). Washington: Govt. Print. Off., 1889. 799p. [Serial Set 2673]

On pp. 31-32 the testimony of Mr. Underhill, a steamboat agent, indicated that he carried Mormons from Liverpool and answers questions about them. Pages 265-266 includes the testimony of Charles N. Tinkor of New York, a book publisher, and the Commissioner of Emigration of New York State. When asked the question regarding whether he or his agents had power to exclude Mormons if they answered that they were polygamists, he responded "No, sir."

[961] U.S. House. 50th Congress. 2d Session. <u>Reports of the
Diplomatic and Consular Officers concerning Emigration
from Europe to the United States</u>. (H. Rept. No. 3792)
Washington: Govt. Print. Off., 1889. 157p. [Serial
Set 2673]

Page 24, the report of Consul Wood, of Dundee, Scotland,
mentions that sometimes the Mormons attempt to induce
emigration. On p. 131, the report of Consul Catlin of
Zurich, Switzerland, indicates that Mormon preaching is
thoroughly organized in Switzerland and that the
Mormons are converted in Switzerland and emigrate of
their own free will. Page 147 is a report from Denmark
which briefly mentions Mormon emigration and the fact
that it has greatly abated, if not wholly ceased. This
entry found at the end of Serial Set 2673 in a separately
paged section and with a separate title page for the
entry above.

[962] U.S. House. 51st Congress. 1st Session. Committee on the
Territories. <u>Amendment to section 5352, Revised
Statutes... Report. [To accompany H.R. 9264] April 29,
1889</u>. (H. Rept. No. 1811) Washington: Govt. Print.
Off., 1891. 28p. [Serial Set 2812]

Amendment to suppress polygamy. Mormons have perverted
the purpose of the oath for intended voters. Appendix
A. Samuel D. Davis (appellant) vs. H. G. Beason
(sheriff). Extensive material on decisions to ban
polygamy. Appendix B. Extract of Utah Commission
Report, 1887. Extensive material on the Mormons and
the Utah situation.

[Flake 9147]

[963] U.S. House. 51st Congress. 1st Session. H. Res. 23,
"Joint Resolution for the amendment of the Constitution
of the United States in regard to polygamy and polygamous
association or cohabitation between the sexes, December
18, 1889." [Washington: Govt. Print. Off., 1889] 2p.

Referred to the Committee on the Judiciary.

DLC, UPB, US1C

[964] United States of America, respondent, v. Byron W. Brown,
appellant <u>Territory of Utah Reports</u> 6 (January 1889)
pp. 115-120.

Byron W. Brown was indicted for perjury after swearing
under oath that he believed polygamy to be wrong and
did not believe it was right. It was proved that Brown
was a member of the Mormon Church and that he had
recently returned from a mission where he had preached
polygamy.
CU-L, DLC, ICU, MH, MiU, UAr, UPB, UU, ViU-L

[965] United States of America, respondent, v. Joseph Clark,
appellant, <u>Territory of Utah Reports</u> 6 (January 1889)
pp. 120-128.

Joseph Clark, who deserted his first wife, Sarah, was
still considered guilty of unlawful cohabitation,
despite the desertion. Joseph also had a second wife
named Hannah and a third wife named Francis.

CU-L, DLC, ICU, MH, MiU, UAr, UPB, UU, ViU-L

[966] U.S. Senate. Committee on Territories. Hearings before
the Committee on Territories in regard to the admission
of Utah as a state. Washington: Govt. Print. Off.,
1889. 55p.

Includes statements by F. S. Richards, E. P. Ferry, C.
C. Bean, Caleb W. West, John T. Caine, J. R. McBride.

Judge McBride gives almost 20 pages of testimony,
admitting he is part of Caine's "Anti-Mormon Ring".
Hawn's Mill, Mormon's independent legislation, distribution
of land by Mormon's theocratic government, and polygamy
are all debated.

[Flake 9179]
DLC, UHi

[967] U.S. Senate. 50th Congress. 2d Session. Letter from the
Secretary of the Interior, transmitting report of the
Commissioner of Schools for Utah. (S. Ex. Doc. No. 87)
Washington: Govt. Print. Off., 1889. 35p. [Serial Set
2612]

History of public schools in Utah and the Mormon's
attitudes toward education.

[Flake 9333]

[968] U.S. Senate. 50th Congress. 2d Session. Letter from the
Secretary of War, transmitting report upon the claim of
James Bridger. January 25, 1889. (S. Ex. Doc. No. 86)
Washington: Govt. Print. Off., 1889. 23p. [Serial Set
2612]

Bridger claims against the Mormons due to the destruction
of Fort Bridger during the Utah Expedition.

[Flake 9248a]

[969] U.S. Senate. 50th Congress. 2d Session. Memorial of the
Legislative Assembly of the Territory of Idaho, protesting
against the admission of Utah as a state. (S. Misc.
Doc. No. 37) Washington: Govt. Print. Off., 1889.
2p. [Serial Set 2615]

Protest predicated on "treasonability" of the L.D.S.
church in Utah.

[Flake 4182]

[969a] U.S. Senate. 50th Congress. 2d Session. S.R. 5, "Joint
Resolution Proposing an amendment to the Constitution
of the United States empowering Congress to legislate
upon the subjects of marriage and divorce, and prohibiting
bigamy and polygamy, December 4, 1889." [Washington:
Govt. Print. Off., 1889] 1p.

Referred to the Committee on the Judiciary.

DLC, UPB, USlC

[970] U.S. Senate. 51st Congress. 1st Session. Report of Utah Commission as to the management of the Industrial Christian Home Association of Utah. (S. Misc. Doc. No. 34) Washington: Govt. Print. Off., 1890. 10p. [Serial Set 2698]

Report of the Industrial Christian Association of Utah for 1889. Mentions polygamy.

[Flake 4240]

[971] Wilson, Jeremiah Morrow. The Mormon question. Utah and statehood. Irrefutable facts and figures. A strong and able argument. [By] Judge Jeremiah M. Wilson for the Applicants. Washington: Gibson Bros., Printers and Bookbinders, 1889. 4p.

"From the New York World, January 27, 1889."
[Flake 9925]
CU-B, UHi, UPB, USlC

[972] "Women's Relief Corps, of James B. McLean Post No. 1, of Salt Lake City, Utah," Congressional Record 50th Congress, 2d session (2 January 1889) vol. 20, pt. 1, p. 450. [X279]

The memorial of this group remonstrates against admittance of Utah as a state because it would be a polygamous state. Unfortunately the entire memorial is not printed.

[973] Woolley v. Watkins (Bennett, Intervenor) Idaho Reports 2 (22 July 1889) 555-578.

Deals rather extensively with polygamy and election laws of Idaho Territory. Quotes at length from the Doctrine and Covenants.

DLC, UPB, USlC

1890

"It is said that the Mormons, who hold the theory that the Indians are the descendants of the suppositious 'ten lost tribes,' cherish, as a part of their faith, the tradition that some of the lost Hebrew emigrants are still ice-bound in the frozen north, whence they will one day emerge to rejoin their brethren in the south. When the news of this Indian revelation came to their ears, the Mormon priests accepted it as a prophecy of speedy fulfillment of their own traditions, and Orson Pratt, one of the most prominent leaders, preached a sermon, which was extensively copied and commented on at the time, urging the faithful to arrange

their affairs and put their houses in order to receive
the long-awaited wanderers."

[Entry 1000]

---

[974] "An act making appropriations for the legislative, executive,
and judicial expenses of the Government..." (Chapter
667, July 11, 1890) United States Statutes at Large 26,
p. 250. [GS4.111:26, AE2.111:26]

On the aforementioned page, reference is made to
funding the salaries of the five commissioners of the
newly formed Utah Commission. The Edmunds Act of 1882
is the statutory reference cited in this appropriations
legislation.

[975] "An act to provide for certain of the most urgent deficiencies
in the appropriations for the service of the Government.
. ." (Chapter 63, April 4, 1890) United States Statutes
at Large 26, p. 38. [GS4.111:26, AE2.111:26]

One small paragraph in this appropriations act deals
with funding for the Industrial Home in Utah Territory.

[976] "Admission of Idaho," Congressional Record 51st Congress,
1st session (2 April 1890) vol. 21, pt. 3, pp. 2932-
2933. [X285]

Discussion on the bill which included the disfranchisement
of Mormons in Idaho.

[977] "Annual report of the Utah Commission, 1890," pp. 397-428.
In Annual Report of the Department of the Interior,
1890, vol. 3. Washington: Govt. Print. Off., 1890.
[I1.1:890/vol.3]

Describes voter registration practices in Utah and a
summary of indictments for polygamous marriages. It
also mentions the Industrial Christian Home Association
and a short synopsis of Mormon Church happenings for
the year, including excerpts from talks by Church
President Wilford Woodruff. Summary of the Commission's
report by the Secretary of the Interior in Vol. I
[Serial Set 2840] pp. CIX-CXI and additional material
on Manifesto vol. I, pp. CLI-CLVI.

Variant ed. U.S. 51st Congress, 2nd session, House
Exec. Doc. No. 1, Pt. 5, Vol. III. Serial Set 2842.

[978] Bassett v. United States, U.S. Reports 137 (22 December
1890) pp. 496-507. [Ju6.8/1:137]

Polygamy trial of William E. Bassett and his wives
Sarah Ann Williams and Kate Smith. Mr. Franklin S.
Richards and Mr. Charles C. Richards for plaintiff in
error. This was an error to the Supreme Court of the
Territory of Utah.

[979] Broadhead, James Overton. Mormon Church property. Argument
of Hon. James O. Broadhead, of St. Louis, on Senate

bill No. 4047, proposing to dispose of the confiscated personal property of the Mormon Church for the use and benefit of the public schools in the Territory of Utah, before the House Committee on the Judiciary, Saturday, July 19, 1890. Washington: Govt. Print. Off., 1890. 16p.

[Flake 870]
NjP, UPB, US1C

[980] Caine, John T. (Utah) "Admission of Idaho," Congressional Record 51st Congress, 1st session (3 April 1890) vol. 21, pt. 11, Appendix, pp. 84-88. [X293]

Defends the character of the Mormons in Idaho, who were to be disenfranchised, regarding H.R. 4562.

[981] Caine, John Thomas. Admission of Idaho: Disfranchisement of Mormons. Argument of Hon. John T. Caine. April 23, 1890. 14p.

Includes an "official declaration" of Dec. 12, 1889 by the L.D.S. church authorities, denying the killing of apostates. A speech apparently given in the Committee on Territories regarding H.R. 9265.

[Flake 1069]
US1C

[982] Caine, John Thomas. Admission of Idaho. Disfranchisement of Mormons because of their Church membership. Speech of Hon. John T. Caine of Utah, in the House of Representatives, Thursday, April 3, 1890, on the bill (H.R. 4562) to provide for the admission of the State of Idaho into the Union. Washington, 1890. 15p.

See entry 981 for annotation.

[Flake 1070]
DLC, UPB, US1C

[983] Caine, John Thomas. Admission of Idaho. Disfranchisement of Mormons because of their Church membership. Speech of Hon. John T. Caine of Utah, in the House of Representatives, Thursday, April 3, 1890, on the bill (H.R. 4562) to provide for the admission of the State of Idaho into the Union. Washington, 1890. 29p.

See entry 981 for annotation.

[Flake 1071]
UPB, US1C

[984] Cannon, George Q. Exhibit of extracts from newspapers relating to proclamation of President Woodruff and conference of Mormon Church, transmitted to Secretary by Governor Thomas...Remarks by President George Q. Cannon. [n.p., 1890]

On pp. 151-154 in Department of Interior. Messages and Documents. 1890. Appendix D.

Remarks by George Q. Cannon and Wilford Woodruff at
General Conference, October 6, 1890, immediately
following adoption of the Manifesto.

[Flake 1151]
DLC, ULA, UPB

[985] Clayton v. Utah Territory, U.S. Reports 132 (January 6,
1890) pp. 632-643. [Ju6.8/1:132]

This appeal from the Supreme Court of the Territory of
Utah decision was denied and the decision of the
Territorial court was upheld regarding the appointment
of Arthur Pratt as Territorial Auditor. The discussion
of the opinion of the court centered in part around the
jurisdiction of the Probate Courts.

[986] Davis v. Beason, U.S. Reports 133 (February 3, 1890) pp.
333-348. [Ju6.8/1:133]

Case deciding the constitutionality of an Idaho statute
which prohibited voting or the holding of office
because of polygamy activities.

[987] "European Emigration: Studies in Europe of emigration
moving out of Europe, especially that flowing to the
United States," pp. 265, 273, 281-289, vol. 16, no. 19.
In Special Consular Reports. Washington: Govt. Print.
Off., 1890. [S4.9:16/no.19]

Brief mention of German and Norwegian Mormon emigration
on the first two page entries. The larger entry deals
with emigration from Liverpool and a brief description
of the character and occupations of the Mormon emigrants
from Liverpool.

[988] George H. Cope, appellant, vs. Janet Cope and Thomas H.
Cope. Appeal from the Supreme Court of the Territory
of Utah. Transcript of Record. Supreme Court of the
United States, October Term, 1890, No. 1327. [Washington:
Judd & Detweiler, Printers, 1890] 18p.

Transcript of record in the Cope v. Cope case 137 U.S.
Reports 682-689, 19 January 1891.

DLC, UPB, US1C

[989] George H. Cope, appellant, vs. Janet Cope, et. al., Brief
for appellant. In the Supreme court of the United
States, October Term, 1890, No. 1327. Attorney for
appellant, J. G. Sutherland. [n.p., 1890?] 21p.

Brief in the Cope v. Cope case 137 U.S. Reports 682-
689, 19 January 1891. Includes some family information.

[Flake add. 8538a]
DLC, UPB, US1C

[990] George H. Cope, appellant, vs. Thomas H. Cope and Janet
Cope, respondents. Brief for respondents. Supreme
Court of the United States, October term, 1890. No.
1327. [n.p., 1890] 19p.

Signed: R. N. Baskin, John M. Zane. (John M. Zane has been crossed out in ink).

Brief for respondents. Cope vs. Cope case, 137 U.S. Reports 682-689, 19 January 1891.

[Flake add. 328a]
DLC, UPB, USlC

[991] Harrison, Benjamin. By the President of the United States. A proclamation [granting amnesty and pardon to all persons liable to penalties by reason of unlawful cohabitation under the color of polygamous or plural marriage, who have since November 1, 1890, abstained from such unlawful cohabitation. Washington? 1893] 2p.

Issued upon recommendation of the Utah Commission after the Mormon Church had pledged faithful obedience to the laws against plural marriage.

[Flake 9227]
CtY, UPB, USlC

[992] Harrison, Benjamin. "Second Annual Message, December 1890," p. 5553. In A Compilation of the Messages and Papers of the Presidents, by James D. Richardson, vol. 7. New York: Bureau of National Literature, 1911, c1897. [GS4.113:7, AE2.114:1-27/v.7]

Harrison views the non-Mormon population increase in Utah with satisfaction. Refers to the Manifesto and cautions that Wilford Woodruff did not denounce the doctrine but that he only refrains from teaching it and advises against its practices because it is against the law.

[993] In re the estate of George Handley, Sarah A. Chapman, and others, appellants, v. John Handley, and others, respondents, Territory of Utah Reports 7 (June 1890) pp. 49-62.

Attempt of Ruth A. Newson, Benjamin T. Handley, Harry L. Handley, and Sarah A. Chapman to receive a share of the estate of George Handley. They were the children of Sarah Chapman, his plural wife. The appellants are entitled to share the estate. A hearing was also June, 1897, 15 Utah Reports p. 212-225.

CU-L, DLC, ICU, MH, MiU, UAr, UPB, UU, ViU-L

[994] In the matter of the estate of George Handley, deceased, Sarah A. Chapman, et. al., appellants, vs. Elizabeth Handley, et. al., respondents. Brief for respondents. [n.p., 1890] 8p.

This brief was filed in regard to the estate of George Handley, Sarah A. Chapman, and others, appellants, v.

John Handley, and others, respondents, 7 Utah Reports
49-62, June 1890.

[Flake add. 4056bb]
UAr, UPB

[995] In the matter of the estate of George Handley, deceased.
Sarah A. Chapman, et. al., appellants, vs. Elizabeth
Handley, et. al. Respondents. Brief for appellants.
In the Supreme Court of the Territory of Utah, June
1890. [n.p.] 1890. 22p.

This brief was filed in regard to the estate of George
Handley, 7 Territory of Utah Reports, 49-62, June 1890.

[Flake add. 8540a]
UAr, UPB

[996] In the matter of the estate of Thomas Cope, deceased.
Appellant's Brief in the Supreme Court of the Territory
of Utah, June Term, 1890. [n.p., 1890?] 14p.

Brief filed in the C.O. Whittemore v. Thomas H. Cope
(and others) 11 Utah Reports 344-362, June 1895.
Polygamous inheritance case.

[Flake add. 8540b]
UAr, UPB

[997] In the matter of the Estate of Thomas Cope, deceased.
Respondent's brief in the Supreme Court of the Territory
of Utah, June 1890. [n.p., 1890?] 10p.

Brief filed in the C.O. Whittemore v. Thomas H. Cope
(and others) case 11 Utah Reports 344-362, June 1895.
Polygamous inheritance case of the Cope family.

[Flake add. 10105c]
UAr, UPB

[998] The Late Corporation of the Church of Jesus Christ of
Latter-day Saints v. United States, U.S. Reports 136
(May 19, 1890), pp. 1-68. [Ju6.8/1:136]

Congress had the power to repeal the Act of Incorporation
of the Church of Jesus Christ of Latter-day Saints.
Referring back to the Morrill Act of 1 July 1862.

[999] "Latter-day Saints," pp. 421-425. In U.S. Bureau of the
Census. Report on statistics of churches in the United
States at the eleventh census: 1890. Washington:
Govt. Print. Off., 1894. [52d Cong. 1st sess. H. Misc.
Doc. No. 340, Pt. 7, Serial Set 3017]

Brief statement of the history and doctrine of the
church; statistics of church membership, etc.

[1000] Mooney, James. The ghost-dance religion and the Sioux
outbreak of 1890. pp. 703-704, 719-790, 792-793, 818,
1108. In U.S. Bureau of American Ethnology. Fourteenth
annual report... 1892-93. Washington: Govt. Print.
Off., 1896. [SI2.1:893/pt.2]

The author quotes, "a curious pamphlet... published
anonymously at Salt Lake City" in 1892 while the Indian
excitement was at its height. The pamphlet is The
Mormons have stepped down and out of Celestial
Government - The American Indians have stepped up and
into Celestial Government, by Angus McDonald.

[Flake 5457]
CU-B, DLC, UHi

[1001] "The Mormon Church Litigation," pp. xvi, 245-258. In
Annual Report of the Attorney General of the United
States for the year 1890. Washington: Govt. Print.
Off., 1890. [J1.1:890]

Litigation regarding the property of the Mormon Church,
which includes the report (Exhibit Q) of the U.S.
Attorney General regarding the status of Mormon Church
litigation. His report deals with the Perpetual
Emigration Fund, Temple Block, the Tithing Yard, and
several individuals who have brought action to recover
parcels of land.

Variant ed. U.S. House. 51st Congress, 2d session.
Serial Set 2851.

DLC, UPB, US1C

[1002] Murphy, N. O. "Report of the Acting Governor of Arizona,
September 1890," pp. 630-639. In Message from the
President of the United States to the Two Houses of
Congress at the beginning of the Second Session of the
Fifty-first Congress. Washington: Govt. Print. Off.,
1891. [Y8.51/2:]

On p. 631 of N. O. Murphy's report, the number of
Mormons in Arizona Territory is mentioned as around
12,000 people. Murphy also mentions that he expects
their numbers to increase due to the restrictive
legislation in Utah and Idaho regarding polygamy.

[1003] "Petition," Congressional Record 51st Congress, 1st
session (26 May, 2 June 1890) vol. 21, pt. 6, p. 5272,
5469. [X288]

Petition from non Mormons in Utah asking that franchise
be given only to people loyal to the government, which
would exclude polygamists.

[1004] "Petition," Congressional Record 51th Congress, 1st
session. (29 May 1890) vol. 21, pt. 6, p. 5418.
[X288]

Petition of 436 non-Mormon citizens of Ogden against
the bill that would disfranchise all believers of the
Mormon creed.

[1005] "Petitions and Memorials," Congressional Record 51st
Congress, 1st session (24, 25 February 1890) vol. 21,
pt. 2, pp. 1668, 1670. [X284]

Two petitions, not printed, from the Woman's Missionary Union of Congregational Churches of Minneapolis praying for laws which would give Utah free public schools.

[1006] "Reorganized Church of Jesus Christ of Latter-day Saints," pp. 427-432. In U.S. Bureau of the Census. Report on statistics of churches in the United States at the eleventh census: 1890. Washington: Govt. Print. Off., 1894. [52d Cong. 1st sess. H. Misc. Doc., No. 340, Serial Set 3017.]

Brief statement of the history and doctrine of the church, statistics of church membership, etc.

[1007] "Report of the Governor of Idaho, October 20, 1890," pp. 639-683. In Message from the President of the United States to the Two Houses of Congress at the Beginning of the Second Session of the Fifty-first Congress. Washington: Govt. Print. Off., 1891. [Y8.51/2:]

Although this report is supposedly identical to the one found in the Report of the Secretary of Interior annual report series, this is not the case for Idaho. It does contain on pp. 651-653 the assessment of the Mormon influence in Idaho politics, but it does not include the Supreme Court case of Samuel D. Davis. However, on pp. 678-683 a section not appearing in the other printed version deals with Mormons and the political situation and the character of the Mormon people especially as regards polygamy.

[1008] "Report of the Governor of Idaho, October 20, 1890," pp. 495-586. In Report of the Secretary of Interior being part of the Messages and documents... vol. III. Washington: Govt. Print. Off., 1890. [I1.1:890]

On pp. 576-578 is a section dealing with the Mormon influence in Idaho politics. Pages 582-586 is an Appendix which recites the Supreme Court case of Samuel D. Davis found in 133 U.S. Reports pp. 333-348. The case dealt with polygamy.

[1009] Report of the Utah Commission to the Secretary of the Interior, 1890. Washington: Govt. Print. Off., 1890. 34p.

See entry 977 for annotation.

[Flake 9239]
CtY, MH, NN, UHi, UPB, USlC

[1010] Sarah A. Chapman, et al., appellants, vs. Elizabeth Handley, et al., respondents. Brief of respondents. In the Supreme court of the Territory of Utah, June 1890. [n.p., 1890] 8p.

This brief was filed in regard to the estate of George Handley, Sarah A. Chapman, and others, appellants, v. John Handley, and others, respondents, 7 Utah Reports 49-62.

UAr, UPB

[1011] Sarah A. Chapman, Ruth Newsom, Benjamin T. Handley, and
Harvey Handley, appellant, vs. Elizabeth Handley, John
Handley, William F. Handley, Charles T. Handley, and
Emma N. Handley. Appeal from the Supreme Court of the
territory of Utah. Record case No. 14,191. Supreme
Court of the United States, October Term, 1891. Term
No. 808 [crossed out and another unreadable number
handwritten in]. [Washington: Judd & Detweiler,
Printers, 1891] 16p.

This appeal was filed September 29, 1890, in the
Chapman v. Handley case 151 U.S. Reports 443-446,
October 1893 session.
                                        [Flake add. 8538b]
                                         DLC, UPB, USlC

[1012] Struble, Isaac S. (Iowa). "Admission of Idaho," Congressional
Record 51st Congress, 1st session (3 April 1890) vol.
21, pt. 11, Appendix, pp. 98-101. [X293]

In favor of admitting Idaho into the Union and maintaining
its constitutional provisions which require the taking
of an oath regarding polygamy prior to being allowed to
vote or hold office.

[1013] Territory v. Evans Idaho Reports 2 (February 24, 1890)
627-634.

Reiterates that a member of the so-called Mormon Church
cannot be a juror.
                                         DLC, UPB, USlC

[1014] Thomas, Arthur L. "Report of the Governor of Utah to the
Secretary of the Interior, 1890," pp. 635-667. In
Annual Report of the Department of the Interior, 1890,
vol. 3. Washington: Govt. Print. Off., 1890. [I1.1:890]

Deals with polygamy, in particular a conversation with
President Wilford Woodruff, and he also includes a
description of the "Mormon Personality", a copy of an
1886 editorial from the Juvenile Instructor by George
Q. Cannon on the men sentenced to the penitentiary for
polygamy.

Summary of the territorial governors report and the
Utah Commission reports appear in vol. 1 pp. cii-cxi.

Variant ed. U.S. 51st Congress, 2d session. H. Ex.
Doc. No. 1, Serial Set 2842.

[1015] Thomas, Arthur L. Report of the Governor of Utah to the
Secretary of the Interior, 1890. Washington: Govt.
Print. Off., 1890. 35p.

Section on the Mormon people; advice for future legislation.
                                         [Flake 9376]
                                      MH, UHi, UPB, USlC

[1016] The United States, appellant, v. S. B. Christensen, respondent, <u>Territory of Utah Reports</u> 7 (June 1890) pp. 26-34.

An attempt to secure a new polygamy trial due to the problem of a juror.
CU-L, DLC, ICU, MH, MiU, UAr, UPB, UU, ViU-L

[1017] U.S. Census, 1890, Part 2. <u>Compendium of the Eleventh Census.</u> Washington: Govt. Print. Off., 1897. [I12.5:2]

Table 2. is a list of Churches, p. 269 includes the Latter-day Saints in statistics for all the states and territories.

[1018] U.S. House. Committee on Territories. <u>Admission of Idaho into the Union: Mr. Mansur submitted the following as the views of the minority on the bill (H.R. 4562) "To provide for the admission into the Union of the State of Idaho and for other purposes."</u> [Washington, 1890?] 16p.

The minority disagree with the deprivation of suffrage based upon polygamy. Because it is a crime of which an individual has not been convicted. Primarily a legal brief citing precedents for their opinion.
[Flake 9140]
Cty, ULA, UPB, US1C

[1019] U.S. House. Committee on Territories. <u>Anti-Mormon test oath.</u> Arguments of Hon. J. M. Wilson, Hon. A. B. Carlton, and Bishop William Budge, in opposition to the constitution of the proposed state of Idaho adopted at Boise City, August 6, 1889, made before the Committee on the Territories of the House of Representatives, January 21 and February 8, 1890. Washington: Govt. Print. Off., 1890. 41p.
[Flake 9148]
ICN, UPB, US1C

[1020] U.S. House. 51st Congress. 1st Session. Committee on the Judiciary. <u>Section 5352 of the Revised Statutes... Mr. Caswell, from the Committee on the Judiciary, submitted the following Report.</u> (H. Rept. No. 3200) Washington: Govt. Print. Off., 1890. 2p. [Serial Set 2816]

The Committee recommends that the Mormon church property, escheated under the Edmunds-Tucker Act, be donated to the public school fund.
[Flake 9133]

[1021] U.S. House. 51st Congress. 1st Session. Committee on the Territories. <u>Admission of Idaho into the Union.</u> (H. Rept. No. 1064) Washington: Govt. Print. Off., 1891. 52p. [Serial Set 2810]

March 26, 1890 ordered to be printed. Includes 16p., views of the minority. Polygamy a reason to restrict its admission.
[Flake 9139]

[1022] U.S. House. 51st Congress. 2d Session. Exhibit of extracts from newspapers relating to proclamation of President Woodruff and conference of Mormon Church, transmitted to Secretary by Governor Thomas...Remarks by President George Q. Cannon. (H. Ex. Doc. No. 1, pt. 5) [n.p., 1890] [Serial Set 2724]

On pp. 151-154 in Department of Interior. Messages and Documents. 1890. Appendix D. Appears to be the same as entry 984.

[Flake 1151]

[1023] U.S. House. 51st Congress. 1st Session. H.R. 4639, "A bill restrictive of the rights of Mormons, January 13, 1890." [Washington: Govt. Print. Off., 1890] 2p.

Referred to the Committee on the Judiciary.

Because the Mormon Church is a theocracy which controls its members in all matters temporal and political, and because its members practice polygamy, they should be prohibited from voting in any election, settling on public lands, holding any office, and they must take an oath to this affect prior to voting.

DLC, UPB, US1C

[1024] U.S. House. 51st Congress. 1st Session. H.R. 9265, [Report No. 1811] April 11, 1890. Reported with amendments... "A bill to amend an act of Congress of March third eighteen hundred and eighty-seven, entitled 'An act to amend an act entitled An act to amend section fifty-three hundred and fifty-two of the Revised Statutes of the United States in reference to bigamy..., April 29, 1890.'" [Washington, 1890] 5p.

Bill to amend the Edmunds-Tucker Act. Known as the Cullom-Strubble bill.

DLC, UPB, US1C

[1025] U.S. House. 52d Congress. 1st Session. Report on statistics of churches in the United States at the 11th Census: 1890. (H. Misc. Doc. No. 340, Pt. 17) Washington: Govt. Print. Off., 1895. 812p. [Serial Set 3017]

Church of Jesus Christ of Latter-day Saints, pp. 422-425. Information on history and doctrine.

[Flake 9103]

[1026] United States, respondent, v. Andrew P. Schow, appellant, Territory of Utah Reports 6 (January 1890) pp. 381-382.

Indicted on a charge of unlawful cohabitation with two wives, unnamed.

CU-L, DLC, ICU, MH, MiU, UAr, UPB, UU, ViU-L

[1027] U.S. Senate. Committee on Territories. Admission of Idaho, Committee on Territories, January 21, 1890. [Washington? Govt. Print. Off.? 1890?] 82p.

Polygamy, euphamistically called "The Mormon question," is discussed and it is commented that Idaho has done more by statute to discourage polygamy than all other legislation combined.

[Flake 9176]
DLC, US1C

[1028] U.S. Senate. Committee on Territories. The constitution of the proposed state of Idaho: Hearing before the Committee on Territories. [Washington: Govt. Print. Off., 1890] 63p.

At head of title: In the Senate of the United States.

Includes the polygamy test oath, and a copy of the Constitution which prohibits bigamy and polygamy (Article VI, Sec. 3). The real problem with the Constitution, according to Jeremiah Wilson, is that it disenfranchises all Mormons.

Includes testimony of Jeremiah M. Wilson, Fred T. Dubois, William Budge, Gov. E. A. Stevenson and John T. Caine.

[Flake 9178a]
UHi, UPB, US1C

[1029] U.S. Senate. Committee on Territories. Hearings before the Committee on Territories in relation to the exercise of the elective franchise in the Territory of Utah. [Washington: Govt. Print. Off.? 1890] 25p.

Consideration of further polygamy legislation.

[Flake 9180]
UPB, US1C

[1029a] U. S. Senate. 51st Congress. 1st Session. Constitution Adopted by a Constitutional Convention held at Boise City, in the Territory of Idaho, August 6, 1889. (S. Misc Doc. No. 39) Washington: Govt. Print. Off., 1890. 23p. [Serial Set 2698]

Article VI, Sec. 3 of the Constitution of Idaho prohibits people who are bigamists, polygamists, or living in patriarchal, plural or celestial marriage from voting, serving as a juror, or holding any civil office.

[1030] U.S. Senate. 51st Congress. 1st Session. S. 3480, "A bill to amend the act of Congress of March third, eighteen hundred and eighty-seven, entitled 'An act to amend section fifty-three hundred and fifty-two of the Revised Statutes of the United States in reference to bigamy, and for other purposes,' approved March twenty-second, eighteen hundred and eighty-two." [Washington: Govt. Print. Off., 1890] 7p.

Reported by Mr. Platt on June 28, 1890, with an amendment. Appears to be a total rewrite of the original bill. Once again a revision of the Edmunds-Tucker, regarding the practice of and counseling or teaching of celestial marriage.

DLC, UPB, US1C

[1031] U.S. Senate. 51st Congress. 1st Session. S. 3480, "A bill to amend the act of Congress of March third, eighteen hundred and eighty-seven entitled 'An act to amend an act entitled "An Act to amend section fifty-three hundred and fifty-two of the Revised Statutes of the United States in reference to bigamy, and for other purposes,' approved March twenty-second, eighteen hundred and eighty-two, April 10, 1890." [Washington: Govt. Print. Off., 1890] 4p.

Another proposed amendment to the Edmunds-Tucker Act. Referred to the Committee on Territories. The sections proposed here are extremely explicit regarding polygamy and celestial marriage and go further than punishing people for violation of, but also for teaching, advising, counseling, aiding, or encouraging any person into such marriages.

DLC, UPB, US1C

[1032] U.S. Senate. 51st Congress. 1st Session. S. 3480, "Senator Cullom's Anti-Mormon bill." [n.p., n.d.] 5p.

Apparently a reprint of S. 3480, 1890 bill to amend the Edmunds-Tucker Act.

See entry 1031 for annotation.

UPB

[1033] U.S. Senate. 51st Congress. 1st Session. S. 3823, "Amendment intended to be proposed by Mr. Butler to the bill (S. 3823) in amendment of and supplementary to the act of Congress approved March twenty-second, eighteen hundred and eighty-two, entitled, 'An act to amend section fifty-three hundred and fifty of the Revised Statutes of the United States in reference to bigamy, and for other purposes,' May 14, 1890." [Washington: Govt. Print. Off., 1890] 1p.

Deals with an amendment to Section 3 of S. 3823 regarding voter registration and the oath regarding polygamy.

DLC, UPB, US1C

[1034] U.S. Senate. 51st Congress. 1st Session. S. 3823, "A bill in amendment of and supplementary to the act of Congress approved March Twenty-second, eighteen hundred and eighty-two entitled 'An Act to amend section fifty-three hundred and fifty of the Revised Statutes of the United States, in reference to bigamy, and for other purposes,' May 14, 1890." [Washington: Govt. Print. Off., 1890] 3p.

Referred to the Committee on the Judiciary. Proposed amendment to the Edmunds-Tucker Act.

DLC, UPB, US1C

[1035] U.S. Senate. 51st Congress. 1st Session. S. 3823, "A bill in amendment of and supplementary to the act of

Congress approved March twenty-second, eighteen hundred and eighty-two, entitled 'An act to amend section fifty-three hundred and fifty of the Revised Statutes of the United States, in reference to bigamy and for other purposes,' May 14, 1890." [Washington: Govt. Print. Off., 1890] 5p.

Reported with amendments by Mr. Edmunds on June 12, 1890. Considerable changes from the May 14th version. Proposed amendment to the Edmunds-Tucker Act.

DLC, UPB, US1C

[1036] U.S. Senate. 51st Congress. 1st Session. S. 4047, "A bill supplemental to the act of Congress passed in March, eighteen hundred and eighty-seven, entitled 'an act to amend an act entitled An act to amend section fifty-three hundred and fifty-two of the Revised Statutes of the United States, in reference to bigamy, and for other purposes approved March twenty-second, eighteen hundred and eighty-two,' June 10, 1890." [Washington: Govt. Print. Off., 1890] 2p.

Referred to the Committee on the Judiciary. Mormon Church property to be devoted to the use of schools in the Territory and invests the Supreme Court of the Territory with power and authority to make orders and decrees for this purpose.

DLC, UPB, US1C

[1037] U.S. Senate. 51st Congress. 1st Session. S. 4047, "A bill supplemental to the Act of Congress passed in March, eighteen hundred and eighty-seven, entitled: 'An act to amend an act entitled An act to amend section fifty-three hundred and fifty-two of the Revised Statutes of the United States, in reference to bigamy, and for to the purposes, approved March twenty-second, eighteen hundred and eighty-two,' June 10, 1890." [Washington: Govt. Print. Off., 1890] 2p.

Referred to the Committee on the Judiciary and reported by Mr. Edmunds with amendments on June 12, 1890. An attempt to amend the Edmunds-Tucker Act.

A slight revision of S. 4047, in regard to Mormon Church property.

DLC, UPB, US1C

[1038] U.S. Senate. 51st Congress. 2d Session. Letter from the Secretary of the Interior, transmitting a letter of the Governor of Utah and a report of the Commissioner of Public Schools. (S. Ex. Doc. No. 46) Washington: Govt. Print. Off., 1891. 14p. [Serial Set 2818]

Report for 1890. Mormons church schools had increased from 6 to 21 in anticipation of free public schools.

[Flake 9331]

[1039] U.S. Senate. 51st Congress. 1st Session. Letter from the Secretary of the Interior, transmitting the second

annual report of the Commissioner of Schools for Utah.
(S. Ex. Doc. No. 27) Washington: Govt. Print. Off.,
1890. 15p. [Serial Set 2682]

A good deal of information on Mormons with regard to
the school situation.

[Flake 9335]

[1040] U.S. Senate. 51st Congress. 1st Session. Petition of
citizens of Utah Territory praying that the elective
franchise in that Territory may be restricted to those
who give unqualified allegiance to the government of
the United States. (S. Misc. Doc. No. 156) Washington:
Govt. Print. Off., 1890. 3p. [Serial Set 2698]

Material on the People's Party of Utah, and its relationship
to the Mormon church.

[Flake 9326]

[1041] U.S. Senate. 51st Congress. 2d Session. Report of the
Commissioners of Registration and Elections on the
Industrial Christian Home Association of Utah. Nov.
12, 1890. (S. Misc. Doc. No. 15) Washington: Govt.
Print. Off., 1891. 6p. [Serial Set 2815]

Report of the Industrial Christian Home Association of
Utah for 1890, including data on polygamy and the
Manifesto.

[Flake 4239]

[1042] "Utah," pp. 841-954. In Treasury Department. Report on
the internal commerce of the United States for the year
1890. (H. Ex. Doc. No. 6, pt. 2) Washington: Govt.
Print. Off., 1891. 1174p. [Serial Set 2854]

Considerable information on Utah History and Mormons in
Utah.

[1043] Washington, Joseph E. (Tennessee). "Admission of Idaho,"
Congressional Record 51st Congress, 1st session (2
April 1890) vol. 21, pt. 11, Appendix, pp. 73-75.
[X293]

Mr. Washington cannot vote for the admission of Idaho
unless its Constitution is amended so that merely
assuming a person to be a Mormon can exclude that
person from holding office or voting.

[1044] William E. Bassett, plaintiff in error, v. The United
States, defendant in error. Brief for plaintiff in
error. Supreme Court of the United States, October
Term, 1890, No. 110. [Attorneys] for plaintiff in
error, Franklin S. Richards, Charles C. Richards. Salt
Lake City: Juvenile Instructor Co., printers and
bookbinders, 1890. 24p.

This brief for plaintiff was filed in regard to the
Bassett v. United States case 137 U.S. Reports 496-507.

DLC, UPB, US1C

[1045] William E. Bassett, plaintiff in error vs. the United
States. In error to the Supreme Court of the Territory
of Utah. Transcript of Record. Supreme Court of the
United States, October Term, 1890, No. 110. [Washington:
Judd & Detweiler, Printers, 1890] 67p.

This transcript was filed, September 23, 1887, regarding
the Bassett v. United States case 137 U.S. Reports 496-
507, 22 December 1890.
[Flake add. 331b]
DLC, UPB, US1C

[1046] William E. Bassett, plaintiff in error, vs. The United
States, No. 110. Error to the Supreme Court of Utah.
Brief for defendant in error. In the Supreme Court of
the United States, October Term, 1890. [n.p., 1890?]
12p.

Brief in the Bassett v. United States case 137 U.S.
Reports 496-507, 22 December 1890.
DLC, UPB, US1C

[1047] William E. Bassett, vs. The United States. Brief for
Plaintiff in Error. [Salt Lake City, 1890] 22p.

At head of title: Supreme Court of the United States.
October Term, 1890, No. 110.

This brief was filed in regard to the Bassett v. United
States case 237 U.S. Reports 496-507, 22 December 1890.
[Flake 7241]
US1C

1891

"This proclamation [the Manifesto], in the
proceedings of the conference, is not called
a revelation, and, perhaps, it is not considered
as strictly such, but it is distinctly
asserted it is put forth by permission of the
Lord, granted in answer to prayer on the
subject, and by the only man on earth who
holds the keys of the sealing power. Whether
it is put forth as a command from the Lord or
only as permissive I have no doubt that, as
they have been led to believe it was put
forth by divine sanction, it will be received
by the members of the Mormon Church as an
authoritative rule of conduct, and that, in
effect, the practice of polygamy is formally
renounced by the people."
[Entry 1066]

[1048] "An act in Amendment to the various acts relative to
immigration and the importation of aliens under contract
or agreement to perform labor" (Chapter 551, March 3,
1891) United States Statutes at Large 26, pp. 1084-
1086. [GS4.111:26, AE2.111:26]

213

This act essentially amends an 1882 act and specifically added a category of undesireable immigrants as polygamists. The report which accompanies this act is found in Serial Set 2888, H. Report 3807.

[1049] "An act making appropriations for the legislative executive, and judicial expences of the Government. . ." (Chapter 541, March 3, 1891) United States Statutes at Large 26, p. 930. [GS4.111:26, AE2.111:26]

Funding for territorial officers cited, along with the Utah Commission, which was formed as a result of the Edmunds Act.

[1050] "Annual report of the Utah Commission, 1891," pp. 415-448. In Annual Report of the Department of the Interior, 1891, vol. 3. Washington: Govt. Print. Off., 1892. [I1.1:891/v.3]

The majority of the report deals with the disbanding of the People's Party (a ruse to gain statehood according to the Commission) and the year's indictments for polygamy. A minority report recounts federal legislation against polygamy. Summary of the Commission's report by the Secretary of the Interior in Vol. I. [Serial Set 2933] pp. CXV-CXVII.

Variant ed. U.S. 52nd Cong. 1st session, House Exec. Doc. No. 1, pt. 5, vol. III. Serial Set 2935.

[1051] Cope v. Cope, U.S. Reports 137 (January 19, 1891), pp. 682-689. [Ju6.8/1:137]

An inheritance case revolving around Thomas Cope, his lawful wife, Janet Cope and his legitimate son Thomas H. and George H. Cope, his illegitimate son by his polygamous or plural wife, Margaret Cope.

[1052] Dwight Peck, et al., plaintiffs and respondents, vs. Cecillia [sic] Rees, defendant and appellant. Appellant's brief. In the Supreme Court of the Territory of Utah, June Term, 1891. Ogden: W. W. Browning & Co., 1891. 7p.

This brief was filed in regard to the Dwight Peck, et. al., v. Cecilia Rees case 7 Utah Reports (June 1891) 467-475.

[Flake add. 6839a]
UAr, UPB

[1053] Dwight Peck, et al., plaintiffs and respondents, vs. Cecelia [sic] Rees, defendant and appellant. Brief for respondents. In the Supreme Court of Utah Territory, June Term, 1891. [n.p., 1891?] 5p.

This brief was filed in regard to the Dwight Peck, et. al., v. Cecilia Rees case 7 Utah Reports (June 1891) 467-475.

UAr, UPB

[1054] Dwight Peck, et al., plaintiffs and respondents, vs. Cecilia Rees, defendant and appellant, Territory of Utah Reports 7 (June 1891) pp. 467-475.

Land dispute concerning a will which left part of the estate to Cecilia Rees for the purpose of having temple work performed in the Logan Temple.

CU-L, DLC, ICU, MH, MiU, UAr, UPB, UU, ViU-L

[1055] Edwin Ayres and Edward A. Kessler, appellants, vs. Mary Ann Jack, respondent, vs. William Leggett, respondent. Brief of Appellants in the Supreme Court of Utah Territory, January Term, 1891. [n.p., 1891?] 11p.

This brief was filed in regard to the C.O. Whittemore v. Thomas H. Cope (and others) case 11 Utah Reports (June 1891) 344-362.

UAr, UPB

[1056] Fergus Ferguson, appellant, v. Clarence E. Allen, respondent, Territory of Utah Reports 7 (January 1891) pp. 263-277.

Voting irregularities as a result of the Edmunds-Tucker Law.

CU-L, DLC, ICU, MH, MiU, UAr, UPB, UU, ViU-L

[1057] Harrison, Benjamin. "Message of the President, 9 December 1891," pp. 32-33. In Messages and Documents, 1891-1892 Abridgement. Washington: Govt. Print. Off., 1892. [Y8.52/1:]

Congressional legislation brought some resistance in Utah, but the Mormons are coming around.

[1058] Harrison, Benjamin F. "Third Annual Message, 9 December 1891," p. 5641. In A Compilation of the Messages and Papers of the Presidents, by James D. Richardson, Vol. 8. New York: Bureau of National Literature, 1911, c1897. [GS4.113:8, AE2.114:1-27/v.8]

Harrison takes a swipe at statehood for Utah as he claims that Congress has successfuly contained polygamy through its laws, but that statehood might reverse this good work.

[1059] In the Matter of the Estate of Orson Pratt deceased. Abstract of Record. Appeal from the District Court of the Third Judicial District. In the Supreme Court of Utah Territory, [January Term, 1891]. [Salt Lake City.], Star Printing Company, [1890] 9p.

This abstract of record was filed in regard to the matter of the estate of Orson Pratt. Milando Pratt, and others, appellants, v. Arthur Pratt and others, respondents, Territory of Utah Reports 7 (October 1891) pp. 278-279.

[Flake add. 404a]
UAr, UPB

[1060] In the Matter of the Estate of Orson Pratt, deceased.
Appellants' Brief. In the Supreme Court of Utah
Territory, [January Term, 1891]. Salt Lake City: Star
Printing Co. [1891] 12p.

This brief was filed in regard to the matter of the
estate of Orson Pratt, Milando Pratt, and others,
appellants, v. Arthur Pratt and others, respondents,
Territory of Utah Reports 7 (October 1891) pp. 278-279.

[Flake add. 404b]
UAr, UPB

[1061] In the Matter of the Estate of Orson Pratt, Milando Pratt,
and others, appellants, v. Arthur Pratt and others,
respondents, Territory of Utah Reports 7 (January 1891)
pp. 278-279.

The decision that both the children of the legal wife
and the polygamist wife should inherit.

CU-L, DLC, ICU, MH, MiU, UAr, UPB, UU, ViU-L

[1062] Minority Report of the Utah Commission, 1891. Presented
by Gen. John M. McClernand. [Salt Lake City?] 1891.
18p.

Summary of election laws, history of polygamy legislation,
and the errors of disfranchisement of the Mormons.

UPB

[1063] "Mormons in Mexico," pp. 60-61. In Reports from the
Consuls of the United States, Vol. XXXVI, nos. 128, May
1891. Washington: Govt. Print. Off., 1891.
[S4.7:36/No.128]

Consul A. J. Sampson of Paso Del Norte describes the
Mormon colonies in Corralitos, Ascension and Casas
Grandes as to the number of inhabitants, occupations
and climate.

[1064] The people of the Territory of Utah, ex relations the
Board of Education of Salt Lake City, v. Utah Commissioners
Territory of Utah Reports 7 (January 1891) pp. 279-288.

Election difficulties as a result of the Edmunds-Tucker
law.
CU-L, DLC, ICU, MH, MiU, UAr, UPB, UU, ViU-L

[1065] Report of the Utah Commission to the Secretary of the
Interior, 1891. Washington: Govt. Print. Off., 1891.
36p.

See entry 1050 for a description.
[Flake 9239]
CtY, DLC, ICN, MH, NN, UHi, UPB, USlC

[1066] Thomas, Arthur L. Report of the Governor of Utah to the
Secretary of the Interior. 1891. Washington: Govt.
Print. Off., 1891. 58p.

Polygamy as affected by the Edmunds-Tucker Act and the political situation in Utah.

[Flake 9377]
UHi, UPB, US1C

[1067] Thomas, Arthur L. "Report of the Governor of Utah to the Secretary of the Interior, 1891," pp. 359-414. In Annual Report of the Department of the Interior, 1891, vol. 3. Washington: Govt. Print. Off., 1892. [I1.1:891/vol.3]

The Mormons' People Party has been disbanded, and he also feels that the Mormons are sincere in abandoning polygamy. Includes copy of the "Manifesto" and the Mormons, ratification of it.

Summary of the report found in vol. 1, pp. CX-CXVII.

Variant ed. U.S. 52d Congress. 1st session, H. Ex. Doc. No. 1, Serial Set 2935.

[1068] U.S. House. 51st Congress. 2d Session. Immigration Investigations. (H. Rept. 3807) Washington: Govt. Print. Off., 1891. 8p. [Serial Set 2888]

The House Report which accompanies the passage of the March 3, 1891 law on the amendment of various immigration and importation of aliens under contract agreement found in the vol. 26, pp. 1084-1086 of the Statutes at Large. This act amended an 1882 act and specifically added a category of undesirable immigrants as polygamists. Surprisingly in this report there is no discussion of that particular category only mention that this is a new category of undesirables.

[1068a] U.S. House. 51st Congress. 2d Session. Report of the Select Committee on Immigration and Naturalization, and Testimony taken by the Committee on Immigration and Naturalization of the House of Representatives under Concurrent Resolution of March 12, 1890. (H. Rept. 3472) Washington: Govt. Print. Off., 1891. 1095p. [Serial Set 2886]

The report to accompany H.R. 13175, which is especially concerned with the regulation of immigration. It is only on preliminary page iv, however, that there is any mention of polygamists as an undesirable group to regulate. They are sandwiched in with persons likely to become a public charge or who are suffering from a loathsome disease.

[1068b] U.S. House. 51st Congress. 2d Session. Report: [To accompany S. 5035.]. (H. Rept. No. 2165) Washington: Govt. Print. Off., 1981. 5p. [Serial Set 2827]

Brief report to accompany S. 5035, to amend various immigration laws. The Appendix includes a chart showing people excluded under current law and those excluded with this new proposal. Polygamists simply listed as a newly excluded group.

"Every person who has a husband or wife
living, who, hereafter marries another,
whether married or single, and any man who
hereafter simultaneously, or on the same day,
marries more than one woman, is guilty of
polygamy, and shall be punished by a fine of
not more than five hundred dollars and by
imprisonment for a term of not more than five
years; but this section shall not extend to
any person by reason of any former marriage
whose husband or wife by such marriage shall
have been absent for five successive years,
and is not known to such person to be living,
and is believed by such person to be dead,
nor to any person by reason of any former
marriage which shall have been dissolved by a
valid decree of a competent court, nor to any
person by reason of any former marriage which
shall have been pronounced void by a valid
decree of a competent court, on the ground of
nullity of the marriage contract."

[Entry 1089]

[1069] "An act making appropriations for sundry civil expenses of
the government..." (Chapter 380, August 5, 1892)
United States Statutes at Large 27, p. 385. [GS4.111:27,
AE2.111:27]

Funding for the Utah Industrial Christian Home cited.

[1070] "An act making appropriations for the legislative, executive,
and judicial expenses of the government. . ." (Chapter
196, July 16, 1892) United States Statutes at Large
27, p. 206. [GS4.111:27, AE2.111:27]

Funding for territorial officers, including the Utah
Commission are given.

[1071] "Annual report of the Utah Commission, 1892," pp. 445-467.
In Annual Report of the Department of the Interior,
1892, vol. 3. Washington: Govt. Print. Off., 1892.
[1.1:892/v.3]

Describes the criticism that it (the Commission)
received from the Mormon Church for asserting that the
Church interfered with the politics of its members.
Report recommends amnesty be granted to the Mormon
people regarding polygamy. Summary of the Commission's
report by the Secretary of the Interior in vol. I.
[Serial Set 3089] pp. CXV-CXVIII.

Variant ed. U.S. 52nd Congress, 2nd session, House
Exec. Doc. No. 1, pt. 5, vol. III. [Serial Set 3089]

[1072] Elbridge Tufts, respondent, v. Eleanor Tufts, appellant
Territory of Utah Reports 8 (June 1892), pp. 142-149.

> A Mormon Church divorce case between Elbridge and
> Eleanor Tufts, who were married in November 1869 at
> Salt Lake City [the Abstract filed earlier indicated
> that the marriage took place at the Endowment House]
> Eleanor Tufts assumed that her Church divorce was a
> valid legal divorce, as a consquence she married again.
> Courts upheld her petition.
> CU-L, DLC, ICU, MH, MiU, UAr, UPB, UU, ViU-L

[1073] Eleanor B. Tufts, plaintiff, vs. Elbridge Tufts, defendant.
Transcript of record. In the District Court of the
Third Judicial District, Salt Lake County, Territory of
Utah. [Chicago: Press of the Irrigation Age, 1892?]
12p.

> Transcript of record in the Elbridge Tufts v. Eleanor
> Tufts case Territory of Utah Reports 8 (June 1892) 142-
> 149. The transcript gives much more detail about the
> marriage, and its mental cruelty. It also indicates
> here that the marriage took place in the Endowment
> House.
> UAr, UPB

[1074] "Industrial Home," Congressional Record 52nd Congress, 1st
session (8 March 1892) vol. 23, pt. 2, p. 1841 [X301]

> The petition of the governor and the Legislative
> Assembly of the Territory of Utah was mentioned regarding
> the grounds and building of the Industrial Home being
> donated to the Territory for school use. The brief
> debate centered around whether it should be sent to the
> Committee on Judiciary or the Committee on Territories
> [Territories won out] because there was a question on
> which committee debated all the Mormon concerns.

[1075] John Blazzard, by his guardian ad litem, Mariam Blazzard
Steers; Thomas Blazzard, James Blazzard and Mariam
Blazzard Steers, plaintiffs, vs. Caleb D. Blazzard and
Richard Howe, defendants, and Mary Jane Hill and Sarah
Jane Stewart, plaintiffs in intervention. Transcript
and abstract in the Supreme Court of Utah Territory.
[n.p., 1892?] 108p.

> No ruling can be found in the Utah Reports for this
> case, but the transcripts, abstracts and briefs are
> nevertheless related to Mormonism, regarding the
> Blazzard family and probate and inheritance problems
> related to polygamy, and the Nauvoo period of the
> Church.
> UAr

[1076] John Blazzard, by his guardian ad litem, Mariam Blazzard
Steers; James Blazzard, Thomas Blazzard and Mariam
Blazzard Steers, plffs and Respd'ts., vs. Lucy D.
Watts, individually and as Administratrix, with the
will annexed of John H. Blazzard, deceased, Caleb D.
Blazzard, Orson D. Blazzard, and Mark H. Blazzard,
defendants and appellants, No. 8248. John Blazzard,

et. al., plaintiffs and respondents, vs. Lucy D. Watts, et. al., defendants and appellants, No. 8247. John Blazzard et. al., plaintiffs and respondents, vs. Orson D. Blazzard, et. al., defendants and appellants, No. 8246. John Blazzard, et. al., plaintiffs and respondents vs. Caleb D. Blazzard, et. al., defendants and appellants, No. 8245. John Blazzard, et. al., plaintiffs and respondents, vs. Mark H. Blazzard et. al., defendants and appellants, No. 8244. Appellants' brief on appeal in the Supreme Court of Utah Territory. [n.p., 1892?] 108p.

See entry 1075 for annotation.

UAr

[1077] John Blazzard, by his guardian ad litem, Mariam Blazzard Steers, Thomas Blazzard, James Blazzard and Mariam Blazzard Steers, plaintiffs, vs. Lucy D. Watts and Richard Howe, defendants, and Mary Jane Hill and Sarah Jane Stewart, plaintiffs in intervention, No. 8247. Transcript and abstract in the Supreme Court of Utah Territory. [n.p., 1892?] 108p.

See entry 1075 for annotation.

UAr

[1078] John Blazzard, by his guardian ad litem, Mariam Blazzard Steers, Thomas Blazzard, James Blazzard and Mariam Blazzard Steers, plaintiffs, vs. Lucy D. Watts individually and as Administratrix, with the Will annexed, of the estate of John H. Blazzard, deceased, Caleb D. Blazzard, Orson D. Blazzard and Mark H. Blazzard, defendants, and Mary Jane Hill and Sarah Jane Stewart, plaintiffs in invention, No. 8248. Transcript and abstract in the Supreme Court of Utah Territory. [n.p., 1892?] 117p.

See entry 1075 for annotation.

UAr

[1079] John Blazzard, by his guardian ad litem, Mariam Blazzard Steers, Thomas Blazzard, James Blazzard and Mariam Blazzard Steers, plaintiffs, vs. Mark H. Blazzard and Richard Howe, defendants, and Mary Jane Hill and Sarah Jane Stewart, plaintiffs in intervention, No. 8244. Transcript and Abstract in the Supreme Court of Utah Territory. [n.p., 1892?] 108p.

See entry 1075 for annotation.

UAr

[1080] John Blazzard, by his guardian ad litem, Mariam Blazzard Steers, Thomas Blazzard, James Blazzard and Mariam Blazzard Steers, plaintiffs, vs. Orson D. Blazzard, J. H. Clive, Walter L. Price and E. A. Kessler, defendants, and Mary Jane Hill and Sarah Jane Stewart, plaintiffs in intervention, No. 8246. Transcript and Abstract in the Supreme Court of Utah Territory. [n.p., 1892?] 112p.

See entry 1075 for annotation.

UAr

[1081] "Memorial," Congressional Record 52d Congress, 1st session
(15 February 1892) vol. 33, pt. 2, p. 1167. [X301]

Memorial, not printed, against the Faulkner-Caine and
Teller bills which would have provided home rule for
Utah.

[1082] "Memorial," Congressional Record 52d Congerss, 1st session
(7 June 1892) vol. 33, pt. 6, p. 5103. [X305]

Memorial, not printed agains the Faulkner-Caine and
Teller bills which would have provided home rule for
Utah.

[1083] "Memorials," Congressional Record 52d Congress, 1st
session (23, 26, 28, 29, 30 March, 1, 4, 5 April 1892)
vol. 33, pt. 3, pp. 2385, 2596, 2597, 2600, 2635, 2682,
2856, 2890, 2943. [X302]

Memorials, not printed, against the Faulkner-Caine and
Teller bills which would have provided home rule for
Utah. Seems to be a predominantly Pennsylvania campaign.

[1084] "Memorials," Congressional Record 52d Congress, 1st
session (11, 13, 15, 19, 22, 25, 26, 27 April 1892)
vol. 33, pt. 4, pp. 3151, 3153, 3234, 3356, 3403, 3435,
3513, 3606, 3641, 3642, 3731. [X303]

Memorials, not printed, against the Faulkner-Caine and
Teller bills which would have provided home rule for
Utah. Seems to be a predominantly Pennsylvania campaign.

[1085] "Memorials," Congressional Record 52d Congress, 1st
session (9, 11, 18, 19 May, 1 June 1892) vol. 33, pt.
5, pp. 4077, 4162, 4403, 4405, 4885. [X304]

Memorials, not printed, against the Faulkner-Caine and
Teller bills which would have provided home rule for
Utah. Seems to be a predominantly Pennsylvania campaign.

[1086] "Mormon church litigation," p. xxi. In Annual report of
the Attorney-general of the United States for the year
1892. Washington: Govt. Print. Off., 1892. [J1.1:892]

Litigation touching the property of the Mormon church.

[1087] "Petition against Utah Statehood," Congressional Record
52d Congress, 1st session (17 February 1892) vol. 23,
pt. 2, p. 1263. [X301]

Memorial of former Iowa residents against Utah statehood.
Not printed in full.

[1088] "Petition against Utah Statehood," Congressional Record
52d Congress, 1st session (29 March 1892) vol. 23, pt.
3, p. 2633. [X302]

Citizens of Pennsylvania memorial, not printed in full,
against admission of Utah as a state.

[1089] "Polygamy" (Chapter 7, February 4, 1892). <u>Laws of Territory of Utah, 1892</u>, Salt Lake City: The Irrigation Age, Co., 1892? pp. 5-6.

Vigorous anti-polygamy legislation aimed to secure statehood.

UPB

[1090] "Report of the Attorney of the United States for the district of Utah upon the Mormon Church," p. 315-317. In <u>Annual report of the Attorney-general of the United States of the United States for the year 1892</u>. Washington: Govt. Print. Off., 1892. [Jl.1:892]

Exhibit P, Mormon church litigation.

[1091] <u>Report of the Utah Commission to the Secretary of the Interior. 1892</u>. Washington: Govt. Print. Off., 1892. 25p.

See entry 1071 for annotation.

[Flake 9239]
CtY, DLC, ICN, MH, NN, UHi, UPB, US1C

[1092] "Statement of John T. Caine, a delegate from the Territory of Utah," pp. 172-177. In <u>Hearings before Subcommittee House, Committee on Appropriations</u>. Washington: Govt. Print. Off, 1892.

John T. Caine requests the abolition of the Utah Commission, based upon its cost to the government and the fact that polygamy has been abolished. He also recommends that the Industrial Christian Home of Utah be turned over to the Territory for a school for the deaf.

Xerox of pp. 172-177 at UPB and US1C, Original in its entirety at DLC.

[1093] Thomas, Arthur L. "Report of the Governor of Utah to the Secretary of the Interior, 1892," pp. 381-443. In <u>Annual Report of the Department of the Interior, 1892</u>, vol. 3. Washington: Govt. Print. Off., 1892. [I1.1:892/vol.3]

Gives a summary of territorial legislation, including the prohibition of polygamy. Governor express his opinion that amnesty be given to polygamous Mormons. Includes the Dec. 18, 1891 petition for amnesty from Church leaders to the governor.

Summary report found in vol. 1, pp. CIX-CXVIII.

Variant ed. of the summary report Report of the Secretary of the Interior for the fiscal year ending June 30, 1892. Washington: Govt. Print. Off., 1892. pp. 113-122.

Variant ed. 52d Congress, 2d session, H. Exec. Doc. No. 1, Serial Set 3089.

[1094] Thomas, Arthur L. Report of the Governor of Utah to the Secretary of the Interior, 1892. Washington: Govt. Print. Off., 1892. 65p.

Report of polygamy and church participation in politics.
[Flake 9378]
UHi, UPB, US1C

[1095] "To the honorable the Senate and House of Representatives of the United States in Congress Assembled," Congressional Rcord 52d Congress, 1st session (10 February 1892) vol. 23, pt. 1, p. 997. [X300]

Polygamy, once practiced by a small minority, has been eliminated, but the Utah Commission continues to interfere with the affairs of the territory.

[1096] U.S. House. Committee on Territories. Arguments made before the Committee on the Territories of the House of Representatives on bill (H.R. 524) "for the Local Government of Utah Territory and to provide for the election of certain officers in said Territories." [Washington? 1892] 71p.

Polygamy hearings after the Manifesto probably same as entry 1099, True Condition of Utah, this item lacks title page.
[Flake 9154]
UHi, UPB, US1C

[1097] U.S. House. Committee on the Territories. Notes of a hearing before the Committee on Territories of the House of Representatives on Bill (H.R. 524) "For the local government of Utah Territory and to provide for the election of certain officers in said Territories." [Washington: Govt. Print. Off., 1892] 97p.

Mormons and politics. Extensive discussion of polygamy after the Manifesto. Party politics and Mormonism.
[Flake 9156]
MH, UPB, US1C

[1098] U.S. House. Committee on the Territories. Notes of a hearing before the Committee on Territories of the House of Representatives on Bill (H.R. 524) for the local government of Utah Territory and to provide for the election of certain officers in said Territories..." Washington, 1892. 104p.

Hearings after the Manifesto.

Prevalence of polygamy and Mormon Church policy. Testimony of individuals such as Caleb West, Franklin S. Richards, Wilford Woodruff, C. E. Allen of the Liberal Party, and others.
[Flake 9157]
US1C

[1099] U.S. House. Committee on the Territories. True condition of Utah. Arguments by delegations from Utah, made

before the House Committee on Territories, First
Session fifty-second Congress, in favor of the passage
of the pending bills providing for statehood or home
rule for the Territory of Utah [H.R. 524 and H.R.
4008]. Washington: Govt. Print. Off., 1892. 71p.

Polygamy hearings after the Manifesto.
[Flake 9160a]
UPB, US1C

[1100] U.S. House. 52d Congress. 1st Session. Committee on the
Territories. Local government for the Territory of
Utah... Report: [To accompany H.R. 7690]. (H. Rept.
No. 943) Washington: Govt. Print. Off., 1892. 28p.
[Serial Set 3044]

Considerable on polygamy and the Mormons.
[Flake 9153]

[1101] U.S. House. 52d Congress. 1st Session. Committee on War
Claims. James Bridger. Report: [To accompany S.
1198] The Committee on War Claims, to whom was referred
the bill (S. 1198) for the relief of the heirs of James
Bridger, deceased, submit the following report. (H.
Rept. No. 1576) Washington: Govt. Print. Off., 1892.
24p. [Serial Set 3046]

Claims from the destruction of Fort Bridger due to the
Utah Expedition.
[Flake 9162]

[1102] U.S. House. 52d Congress. 1st Session. Enforcement of
Immigration and Contract-Labor laws. (H. Rept. No.
1573) Washington: Govt. Print. Off., 1892. 3p.
[Serial Set 3046]

A form was utilized to enforce the Immigration and
Contract-Labor laws which was entitled "Passenger List,
List or manifest of Immigrants. . ." one of the columns
in this form was entitled "whether a polygamist" An
example of this form, used repeatedly, is found in this
report.

[1103] U.S. House. 52d Congress. 1st Session. H. Res. 77,
"Joint Resolution proposing an amendment to the Constitution
prohibiting polygamy within the United States, and all
places subject to their jurisdiction, to be known as
the sixteenth amendment, February 1, 1892." [Washington:
Govt. Print. Off., 1892] 3p.

Referred to the Committee on the Judiciary.

DLC, UPB, US1C

[1104] U.S. House. 52d Congress. 1st Session. H.R. 9689, "A
bill to enable the people of Utah to form a constitution
and State government, and to be admitted into the Union
on an equal footing with the original states, July 30,
1892." [Washington: Govt. Print. Off., 1892] 15p.

Referred to the Committee on the Territories.

In section 3, line 17, "no inhabitant of said state
shall ever be molested in person or property on account
of his or her mode of religious worship."
                                    DLC, UPB, USlC

[1105] U.S. House. 52d Congress. 1st Session. Immigration
       Investigation (H. Rept. No. 2090) Washington: Govt.
       Print. Off., 1892. 798p. [Serial Set 3053]

       In the testimony of Dr. Walter Kempster, he indicated
       that various steamship companies made up their own form
       to implement their interpretation of the United States
       Immigration Act. He refers to the Hamburg American
       Packet Co., the Nord Deutscher Lloyd and the Red Star
       Line. On pp. 769-770 Kempster refers to the form of
       the Hamburg American Packet Co., who interpret Question
       #6, polygamists, as person having several wives, for
       example, Mormons.

[1106] U.S. House. 52d Congress. 1st Session. Letter from
       Governor of Utah, transmitting the fourth annual report
       of the Commissioner of Schools for Utah Territory. (H.
       Misc. Doc. No. 47) Washington: Govt. Print. Off.,
       1892. 16p. [Serial Set 2959]

       Signed: Dec. 31, 1891.

       Mentions Mormons and Mormon schools. Report of Commissioner
       of Schools for Utah, 1890.
                                          [Flake 9330]

[1107] U.S. House. 52d Congress. 1st Session. Letter from the
       chairman of the Utah Commission acting as a board for
       the mangement and control of the Industrial Christian
       Home Association of Utah, transmitting the report of
       the Commission respecting the operations of that
       Association. (H. Misc. Doc. No. 104) Washington:
       Govt. Print. Off., 1892. 5p. [Serial Set 2959]

                                          [Flake 9235]

[1108] U.S. House. 52d Congress. 1st Session. Letter from the
       Secretary of the Treasury, transmitting a Report of the
       Commissioners of Immigration upon the Causes which
       incite immigration to the United States. (H. Ex. Doc.
       235, Part I) Washington: Govt. Print. Off., 1892.
       331p. [Serial Set 2957]

       Three entries in this massive report contain information
       about Mormon immigration. (1) p. 143 in the report
       contains a circular from the Hamburg-American Packet
       Company which contains the March 3, 1891 Immigration
       Act and its clause on no polygamists. The circular
       pointedly draws attention by saying i.e. Mormons. (2)
       p. 147 contains a letter from the Red Star Line Royal
       Belgian Mail Steamers which in a brief passage describes
       the category of U.S. immigrants which are excluded
       under U.S. law, one of which is polygamists. (3) pp.
       185-187 entitled "The Mormon Movement," gives a brief

background on Mormon emigration from England, especially from Liverpool.

[1109] U.S. House. 54th Congress. 2d Session. Fourteenth annual report of the Bureau of Ethnology to the Secretary of the Smithsonian Institution, 1892-93. By J. W. Powell, Director. (H. Doc. No. 230, Pt. 2) Washington: Govt. Print. Off., 1896. [Serial Set 3531]

Appendix, pp. 792-799, The Mormons, the Indians and the coming of the Messiah, Deseret Evening News, made January, 1892, "1890 has passed, and no Messiah had come. 1891 has passed, and no pruning of the vineyard."

[Flake 9101a]

[1110] United States of America, appellant, vs. The Late Corporation of the Church of Jesus Christ of Latter-day Saints, and others, appellees, No. 1287. Appeal from the Supreme Court of Utah Territory. Motion to Advance Cause. Supreme Court of the United States, October Term, 1892. [n.p., 1893?] 6p.

This appeal was filed in the United States v. The Late Corporation of the Church of Jesus Christ of Latter-day Saints 150 U.S. Reports, 6 November 1893, 145-149.

[Flake add. 7237a]
DLC, UPB, US1C

[1111] United States of America, plaintiff, v. The Late Corporation of the Church of Jesus Christ or [sic.] Latter-day Saints, et al., defendants. Brief for the Petitioners, Wilford Woodruff, George Q. Cannon and Joseph F. Smith. Franklin S. Richards of counsel for Petitioners. [Salt Lake City? 1892] 13p.

At head of title: In the Supreme Court of Utah Territory.

Brief filed in the United States vs. The Late Corporation of the Church of Jesus Christ of Latter-day Saints Territory of Utah Reports 8 (June 1892) pp. 310-352.
UAr, UPB, US1C

[1111a] United States of America, plaintiff vs. The Late Corporation of the Church of Jesus Christ of Latter-day Saints, and others, defendents, June Term 1892. Opinion. Salt Lake City: Star Print, 1892. 43p.

Certified copy. Signed: John W. Blackburn, James A. Miner.

At head of title: In the Supreme Court, Territory of Utah...Brief filed in regard to the United States respondent vs. The Late Corporation of the Church of Jesus Christ of Latter-day Saints and others appellants, Territory of Utah Reports 8 (June 1892) pp. 310-352.
US1C

[1112] United States of America, vs. The Late Corporation of the Church of Jesus Christ of Latter-day Saints, et. al.,

Brief of W. H. Dickson, of counsel for defendants. [Salt Lake? Star Print, Herald Block, 1892?] 28p.

Brief filed in regard to the United States, respondent, v. the late Corporation of the Church of Jesus Christ of Latter-day Saints and others, appellants, Territory of Utah Reports 8 (June 1892) pp. 310-352.

This brief of W. H. Dickson proposed the argument that property should be vested in a trustee to be used for church purposes which were legal. This brief and the decision in the Territorial Supreme Court played an important role in the later Supreme Court decision of United States v. the Late Corporation of the Church of Jesus Christ of Latter-day Saints, U.S. Reports, 105 pp. 145-149, which reversed the act of May 19, 1890 wherein the Church was dissolved.

UPB, USlC, UHi, UU

[1113] United States, respondent, v. The late Corporation, the Church of Jesus Christ of Latter-day Saints and others, appellants, Territory of Utah Reports 8 (June 1892) pp. 310-352.

After the church was disincorporated its real estate was escheated to the U.S., but the church personal property was not disposed of. The decision held that such property should be vested in a trustee to be used for church purposes which were legal.

CU-L, DLC, ICU, MH, MiU, UAr, UPB, UU, ViU-L

[1114] U.S. Senate. Committee on Territories. Hearings before the Committee on Territories of the U. S. Senate in relation to the Bill (S. 1306) for the local government of Utah Territory, and to provide for the election of certain officers in said territory. Washington: Govt. Print. Off., 1892. 166p.

Franklin S. Richards, Caleb West, John T. Caine, John H. Smith and many others gave testimony on polygamy, church & state, Edmunds Act, People's Party of Utah and the Liberal Party.

[Flake 9181]
CU-B, MH, UHi, UPB, USlC

[1115] U.S. Senate. Committee on Territories. Home rule for Utah: arguments made by a delegation from Utah before the Senate Committee on Territories, First Session, 52nd Congress, in favor of passage of S. 1306, "A bill for the local government of Utah Territory and to provide for the election of certain officers in the said territory." Washington: Govt. Print. Off., 1892. 113p.

Same as above entry, except session of February 18, 23 is omitted.

[Flake 9182]
CU-B, UHi, UPB, USlC

[1116] U.S. Senate. Committee on Territories. Utah as it is: Arguments made by delegations from Utah before the

Senate Committee on Territories, First Session, Fifty-second Congress, in favor of the passage of the pending bills providing for statehood or local government for the Territory of Utah [S. 1306 and S. 1653] Washington: govt. Print. Off., 1892. 131p.

Discusses polygamy and the domination of the Mormon hierarchy. Discussion of the composition of the Democratic and Republican parties in regards to Mormons.

[Flake 9185]
MH, UPB, US1C

[1117] U.S. Senate. 52d Congress. 1st Session. Committee on Claims. In the Senate of the United States... Report: [To accompany S. 1198.] (S. Rept. No. 625) Washington: Govt. Print. Off., 1892. 23p. [Serial Set 2913]

Heirs of James Bridger attempt to secure reparation for Fort Bridger, burned during the Utah Expedition.

[Flake add. 9166d]

[1118] U.S. Senate. 52d Congress. 1st Session. In the Senate of the United States. . . from the Committee on Immigration. . . Report (to accompany S. 3240). (S. Rept. 787) Washington: Govt. Print. Off., 1892. 3p. [Serial Set 2914]

The report accompanying S. bill 3240 which resulted in the passage of the March 3, 1893 act found in v. 27, pp. 569-571 of the Statutes at Large. The act was a follow-up to the 1891 act which added the group of undesirable immigrants of polygamists. In this report there is an interesting "List of manifest of Immigrants" form reproduced which the ships' captains would fill out on each immigrant. One of the columns is for the question "Whether a polygamist."

[1119] U.S. Senate. 52d Congress. 1st Session. S. 2263, "In the United States, February 17, 1892, Mr. Paddock introduced the following bill; which was read twice and referred to the Committee on Territories. A bill to amend an act entitled 'An act to amend section fifty-three hundred and fifty-two of the Revised Statutes of the United States, in reference to bigamy, and for other purposes.'" [Washington, 1892] 1p.

[Flake 9166c]
US1C

[1120] United States, vs. The Late Corporation of the Church of Jesus Christ of Latter-day Saints, and others. Brief of J. W. Judd, for the petitioners, the Trustees of Brigham Young Academy, at Provo, Utah County... [Salt Lake City? 1892] 9p.

At head of title: In the Supreme Court, Utah Territory. June term, 1892.

Brief filed in the United States vs. the Late Corporation
of the Church of Jesus Christ of Latter-day Saints.
Territory of Utah Reports 8 (June 1892) pp. 310-352.
[Flake add. 4510b]
UAr, UHi, US1C

1893

"Now, therefore, I, Benjamin Harrison,
President of the United States, by virtue of
the powers in me vested, do hereby declare
and grant a full amnesty and pardon to all
persons liable to the penalties of said act
by reason of unlawful cohabitation under the
color of polygamous or plural marriage who
have since November 1, 1890, abstained from
such unlawful cohabitation, but upon the
express condition that they shall in the
future faithfully obey the laws of the United
States hereinbefore named, and not otherwise.
Those who shall fail to avail themselves of
the clemency hereby offered will be vigorously
prosecuted."
[Entry 1126]

[1121] "An act making appropriations for the legislative, executive,
and judicial expenses of the government. . ." (Chapter
211, March 3, 1893) United States Statutes at Large
27, p. 697 [G4.111:27, AE2.111:27]

Funding for territorial officers, including the Utah
Commission.

[1122] "An act to facilitate the enforcement of the immigration
and contract-labor laws of the United States" (Chapter
206, March 3, 1983) United States Statutes at Large 27,
pp. 569-571. [GS4.111:27, AE2.111:27]

The act was a follow-up to the 1891 immigration act
which added the group of undesirable immigrants of
polygamists. The report which accompanies this act is
found in Serial Set 2914 as Senate Report 787. See
entry 1119.

[1123] "Admission of Utah," Congressional Record 53rd Congress,
2d session (8, 12, 13 December 1893) vol. 26, pt. 1,
pp. 118, 174-187, 209-220. [X317]

Morse and other representatives depict the Mormons as
undependable scoundrels, while Rawlins from Utah and
others laud the Mormons. See also entry 1157 where the
Hon. J. E. Washington eulogizes the Mormons.

[1124] "Annual report of the Utah Commission, 1893," pp. 407-
451. In Annual Report of the Department of the Interior,
1893, vol. 3. Washington: Govt. Print. Off., 1893.
[I1.1:893/v.3]

Includes information on the closing of the Industrial Christian Home Association, the voter registration of the Mormons granted amnesty by President Harrison, and a brief history of the Mormons in Utah. Summary of Commission's report by the Secretary of Interior in vol. 1. [Serial Set 3209] pp. LIII-LV.

Variant ed. U.S. 53rd Congress, 2d session, House Exec. Doc. No. 1. Serial Set 3211.

[1125] Chapman v. Handley, U.S. Reports, 151 (October 1893) 443-446. [Ju 6.8/1:151]

The rights of the heirs of a second or polygamist wife to inherit part of the estate.

[1126] Harrison, Benjamin F. "By the President of the United States of America: A Proclamation, 4 January 1893," pp. 5803-5804. In A Compilation of the Messages and Papers of the Presidents, by James D. Richardson, vol. VIII. New York: Bureau of National Literature, 1911, c1897. [GS4.113:8, AE2.114:1-27/v.8]

This proclamation provided amnesty and pardon to those who have "abstained from unlawful cohabitation".

[1127] Joseph P. Ledwidge, as County Clerk and Clerk of the Probate Court of Weber County, Utah, plaintiff and respondent, George H. Matson, as County Registration Officer of Weber County, Utah, and F. L. Chapin, O. P. Herriman, George L. Corey, Jr., A. I. Stone and H. M. Dubrow, as Deputy Registrars, defendants and appellants. Brief for appellants. In the Supreme Court of the Territory of Utah, January term, 1893. Ogden: Acme Printing, 1893. 10p.

This brief was filed in the Joseph P. Ledwidge respondent, v. George H. Matson and other, appellants 9 Utah Reports (June 1893) 106-110.

UAr, UPB

[1128] Joseph P. Ledwidge, respondent, v. George H. Matson and others, appellants. Territory of Utah Reports 9 (June, 1893) pp. 106-110.

How the Edmunds and Edmunds-Tucker laws affected elections.
CU-L, DLC, ICU, MH, MiU, UAr, UPB, USlC, UU, ViU-L

[1129] Lester T. Rogers appellant, vs. Jennie V. Thompson, et al., respondents. Brief. Appeal from Third Judicial District. The Supreme Court of Utah. [n.p., 1893?] 11p.

In the brief for the case 9 Utah Reports 46-48, The United States vs. The Church of Jesus Christ of Latter-day Saints is used as authority for this case.

UAr, UPB

[1130] "Memorial," Congressional Record 53d Congress, 2d session (13 December 1893) vol. 26, pt. 1, p. 188. [X317]

Memorial, not printed, against admission of Utah as a
state.

[1131] "The Mormon Church Litigation," in U.S. Attorney Generals
Opinions. Official Opinions of the Attorney General of
the United States. Vol. 20. Washington: Govt. Print.
Off., 1893, p. xviii. [Jul.5:20]

Brief paragraph which mentions that Mormon Church
litigation was the subject of an act of Congress which
was passed at a special session begun August 7. The
Act referred to is Joint Resolution no. 11, October 25,
1893 in U.S. Statutes at Large, v. 28, p. 980.

DLC, UPB, US1C

[1132] Morse, Elijah Addison. Admission of Utah as a state.
Polygamy and Mormonism, the foulist blot upon American
civilization. The Territory of Utah unfit for statehood
and should wait until anti-Mormons are in the majority.
Speech of Hon. Elijah A. Morse... Of Massachusetts, in
the House of Representatives, Tuesday, December 12,
1893. Washington, 1893. 13p.

See entry 1123 for annotation.

[Flake 5590]
MH, UPB

[1133] "Providing for the disposition of certain personal property
and money now in the hands of a receiver of the Church
of Jesus Christ of Latter-day Saints, appointed by the
supreme court of Utah, and authorizing its application
to the charitable purposes of said church. (Joint
resolution, No. 11, October 25, 1893) United States
Statutes at Large, v.28, p. 980. [GS4.111:28]

This resolution led to the Supreme Court case U.S. v.
The Late Corporation of the Church of Jesus Christ of
Latter-day Saints, 150 U.S. Reports 145-149.

[1134] Rawlins, Joseph Lafayette. Admission of Utah. Speech of
Hon. Joseph L. Rawlins, of Utah, in the House of
Representatives, Tuesday, December 12, 1893. Washington,
1893. 23p.

Concerning polygamy and statehood. See entry 1123 for
annotation.

[Flake 6825]
DLC, UPB, US1C

[1135] Report of the Utah Commission to the Secretary of the
Interior, 1893. Washington: Govt. Print. Off., 1893.
16p.

See entry 1124 for annotation.

[Flake 9239]
CtY, DLC, ICN, MH, NN, UHi, UPB, US1C

[1136] Sarah A. Chapman et al., appellants vs. Elizabeth Handley,
respondent. Respondent's brief. Record Case no.

14,191. Attorneys for respondents E. D. Hoge, Arthur Brown. Supreme Court of the United States. [n.p., 1893] 14p.

This brief was filed in regard to the Chapman v. Handley case 151 U.S. Reports 443-446, October 1893 session.

[Flake add. 4056ba]
DLC, UPB, US1C

[1137] The United States, appellant, vs. The late Corporation of the Church of Jesus Christ of Latter-day Saints et al., Appeal from the Supreme Court of the Territory of Utah. [Washington: Govt. Print. Off., 1893] 217p.

At head of title: Record Case No. 15257.

Property suits resulting from polygamy legislation.

This appeal was filed in the Late Corporation of the Church of Jesus Christ of Latter-day Saints v. The United States 150 U.S. Reports (6 November 1893) 145-149.

[Flake 9230]
DLC, NjP, UHi

[1138] The United States, appellant, v. The Late Corporation of the Church of Jesus Christ of Latter-day Saints, et al., No. 887. Appeal from the Supreme Court of the Territory of Utah. Brief for the United States. In the Supreme Court of the United States, October term, 1893. [n.p., 1893?] 22p.

This brief was filed in regard to the United States v. The Late Corporation of the Church of Jesus Christ of Latter-day Saints case 150 U.S. Reports (6 November 1893) 145-149.

[Flake add. 1450c]
DLC, UPB, US1C

[1139] U.S. House. 52d Congress. 2d Session. Committee on the Territories. Admission of Utah... Mr. Mansur, from the Committee of the Territories, submitted the following report: [To accompany H.R. 10190.] (H. Rept. No. 2337) Washington: Govt. Print. Off., 1893. 20p. [Serial Set 3141]

Recommends the passage of the bill to admit Utah as a state. With the Manifesto, which is included, and along with the petition of amnesty, etc., statehood should be granted.

[Flake 9142]

[1140] U.S. House. 52d Congress. 2d Session. Industrial Christian Home of Utah. Communication from the Utah Commissioners transmitting their annual report to Congress. (H. Misc. Doc. No. 6) Washington: Govt. Print. Off., 1893. 4p. [Serial Set 3110]

Report of the Industrial Christian Home Association of Utah for 1892.

[Flake 9234]

[1141] U.S. House. 53d Congress. 1st Session. Committee on the Judiciary. Church of Jesus Christ of Latter-day Saints... Report: [To accompany H. Res. 34.] (H. Rept. No. 50) Washington: Govt. Print. Off., 1893. 1p. [Serial Set 3157]

Disposition of church property after the Manifesto.

[1142] U.S. House. 53d Congress. 1st Session. Committee on the Territories. Admission of Utah... Mr. Kilgore, from the Committee on the Territories, submitted the following report: [To accompany H.R. 352) (H. Rept. No. 162] Washington: Govt. Print. Off., 1893. 2 parts (24, 15p.) [Serial Set 3157]

The majority report recommends the passage of the bill, showing that the Mormon church has given up polygamy. The minority report puts forth its own bill that prohibits polygamy.

Pt. 2. "Views of the minority" submitted by Mr. Wheeler.

[Flake 9146]

[1143] U.S. House. 53d Congress. 1st Session. H. Res. 34, "Joint resolution providing for the disposition of certain personal property and money now in the hands of a receiver of the Church of Jesus Christ of Latter-Day Saints, appointed by the Supreme Court of Utah, and authorizing its application to the charitable purposes of said church, September 9, 1893." [Washington: Govt. Print. Off., 1893] 2p.

Referred to the Committee on the Judiciary.

Mr. Rawlins presented this resolution stating that the church no longer practiced polygamy and therefore the church's property sould be returned to it from the receivership.

DLC, UPB, US1C

[1144] The United States of America, appellant, v. The Late Corporation of the Church of Jesus Christ of Latter-day Saints, et. al., appellees, No. 887. Appeal from the Supreme Court of Utah Territory. Brief for Appellees. [Attorney] for appellees Franklin S. Richards. Supreme Court of the United States, October Term, 1893. Washington: Gibson Bros., Printers and Bookbinders, 1893. 43p.

Brief in the United States v. the Late Corporation of the Church of Jesus Christ of Latter-day Saints 150 U.S. Reports (6 November 1893) 145-149.

DLC, UPB, US1C

[1145] The United States of America, appellant, v. The Late Corporation of the Church of Jesus Christ of Latter-day Saints et. al., appellees, No. 887. Appeal from the

Supreme Court of Utah Territory. Motion for decree.
[Attorney] for appellees Franklin S. Richards. Supreme
Court of the United States, October Term, 1893.
Washington: Gibson Bros., Printers and bookbinders,
1893. 2p.

This motion was filed in regard to the United States v.
The Late Corporation of the Church of Jesus Christ of
Latter-day Saints case 150 U.S. Reports (6 November
1893) 145-149.

DLC, UPB, US1C

[1146] The United States of America, appellant, v. The Late
Corporation of the Church of Jesus Christ of Latter-day
Saints, et. al., appellees, No. 887. Appeal from the
Supreme Court of Utah Territory. Motion for decree.
[Attorney] for appellees Franklin S. Richards. Supreme
Court of the United States, October Term, 1893.
Washington: Gibson Bros., Printers and Bookbinders,
1893. 6p.

This motion was filed in regard to the United States v.
The Late Corporation of the Church of Jesus Christ of
Latter-day Saints case 150 U.S. Reports (6 November
1893) 145-149.

[Flake add. 7237b]
DLC, UPB, US1C

[1147] United States, respondent, v. Church Coal Lands and Angus
M. Cannon, treasurer, appellant, Territory of Utah
Reports 9 (June 1893), pp. 288-289.

Church first obtained an interest in the land in April
1880 and in accordance with the opinion of the U.S. v.
Tithing Yard, this land escheated to the United States
and that action is affirmed by the court.
CU-L, DLC, ICU, MH, MiU, UAr, UPB, UU, ViU-L

[1148] United States, respondent, v. Church Farm and Francis
Armstrong and another, Trustees, appellants, Territory
of Utah Reports 9 (June 1893) p. 289.

The Church first acquired an interest in the Church
Farm in 1874 and based upon the decision of the U.S.
vs. Tithing Yard, the property escheated to the United
States and this decision is affirmed by the court.

CU-L, DLC, ICU, MH, MiU, UAr, UPB, UU, ViU-L

[1149] United States, respondent, v. Gardo House and Historian
Office and James P. Freeze . . . Territory of Utah
Reports 9 (June 1893) pp. 285-288.

The Gardo House and Historian Office were subject to
forfeiture by the church based upon the 1862 Morrill
Act and the U.S. vs. Tithing Yard decision. The
property was acquired after 1862.

CU-L, DLC, ICU, MH, MiU, UAr, UPB, UU, ViU-L

[1150] United States, respondent, v. Tithing Yard and Offices and James P. Freeze. . . Territory of Utah Reports 9 (June 1893) pp. 273-285.

Overturned a lower court ruling which claimed that the Tithing Yard should be divested from the Mormon Church based upon the proviso of the 1862 Anti-Polygamy law which escheated real estate owned by religious corporations in excess of $50,000. Court decision was that "existing vested rights in real estate shall not be impaired" by this section of the 1862 law, and because property was bought or acquired prior to existence of law or U.S. Land office.

CU-L, DLC, ICU, MH, MiU, UAr, UPB, UU, ViU-L

[1151] U.S. Senate. 52d Congress. 2d Session. Committee on Claims. Report: [To accompany S. 3863]. (S. Rept. No. 1295) Washington: Govt. Print. Off., 1893. 5p. [Serial Set 3073]

Recommends the refunding to George Q. Cannon of forfeited bail, in regard to his unlawful cohabitation indictments.
[Flake 9167]

[1152] U.S. Senate. 52d Congress. 2d Session. Letter from the Secretary of the Interior, transmitting the report of the Commissioner of Schools for Utah. (S. Ex. Doc. No. 30) Washington: Govt. Print. Off., 1893. 20p. [Serial Set 3056]

Some information on Mormon schools.
[Flake 9334]

[1153] U.S. Senate. 52d Congress. 2d Session. Letter from the Secretary of the Treasury, inclosing [sic] papers in the claim of George Q. Cannon for money covered in the Treasury on a forfeited bond. (S. Ex. Doc. No. 43) Washington: Govt. Print. Off., 1893. 4p. [Serial Set 3056]

Some information of George Q. Cannon's arrest and circumstances of his unlawful cohabitation.
[Flake 9195]

[1154] U.S. Senate. 53rd Congress. 2d Session. The Vice-President presented the following report of the Utah Commission, with copies of correspondence between said commission and various officials of the govt. and others, relative to the occupancy of the Industrial Christian Home Building at Salt Lake City, Utah. (S. Misc. Doc. No. 7) Washington: Govt. Print. Off., 1895. 7p. [Serial Set 3167]

Referred to the Committee on Territories on December 5, 1893.
[Flake 9243]

[1155] U.S. Utah Commission. Sir: I enclose herewith a commission appointing you a Judge of Election for the General Election in November, 1893. Upon your acceptance of the appointment, please subscribe and swear to the oath enclosed, and return the same to me. The following has been prepared by the Commission for the information of Election Judges. Salt Lake City, 1893. 2p.

Contains in Sec. VI, a paragraph regarding the prohibition of polygamists as voter.

Signed at end: A. B. Williams, Chairman.

[Flake 9241]
UPB

[1156] United States v. The Late Corporation of the Church of Jesus Christ of Latter-day Saints, U.S. Reports 150 (6 November 1893) 145-149. [JU6.8/1:150]

Reversed the act, May 19, 1890 wherein the Church of Jesus Christ of Latter-day Saints was dissolved.

[1157] Washington, Joseph E. (Tennessee) "Admission of Utah," Congressional Record 53rd Congress, 2d session (13 December 1893) vol. 26, pt. 9, Appendix, pp. 34-36. [X325]

Defends the Mormons, especially as to the paucity of polygamy being practiced in the Territory.

[1158] West, Caleb W. "Report of the Governor of Utah to the Secretary of the Interior, 1893," pp. 389-405. In Annual Report of the Department of the Interior, 1893, vol. 3. Washington: Govt. Print. Off., 1893. [I1.1:893]

Governor believes that polygamy has been abandoned, the People's Party dissolved and that Mormon-Gentile relations were harmonious.

Recommends that the Mormon Church's land confiscated under the 1887 Edmunds-Tucker law be returned.

[1159] West, Caleb W. Report of the Governor of Utah to the Secretary of the Interior, 1893. Washington: Govt. Print. Off., 1893. 19p.

See entry 1158 for annotation.

[Flake 9382]
MH, UPB, US1C

1894

"Partridge left the State about that time and died in 1841. One Poole, who lived at Independence, Missouri, in 1848 hunted up the heirs, five in number, of said Partridge, in the State of Iowa, and obtained from three of them a purported deed (acknowledged in Missouri) to the sixty-three acres of land at Independence, so deeded by said Partridge to

Oliver Cowdery, including the Temple Lot,
which lot contains about two and one half acres."
[Entry 1175]

[1160]   "An act to enable the people of Utah to form a constitution
and state government, and to be admitted into the union
on an equal footing with the original states." (Chapter
138, July 16, 1894) United States Statutes at Large
vol. 28, pp. 107-112. [GS4.111:28, AE2.111:28]

Statehood would be granted provided that polygamous
marriages are forever prohibited.

[1161] "Brigham Young Memorial," (Chapter XXVIII, March 7, 1894)
Laws of the Territory of Utah, 1894, pp. 24-5.

The Brigham Young Memorial Association contracted with
Cyrus E. Dallin to construct a monument upon the
capitol grounds in Salt Lake.

UPB

[1162] Cleveland, Grover. "By the President of the United States
of America: A Proclamation (No. 14, September 25,
1894) United States Statutes at Large 28, p. 1257.
[GS4.111:28, AE2.111:28]

Proclamation of amnesty for the Mormons after the
Manifesto.

[1163] Cleveland, Grover. "By the President of the United States
of America: A Proclamation, 25 September 1894," pp.
5942-5943. In A Compilation of the Messages and Papers
of the Presidents, by James D. Richardson, Vol. 8. New
York: Bureau of National Literature, 1911, c1897.
[GS4.113:8, AE2.114:1-27/v.8]

In this proclamation, Cleveland echoes Harrison's
amnesty proclamation for polygamy for those people not
illegally cohabitating.

[1164] "Communication from the Secretary of the Territory of
Utah," Congressional Record 53d Congress, 2d session
(12 February 1894) vol. 26, pt. 3, p. 2074. [X319]

The Secretary transmitted a petition, not printed, of
the governor and the Legislative Assembly praying for
the restoration to the Church of Jesus Christ of
Latter-day Saints of certain real property.

[1165] "Memorial," Congressional Record 53d Congress, 2d session
(3 February 1894) vol. 26, pt. 2, p. 1853. [X318]

Memorial, not printed, to suppress and punish polygamy.

[1166] "Memorial," Congressional Record 53d Congress, 2d session
(16 June 1894) vol. 26, pt. 7, p. 6389. [X323]

Memorial, not printed, against admission of Utah as a
state.

[1167] "Memorial of the Citizens of Wooster, Ohio," Congressional Record 53rd Congress, 2d session (19 March 1894) vol. 26, pt. 4, p. 3073. [X320]

Unfortunately the entire memorial is not printed, but the citizens are remonstrating against admission of Utah, Arizona and New Mexico as states until the entire Mormon question is resolved.

[1168] "Memorials," Congressional Record 53d Congress, 2d session (26 February, 5, 13 March 1894) vol. 26, pt. 3, pp. 2407, 2576, 2578, 2927. [X319]

Memorials, not printed, against admission of Utah as a state until the Mormon question has been resolved.

[1169] Memorials," Congressional Record 53d Congress, 2d session (19 March, 14, 17, 24 April 1894) vol. 26, pt. 4, pp. 3073, 3751, 3764, 4016. [X320]

Memorials, not printed, against admission of Utah as a state until the Mormon question has been resolved.

[1170] "Memorials," Congressional Record 53d Congress, 2d session (28 April, 8, 15 May 1894) vol. 26, pt. 5, pp. 4214, 4472, 4746. [X321]

Memorials, not printed, against admission of Utah as a state until the Mormon question has been resolved.

[1171] "Memorials," Congressional Record 53d Congress, 2d session (24, 31 May, 5, 7 June 1894) vol. 26, pt. 6, pp. 5192, 5498, 5746, 5948. [X322]

Memorials, not printed, against admission of Utah as a state until the Mormon question has been resolved.

[1172] "Parochial Schools," pp. 1618-1619. In Report of the Commissioner of Education for the Year 1894-95, vol. 2. Washington: Govt. Print. Off., 1896. [FS5.1:894-895]

Reports the Mormon view of denominational education for their children. Quotes Juab Stake Academy and Wilford Woodruff on religious education philosophy.

[1173] Report of the Utah Commission to the Secretary of the Interior for the fiscal year ending June 30, 1894. Washington: Govt. Print. Off., 1894. 12p.

See entry 1174 for annotation.

[Flake 9239]
CtY, ICN, NN, UHi, UPB, USlC

[1174] "Thirteenth Annual Report of the Utah Commission, 1894," pp. 475-484. In Annual Report of the Department of the Interior, 1894, vol. 3. Washington: Govt. Print. Off., 1895. [I1.1:894/v.3]

Discusses new election laws, registration for 1893-94 and attempted changes in election laws. No Summary.

Variant ed. U.S. 53rd Congress, 3rd session. House
Exec. Doc. No. 1, pt. 5, vol. 16, Serial Set 3307.

[1175] U.S. Circuit Court (8th Circuit). Decision of John F.
Philips, judge, in Temple Lot case. The Reorganized
Church of Jesus Christ of Latter Day Saints versus the
Church of Christ, et. al., Lamoni, Ia., Reorganized
Church of Jesus Christ of Latter Day Saints, 1894.
Lamoni, Iowa: Reorganized Church of Jesus Christ of
Latter Day Saints, 1894. 28p.

Decision in favor of the complainant.
[Flake 9105]
CSmH, CtY, CU-B, DLC, MoInRC, NjP, NN, UPB, USlC, WHi

[1176] U.S. House. 53d Congress. 2d Session. Henry Page.
Letter from the acting Secretary of the Treasury,
transmitting a communication from the first Comptroller
in relation to the sum expended by the late disbursing
agent of the Industrial Christian Home Association of
Utah. (H. Ex. Doc. No. 220) Washington: Govt.
Print. Off., 1894. 2p. [Serial Set 3226]

[1177] U.S. Senate. 53rd Congress. 2d Session. Committee on
Territories. Admission of Utah, report [To accompany
H.R. 352] May 17, 1894. (S. Rept. No. 414) Washington:
Govt. Print. Off., 1895. 29p. [Serial Set 3183]

Some information on the character of Mormons and
polygamy.
[Flake 9184]

[1178] U.S. Senate. 53d Congress. 2d Session. Letter from the
Secretary of the Interior, transmitting annual report
of Commissioner of Schools for Utah. (S. Ex. Doc. No.
24) Washington: Govt. Print. Off., 1895. 18p.
[Serial Set 3160]

Signed: Jan. 10, 1894.

Segregation of Mormon and non-Mormon students no longer
practicable.
[Flake 9332]

[1179] U.S. Senate. 53d Congress. 2d Session. The Vice President
presented the following letter from the Secretary of
the Territory of Utah forwarding memorial of the
Territorial Legislature in favor of restoring certain
real estate to the Mormon Church. (S. Misc. Doc. No.
81) Washington: Govt. Print. Off., 1895. 2p. [Serial
Set 3167]

February 4, 1894 referred to the Committee on the
Judiciary. A memorial from the Territorial Legislature
and the Governor requesting that Mormon Church property
be returned because polygamy has been abandoned.

[Flake 9393]

[1180] West, Caleb W. "Governor's Message to the Legislative
        Assembly, January 8, 1894," pp. 16-20. In The House
        Journal of the Thirty-first session of the Legislative
        Assembly of the Territory of Utah. Salt Lake City:
        Star Printing Co., 1894.

        Supports the memorial which has been inaugurated by a
        number of citizens to erect a suitable monument to
        Brigham Young. He feels that it would be especially
        fitting to have it erected at the Capitol Grounds where
        Young was the first Governor and where he was the
        pioneer statesman and founder.

                                                    UPB, USlC

[1181] West, Caleb W. Message of Governor Caleb W. West and
        Accompany documents to the Thirty-first Session of the
        Legislative Assembly of the Territory of Utah, 1894.
        Salt Lake City: James B. Bloor, Public Printer, 1894.
        51p.

        See entry 1183 for annotation.

                                             [Flake 9380]
                                      MH, UHi, UPB, USlC

[1182] West, Caleb W. Report of the Governor of the Territory of
        Utah to the Secretary of the Interior, 1894. Washington:
        Govt. Print. Off., 1894. 22p.

        See entry 1183 for annotation.

                                             [Flake 9381]
                                                 MH, UPB

[1183] West, Caleb W. "Report of the Governor of Utah to the
        Secretary of the Interior, 1894," pp. 455-474. In
        Annual Report of the Department of the Interior, 1894.
        Washington: Govt. Print. Off., 1895. [I1.1:894]

        Briefly discusses polygamy, and President Cleveland's
        granting of amnesty to those Mormons liable to conviction
        under the Edmunds-Tucker Act.

        The Secretary of the Interior's summary of the Utah
        territorial governors report appears in vol. 1 pp.
        XXXIX-XL.

        Variant edition, U.S. 53d Congress, 3d session. H. Ex.
        Doc. No. 1, Serial Set 3307.

                                                      1895

        "It should be, and I trust is, a matter of
        infinite satisfaction to the whole country,
        as it is to the people of this Territory,
        that the movement begun in 1886 to obliterate
        the divisions, remove the bitterness, and
        heal the strife existing in Utah, which had
        so long prevented its admission as a State,
        are about to be consummated in the entrance
        of Utah into the Union as a great and prosperous

                            240

State, with a homogeneous, thriving, contented, peaceful, and happy people."

[Entry 1200]

[1184] C. O. Whittemore, appellant, v. Thomas H. Cope, and others, respondents, and George H. Cope, appellant, Territory of Utah Reports 11 (June 1895) pp. 344-362.

Problems with land division due to the legality of children of polygamist marriage.

CU-L, DLC, ICU, MH, MiU, UAr, UPB, UU, ViU-L

[1185] C. O. Whittemore, appellant, vs. Thomas H. Cope, et. al., respondents, and George H. Cope, appellant. Brief for appellants in the Supreme Court of Utah Territory, January Term, 1895. [n.p., 1895?] 17p.

Brief filed in regard to C. O. Whittemore v. Thomas H. Cope (and others) 11 Utah Reports 344-362. The family genealogy of Thomas Cope, wife Jeannette and legitimate son, Thomas H., and Thomas Senior's polygamous wife Margaret was reiterated relating to an inheritance and polygamous family case.

[Flake add. 9798a]
UAr, UPB

[1186] C.O. Whittemore, Appellant, vs. Thomas H. Cope, Mary Ann Jack and B. S. Young, Respondents and George H. Cope, Appellant. Brief of Respondent Thomas H. Cope, In the Supreme Court of Utah Territory, January Term, 1895. Salt Lake City: Star Print, 1895? 23p.

This brief was filed in regard to the C. O. Whitmore, v. Thomas H. Cope (and others) 11 Utah Reports (June 1895) 344-362.

[Flake add. 2514a]
UAr, UPB

[1187] Edwin B. Ayers and Edward A. Kessler, appellants, vs. Mary Ann Jack, respondent, vs. William Leggett, respondent. Additional Abstract in the Supreme Court of Utah Territory. [n.p., 1895] 37p.

Abstracts filed in the C. O. Whittemore v. Thomas H. Cope (and others) case 11 Utah Reports (June 1895) 344-362. Polygamous inheritance case of the Cope family.

[Flake add. 10,105a]
UAr, UPB

[1188] Edwin B. Ayers and Edward A. Kessler, appellants vs. Mary Ann Jack, respondent, vs. William Leggett, respondent. Brief for respondents in the Supreme Court of Utah Territory. Salt Lake: Star Print [1895?]

Brief filed in regard to the C. O. Whitemore v. Thomas H. Cope (and others) 11 Utah Reports (June 1895) 344-

241

362. Interesting family genealogy of Thomas Cope, wife
Jeannette, and legitimate son, Thomas H., but not son
of polygamous wife Margaret, and her son by such
marriage, George H. Cope. All relate to an inheritance
and land case in Salt Lake.

[Flake add. 5282b]
UAr, UPB

[1189] The enabling act. Washington, 1895. 12, III, 48p.

The enabling act is 12p; and To the People of Utah is
3p. and the Constitution is 48p. Includes a provision
against polygamy.

[Flake 9274]
ULA, US1C

[1190] "Fourteenth Annual Report of the Utah Commission," pp.
575-646. In Annual Report of the Department of the
Interior, 1895, vol. 3. Washington: Govt. Print.
Off., 1895. [I1.1:895/v.3]

Contains the proclamations of amnesty by Pres. Harrison,
and Cleveland, regarding polygamy. Summary of the
Commissions report by the Secretary of the Interior
vol. 1, [Serial Set 3381] pp. LXI-LXII.

Variant ed. U.S. 54th Congress, 1st session. House
Exec. Doc., No. 5, vol. III, Serial Set 3383.

[1191] In the matter of the estate of Oscar A. Amy, deceased,
Jennie Amy, appellant, vs. Royal D. Amy et. al.,
appellants, vs. Adelia Young, et. al., respondents.
Appeal from Third District Court in the Supreme Court
of Utah Territory, June Term, 1895. [Salt Lake City:
Tribune Job Printing Co., 1895?] 40p.

Appeal filed concerning the case "In the matter of the
estate of Oscar A. Amy, deceased, Jennie Amy, appellant,
v. Royal D. Amy and others appellants, v. Adelia Young
and others, respondents 12 Utah Reports (1896) 278-336.
Excellent family history material on the Amy family.

[Flake add. 2834a]
UAr, UPB

[1192] In the matter of the estate of Oscar A. Amy, deceased;
Jennie Amy, appellant, vs. Royal D. Amy et. al.,
appellants, vs. Adelia Young et. al., respondents.
Brief of appellant Jennie Amy, appeal from Third
District Court in the Supreme Court of Utah Territory,
June Term, 1895. [Salt Lake City: Tribune Job Printing
Co., 1895?] 32p.

Brief filed concerning the case "In the matter of the
estate of Oscar A. Amy, deceased. . ." 12 Utah Reports
(1896) 278-336. Inheritance rights of polygamous wives
and children in the case of Oscar A. Amy's family.

UAr, UPB

[1193] In the Matter of the Estate of Oscar A. Amy, deceased;
Jennie Amy, appellant, vs. Royal D. Amy, et. al.,
appellants, vs. Adelia Young, et. al., respondents.

Brief of respondents, Adelia Young, et. al., appeal
from Third District Court in the Supreme Court of Utah
Territory, June Term, 1895. [n.p., 1895?] 36p.

Brief filed in the case of "In the matter of the estate
of Oscar A. Amy, deceased. . ." 12 Utah Reports (1896)
278-336. Polygamous inheritance case regarding the Amy
family.
[Flake add. 10,105b]
UAr, UPB

[1194] In the Matter of the Estate of Oscar A. Amy, deceased;
Jennie Amy, appellant, vs. Royal D. Amy et. al.,
appellants, vs. Adelia Young et. al., respondents.
Jennie Amy's brief in reply. Appeal from Third District
Court in the Supreme Court of Utah Territory, June
Term, 1895. [Salt Lake City: Tribune Job Printing
Co., 1895?] 7p.

Brief filed in the case "In the matter of the estate of
Oscar A. Amy, deceased . . ." 12 Utah Reports (1896)
278-336. Polygamous inheritance case.
UAr, UPB

[1195] J.D. Page, plaintiff and applicant, vs. J. R. Letcher,
Geo. W. Thatcher, A. G. Norrell, Hoyt Sherman, Jr., and
E. W. Tatlock, defendants. Proceedings in Prohibition,
Brief of respondent in the Supreme Court of Utah
Territory. [Salt Lake City: Star Print, 1895?] 8p.

Brief filed in the J. D. Page, respondent, v. the Utah
Commission. . . case in 11 Utah Reports (1895) 119-134,
which dealt with the problems of canvassing of votes
due to rulings of the Utah Commission.
[Flake add. 10,120a]
UAr, UPB

[1196] J. D. Page, plaintiff and respondent, vs. J. R. Letcher,
et. al., defendants and appellants. Brief and points
and authorities for respondent on application for writ
of mandate [n.p., 1895?] 20p.

Brief filed in the J. D. Page, respondent, v. the Utah
Commission case 11 Utah Reports (1895) 119-134, regarding
problems of canvassing votes due to rulings of the Utah
Commission.
[Flake add. 6064a]
UAr, UPB

[1197] J. D. Page, respondent, v. The Utah Commission, consisting
of Jerrold R. Letcher, Erasmus W. Tatlock, Albert G.
Norrell, Hoyt Sherman, Jr., George W. Thatcher, appellant.
Territory of Utah Reports 11 (1895) pp. 119-134.

Problems with canvassing of votes due to rulings of the
Utah Commission.
CU-L, DLC, ICU, MH, MiU, UAr, UPB, UU, ViU-L

[1198] James Thomson, respondent, vs. Franklin C. Avery, appellant...
Brief of respondent. In the Supreme Court of Utah

Territory. Salt Lake City: Press of the Salt Lake Lithographing Co., 1895. 33p.

This brief was filed in regard to the Thomson v. Avery case 11 Utah Reports (January 25, 1895) 214-241. The land in question had formerly been owned by John Bergen who had been indicted for unlawful cohabitation.

UAr, UPB

[1199] Official report of the proceedings and debates of the convention assembled at Salt Lake City, on the fourth day of March, 1895 to adopt a constitution for the State of Utah. Salt Lake City: Star Printing Co., 1898. 2v.

Includes an anti-polygamy clause.

[Flake 9342]
CU, DLC, NN, UHi, UPB, US1C, UU

[1200] Report of the Utah Commission to the Secretary of the Interior for the fiscal year ending June 30, 1895. Wasington: Govt. Print. Off., 1895. 74p.

See entry 1190 for annotation.

[Flake 9239]
CtY, ICN, MH, NN, UHi, UPB, US1C

[1201] U.S. House. 53d Congress. 2d session. Administration of Immigration and Contract Labor Laws, letter from the Secretary of the Treasury. (H. Ex. Doc. 247) Washington: Govt. Print. Off., 1895. 33p. [Serial Set 3226]

Sporadic references throughout this publication to the 1891 and 1892 laws which prohibit that class of immigrant--polygamists.

[1202] West, Caleb W. "Report of the Governor of Utah to the Secretary of the Interior, 1895," pp. 529-573. In Annual Report of the Department of the Interior, 1895, vol. 3. Washington: Govt. Print. Off., 1895. [I1.1:895]

Deals primarily with the state constitution, and includes a copy of the ratified constitution.

Variant ed. U.S. 54th Congress, 1st session. H. Doc. No. 5, Serial Set 3383.

1896

"The Latter-Day Saints accept the Scriptures of the Old and New Testaments, and, in general, the precepts of conduct and the ordinances therein prescribed. They baptize by immersion. The distinction between Latter-Day Saints and most others who accept the Christian Scriptures begins with their claims of recent and continued revelations largely embodied in the Book of Mormon, from

which has grown the common name of Mormons,
distasteful to them."

[Entry 1206]

[1203] Cleveland, Grover. "By the President of the United States
of America: A Proclamation, 4 January 1896," pp. 6120-
6121. In A Compilation of the Messages and Papers of
the Presidents, by James D. Richardson, Vol. 8. New
York: Bureau of National Literature, 1911, c1897.
[GS4.113:8, AE2.114:1-27/v.8]

The admission of Utah into statehood is proclaimed.

[1204] "Government in the territories," (Chapter 373, June 8,
1896) United States Statutes at Large 29, pp. 277-278.
[GS4.111:29, AE2.111:29]

Provides money for the payment of the Utah Commission
and for the publication of the proceedings of the Utah
Constitutional Convention.

[1205] In the matter of the estate of Oscar A. Amy, deceased,
Jennie Amy, appellant, v. Royal D. Amy and others,
appellants, v. Adelia Young and others, respondents,
Territory of Utah Reports 12 (1896) pp. 278-336.

Concerning inheritance of polygamist children.

CU-L, DLC, ICU, MH, MiU, UAr, UPB, UU, ViU-L

[1206] "Latter Day Saints sunday schools," pp. 415-425. In
Report of the Commissioner of Education for the year
1896-1897, vol. 1. Washington: Govt. Print. Off.,
1898. [FS5.1:897/Vol. 1]

Discussion of Mormon sunday schools being different due
to the Book of Mormon.

[1207] "Mormon colonists in Mexico," p. 409. In Consular Reports,
Vol. LI, No. 190, July, 1896. Washington: Govt.
Print. Off., 1896. [S4.7:51/No.190]

Louis M. Buford, Consul-General, Paso Del Norte,
reports that there are ten Mormon colonies in northern
Mexico, and that the Mormons would prefer purchasing
American goods because they are of superior quality.

[1208] "Report of the Utah Commission, 1896," pp. 447-535. In
Annual Report of the Department of the Interior, 1896,
vol. 3. Washington: Govt. Print. Off., 1896.
[I1.1:896/v.3]

This is the final report of the Utah Commission and it
deals primarily with various voting issues. The Mormon
Church is discussed, mainly in regard to its influence
on politics. Summary of the Commission report by the
Secretary of the Interior in vol. 1. [Serial Set
3488], p. XCVII - XCVIII.

Variant ed. U.S. 54th Congress, 2nd session, House
Exec. Doc. No. 5, vol. III. Serial Set 3490.

[1209] Report of the Utah Commission to the Secretary of the
Interior, 1896. Washington: Govt. Print. Off., 1896.
91p.

See entry 1208 for annotation.

[Flake 9239]
CtY, DLC, ICN, MH, UHi, UPB, US1C

[1210] U.S. House. 54th Congress. 1st Session. Committee on
the Judiciary. Church of Jesus Christ of Latter-day
Saints... Report [To accompany H. Res. 96]. (H. Rept.
No. 519) Washington: Govt. Print. Off., 1896.
1p.[Serial Set 3458]

Report from the Committee amending joint resolution 98,
providing for restoration of church property taken
under the Edmunds Act.

[Flake 9123]

[1211] U.S. House. 54th Congress. 1st Session. Industrial
Christian Home building Salt Lake City, Utah. Letter
from the acting Secretary of the Treasury, transmitting
an estimate of appropriation for repairs of the Industrial
Christian Home building, Salt Lake City, Utah. (H.
Doc. No. 327) Washington: Govt. Print. Off., 1896.
3p. [Serial Set 3428]

Permission for the home, which was originally designed
to house and employ female polygamists, to be used as
federal offices.

[1212] U.S. Senate. 54th Congress. 1st Session. S. 3296, "A
bill to grant the State of Utah the Industrial Christian
Home in Salt Lake City, June 10, 1896." [Washington:
Govt. Print. Off., 1896] 1p.

Referred to the Committee on Public Buildings and
Grounds.

DLC, UPB, US1C

1897

"Representing as we do the Church of Jesus
Christ of Latter-day Saints, we desire to
state that for the past few years our missionaries
have from time to time been subject to
arrests and banishment, and that through a
procedure which we do not think is warranted
under the constitution of this country--that
is, they have been summoned to appear before
the officers of the law simply to hear the
decree of banishment read to them, with a
demand for them to leave the country at once,
and as a rule they have been escorted out by
the police officials, having had no specific

charges preferred against them or been given
any chance of a defense."

[Entry 1215]

[1213] In the Matter of the Estate of George Handley, deceased,
on petition of Sarah Chapman, et. al., for a Rehearing.
Brief for Respondent. [Salt Lake City] Star Printing
Co. [1897?] 12p.

Polygamy inheritance case. This brief was filed in the
Chapman v. Handley case 151 U.S. Reports 443-446,
October 1893.

[Flake add. 2827a]
DLC, UPB, US1C

[1214] "Industrial Home," Congressional Record 55th Congress, 1st
session (12 May 1897) vol. 30, pt. 1, p.1037. [X345]

A petition from the Governor and Legislative Assembly
of Utah requesting that the Industrial Home property of
Salt Lake City be granted to the state for educational
and charitable purposes. The memorial is printed and
mentions the purpose of the home which was to provide a
home for dependent women who renounced polygamy, and
for their children.

[1215] "Protection of Mormon Missionaries," pp. 121-124. In
Foreign Relations of the United States, 1897. Washington:
Govt. Print. Off., 1898. [S1.1:897]

Correspondence of C. N. Lund, President of the Scandinavian
Mission of the Mormon Church, with affidavits from Jens
Jorgen Jensen and Joseph Larsen, to the U.S. Legation
in Denmark, regarding the problem of arrests and
banishment of Mormon missionaries by the Danish government
over alleged problems of misconduct. The problem
apparently relates to polygamy.

[1216] U.S. House. 54th Congress. 2d session. Expenses of Utah
Commission, etc. Letter from the acting Secretary of
the Treasury, transmitting, with a communication from
G. W. Parks, a recommendation for an appropriation for
compensation of officers of election in Utah and of the
Utah Commission. (H. Doc. No. 197) Washington: Govt.
Print. Off., 1897. 4p. [Serial Set 3524]

[1217] U.S. Senate. 55th Congress. 1st Session. S. 689, "A
bill to grant to the State of Utah the Industrial
Christian Home in Salt Lake City, March 18, 1897."
[Washington: Govt. Print. Off., 1897] 1p.

Referred to the Committee on Public Buildings and
Grounds. Transferring of the Industrial Christian Home
property, originally set up to assist polygamous wives,
to the state.

DLC, UPB, US1C

[1218] U.S. Senate. 67th Congress. 2d Session. Federal aid in
domestic disturbances, 1897-1903. (In Federal Aid in

domestic disturbances, 1903-1922. Prepared under the
direction of the Secretary of War). (S. Doc. No. 263)
Washington: Govt. Print. Off., 1922. 322p. [Serial
Set 7985]

Utah Expedition, pp. 78-80, disturbances at Provo, pp.
81-82. Disorders at Salt Lake City, pp. 183-184.

1898

"Few, if any, persons availed themselves of
the shelter afforded by the building. It was
not occupied, and became and is a source of
expense to the Government. As stated, the
building was constructed as a dwelling house,
and only by a large expense can it be made
available for any other purpose."

[Entry 1222]

[1219] Baldwin, Simeon E. "The Constitutional Questions incident
to the acquisition and government by the United States
of Island Territories," pp. 326-328. In Annual Report
of the American Historical Association for the year
1898. Washington: Govt. Print. Off., 1899. [SI4.1:898]

Reference is made to the various acts of Congress
passed to suppress polygamy and some of the Supreme
Court decisions which relate to enforcement of these
laws, i.e. Mormon Church v. United States, and Reynolds
v. United States.

[1220] "Expulsion of Mormon Missionaries," pp. 347-354. In
Foreign Relations of the United States, 1898. Washington:
Govt. Print. Off., 1901. [S1.1:898]

Deals with the expulsion of Charles Richards and Elijah
A. Larkin, Mormon missionaries of Ogden, Utah, and
their expulsion from Hanover, Germany, for "preaching
the doctrine of their sect." Polygamy, of course, is
the main issue here.

[1221] "Protection to Mormon agents," p. 1112. In Foreign
Relations of the United States, 1898. Washington:
Govt. Print. Off., 1901. [S1.1:898]

Brief letter introducing Apostle Anthon H. Lund and
Elder F. F. Hintze, of the Mormon Church, to the
diplomatic and consular offices in Turkey. Lund and
Hintze were visiting Turkey to look after the welfare
of its members.

[1222] U.S. House. 55th Congress. 2d session. Committee on the
Judiciary. Industrial Home, Salt Lake City, Utah...
Report: [To accompany H.R. 7935]. (H. Rept. No. 1247)
Washington: Govt. Print. Off., 1898. 2p. [Serial Set
3721]

Report from the Committee on the Judiciary, favoring H. 7935, to grant the State of Utah an Industrial Christian Home in Salt Lake City.

[Flake 9125]

[1223] U.S. House. 55th Congress. 2d Session. H.R. 7935, "A bill to grant to the State of Utah the Industrial Christian Home in Salt Lake City, February 9, 1898." [Washington: Govt. Print. Off., 1898] 1p.

Referred to the Committee on the Judiciary.

Disposal of the home built to house polygamist women.

DLC, UPB, US1C

[1224] U.S. Senate. 55th Congress. 2d Session. S. 4299, "A bill ta [sic] grant to the State of Utah the Industrial Christian Home in Salt Lake City, March 31, 1898." [Washington: Govt. Print. Off., 1898] 1p.

Referred to the Committee on Public Buildings and Grounds. Transferring the Industrial Christian Home, set up on behalf of polygamous wives, to the state for use as a high school.

DLC, UPB, US1C

1899

"According to our creed, the head of the church receives from time to time revelations for the religious guidance of his people. In September, 1890, the present head of the church in anguish and prayer cried to God for help for his flock, and received permission to advise the members of the Church of Jesus Christ of Latter-Day Saints that the law commanding polygamy was henceforth suspended."
[Entry 1225]

[1225] Brown, Clarence T. In the matter of Brigham H. Roberts, Member-elect from the State of Utah: Protest and Petition of C. T. Brown, Wm. Paden and T. C. Iliff. [Salt Lake City? 1899] 18p.

Signed: Salt Lake City, Utah, January 6th, 1899.

At head of title: House of Representatives. Fifty-sixth Congress.

Lengthy and moving appeal to show that legally the Mormon Church had moved away from polygamous marriage. Includes the amnesty proclamation of Harrison, and Cleveland and the Enabling Act for Utah. Concludes with the idea that B. H. Roberts is living with at least 3 wives, Louisa, Cecelia Dibbles and Dr. Maggie C. Shipp.

[Flake 893]
OO, UPB

[1226] Dinsmore, Hugh Anderson. The Roberts case. Speech of
       Hon. Hugh A. Dinsmore, of Arkansas, in the House of
       Representatives, December 5, 1899. Washington: Govt.
       Print. Off., 1899. 7p.

       See entry 1235 for annotation.

                                          [Flake 2841]
                                          DLC, NjP

[1227] "Memorial," Congressional Record 55th Congress, 3d session
       (22 February 1899) vol. 32, pt. 3, pp. 2203. [X360]

       Memorial, not printed, from the Delaware State Assembly
       favoring exclusion of polygamists from Congress.

[1228] "Memorial of Legislature of Nebraska Against Seating of
       Polygamist in Congress," Congressional Record 55th
       Congress, 3d session (17, 18, 20 February 1899) vol.
       32, pt. 2, 2036, 2080, 2122. [X359]

       Not printed in full.

[1229] "Memorial of the Legislature of Connecticut Against
       Seating of Brigham H. Roberts," Congressional Record
       56th Congress, 1st session (7, 11 December 1899, 8
       January 1900) vol. 33, pt. 1, pp. 152-177, 694. [X362]

       The December 11 memorial only entry printed in full.

[1230] "Memorial of the Legislature of the State of Wisconsin
       protesting the Seating of Brigham H. Roberts," Congressiona
       Record 56th Congress, 1st session (7 December 1899)
       vol. 33, pt. 1, p. 152 [X362]

       Five memorials not printed in full.

[1231] "Memorials Against Seating of Brigham H. Roberts," Congression
       Record 55th Congress, 3d session (17, 20 February 1899)
       vol. 32, pt. 2, pp. 2036, 2122. [X359]

       Twelve separate entries none printed in full.

[1232] "Memorials Praying the Adoption of an Amendment to the
       Constitution to Prohibit Polygamy," Congressional
       Record 56th Congress, 1st session (11 December 1899)
       vol. 33, pt. 1, p. 177. [X362]

       Six memorials not printed in full.

[1233] "Petitions and Memorials," Congressional Record 56th
       Congress, 1st session (7, 11 December 1899, 8 January
       1900) vol. 33, pt. 1, pp. 152, 176-177, 694. [X362]

       Numerous petitions requesting an amendment to the
       constitution to prohibit polygamy. A brief petition
       from the state of Connecticut is printed in full on p.
       177.

[1234] Rawlins, Joseph L. (Utah) "Practice of Polygamy and Paper
       on Polygamy," Congressional Record 56th Congress, 1st

session (6 December 1899, 16 January 1900) vol. 33,
pt. 1, pp. 98, 849-850. [X362]

Inquiry by congress into public offices held by polygamists
in Utah. Also extent of polygamy since the admittance
of Utah as a state.

[1235] "Representative-elect from Utah," Congressional Record
56th Congress, 1st Session (4, 5 December 1899) vol.
33, pt. 1, pp. 5-6, 38-53. [X362]

The consideration of the election of B. H. Roberts to
congress again addresses the practice of polygamy in
Utah. H. Res. 1 printed in full.

[1236] Roberts, Brigham Henry, defendant. Brief on demurrer in
Roberts' Case. Representative from Utah demurs to the
jurisdiction of the House and its Special Committee in
its Proceedings to unseat him. Fifty-Sixth Congress.
1899. [Washington? 1899] 22p.

Defends himself against polygamy and other charges.

[Flake 7312]
UPB, US1C

[1237] Taylor, Robert Walker. The case of Brigham H. Roberts...
Can a polygamist be excluded from the House of Repre-
sentatives. Speeches of Hon. Robert W. Taylor of Ohio,
in the House of Representatives, December 4 & 5, 1899,
January 23 & 25, 1900. 64p. Washington: Govt. Print.
Off., 1900.

See entry 1235 and 1262 for annotation.
[Flake 8857]
DLC, UHi, UPB, US1C

[1238] U.S. House. 55th Congress. 3d Session. Committee on
Election of President, Vice-President, and Representatives
in Congress. Amendments to the constitution prohibiting
polygamy, etc. (H. Rept. No. 2307) Washington: Govt.
Print. Off., 1899. 16p. [Serial Set 3841]

The election of Brigham H. Roberts in 1899 started new
efforts to have a constitutional amendment against
polygamy. Includes a summary of polygamy and legislation
against it.
[Flake add. 9113h]

[1239] U.S. House. 55th Congress. 3d Session. H. Res. 354,
"Joint Resolution proposing amendments to the Constitution
prohibiting polygamy within the United States and all
places subject to their jurisdiction, and disqualifying
polygamists for election as Senators or Representatives
in Congress, February 6, 27, 1899." [Washington:
Govt. Print. Off., 1899] 4p.

Referred to the Committee on Election of President,
Vice-President, and Representatives in Congress.

This is the reported bill, with amendments.

DLC, UPB, US1C

[1240] U.S. House. 55th Congress. 3d Session. H.R. 11735, "A bill providing that no polygamist shall be a Senator or Representative, January 23, 1899." [Washington: Govt. Print. Off., 1899] 1p.

Referred to the Committee on the Judiciary.

DLC, UPB, US1C

[1241] U.S. House. 56th Congress. 1st Session. H.J. Res. 1, "Joint Resolution proposing amendments to the Constitution disqualifying polygamists for election as Senators and Representatives in Congress, and prohibiting polygamy and polygamous association or cohabitation between the sexes, December 4, 1899." [Washington: Govt. Print. Off., 1899] 3p.

Referred to the Committee on Election of President, Vice-President, and Representatives in Congress.

DLC, UPB, US1C

[1242] U.S. House. 56th Congress. 1st Session. H.J. Res. 10, "Joint resolution providing for an amendment to the Constitution of the United States prohibiting polygamy, December 4, 1899." [Washington: Govt. Print. Off., 1899] 2p.

Referred to the Committee on the Judiciary.

DLC, UPB, US1C

[1243] U.S. House. 56th Congress. 1st Session. H.J. Res. 45, "Joint Resolution [providing for a] constitutional amendment to prohibit polygamy or polygamous cohabitation in the United States and all territory subject to its jursdiction, and to prohibit all persons guilty of polygamy or polygamous cohabitation from holding offices of trust, December 5, 1899." [Washington: Govt. Print. Off., 1899] 2p.

Referred to the Committee on the Judiciary.

DLC, UPB, US1C

[1244] U.S. House. 56th Congress. 1st Session. H. J. Res. 93, "Proposing an amendment to the Constitution of the United States prohibiting polygamy." [Washington, 1899] 2p.

[Flake 9112]
NjP, NN

[1245] U.S. House. 56th Congress. 1st Session. Joint Res. 69, "Proposing an amendment to the Constitution of the United States prohibiting polygamy and polygamous cohabitation within the bound of a state or territory of the United States, December 11, 1899." [Washington, 1899] 2p.

[Flake 9113]
NjP, NN

1900

"In the proceedings by which the Mormon Church secured the return of certain church property escheated to the United States an interpretation of that was made by Mr. Wilford Woodruff, the president of the church, who signed it, and several of the leading apostles, who under oath, testified that the manifesto was a pledge not only against the contraction of future polygamous marriages, but that it covered all marriages already contracted, and prohibited polygamous or unlawful cohabitation with prior acquired wives."

[Entry 1257]

[1246] "Alleged Polygamous Officeholders, Utah," Congressional Record 56th Congress, 1st session (8 January 1900), vol. 33, pt. 1, pp. 685-686. [X362]

Brief debate on the ineligibility of John C. Graham, postmaster of Provo, and Orson Smith, postmaster of Logan to hold federal office for same reason that B. H. Roberts was ineligible.

[1247] Brownlow, Walter P. (Tennessee). "Representative-Elect from Utah," Congressional Record 56th Congress, 1st session (25 January 1900) vol. 33, pt. 8, Appendix, pp. 23-25. [X369]

In lively rhetoric, Mr. Brownlow comes out against the seating of B. H. Roberts.

[1248] "The Case of Brigham H. Roberts, Representative from Utah," Congressional Record 56th Congress, 1st Session, (20 January 1900) vol. 33, pt. 2, pp. 1012-1013. [X363]

Continued debate whether to seat B. H. Roberts in Congress.

[1249] Crumpacker, Edgar Dean. Case of Brigham H. Roberts, of Utah. Speech of Hon. Edgar D. Crumpacker of Indiana in the House of Representatives, January 24, 1900. Washington: [Govt. Print. Off.], 1900. 16p.

See entry 1262 for annotation.

[Flake 2601]
DLC

[1250] DeArmond, David Albaugh. Case of Brigham H. Roberts of Utah. Speech of Hon. David A. DeArmond, of Missouri,

253

in the House of Representatives...January 25, 1900.
Washington: [Govt. Print. Off., 1900] 16p.

See entry 1262 for annotation.

[Flake 2739]
CU-B, US1C

[1251] "Expulsion of Mormon Missionaries," pp. 413-422. In
Foreign Relations of the United States, 1900. Washington:
Govt. Print. Off., 1902. [S1.1:900]

Relates in considerable detail the expulsion of Charles
C. Ronnow and Thomas P. Jensen, Mormon missionaries,
from Denmark. The ostensible reason for the expulsion
was the continued concern that the Mormons were preaching
immoral doctrine regarding marriage, especially polygamy.

[1252] "Fifth Annual Report of the Historical Manuscripts Commission,"
p. 605. In Annual Report of the American Historical
Association for the year 1900, vol. 1. Washington:
Govt. Print. Off., 1901. [SI4.1:900]

Reference to the letter of Gen. Thomas Williams to his
wife, which includes information about the Utah Expedition.

[1253] Freer, Romeo Hoyt. The Roberts case... Speech of Hon.
R. H. Freer, of West Virginia, in the House of Repre-
sentatives... January 25, 1900. Washington: Govt.
Print. Off., 1900. 8p.

See entry 1262 for annotation.

[Flake 3448]
DLC, UHi

[1254] Gannett, Henry. A gazatteer of Utah. Washington: Govt.
Print. Off., 1900. 43p. [I19.3:166]

(Geological survey. Bulletin No. 166)

Brief mention of Mormons as a part of exploration and
settlement of Utah. Population briefly discussed where
Mormon immigration and polygamy are mentioned.

[Flake 3503]

[1255] Grout, William Wallace. Case of Brigham H. Roberts, of
Utah. Speech of Hon. William W. Grout, of Vermont, in
the House of Representatives, Thursday, January 25,
1900. Washington, 1900. 13p.

Speech concerning Robert's exclusion from Congress.

See entry 1262 for annotation.

[Flake add. 3733e]
UPB

[1256] Johnston, David Emmons. Representative-elect from Utah.
Speech of Hon. David E. Johnston of West Virginia in
the House of Representatives, January 25, 1900.
Washington: Govt. Print. Off., 1900. 7p.

See entry 1262 for annotation.

[Flake 4449]
DLC

[1257] Landis, Charles Beary. The Roberts case. Speech of Hon. C. B. Landis of Indiana, in the House of Representatives, Wednesday, January 24, 1900. Washington, 1900. 18p.

See entry 1262 for annotation.

[Flake 4736]
CU-B, DLC, NjP, NN, PHi, UHi, UPB, USlC, UU

[1258] Littlefield, Charles Edgar. Representative-elect from Utah... Speech of Hon. Charles E. Littlefield of Maine, in the House of Representatives... January 23, 1900. Washington: Govt. Print. Off., 1900. 52p.

A very legalistic argument on the seating of B. H. Roberts which stems from polygamy. See entry 1262.

[Flake 4958]
CU-B, DLC, UHi, UPB

[1259] McCall, Samuel W. (Mass.) "Representative-Elect from Utah," Congressional Record 56th Congress, 1st session (25 January 1900) vol. 33, pt. 8, Appendix, pp. 25-26. [X369]

Believes the House of Representatives powers of expulsion should be exercised in the B. H. Roberts case.

"Memorial of the Legislature of Connecticut Against Seating of Brigham H. Roberts," Congressional Record, 1900, see entry 1229.

[1260] "Mormon Colonies," pp. 198-199. In American Republics Bureau. Monthly Bulletin, May 1900, Vol. i, Whole No. 80, No. 15 Message of President Diaz of Mexico.

President Diaz mentions that the arrival of 500 Mormons from Utah in Chihuahua has attracted attention to the prosperous condition of the Mormons in the colonies. He goes on to say that for 20 years there has never been the slightest problem between the Mormons and the Mexicans.

Xerox of the two pages at UPB, USlC. Original in full at DLC.

"Petitions and Memorials," Congressional Record, 1900, see entry 1233.

[1261] Powers, Horace Henry. Remarks of Hon. H. Henry Powers of Vermont, on the resolution to exclude B. H. Roberts, Member-elect from Utah, from his seat in the House of Representatives, January 24, 1900. Washington, 1900. 8p.

Cover-title: In favor of unseating B. H. Roberts.

See entry 1262 for annotation.

[Flake 6433]
UHi

Rawlins, Joseph L. (Utah) <u>Congressional Record</u>, 1900,
see entry 1234.

[1262] "Representative-elect from Utah," <u>Congressional Record</u>
56th Congress, 1st session (23, 24, 25 January 1900)
vol. 33, pt. 2, pp. 1012-1013, 1072-1116, 1123-1149,
1175-1182, 1184-1217. [X363]

The debate whether to seat B. H. Roberts in Congress.

[1263] "Smith, David H. (Kentucky). "Case of Brigham H. Roberts,
of Utah," <u>Congressional Record</u> 56th Congress, 1st
session (24 January 1900) vol. 33, pt. 8, Appendix, pp.
40-41. [X369]

Mr. Smith feels he cannot violate the Constitution in
order to get rid of B. H. Roberts.

[1264] <u>U.S. Census, 1900: Census Bulletin No. 50</u>. "Population
of Utah Counties and Minor Civil Divisions." Washington:
Govt. Print. Off., 1901. 7p. [C3.3:50]

No specific Mormon material, however, valuable comparative
statistics for a number of years are included.

[1265] U.S. House. Committee on the Judiciary. <u>Hearing before
the Committee on the Judiciary on the proposed amendment
to the Constitution of the United States prohibiting
polygamy</u>. Statement of Rev. William R. Campbell.
[Washington] 1900. 15p.

[Flake 9124]
NN

[1266] U.S. House. 56th Congress. 1st Session. Committee on
Election of President, Vice President, and Representatives
in Congress. <u>Disqualifying polygamists for election as
senators, etc...</u> Report: [To accompany H. J. Res. 1.
Washington] February 16, 1900. (H. Rept. No. 348)
Washington: Govt. Print. Off., 1900. 17p. [Serial Set
4022]

Proposing amendments to the constitution prohibiting
polygamists from election to public office.

[Flake 9114]

[1267] U.S. House. 56th Congress. 1st Session. Committee on
the Post-Office and Post-Roads. <u>John C. Graham and
Orson Smith</u>. (H. Rept. No. 611) Washington, 1900.
40, 14p. [Serial Set 4023]

Investigation to see if these postmasters are polygamists.
[Flake 9137]

[1268] U.S. House. 56th Congress. 1st Session. H. Res. 35,
"Resolution to remove John C. Graham." [Washington,
1900]. 2p.

Resolution to remove a postmaster, John C. Graham,
because of suspected polygamy.

                                        NjP, NN, ULA

[1269] U.S. House. 56th Congress. 1st Session. H. J. Res. 112,
"Joint resolution, proposing an amendment to the
Constitution to disqualify persons found guilty of
polygamy or polygamous cohabitation from holding
office." [Washington, 1900] 2p.

                                        [Flake 9111]
                                        NjP, NN, ULA

[1270] U.S. House. 56th Congress. 1st Session. Special Committee
on the case of Brigham H. Roberts. Case of Brigham H.
Roberts of Utah... Report [to accompany H. Res. 107]
January 20, 1900. (H. Rept. No. 85, 2 parts) Washington:
Govt. Print. Off., 1900. 77p. [Serial Set 4021]

Second part: "Views of minority," pp. 53-77.
                                        [Flake 9163]

[1271] U.S. House. 56th Congress. 1st Session. Special Committee
to Investigate the Eligibility of Brigham H. Roberts,
of Utah, to a seat in the House of Representatives.
Election case of Brigham H. Roberts, of Utah. [Washington:
Govt. Print. Off., 1900?] 245p.

Contains: Election case of B. H. Roberts; Case of B.
H. Roberts... Report: Speeches of Hon. Robert W.
Taylor, Hon. Charles E. Littlefield, Hon. R. H. Freer,
and Hon. Samuel W. T. Lanham.
                                        [Flake 9165]
                                        CU-B, NN, UHi, UPB

[1272] U.S. House. 56th Congress. 1st Session. Special Committee
to Investigate the Eligibility of Brigham H. Roberts,
of Utah, to a seat in the House of Representatives.
Election case of Brigham H. Roberts, of Utah. Statement
of Mr. Roberts before the Committee January 5 and 6,
1900. [Washington, 1900] 173-239p.

Reprint of a section of the longer report above.

                                        [Flake 9166]
                                        UPB, USlC

[1273] Wilson, Edgar. Representative-elect from Utah. Speech of
Hon. Edgar Wilson, of Idaho, in the House of Representatives,
Wednesday, January 24, 1900. Washington: Govt. Print.
Off., 1900. 8p.

See entry 1262 for annotation.
                                        [Flake 9908]
                                        DLC, NjP, UHi

                                                1901

"I have the honor to inform you that in
December last, under general instructions
from the Department, intervention was made in
behalf of Lewis T. Cannon and Jacob Muller,

American citizens, who had been residing in
Cologne, `in the capacity of missionaries of
the Church of Jesus Christ of Latter Day
Saints (otherwise known as the Mormon Church),'
who had been found `lastig' (troublesome,
objectionable) by the local authorities
`because of the preaching and practice' of
their religion, and who had consequently been
expelled from Prussia."

[Entry 1274]

[1274] "Expulsion of Mormon missionaries from Germany," pp. 165-
166. In Foreign Relations of the United States, 1901.
Washington: Govt. Print. Off., 1902. [S1.1:901]

Brief correspondence regarding the expulsion of Lewis
T. Cannon and Jacob Muller, Mormon missionaries, from
Prussia.

[1275] "Permission for Mormon Missionary to Visit Denmark," pp.
140-141. In Foreign Relations of the United States,
1901. Washington: Govt. Print. Off., 1902. [S1.1:901]

Series of brief letters on the request of Charles C.
Ronnow, a Mormon missionary, to visit Denmark before
returning to the United States.

See entry 1251 in 1900 entitled "Expulsion of Mormon
Missionaries," which details the original problem.

[1276] U.S. House. 57th Congress. 1st Session. H.J. Res. 40,
"Joint resolution proposing an amendment to the Constitution
of the United States prohibiting polygamy and polygamous
cohabitation within the bounds of a State or Territory
of the United States, December 3, 1901." [Washington:
Govt. Print. Off., 1901] 2p.

Referred to the Committee on the Judiciary.

DLC, UPB, US1C

[1277] U.S. House. 57th Congress. 1st Session. H.J. Res. 55,
"Joint resolution proposing amendment to the Constitution
disqualifying polygamists for election as Senators and
Representatives in Congress, and prohibiting polygamy
and polygamous association or cohabitation between the
sexes, December 6, 1901." [Washington: Govt. Print.
Off., 1901. 3p.

Referred to the Committee on the Judiciary.

DLC, UPB, US1C

[1278] U.S. House. 57th Congress. 1st Session. H.J. Res. 68,
"Joint resolution proposing an amendment to the Constitution
to disqualify persons found guilty of polygamy or
polygamous cohabitation from holding office, December
10, 1901." [Washington: Govt. Print. Off., 1901] 1p.

Referred to the Committee on the Judiciary.

DLC, UPB, US1C

1902

"Mrs. Hamblin is a simple-minded person of
about 45, and evidently looks with the eyes
of her husband at everything. She may really
have been taught by the Mormons to believe it
is not great sin to kill Gentiles and enjoy
their property. Of the shooting of the
emigrants, which she had herself heard, and
knew at the time what was going on, she
seemed to speak without a shudder, or any
very great feeling; but when she told of the
17 orphan children who were brought by such a
crowd to her own house of one small room
there in the darkness of night, two of the
children cruelly mangled and the most of them
with their parents' blood still wet upon
their clothes, and all of them shrieking with
terror and grief and anguish, her own mother
heart was touched. She at least deserved
kind consideration for her care and nourishment
of the three sisters, and for all she did for
the little girl `about 1 year old who had
been shot through one of her arms, below the
elbow, by a large ball, breaking both bones
and cutting the arm half off.'"

[Entry 1281]

[1279] The Corporation of the members of the Church of Jesus
Christ of Latter-day Saints, residing in the Fiftieth
Ecclesiastical [sic] Ward of Salt Lake Stake of Zion,
Plaintiff and Respondent, vs. Helen Watson, Defendant
and Appellant. Brief for Respondent, F. S. Richards,
J. T. Richards, Attorneys for Respondent. [Salt Lake
City, 1902?] 13p.

Property dispute.

[Flake 7231]
MH

[1280] U.S. House. Committee on the Judiciary. Polygamy [Hearing,
February 25, 1902]. Washington: Govt. Print. Off.,
1914 16p. [Y4.J89/1:P76]

[Flake 9127]

[1281] U.S. House. 57th Congress. 1st Session. Mountain Meadow
Massacre... Special report of the Mountain Meadow
Massacre, by J. H. Carleton, Brevet Major, United
States Army, Captain, First Dragoons. (H. Doc. No.
605) Washington: Govt. Print. Off., 1902. 17p.
[Serial Set 4377]

Dated: Camp at Mountain Meadows, Utah Territory, May 25, 1859, and addressed to the Assistant Adjutant-General, U.S.A., San Francisco, Cal.

Reprinted from U.S. 40th Cong. 2d Sess. Report No. 79, p. 26-40. See entry 315 for original government printing. Originally printed in two printings in Little Rock, Arkansas in 1860.

[Flake 1188]

1903

"'After we were taught a good many things that had transpired and passed up to the present, the oath was taken that we should avenge the blood of Joseph Smith on this nation, down from the President to the last man; and after we had done that we was talked to a little bit more in another room, and we took another oath, that if we divulged any of the secrets we should have our throats cut, and our bowels ripped out; that is to be teached to the children and the children's children down to the third and fourth generations.'"

[1283a]

[1282] Depew, Chauncey M. (New York) "Statehood Bill," Congressional Record 57th Congress, 2d session (11, 13, 17 February 1903) vol. 36, pt. 3, Appendix, pp. 87-114. [X387]

Pages 96-102 includes a debate on the Mormon population in Arizona (which is being considered for statehood) and the concerns regarding polygamy among this group are aired. Colonization policies of the Mormons, Reed Smoot's role, economic value of Arizona are discussed.

[1283] Mead, Elwood. Report of irrigation investigations in Utah, under the direction of Elwood Mead... Assisted by R. P. Teele, A. P. Stover, A. F. Doremus, J. D. Stannard, Frank Adams, and G. L. Swendsen. Washington: Govt. Print. Off., 1903. 330p. [A10.3:124]

U.S. Dept. of Agriculture. Office of Experiment Stations. Bulletin No. 124.

Brief mention of the influence of the Mormon church on the history of irrigation in Utah and settlement of controversies, pp. 7, 8, 19, 22, 132, 136, 137, 155, 164, 227, 236, 257.

[Flake add. 5321a]

[1283a] U.S.District Court. Utah. (Third District). The Inside of Mormonism: A Judicial Examination of the Endowment oaths Administered in all the Mormon Temples . . . for the Third Judicial District of Utah, to Determine Whether Membership in the Mormon Church is consistent

with citizenship in the United States. Salt Lake City:
Utah Americans, 1903. 93p.

Although technically this publication is not governmentally
published, it transcribes the proceedings in the
District Court which began in 1889 and ended in 1903.
A fascinating array of testimony from temple garments
to hostility to the United States.

[Flake 5231]
CsmH, ICN, MoInRC, NjP, NN, UHi, UPB, USlC, UU, Whi

[1284] U.S. House. 57th Congress. 2d Session. H.J. Res. 240,
"Joint resolution proposing an amendment to the Constitution
of the United States, January 5, 1903." [Washington:
Govt. Print. Off., 1903] 1p.

Referred to the Committee on the Judiciary. Another
amendment to the constitution regarding bigamy or
polygamy.
DLC, UPB, USlC

[1285] U.S. House. 57th Congress. 2d Session. H.J. Res. 258,
"Joint Resolution proposing an amendment to the Constitution
of the United States Prohibiting bigamy and polygamy,
January 3, 1903." [Washington: Govt. Print. Off.,
1903] 1p.

Referred to the Committee on the Judiciary. A proposal
for a 16th Amendment to the Constitution.
DLC, UPB, USlC

[1286] U.S. Senate. 57th Congress. 2d Session. Federal aid in
domestic disturbances, 1787-1903. Prepared...by
Frederick T. Wilson. (S. Doc. No. 209) Washington:
Govt. Print. Off., 1903. 394p. [Serial Set 4430]

The Mormon rebellion 1851-1858, pp. 94-96; disturbances
in Provo, pp. 96-99; disorders at Salt Lake City, pp.
183-184.
[Flake 9914]

[1287] U.S. Senate. 57th Congress. 2d Session. S. R. 164,
"Joint resolution proposing an amendment to the Constitution
of the United States prohibiting bigamy and polygamy,
February 5, 1903." [Washington: Govt. Print. Off.,
1903] 1p.

Referred to the Committee on the Judiciary.

DLC, UPB, USlC

1904

"It has been the constant practice with
officers of the church to consult, or to use
our language, to `counsel,' with their
brethren concerning all questions of this
kind. They have not felt that they were
sacrificing their manhood in doing so, nor

that they were submitting to improper dictation,
nor that in soliciting and acting upon the
advice of those over them they were in any
manner doing away with their individual
rights and agency, nor that to any improper
degree with their right and duties as American
citizens being abridged or interfered with.
They realize that in accepting ecclesiastical
office they assumed certain obligations; and
among these was the obligation to magnify the
office which they held, to attend to its
duties in preference to every other labor,
and to devote themselves exclusively to it
with all the zeal, industry, and strength
they possess, unless released in part or for
a time by those who preside over them. Our
view--and it has been the view of all our
predecessors--is that no officer of our
church, especially those in high standing,
should take a course to violate this long-
established practice. Rather than to disobey
it and declare himself independent of his
associates and his file leaders, it has
always been held that it would be better for
a man to resign the duties of his priesthood;
and we entertain the same view to-day."

[Entry 1293]

[1288] "Emigration to the United States", pp. 114-115, 134-135.
In Special Consular Reports, vol. XXX. Washington:
Govt. Print. Off., 1904. [S4.9:30]

The entire volume is a special study of emigration to
the U.S. and the two brief entries listed discuss the
Mormon missionary influence on emigration in Norway and
Switzerland.

[1289] "Petitions Against the Seating of Reed Smoot," Congressional
Record 58th Congress, 3d session (7, 8, 12, 13, 14, 15,
16 December 1904) vol. 39, pt. 1, pp. 43, 44, 45, 63,
120, 186, 190, 253, 295, 340, 395. [X397]

None of these petitions, and there are many more than
it would appear from the paging, are printed in full.

[1290] "Postmasters in Idaho," Congressional Record 58th Congress,
2d session (20 April 1904) vol. 38, pt. 6, p. 5161. [X395]

Petition to determine if postmasters in Idaho are
living in polygamy.

[1291] "Protest," Congressional Record 58th Congress, 2d Session.
(6 April 1904) vol. 38, pt. 5, p. 4345. [X394]

Remonstrance of 640 non Mormon citizens of Salt Lake
condemning the testimony of Joseph F. Smith at the
Smoot hearings.

[1292] U.S. Senate. Committee on Privileges and Elections.
Extracts from Proceedings before the Committee on
Privileges and Elections of the United States Senate in
the matter of the protests against the right of Hon.
Reed Smoot, a Senator from the State of Utah, to hold
his Seat: Testimony taken during the months of January,
February and March 1904. New York: The Interdenominational
Council of Women for Christian and Patriotic Service
[1904?] 9p.

Although technically not a government publication, this
brief extract provides an interesting index to the
oversized polygamy document.

[Flake 9171]
UPB, USlC

[1293] U.S. Senate. 59th Congress. 1st Session. Committee on
Privileges and Elections. Proceedings before the
Committee on Privileges and Elections of the United
States Senate in the Matter of the Protests against the
Right Hon. Reed Smoot, a senator from the State of
Utah, to hold his seat. (S. Rept. No. 486) Washington:
Govt. Print. Off., 1904-6. 4v. [Serial Set 2932-2935]

This four-volume set submitted by Mr. Julius Caesar
Burrows with Views of the minority, submitted by Mr.
Joseph B. Foraker v. 4, pp. 467-542.

Contents of testimony taken before the committee in the
matter of the protest against the right of Reed Smoot,
a Mormon Apostle to hold his seat. Classified into
eighteen subdivisions and indexed as to witnesses. The
Committee voted to have Smoot expelled, but Congress
voted otherwise. Pivotal documents in the history of
the Church: After testifying Joseph F. Smith returned
to Salt Lake City and issued the second Manifesto.

[Flake 9173]

[1294] "Utah Senatorial Investigation," Congressional Record 58th
Congress, 2d Session (25, 27 January 1904) vol. 38, pt.
2, pp. 1100, 1239. [X391]

The initial requests from the Committee on Privileges
and Elections to investigate the seating of Reed Smoot.

[1295] "Utah Statehood Investigation," Congressional Record 58th
Congress, 2d Session (25, 27 January 1904) vol. 38, pt.
2, pp. 1100, 1239. [X391]

The initial requests from the Committee on Privileges
and Elections to investigate the seating of Reed Smoot.

1905

"Brigham Young succeeded Joseph Smith and he
set up a kind of kingly rulership, not
unbecoming to a man of his vast empire-
building power. The Mormons have been taught
to revere Joseph Smith as a direct prophet
from God. He saw the fact of the All Father.

He held communion with the Son. The Holy
Ghost was his constant companion. He settled
every question, however trivial, by revelation
from Almighty God. But Brigham was different.
While claiming a divine right of leadership,
he worked out his great mission by palpable
and material means. I do not know that he
ever pretended to have received a revelation
from the time that he left Nauvoo until he
reached the shores of the Dead Sea, nor
through all the thirty years of his leadership
there. He seemed to regard his people as
children who had to be led through their
serious calamities by holding out to them the
glittering thought of divine guardianship.
So firmly did Brigham establish the social
order in Utah that all of the people were
equal, except the governing body."

[Entry 1296]

[1296] Kearns, Thomas. <u>Conditions in Utah. Speech of Hon.
Thomas Kearns, of Utah, in the Senate of the United
States, Tuesday, February 28, 1905</u>. Washington, 1905.
14p.

Social conditions in Utah, polygamous marriages and
plural cohabitation. Statehood was gained by a compact
against polygamy which has been repeatedly broken.
"Mormons as a community are ruled by a special privileged
class... the church monarchy."

[Flake 4530]
CSmH, CU-B, MH, MoInRC, MoU, NjP, NN, OO, PHi, UHi, UPB,
USl, USlC, UU

[1297] Kearns, Thomas (Utah) "Polygamous Marriages and Plural
Cohabitation," <u>Congressional Record</u> 58th Congress, 3d
session (27, 28 February 1905) vol. 39, pt. 4, pp.
3474, 3608-3613. [X400]

Sen. Kearns of Utah discusses polygamy; the character
of the people in Utah; pledges of the Mormon Church
concerning polygamy; the social aspect of polygamy; the
Mormon church as a business monopoly; the general
situation in Utah; and the remedy for evils existing in
polygamy.

[1298] "Petitions Against the Seating of Reed Smoot," <u>Congressional
Record</u> 58th Congress, 3d session (4, 5, 6, 10, 11, 13,
January 1905) vol. 39, pt. 1, pp. 434, 435, 456, 457,
510, 621, 674, 769. [X397]

None of these petitions, and there are many more than
it would appear from the pages, are printed in full.

[1299] "Petitions Against the Seating of Reed Smoot," <u>Congressional
Record</u> 58th Congress, 3d session (20, 23, 25, 26, 27,
28, 30, 31 January, 1, 3, 4, 6, 8 February 1905) vol.
39, pt. 2, pp. 1116, 1121, 1218, 1326, 1382, 1440,
1441, 1442, 1502, 1572, 1573, 1622, 1667, 1814, 1815,
1860, 1910, 2057. [X398]

None of these petitions are printed in full.

[1300] "Petitions Against the Seating of Reed Smoot," Congressional
Record 58th Congress, 3d session (9, 10, 11, 13, 14,
16, 18, 20, 22 February 1905) vol. 39, pt. 3, pp. 2143,
2144, 2224, 2388, 2446, 2511, 2512, 2707, 2816, 2887,
2888, 3017. [X399]

None of these petitions are printed in full.

[1301] "Petitions Against the Seating of Reed Smoot," Congressional
Record 58th Congress, 3d session (25, 28 February, 1,
2, 3, March 1905) vol. 39, pt. 4, pp. 3361, 3598, 3599,
3600, 3718, 3821, 3927. [X400]

None of these petitions are printed in full.

[1302] U.S. Senate. Committee on Privileges and Elections. In
the matter of the protests against the right of Hon.
Reed Smoot, a Senator from the State of Utah, to hold
his seat: Arguments of A. S. Worthington and Waldemar
Van Cott, on behalf of the respondent. Washington:
Govt. Print. Off., 1905. 164p.
                                        [Flake 9172a]
                                        DLC, US1C

[1303] U.S. Senate. 58th Congress. 3d Session. Postmasters in
Idaho living in Polygamy. Letter from the Postmaster
General transmitting, in response to a Senate resolution
of April 20, 1904, the report of Post-Office Inspector
M. C. Fosnes relative to what, if any, postmasters in
Idaho are living in polygamy. Jan. 4, 1905. (S. Doc.
No. 62) Washington: Govt. Print. Off., 1905. 19p.
[Serial Set 4764]

Considerable historical information on Joseph Smith,
the Mormons, and the polygamy question. Concerns Miss
Dora Clegg, postmistress of Rexburg, and her alleged
polygamous relationship with Ben E. Rich.
                                        [Flake 9211]

                                             1906

"During this period of disintegration one
Brigham Young, who had identified himself
with the Mormon organization as early as
1832, a man of indomitable will and undaunted
courage, bold and unscrupulous, seized upon
the occasion of the demoralization incident
to the death of the prophet to place himself
at the head of some 5,000 Mormons, and
marching over desert and mountain, established
himself with his adherents in the valley of
Salt Lake, July 24, 1847, then Mexican
territory, where he undoubtedly indulged the
hope that the new doctrine of polygamy about
to be publicly proclaimed by him might be
promulgated with impunity and practiced and
maintained without interference by the United
States. These hopes, however, were destined

> to be blasted, for by the treaty of Guadalupe-
> Hidalgo of February 2, 1848, this territory
> passed from the jurisdiction of Mexico to the
> sovereignty of the United States, and its
> inhabitants thereupon became amenable to its
> laws."
>
> [Entry 1312]

[1304] Burrows, Julius Caeser. The Burrows and Dubois speeches, the difference between the Reorganized Church of Jesus Christ of Latter Day Saints and the Brighamite Mormon Church clearly stated in speeches delivered in the United States Senate by two distinguished statesmen. [n.p., 1906?] 4p.

The question of succession as raised during the Smoot hearings.

[Flake 1023]
MoInRC

[1305] Burrows, Julius Caeser. In support of the resolution reported from the Committee on Privileges and Elections "That Reed Smoot is not entitled to a seat as a senator of the United States from the State of Utah." Speech of Hon. Julius C. Burrows, of Michigan, in the Senate of the United States, Tuesday, December 11, 1906. Washington, 1906. 44p.

See entry 1312 for annotation.

[Flake 1024]
CU-B, MoInRC, UPB, USlC

[1306] Dubois, Fred Thomas. Senator from Utah. Speech of Hon. Fred T. Dubois, of Idaho, in the senate of the United States, Thursday, December 13, 1906. Washington, 1906. 57p.

Concerning the Reed Smoot hearings. See entry 1312 for annotation.

[Flake 3017]
MoInRC, UPB, USlC

[1307] "Latter-day Saints," pp. 327-335. In U.S. Bureau of the Census. Special Reports. Religious bodies: 1906. Pt. 2. Washington: Govt. Print. Off., 1910. [C3.2:1906, C3.35:R27/2]

General statement of the history and doctrine of the church, statistics of church membership, etc.

[1308] "Latter-day Saints (Reorganized)," pp. 335-340. In U.S. Bureau of the Census. Special Reports. Religious bodies: 1906. Pt. 2. Washington: Govt. Print. OFf., 1910. [C3.2:1906, C3.35:R27/2]

Brief statement of the history and doctrine of the church; statistics of church membership, etc.

[1309] "Memorial," <u>Congressional Record</u> 59th Congress, 1st
    session (20 April 1906) vol. 40, pt. 6, p. 5638. [X407]

Peition, not printed, from Legislature of New York
praying a constitutional amendment to prohibit polygamy.

[1310] "Memorial from the Legislature of New York," <u>Congressional</u>
    <u>Record</u> 59th Congress, 1st session (30 March, 2, 4, 5
    April 1906) vol. 40, pt. 5, pp. 4517, 4551, 4627, 4757,
    4828. [X406]

Petitions, one printed in full on p. 4551, praying a
constitutional amendment to prohibit polygamy.

[1311] "Petitions and Memorials," <u>Congressional Record</u> 59th
    Congress, 2d session (10, 11, 13, 17, 18, 20 December
    1906) vol. 41, pt. 1, pp. 185, 237, 295, 328, 444, 488,
    566. [X413]

Petitions from various organizations throughout the
United States, such as the Women's Reading Club of
Rutherford, N.J. or the Woman's Christian Temperance
Union of Esceola, [i.e. Osceola] Nebraska, requesting,
or praying, that Reed Smoot be investigated as to the
charges against him. Unfortunately the full petitions
are never printed in full.

[1312] "Senator from Utah," <u>Congressional Record</u> 59th Congress,
    2d Session (11, 13, 18 December 1906) vol. 41, pt. 1,
    pp. 241-255, 330-348, 498. [X413]

Extensive debate on the seating of Reed Smoot as a
Senator. Detailed history of the Mormon Church,
priesthood authority, polygamy, theocratic nature of
Mormonism, Supreme Court decisions, the influence of
the Mormons in Idaho politics, etc.

[1313] "Senator from Utah," <u>Congressional Record</u> 59th Congress,
    1st session (11 June 1906) vol. 40, pt. 9, pp. 8218-
    8238. [X410]

Strong protest against seating of Reed Smoot, based
primarily on polygamy and church and state issues.

[1314] Smoot, Reed (Utah) "Correspondence," <u>Congressional Record</u>
    59th Congress, 1st session (13 June 1906) vol. 40, pt.
    9, pp. 8402-8403. [X410]

Correspondence between Reed Smoot and the Department of
Justice regarding polygamy in Arizona.

[1315] U.S. Senate. Committee on Privileges and Elections.
    <u>Contents of testimony taken before the Committee on</u>
    <u>Privileges and Elections of the United States Senate in</u>
    <u>the matter of the protests against the right of Hon.</u>
    <u>Reed Smoot a Senator from the State of Utah, to hold</u>
    <u>his seat.</u> Comp. for Mr. Smoot. Washington: Judd &
    Detweiler [1906?] 149p.

The index to the 4 volume investigation, for the
investigation see Entry 1293.

[Flake 9170]
NjP, UHi, ULA, UPB

[1316] U.S. Senate. 59th Congress. 1st Session. Committee on
Privileges and Elections. In re Reed Smoot. (S. Rept.
No. 4253, pt. 1, 2) Washington: Govt. Print. Off.,
1906. 2 parts (32, 44, p.) [Serial Set 4905-G]

Pt. 1. Reed Smoot. Pt. 2. Views of the minority.

Right of Reed Smoot to hold his seat as Senator from
Utah.

[Flake 9172]

[1316a] U.S. Senate. 59th Congress. 1st Session. Immigration
of Aliens into the United States. (S. Rept. 2186)
Washington: Govt. Print. Off., 1906. 10p. [Serial
Set 4905]

Report accompanying Senate bill 4403 which was to amend
an act entitled "An act to regulate the immigration of
aliens into the United States," approved March 3,
1903. Only a small portion on p. 3 apparently relates
to Mormons with the section on undesirables expanded
from simply polygamists to include "or persons who
admit their belief in the practice of polygamy."

[1317] U.S. Senate. 59th Congress. 1st Session. S.R. 56.
"Joint Resolution proposing an amendment to the Constitution
of the United States prohibiting polygamy and polygamous
cohabitation within the United States, May 9, 1906."
[Washington: Govt. Print. Off., 1906] 2p.
DLC, UPB, US1C

1907

"But should the Senate expel Senator Smoot,
and why? He should not be expelled for
believing in the Mormon religion. The
irrevocable ordinance expressly, and with
Mormonism in view, guaranteed religious
toleration in the State of Utah. He should
not be expelled for being a member or officer
of the Mormon Church for the same reason. He
should not be expelled for the vindication of
Utah's law, violated by certain Mormons
continuing polygamous relations with Senator
Smoot's consent or approval; supposing he did
consent or approve; for Utah, without being
ignorant of the facts, elected him and the
Senate would not be justified in going out of
its way to enforce respect for the formerly
expressed will of Utah embodied in its law
against polygamous relations by defeating its
later expressed will shown in its electing
Smoot."

[Entry 1330]

"Senator Smoot is a son of a polygamist. His
father had four wives, and he was raised in
this polygamous atmosphere with polygamous
half brothers and sisters. When he reached
the age of manhood he married a polygamous
child, his wife being the daughter of the
fourth wife of her father. I do not say this
in disparagement to them. It is a badge of
distinction for them in Utah. It does not
interfere with their social standing in the
slightest degree. I would not say it if it
hurt the feelings of the Senator from Utah,
but it does not. Few in Utah will blame him
for that; man, most, will honor him for it.
That was his youth. He is an apostle of the
Mormon Church."

[Entry 1324]

[1318] Berry, James Henderson. Speech of Hon. James H. Berry, of
Arkansas, in the Senate of the United States, on the
question of excluding Hon. Reed Smoot of Utah, from the
United States Senate, Monday, February 11, 1907.
Washington, 1907. 23p.

See entry 1312 for annotation and 1339 for Congressional
Record entry.

[Flake 442]
UPB

[1319] Beveridge, Albert Jeremiah. The Reed Smoot case. Speech
of Hon. Albert J. Beveridge, of Indiana, in the Senate
of the United States, in support of the minority report
on the resolution that Reed Smoot is not entitled to a
seat in the Senate as a senator from Utah. February
20, 1907. Washington, 1907. 15p.

See entry 1312 for annotation and 1340 for Congressional
Record entry.

In favor of seating Mr. Smoot.

[Flake 449]
MH, UPB, USlC, UU

[1320] Burrows, Julius Caeser. Senator from Utah. The scope of
the power of the Senate, under the Constitution, to
"judge of the elections, returns, and qualifications of
its own members," and the grounds upon which Reed Smoot
is disqualified. Speech of Hon. Julious C. Burrows, of
Michigan, Senate of the United States, Wednesday,
February 20, 1907. Washington, 1907.

Gives some of the testimony of John Taylor, Charles E.
Merrill, B. H. Roberts, Andrew Jenson, Angus M. Cannon,
John Henry Hamlin, George H. Brimhall, Josiah Hickman,
Mrs. Wilhelmina C. Ellis, John Henry Smith, and others,
with focus on polygamy.

See entry 1340 for <u>Congressional Record</u> entry.

[Flake 1025]
CU-B, MH, UHi, UPB, US1C, UU

[1321] "Constitutional amendment against polygamy," <u>Congressional
Record</u> 59th Congress, 2d Session (21, 22 February 1907)
vol. 41, pt. 4, pp. 3511, 3591, 3604. [X416]

Resolved that the Committee on the Judiciary prepare a
report to have a Constitutional convention to prohibit
polygamy.

[1322] "Constitutional Amendment to Prohibit Polygamy,"
<u>Congressional Record</u> 56th Congress, 2d session (15
February 1907) vol. 41, pt. 3, p. 3011. [X415]

Resolution, printed in full, from the Legislature of
Delaware proposing an amendment to the constitution to
prohibit polygamy.

[1323] Dillingham, William Paul. <u>The senator from Utah</u>. Speech
of Hon. Wm. P. Dillingham, of Vermont, in the Senate of
the United States, Tuesday, February 19, 1907.
Washington, 1907. 34p.

Reed Smoot hearings.

See entry 1312 for annotation and 1340 for <u>Congressional
Record</u> entry.

[Flake 2840]
CU-B, UPB, US1C, UU

[1324] Dubois, Fred Thomas. <u>Senator from Utah</u>. Speech of Hon.
Fred T. Dubois, of Idaho, in the Senate of the United
States, Wednesday, February 20, 1907. Washington,
1907. 13p.

Mormon domination and priestly rule.

See entry 1312 for annotation and 1340 for <u>Congressional
Record</u> entry.

[Flake 3018]
CU-B, UPB, US1C

[1325] Du Pont, Henry A. (Delaware) "Presenting a joint resolution
of the legislature of Delaware," <u>Congressional Record</u>
59th Congress, 2d Session (15 February 1907) vol. 41,
pt. 3, p. 3011. [X415]

A call for a Constitutional convention to prohibit
polygamy. This revival of the polygamy problem was
probably due to the Reed Smoot hearings.

[1326] Foraker, Joseph Benson. <u>Senator from Utah</u>. Remarks of
Hon. Joseph B. Foraker, of Ohio, in the Senate of the
United States, February 20, 1907. Washington, 1907.
8p.

The seating of Reed Smoot. It is not the Mormon church
or Joseph F. Smith, but Reed Smoot who is on trial.
Discusses polygamy, and he defends Smoot.

See entry 1312 for annotation.

[Flake 3393]
UHi, UPB

[1327] Hopkins, Albert Jarvis. <u>Senator Reed Smoot and the Mormon
Church.</u> Speech of Hon. Albert J. Hopkins, of Illinois,
in the Senate of the United States, Friday, January 11,
1907. Washington, 1907. 36p.

See entry 1312 and 1337 for <u>Congressional Record</u> entry.

[Flake 4087]
CU-B, NjP, UHi, UPB, USlC

[1328] Knox, Philander Chase. <u>In opposition to the resolution
reported from the Committee on Privileges and Elections
"that Reed Smoot is not entitled to a seat as a Senator
of the United States from the State of Utah."</u> Speech
of Hon. Philander C. Knox, (of Pennsylvania) in the
Senate of the United States, Thursday, February 14,
1907. Washington: Govt. Print. Off., 1907. 14p.

See entry 1312 for annotation and 1339 for <u>Congressional
Record</u> entry.

[Flake 4670]
CU-B, MH, UPB

[1329] Knox, Philander Chase. <u>In opposition to the resolution
reported from the Committee on Privileges and Elections
"that Reed Smoot is not entitled to a seat as a Senator
of the United States from the State of Utah."</u> Speech
of Hon. Philander C. Knox of Pennsylvania, in the
Senate of the United States, Thursday, February 14,
1907. Washington, 1907. 19p.

See entry 1312 annotation and 1339 for <u>Congressional
Record</u> entry.

[Flake 4671]
UPB, USlC

[1330] Knox, Philander Chase. <u>In opposition to the resolution
reported from the Committee on Privileges and Elections
"that Reed Smoot is not entitled to a seat as a senator
of the United States from the State of Utah."</u> Speech
of Hon. Philander C. Knox, of Pennsylvania, in the
Senate of the United States, Thursday, February 14,
1907. Washington: Govt. Print. Off., 1907. 30p.

See entry 1312 for annotation and 1339 for <u>Congressional
Record</u> entry.

[Flake 4669]
DLC, UPB

[1331] "Memorial from the Legislature of North Dakota," <u>Congressional
Record</u> 59th Congress, 2d session (3, 4 March 1907) vol.
41, pt. 5, pp. 4633, 4634, 4672. [X417]

Proposal for an amendment to the Constitution to
prohibit polygamy. The resolution is printed in full
on p. 4634.

[1332] "Memorial to Congress for constitutional amendment,"
Congressional Record 59th Congress, 2d session (4 March
1907) vol. 41, pt. 5, p. 4634, 4672. [X417]

As a result of the Reed Smoot hearings the House of
Representatives of North Dakota asks that a Constitutional
amendment to prohibit polygamy.

[1333] "Petitions and Memorials," Congressional Record 59th
Congress, 2d session (10, 11 January 1907) vol. 41, pt.
1, pp. 863, 922. [X413]

Petitions of individuals and organizations, such as the
Western College of Women of Oxford, Ohio, praying for
an investigation of the charges against Reed Smoot.
Unfortunately the full petitions are never printed in
full.

[1334] "Petitions and Memorials," Congressional Record 59th
Congress, 2d session (17, 22 January 1907) vol. 41, pt.
2, pp. 1250, 1481. [X414]

See entry 1332 for annotation.

[1335] "Petitions and Memorials," Congressional Record 59th
Congress, 2d Session (31 January, 1, 4, 6, 7, 8, 13, 15
February 1907) vol. 41, pt. 3, pp. 2061, 2141, 2187,
2332, 2396, 2496-2497, 2804, 3008-3009, 3011. [X415]

See entry 1333 for annotation. The entry for 15
February is for a Constitutional amendment to prohibit
polygamy and it does include the full text of the
resolution.

[1336] "Petitions and Memorials," Congressional Record 59th
Congress, 2d Session (16, 18, 19, 20 February 1907)
vol. 41, pt. 4, pp. 3075, 3171, 3261, 3262, 3263, 3399.
[X416]

See entry 1332 for annotation.

[1337] "Senator from Utah," Congressional Record 59th Congress,
2d Session (11 January 1907) vol. 41, pt. 1, pp. 933-
945. [X413]

See entry 1312 for annotation.

[1338] "Senator from Utah," Congressional Record 59th Congress,
2d Session (22, 30 January 1907) vol. 41, pt. 2, pp.
1486-1501, 1933-1934. [X414]

See entry 1312 for annotation.

[1339] "Senator from Utah," Congressional Record 59th Congress,
2d Session (11, 14 February 1907) vol. 41, pt. 3, pp.
2681-2688, 2934-2939. [X415]

See entry 1312 for annotation.

[1340] "Senator from Utah," Congressional Record 59th Congress,
2d Session (19, 20 February 1907) vol. 41, pt. 4, pp.
3268-3281, 3404-3430. [X416]

Includes testimony from a number of Mormons regarding
polygamy and Reed Smoot. See entry 1312 for rest of
annotation.

[1341] Senator from Utah. Speech of Hon. Reed Smoot of Utah in
the Senate of the United States, Tuesday, February 19,
1907. Washington: Govt. Print. Off., 1907. 8p.

The Mormon church and its allegiance to the country.

See entry 1312 for annotation and entry 1340 for
Congressional Record entry.
[Flake 8151]
CU-B, UPB, USlC

[1342] U.S. Senate. 60th Congress. 1st Session. S.R. 13,
"Joint Resolution to amend the Constitution of the
United States prohibiting polygamy, December 16, 1907."
[Washington: Govt. Print. Off., 1907] 1p.

Referred to the Committee on the Judiciary.

DLC, UPB, USlC

[1343] Veatch, Arthur Clifford. Geography and geology of a
portion of Southwestern Wyoming, with special reference
to coal and oil. Washington: Govt. Print. Off., 1907.
178p. [I19.16:56]

(U.S. Geological Survey. Professional paper. No. 56)

References to Mormons and Mormon trail, pp. 10, 18-19,
139-140.
[Flake 9450]
CU-B, DLC, UPB

1908

"Sir: I have the honor to acknowledge the
receipt of your note of the 30th ultimo,
wherein you quote from a communication
addressed to Her Majesty the Queen of the
Netherlands by the Interdenomination Council
of Women for Christian and Patriotic Service
urging legislation to prohibit in the Netherlands
the missionary propaganda of the Mormon
Church, and request, by direction of your
Government, information on the points raised
in said communication with reference to the
position of the Mormon Church on the question
of polygamy."
[Entry 1347]

[1344] "Expulsion of Mormon missionaries from Germany," pp. 366-371. In Foreign Relations of the United States, 1908. Washington: Govt. Print. Off., 1912. [Sl.1:908]

A series of letters which discusses the expulsion of two Mormon missionaries, Adelbert A. Taylor and Henry A. Rich who spoke in Breslau on August 12, 1908 and who were subsequently arrested. The arrest was allegedly made because of the practice of polygamy. Serge F. Ballif, President of the Swiss and German Mission, was one of the correspondents.

[1345] "Memorial of the Baptist Church and congregation of Lamoille, Ill.," Congressional Record 60th Congress, 1st session (20 March 1908) vol. 42, pt. 4, p. 3624. [X422]

Another memorial supporting a constitutional amendment prohibiting polygamy.

[1346] "Petitions and Memorials," Congressional Record 60th Congress, 1st session (27 February 1908) vol. 42, pt. 3, p. 2577. [X421]

A letter addressed to Sen. Shelby M. Cullom of Illinois from the Secretary of the Rock River Conference of the Methodist Episcopal Church, J. A. Matlack, was in the form of a resolution prohibiting polygamy and impugning the character of Joseph F. Smith.

[1347] "Status of Mormon missionaries," pp. 659-660. In Foreign Relations of the United States, 1908. Washington: Govt. Print. Off,. 1912. [Sl.1:908]

The Interdenominational Council of Women for Christian and Patriotic Service, based in New York, are especially concerned about Mormon propaganda because of the practice of polygamy and the recruitment of European women to practice polygamy among the Mormons in the United States.

[1348] U.S. Senate. 60th Congress. 1st Session. S.R. 19, "Joint Resolution proposing an amendment to the Constitution of the United States prohibiting polygamy and polygamous cohabitation within the United States, January 7, 1908." [Washington: Govt. Print Off., 1908] 2p.

Referred to the Committee on the Judiciary.

DLC, UPB, US1C

[1349] U.S. Senate. 60th Congress. 1st Session. S.R. 46, "Joint Resolution to amend the Constitution of the United States, prohibiting polygamy and polygamous cohabitation, January 29, 1908." [Washington: Govt. Print. Off., 1908] 1p.

Referred to the Committee on the Judiciary.

DLC, UPB, US1C

"Whereas by reason of such area being isolated
from the rest of the Territory of Arizona it
is impossible to administer the laws of said
Territory or enforce the criminal statutes or
the legal ordinances or provisions or preserve
peace and order, as a result of which criminals
rendezvous therein and obtain immunity from
prosecution; and Whereas such area by reason
of its physical situation and of the interests
of the people owning property therein should
belong to the State of Utah, and its annexation
to the State of Utah would be productive of the
greatest good to all interests and would be
of advantage to the people residing in and
who are interested in said tract of land, the
majority of said residents having petitioned
the congress of the United States to annex
said tract to the State of Utah."

[Entry 1352]

[1350] "House Joint Resolution 7," Congressional Record 60th
Congress, 2d session (19, 20 February 1909) vol. 43,
pt. 3, p. 2670, 2761, 2826. [X430]

The House of Representatives of the state of South
Dakota submits a memorial in support of a constitutional
amendment prohibiting polygamy.

[1351] "House Memorial 6," Congressional Record 61st Congress,
1st session (16 March 1909) vol. 44, pt. 1, p. 52.
[X433]

Memorial from the Arizona Territorial Legislature
protesting annexation to Utah.

[1352] "Memorial," Congressional Record 60th Congress, 2d session
(6 February 1909) vol. 44, pt. 2, p. 1972. [X429]

A memorial from the Utah State Legislature requesting
annexation of Arizona Territory north of the Colorado
River to Utah because the interests of the inhabitants
have more in common with the people of Utah.

[1353] "Mormon bibliography," pp. 515, 677, 691-692. In Annual
report of the American Historical Association for the
Year 1909. Washington: Govt. Print. Off., 1911.
[SI4.1:909]

Entries in writings on American History published as a
part of Annual Report of the American Historical
Association.

[1354] "Senate Concurrent Resolution 17," Congressional Record
61st Congress, Special session (16, 22 March 1909) vol.
44, pt. 1, p. 50, 127. [X433]

Another memorial, from the state of Washington supporting a constitutional amendment prohibiting polygamy.

[1355] U.S. House. 61st Congress. 1st Session. H.R. 4317, "A bill to extend the pension laws of the United States to the soldiers engaged in the Utah Expedition of eighteen hundred and fifty-seven and eighteen hundred and fifty-eight, and to the widows and children of such soldiers, March 24, 1909." [Washington: Govt. Print. OFf., 1909] 1p.

Referred to the Committee on Pension.

DLC, UPB, US1C

1910

"The first permanent settlement of the Utah country was not made, however, until July, 1847, when Salt Lake City was founded by a band of Mormons from Illinois under the leadership of Brigham Young. . . For two years after the founding of Salt Lake City the new colony had no secular government. In 1849 the Mormons organized the so-called state of Deseret and requested admission to the Union."

[Entry 1356]

[1356] "Supplement for Utah." In U.S. Census, 1910: Thirteenth Census of the United States. . . Abstract of the Census. Washington: Govt. Print. Off., 1913. [C3.15:Ab89]

Brief mention of the Mormons, but the main emphasis is on demographics, extensive material pp. 567-659.

1911

"Whereas it appears from an investigation recently made by the Senate of the United States, and otherwise, that polygamy still exists in certain places in the United States, notwithstanding prohibitory statutes enacted by the several States thereof; and Whereas the practice of polygamy is generally condemned by the people of the United States, and there is a demand for the more effectual prohibition thereof by placing the subject under the Federal jurisdiction and control, at the same time reserving to each State the right to make and control its own laws relating to marriage and divorce: Now therefore be it Resolved by the senate (the house of representation concurring), That the application be made, and hereby is made, to Congress, under the provisions of Article V of the Constitution of the United States, for the calling of a convention to propose an amendment to the Constitution of the United States whereby polygamy and polgamous cohabitation

276

shall be prohibited, and Congress shall be
given power to enforce such prohibition by
appropriate legislation."

[Entry 1362]

[1357] "House Joint Memorial 7," Congressional Record 62d Congress,
1st session (6 April 1911) vol. 47, pt. 1, p. 98. [X453]

Joint Memorial of the Legislature of Montana supporting
a Constitutional amendment against polygamy. Memorial
printed in full.

[1358] "Memorial of the Legislature of Nebraska for a Constitutional
Amendment prohibiting Polygamy," Congressional Record
62d Congress, 1st session (6, 10 April 1911) vol. 47,
pt. 1, pp. 99, 148. [X453]

The memorial is printed in full on p. 99.

[1359] "Memorial of the Legislature of Nebraska," Congressional
Record 62d Congres, 1st session (13 June 1911) vol. 47,
pt. 2, p. 2000. [X454]

Brief mention made to the memorial cited above.

[1360] "Memorial of the Legislature of Ohio for Prohibition of
Polygamy," Congressional Record 62d Congress, 1st
session (5, 6, 10, 27 April 1911) vol. 47, pt. 1, pp.
85, 114, 148, 661. [X453]

House Joint Resolution 13 to define the law against
polygamy, is printed in full on p. 661. A little more
detailed resolution than most at this time.

[1361] "Memorial of the Legislature of the State of Washington,"
Congressional Record 61st Congress, 3d session (9
January 1911) vol. 46, pt. 1, p. 651. [X448]

Another state memorial, printed in full, supporting a
constitutional amendment prohibiting polygamy, S. Con.
Res. 17.

[1362] "Memorial of the Legislature of Tennessee for Prohibition
of Polygamy," Congressional Record 62d Congress, 1st
session (13 April 1911) vol. 47, pt. 1, pp. 187, 246.
[X453]

The memorial, Senate Joint Resolution 43, printed in
full on p. 187, is asking for the usual Constitutional
amendment to prohibit polygamy.

[1363] U.S. House. 62d Congress. 1st Session. H.R. 8382, "A
bill to provide for the refunding of certain moneys
illegally assessed and collected and ordered to be
printed, April 29 (calendar day May 1), 1911." [Washington:
Govt. Print. Off., 1911] 2p.

Referred to the Committee on Claims. Included because
it refers to taxes held illegally by the U.S. Supreme
Court on ZCMI.

DLC, UPB, US1C

[1364] U.S. Senate. 62d Congress. 1st Session. S. 412, "A bill
to provide for the refunding of certain moneys illegally
assessed and collected in the district of Utah, April
10, 1911." [Washington: Govt. Print. Off., 1911] 2p.

Referred to the Committee on Finance.

Refers to a tax on Zion's Cooperative Mercantile
Institute, which was illegally held by the Supreme
Court of the United States.

DLC, UPB, US1C

[1365] U.S. Senate. 62d Congress. 1st Session. S. 412, "A bill
to provide for the refunding of certain moneys illegally
assessed and collected in the district of Utah, April
10, 1911, February 6, 1912." 2p.

Referred to the Committee on Finance. See entry 1364
for annotation.

DLC, UPB, US1C

1912

"Night letter telegram from Haymore, dated
last night, received this morning, states
that courier arriving at Aguaprieta from
Morelos Sunday night reports conditions
normal at Morelos, and that Bishop Brown, who
went to investigate Morelos matter, would
communicate with me this morning. Bishop
Brown telegraphs this morning from Douglas,
merely saying that Bishop Lillywhite would be
in Douglas to-day to substantiate his accusations
against Mexican Federals at Colona, Morelos.
Apparently Mormons differ among themselves as
to policy of making representations against
the Mexican authorities."

[Entry 1368]

[1366] "American Samoa," pp. 455-456. In Report of the Commissioner
of Education for the year ended June 30, 1912. Washington:
Govt. Print. Off., 1913. [FS5.1:912, HE5.1:912]

Reports that the Mormons were conducting three schools
in Tutuila, and they were the only teachers teaching
English.

[1367] "Mexico," p. 816. In Foreign Relations of the United
States, 1912. Washington: Govt. Print. Off., 1919.
[S1.1:912]

Murder of William Adams, an American citizen, at
Colonia Diaz by rebel soldiers was reported. Included

as a part of the material on protecting American
citizens in Mexico.

[1368] United States. Department of State. Division of Information.
Disorders in Mexico. (Series A, No. 87, Mexico, No. 13,
Confidential, no. 63, Printed and distributed Sept. 17,
1912) pp. 32, 34, 35, 37.

Condition of colonists in Mormon colonies discussed,
Senator Smoot, Bishop Lillywhite and M. S Haymore, are
involved in the discussion.

Page 32 is the only entry later found in Foreign
Relations 1812, p. 816, edited.

DNA, UPB

[1369] United States. Department of State. Division of Information.
Disorders in Mexico. (Series A, No. 89, Mexico, No.
15, Confidential no. 46. Printed and distributed Nov.
21, 1912). pp. 4, 9, 19, 20.

Problems in the Mormon colonies in Mexico in 1912.

DNA, UPB

[1370] U.S. House. 62d Congress. 2d Session. H.J. Res. 277,
"Joint Resolution proposing an amendment to the Constitution
prohibiting polygamy, March 22, 1912." [Washington:
Govt. Print. Off., 1912] 1p.

Referred to the Committee on the Judiciary.

DLC, UPB, US1C

[1371] U.S. Senate. 62d Congress. 2d Session. Occupation of
Mexican Territory. Message from the President of the
United States transmitting in answer to a resolution of
the House of Representatives of December 15, 1846,
reports from the Secretary of the Navy relative to the
occupation of Mexican territory. (S. Doc. No. 896)
Washington: Govt. Print. Off., 1912. 76p. [Serial Set
6179]

Includes material on the Mormon Battalion and the
Mormon exodus to California, pp. 6-7, 21.

[Flake 9212]

[1372] U.S. Senate. 62d Congress. 2d Session. S. 412, "An act
to provide for the refunding of certain moneys illegally
assessed and collected in the district of Utah, February
13, 1912." [Washington: Govt. Print. Off., 1912] 2p.

Referred to the Committee on Claims.

See entry 1364 for annotation.

DLC, UPB, US1C

[1373] "Zion's Cooperative Mercantile Institution," Congressional
Record 62d Congress, 2d session (12 February 1912) vol.
48, pt. 2, pp. 1957-1958. [X459]

Debate on moneys illegally held by the IRS, stemming
from the use of script by ZCMI back in 1879.

1913

"The school system of the Mormon Church began
with the establishment of the church at
Fayette, N.Y., on the 6th day of April, 1830.
Among the earliest utterances of the founder,
Joseph Smith, were declarations that the
glory of God is intelligence; that men can
not be saved in ignorance; that a man can be
saved no faster than he gains knowledge; and
that 'whatever principles of intelligence we
attain unto in this life, it will rise with
us in the resurrection; and if a person gains
more knowledge and intelligence in this life
through his diligence and obedience than
another, he will have so much the advantage
in the world to come.'"

[Entry 1389]

[1374] "The Commonwealth of Massachusetts," Congressional Record
63d Congress, Special session (28 April 1913) vol. 50,
pt. 1, pp. 606-607. [X476]

Another memorial from a state legislature, printed in
the Record, which supports a constitutional amendment
prohibiting polygamy.

[1375] "Legislature of the state of Wisconsin," Congressional
Record 63d Congress, Special session (7, 8 April 1913)
vol. 40, pt. 1, pp. 42-43, 116. [X476]

Memorial of the legislature of Wisconsin in favor of a
constitutional amendment prohibiting polygamy. The
memorial is printed in full.

[1376] "Memorial of the General Assembly of Illinois," Congressional
Record 63d Congress, Special session (8 April 1913)
vol. 50, pt. 1, pp. 120-121. [X476]

The Memorial, printed in the Record, of the General
Assembly of Illinois which supports a constitutional
amendment prohibiting polygamy.

[1377] "Memorial of the Legislature of Michigan," Congressional
Record 63d Congress, 1st session (2 July 1913) vol. 50,
pt. 3, p. 2290. [X478]

The brief resolution, printed in full, is in support of
a consitutional amendment prohibiting polygamy.

[1378] "Memorial of the Legislature of Oregon," Congressional
Record 62d Congress, 3d session (31 January, 3, 5,
February 1913) vol. 49, pt. 3, pp. 2400, 2463, 2634.
[X473]

Another memorial praying for a Constitutional amendment to prohibit polygamy. Page 2463 includes full text of the memorial.

[1379] "Memorial of the Legislature of the State of Wisconsin," Congressional Record 63d Congress, 1st session (7, 8 April 1913) vol. 50, pt. 1, pp. 42-43, 116. [X476]

Two memorials printed in full requesting a constitutional amendment to prohibit polygamy.

[1380] "Memorial of the Legislature of the State of Vermont," Congressional Record 62d Congress, 3d session (13, 14 January 1913) vol. 49, pt. 2, pp. 1433, 1530. [X472]

Page 1433 includes full text of a memorial to prohibit polygamy through a constitutional amendment.

[1381] "Memorial of the Legislature of the State of Vermont," Congressional Record 62d Congress, 3d session (3 February 1913) vol. 49, pt. 3, p. 2464. [X473]

Includes full text of resolution to prohibit polygamy through a constitutional amendment.

[1382] "Memorial of the Legislature of Wisconsin," Congressional Record 63d Congress, 1st session (7, 8 April 1913) vol. 50, pt. 1, pp. 42-43, 116. [X476]

Two memorials printed in full, condemning polygamy and asking for a constitutional amendment to prohibit it.

[1383] U.S. House. 63d Congress. 1st Session. H.J. Res. 91, "Joint resolution proposing an amendment of the Constitution of the United States, June 2, 1913." [Washington: Govt. Print. Off., 1913] 1p.

Referred to the Committee on the Judiciary.

"Congress shall have power to prohibit polygamy and polygamous cohabitation in all the states..."

DLC, UPB, US1C

[1384] U.S. House. 63d Congress. 1st Session. H.R. 2448, "A bill to provide for the refunding of certain moneys illegally assessed and collected in the district of Utah, April 14, 1913." [Washington: Govt. Print. Off., 1913] 2p.

Money held illegally from Zion's Cooperative Mercantile Institution.

Referred to the Committee on Claims.

DLC, UPB, US1C

[1385] U.S. House. 63d Congress. 1st Session. H.J. Res. 144, "Joint resolution proposing an amendment to the Constitution of the United States, October 28, 1913." [Washington: Govt. Print. Off., 1913] 1p.

Referred to the Committee on the Judiciary.

"Polygamy shall not exist within the United States."

DLC, US1C, UPB

[1386] U.S. House. 63d Congress. 2d Session. S.J. Res. 91, "Joint resolution proposing an amendment to the Constitution, December 20, 1913." [Washington: Govt. Print. Off., 1913] 1p.

Referred to the Committee on the Judiciary.

"Polygamy shall not exist within the United States..."

DLC, UPB, US1C

[1387] U.S. Senate. Committee on the Judiciary. Maintenance of a lobby to influence legislation: Hearings before a Subcommittee of the Committee on the Judiciary, United States Senate, sixty-third Congress, first session pursuant to S. Res. 92, a resolution instructing the Committee on the Judiciary to investigate the charge that a lobby is maintained to influence legislation pending in the Senate. Part 4. Washington: Government Printing Office, 1913. pp. 379-504. [Y4.J89/2:L78/v.4]

Reed Smoot testimony with Mormon references, pp. 445-450. The Mormon Church's interests in the Utah-Idaho Sugar Co. are explored, and their interest as stockholders in other businesses such as the Knight Woolen Mills Company.

[Flake 9187a]
DLC, US1C

[1388] U.S. Senate. 63d Congress. 1st Session. S. 1213, "A Bill to provide for the refunding of certain moneys illegally assessed and collected in the district of Utah, April 17, 1913." [Washington: Govt. Print. Off., 1913] 1p.

Referred to the Committee on Finance. Included because it refers to illegally held taxes of ZCMI by the U.S. Supreme Court.

DLC, UPB, US1C

[1389] Widstoe, Osborne J. P. "The Schools of the Mormon Church," pp. 409-413. In Report of the Commissioner of Education, 1913, vol. 1. Washington: Govt. Print. Off., 1914. [FS5.1:913, HE5.1:913]

Brief history of the school system of the Mormon Church.

[Flake 9835]

1914

"I move to strike out the words, `admit their belief in the practice of polygamy' and to insert in lieu thereof `believe in, advocate, or practice polygamy.' Mr. President, just a

word in explanation. There are two different
phraseologies employed in various places in
this bill. In one case we find that it
requires that the immigrant shall admit his
belief in a certain doctrine; in the other
case the fact that he does believe in a
certain doctrine is all that is required."

[Entry 1393]

[1390] Cummings, Horace H. "The schools of the Mormon Church,"
pp. 609-610. In Report of the Commissioner of Education
for the year ended June 30, 1914, Vol. 2. Washington:
Govt. Print Off., 1915. [FS5.1:914, HE5.1:914]

Contemporary church schools.

[1391] "Monaghan Baptist Church of Greenville, S. C. regarding
Constitutional Amendment prohibiting Polygamy,"
Congressional Record 63d Congress, 2d session (7 May
1914) vol. 51, pt. 8, p. 8204. [X490]

The resolution against polygamy was printed in full. A
P.S. indicates that the resolution was read before an
audience of 1800 to 2000 people in the tent of the Red
Hall, Chautauqua and was unanimously adopted.

[1392] "Polygamy," Congressional Record 63d Congress, 2d session
(29 May 1914) vol. 51, pt. 10, p. 9424. [X492]

The Erwin Cotton Mills Co. of West Durham, N.C. had a
resolution read into the record which gives support to
the constitutional amendment prohibiting polygamy Mr.
Sutherland of Utah responds and inserts in the record a
statement of Bishop F. S. Spalding, bishop of the
Episcopal Church in the State of Utah, in support of
the Mormons. In Spalding's statement the work of the
National Reform Association in Pittsburgh is alluded
to.

[1393] "Regulation of Immigration," Congressional Record 63d
Congress, 3d session (31 December 1914) vol. 52, pt. 1,
pp. 807-812. [X501]

In the middle of the debate on H.R. 6060 to regulate
the immigration of aliens, a portion of the discussion
centered around polygamy and a section of the bill, or
an amendment to the bill, which was worded "Polygamists
or persons who admit their belief in the practice of
polygamy."

[1394] U.S. House. 63d Congress. 2d Session. H.J. Res. 200,
"Joint resolution proposing an amendment to the Constitution
of the United States, January 24, 1914." [Washington:
Govt. Print. Off., 1914] 1p.

Referred to the Committee on the Judiciary.

"Neither polygamy nor polygamous cohabitation shall exist within the United States."

DLC, UPB, US1C

[1395] U.S. House. 63d Congress. 2d Session. H.J. Res. 201, "Joint resolution proposing an amendment to the Constitution of the United States, January 24, 1914." [Washington: Govt. Print. Off., 1914] 1p.

Referred to the Committee on the Judiciary.

"Polygamy and polygamous cohabitation shall not exist within the United States."

DLC, UPB, US1C

[1396] U.S. House. 63d Congress. 2d Session. S. 1213, "An act to provide for the refunding of certain moneys illegally assessed and collected in the district of Utah, April 1, 1914." [Washington: Govt. Print. Off., 1914] 2p.

Included because it refers to taxes held illegally by the U.S. Supreme Court on ZCMI.

DLC, UPB, US1C

[1397] U.S. Senate. 63d Congress. 2d Session. S.J. Res. 96, "Joint resolution proposing an amendment to the Constitution of the United States, January 13, 1914." [Washington: Govt. Print. Off., 1914] 1p.

"Polygamy and polygamous cohabitation shall not exist within the United States..."

DLC, UPB, US1C

1915

"Just before entering the town of Echo the train passes close to Pulpit Rock... which may be seen on the right. As the name implies, this rock bears some resemblance to a pulpit, and the story has been somewhat widely circulated that from it Brigham Young preached his first sermon on entering the 'promised land' in 1847. However, those in a position to speak with authority on this subject say that the first company of Mormon emigrants did not stop at Pulpit Rock and that Young was sick with mountain fever during this part of the journey."

[Entry 1398]

[1398] Lee, Willis Thomas, Ralph W. Stone and Hoyt S. Gale. Guidebook of the Western United States, part B. The Overland route with a side trip to Yellowstone Park. Washington: Govt. Print. Off., 1915. 244p. [I19.3:612]

(U.S. Geological Survey. Bulletin 612)

Detailed geographic information along the line of the Union Pacific Railroad with material on cities, etc.

Primarily geographic in focus, although on p. 77 Mormon pioneers are briefly discussed.

[Flake 4866]

[1399] U.S. House. 64th Congress. 1st Session. H.J. Res. 9, "Joint resolution proposing an amendment to the Constitution of the United States, December 6, 1915." [Washington: Govt. Print. Off., 1915] 1p.

Referred to the Committee on the Judiciary.

"Polygamy and polygamous cohabitation shall not exist with in the United States..."

DLC, UPB, US1C

1916

"Prof. Young stated that the records of meetings of 62 of these committees are extant. He compared them to the town meetings of New England. Both civil and religious matters were dealt with at the same session. He cited instances of ward meetings in Salt Lake City in 1853, which were called to order by the bishop and which considered the setting of shade trees and the supplying of water to irrigate them. The stimuli holding people together were two--religious and economic."

[Entry 1404]

[1400] "Concurrent resolution," Congressional Record 64th Congress, 1st session (12 February 1916) vol. 53, pt. 3, p. 2442. [X509]

Call to convene a Constitutional Convention to abolish polygamy which is still begin practiced in some places.

[1401] Cummings, Horace H., "Latter-day Saints' Schools", in Biennial Survey of Education, 1916-18, vol. I, Bulletin 1919, No. 88. Washington: Govt. Print. Off., 1921, pp. 590-594. [I16.3:916-918/88]

Cummings, General Superintendent of L.D.S. Schools gives a history of Mormon Schools, a statistical report and names the schools and their enrollment, and discusses a home work project, as well as textbooks used and offered.

Xerox of relevant pages at UPB, US1C and entire original Bulletin at DLC

[1402] Cummings, Horace H. "Latter-day Saints' Schools." In Educational Work of the Churches in 1916-1918 Bulletin, 1919, no. 10, pp. 40-44. [I16.3:916-918/10]

A brief and preliminary report on Mormon schools. Gives a statistical table, with names of institutions, location, number of teachers, enrollment and average attendance.

[1403] "Latter Day Saints," pp. 333-340. In U.S. Bureau of the
Census. Religious Bodies. 1916. pt. 2. Separate
denominations. Washington: Govt. Print. Off., 1919.
[C3.2:916, C3.35:916/pt.2]

General statement of the history and doctrine of the
church, statistics of church membership, etc.

[1404] Morris, William A. "Report of the proceedings of the
thirteenth annual meeting of the Pacific Coast Branch
of the American Historical Association," p. 126. In
Annual report of the American Historical Association
for the year 1916. Vol. 1. Washington: Govt. Print.
Off., 1919. [SI4.1:916]

Summarizes a paper by Levi E. Young on town government
in the early days of Utah.

[1405] "Reorganized Church of Jesus Christ of Latter Day Saints,"
pp. 341-346. In U.S. Bureau of the Census. Religious
bodies. 1916. Pt. 2. Separate Denominations.
Washington: Govt. Print. Off., 1919. [C3.2:916,
C3.35:916/Pt.2]

General statement of the history and doctrine of the
church, statistics of church membership, etc.

Part 1 is a Summary and General Tables, and in the
index there are various pages listed under either
Church of Jesus Christ of Latter-day Saints or Mormons.
The pages lead to a variety of tables where the Mormons
are included along with other denominations.

[1406] U.S. Senate. 64th Congress. 1st Session. S 3000, "A
bill to amend the Constitution of the United States,
January 5, 1916." [Washington: Govt. Print. Off.,
1916] 1p.

Referred to the Committee on the Judiciary.

"Polygamy and polygamous cohabitation shall not exist
within the United States..."

DLC, UPB, USlC

[1407] "Withdrawal of American consular officers and other
Americans from Mexico," pp. 683-685. In Foreign
Relations of the United States, 1916. Washington:
Govt. Print. Off., 1925. [S1.1:916]

Problems of Mormons in the colonies during Pancho
Villa's raids, especially in the Casas Grandes area.

1917

"`We shall never secede from the Constitution
of the United States. We shall not stop on
the way of progress, but we shall make
preparations for future events. The South
will secede from the North, and the North
will secede from us, and God will make this

people free as fast as we are able to bear
it. They send their poor miserable creatures
to rule us. Why, it would be upon the same
principle that this church and authority
should send some poor cuss to rule me and my
family in may own house . . . But let me
tell you the yoke is now off our neck, and it
is on theirs, and the bow key is in. The day
is not far distant when you will see us as
free as the air we breathe . . . President
Young is our leader and has been ever since
the death of Joseph the Prophet. He can
govern this people with his hands in his
pockets, and they are not governed one whit
by the men that are sent here . . . We are
going to be ruled by our Father in heaven,
and the agents He sends out and appoints for
us, from this day henceforth and forever.'"

[Entry 1408]

[1408] Daines, Franklin D. "Separatism in Utah, 1847-1870," pp.
333-343. In Annual report of the American Historical
Association for the year 1917. Washington: Govt.
Print. Off., 1920. [SI4.1:917]

Mormon relations with the federal government. The
article is summarized on pp. 97-98.

[Flake 2645]

[1409] U.S. House. 65th Congress. 2d Session. H.J. Res. 177,
"Joint resolution proposing an amendment to the Constitution
of the United States, December 7, 1917." [Washington:
Govt. Print. Off., 1917] 1p.

Referred to the Committee on the Judiciary.

"Polygamy and polygamous cohabitation shall not exist
within the United States..."

DLC, UPB, US1C

[1410] U.S. Senate. 65th Congress. 1st Session. S. 109, "A
bill to provide for the refunding of certain moneys
illegally assessed and collected in the district of
Utah, April 4, 1917." [Washington: Govt. Print. Off.,
1917] 2p.

Referred to the Committee on Finance. Money collected
in 1879 from Zion's Cooperative Mercantile Institution.

DLC, UPB, US1C

1918

"The recent action of the women of the Church
of Jesus Christ of Latter Day Saints, in
Utah, in releasing wheat and flour for the
use of our allies and our own soldiers abroad
is so commendable that I wish to drop you
this line merely to assure you of my appreciation

of this service performed by the Church. It
has given me pleasure to write about this
matter to Joseph F. Smith, Anthon H. Lund,
and C. W. Penrose, first presidency, Church
of Jesus Christ of Latter Day Saints, and to
assure them of the renewed courage we get
from this generous act, both because it
yields a substantial addition of food sorely
needed by our hard-pressed allies and also
because the example is felt far outside the
field of its immediate application."

[Entry 1412]

[1411] U.S. Senate. 65th Congress. 2d Session. S. J. Res. 147,
"Joint resolution proposing an amendment to the
Constitution of the United States. April 5, 1918."
[Washington: Govt. Print. Off., 1918] 1p.

Referred to the Committee on the Judiciary.

"Polygamy and polygamous cohabitation shall not exist
within the United States..."

DLC, UPB, US1C

[1412] Welling, Milton H. (Utah) "Speech of," Congressional
Record 65th Congress, 2d session (7 June 1918) vol. 56,
pt. 8, pp. 7498-7499. [X544]

Concerning the wheat collected by the Mormon women to
feed the poor caused by the war. Some 12,331,000
pounds of wheat was supplied. Includes a letter by
Herbert Hoover thanking the women.

1919

"Winifred Graham, the well-known English
authoress, who has done much in this country
to expose Mormonism, told the World correspondent
to-day that fully 1,200 English girls have
recently been persuaded by Mormon propagandists
here to go to Utah. 'During the war,' she
said, 'the Mormons made great headway in the
United Kingdom. I hope the American authorities
will prevent the departure of these girls for
America. From reliable sources I learn that
there are 1,200 of them anxious to sail
immediately. Only last week one was bound
over in a London police court for falsification
of a passport in her efforts to go to Utah.'"

[Entry 1413]

[1413] "The Mormon Church," Congressional Record 66th Congress,
1st session (11 November 1919) vol. 58, pt. 8, pp.
8269-8270. [X561]

Speech of Reed Smoot against false articles in the
newspapers. He quotes an article by Winifred Graham,

English authoress, concerning the Mormons trying to get girls to come to Utah. Quotes The Salt Lake Commercial Club on the same subject. Mr. Henry F. Ashurst then speaks and concurs with Smoot.

[1414] "Proceedings of the Fifteenth Annual Meeting of the Pacific Coast Branch of the American Historical Association," pp. 112-113. In Annual Report of the American Historical Association for the year 1919, vol. I. Washington: Govt. Print. Off., 1923. [SI4.1:919]

Synopsis of a paper presented by A. Harvey Collins, Redlands University on "The Mormon Outpost of San Bernardino Valley."

[1415] Smoot, Reed. The Mormon Church. Speech given in the Senate of the United States, Tuesday, November 11, 1919. Washington: Govt. Print. Off., 1919. 8p.

See entry 1413 for annotation.

[Flake 8150]
UPB, US1C

[1416] U.S. House. Committee on the Public Lands. Homes for Soldiers: Hearings on H.R. 487, May 27 to June 28, 1919. Washington: Govt. Print. Off., 1919.

Pages 728-794 deals with the needs in Utah for homes for soldiers. There is some mention made, especially by William L. Hansen a Bishop in Salt Lake City, of the history of Mormon colonization in Utah.

Xerox copy of the specific pages only in UPB, US1C, Original in DLC

[1417] U.S. House. 66th Congress. 1st Session. H.J. Res. 74, "Joint resolution proposing an amendment to the Constitution of the United States, May 28, 1919." [Washington: Govt. Print. Off., 1919] 1p.

Referred to the Committee on the Judiciary.

"Polygamy and polygamous cohabitation shall not exist within the United States..."

DLC, UPB, US1C

[1418] U.S. House. Special Committee on the Case of Brigham H. Roberts. Report of the Special Committee on the case of Brigham H. Roberts of Utah, being report No. 85. 56th Congress, 1st Session: Reprinted for the use of the Special Committee appointed under authority of H.R. No. 6, concerning the right of Victor L. Berger to be sworn in as a member of the 66th Congress. Washington: Govt. Print. Off., 1919. 83p.

[Flake 9164]
CU-B, DLC

1920

"In my investigation I learned that when they first went there the country was generally barren, much the same as our own country was in the West. The same great range of mountains, the Rocky Mountains in our country, extends down through Mexico and becomes the `Sierra de Sur and Sierra Madre.' They began to cultivate the land and build homes, and soon began to have large tracts of land under cultivation, and they organized town sites and built up towns. The towns of Colonia Diaz, Colonia Juarez, Colonia Dublan, Colonia Garcia, Colonia Pacheco, Colonia Chuachupa, Colonia Morelos, Colonia San Jose, were all towns of that character, which were built up principally by the Mormon people, although, of course, a good many Mexicans live there also. When they went in there at first, especially at Colonia Pacheco, and Colonia Chuachupa, they did a good deal of trouble with the Apache Indians. That was in their early history. They got rid of those, and got the country in a condition that it could be settled.

[Entry 1421]

[1419] "The story of the theft of the land of the Colony Morelos (Mormon) in the state of Sonora, Mexico..." pp. 3253-3255. In Investigation of Mexican Affairs: Hearing before a subcommittee of the Committee on Foreign Relations, United States Senate. Washington: Govt. Print. Off., 1920. [Y4.F76/2:M57/2/v.2]

The abandonment of the colony due to the revolution in 1912.

[1420] "Testimony of Capt. S. H. Veater," pp. 1478-1494. In Investigation of Mexican Affairs: Hearing before a subcommittee of the Committee on Foreign Relations, United States Senate. Washington: Govt. Print. Off., 1920. [Y4.F76/2:M57/2/v.2]

Destruction of property in the Mormon colonies in 1912.

[1421] "Testimony of G. W. Bartch," pp. 2719-2750. In Investigation of Mexican Affairs: Hearing before a subcommittee of the Committee on Foreign Relations, United States Senate. Washington: Govt. Print. Off., 1920.
[Y4.F76/2:M57/2/v.2]

His testimony includes a discussion of the Mormon colonies in Mexico.

[1422] "Testimony of Junius Romney," pp. 2574-2590. In Investigation of Mexican Affairs: Hearing before a subcommittee of the Committee on Foreign Relations, United States Senate. Washington: Govt. Print. Off., 1920. [Y4.F76/2:M57/2/v.2]

His testimony includes the history of Mormon colonization in Mexico.

[1423] "Zion National Park, 1920," pp. 141-142. In The Annual
Report of the Secretary of the Interior for the Fiscal
Year ended June 30, 1920. Washington: Govt. Print.
Off., 1920. [I1.1:920]

The separately paged section of the Interior Departments
annual report from the Director of the National Park
Service includes a brief mention of the establishment
of Zion National Park and the discovery of Little Zion
Canyon by early Mormon pioneers as a refuge.

1921

"I am in favor of that. But I am not in
favor that even now our distinguised Speaker
should do away with our prohibition amendment
and substitute therefore an amendment prohibiting
polygamy [laughter], though I am strongly
against polygamy."

[Entry 1424]

[1424] "House Joint Res. 131," Congressional Record 67th Congress,
1st session (26 May 1921) vol. 61, pt. 2, p. 1812. [X578]

Brief debate, with much laughter over, what was apparently
an error, to substitute this polygamy constitutional
amendment for the existing prohibition amendment.

[1425] U.S. House. 67th Congress. 1st Session. H.J. Res. 131,
"Joint resolution proposing an amendment to the
Constitution of the United States, May 24, 1921."
[Washington: Govt. Print. Off., 1921] 1p.

Referred to the Committee on the Judiciary.

"Polygamy and polygamous cohabitation shall not exist
within the United States..."

DLC, UPB, US1C

[1426] U.S. House. 67th Congress. 1st Session. H.J. Res. 137,
"Joint resolution proposing an amendment to the
Constitution of the United States, May 27, 1921."
[Washington: Govt. Print. Off., 1921] 1p.

Referred to the Committee on the Judiciary.

"Polygamy and polygamous cohabitation shall not exist
within the United States..."

DLC, UPB, US1C

[1427] U.S. Senate. 67th Congress. 1st Session. S. 448, "A
bill to provide for the refunding of certain moneys
illegally assessed and collected in the district of
Utah, April 12, 1921." [Washington: Govt. Print.
Off., 1921] 1p.

Referred to the Committee on Finance.

Tax held illegally from Zion's Cooperative Mercantile
Institution, in 1879.

DLC, UPB, US1C

1922

"'It was now established, as was supposed, on
sufficient evidence, that the Mormons refused
obedience to Gentile law; that Federal
officials had been virtually driven from
Utah, and that one at least of the Federal
judges had been threatened with violence
while his court was in session; and that the
records of the court had been destroyed or
concealed. With the advice of his cabinet,
therefore, and yielding perhaps not unwillingly
to the outcry of the Republican party,
President Buchanan determined that Brigham
Young should be superseded as governor, and
that a force should be sent to the Territory,
ostensibly as a posse comitatus, to sustain
the authority of his successor.'"

[Entry 1428]

[1428] Campbell, Marius Robinson. Guidebook of the Western
United States, Part E. The Denver & Rio Grande Western
route. Washington: Govt. Print. Off., 1922. 266p.
[I19.3:707]

U.S. Geological survey, Bulletin 707.

Continuation of U.S. Geological survey, Bulletins 614.

Detailed geological information on Utah with some
historical information, pp. 218-257.

[Flake 1118]

1923

"To grant certain lands to Brigham Young
University for educational purposes . . .
Provided, That the grant hereby made is, and
the patent issued hereunder shall be, subject
to all legal rights heretofore acquired by
any person or persons in or to the above-
described premises, or any part thereof, and
now existing under and by virtue of the laws
of the United States.

[Entry 1429]

[1429] U.S. Senate. 68th Congress. 1st Session. S. 1222, "A
bill to grant certain lands to Brigham Young University
for educational purposes, December 15, 1923." [Washington:
Govt. Print. Off., 1923] 2p.

Referred to the Committee on Public Lands and Surveys.

A bill, introduced by Mr. Smoot, to grant some Wasatch
National Forest Lands to Brigham Young University.

DLC, UPB, US1C

1924

"There can be no possible reason for discriminating
against this class of American citizens. I
explained to you yesterday more in detail the
situation as it exists, and I now ask you to
direct the proper American representatives to
the above named countries to secure an order
from the proper officials of each country
named to their American representatives,
authorizing them to visa the American passports
issued to members of said Church when called
to do missionary works therein. The recent
and present policy has been very embarrassing
and burdensome to the work of the Church, and
I ask you to endeavor to have it corrected."
[Entry 1430]

[1430] "Representations by the United States against the exclusion
of American Mormon missionaries from certain European
countries," pp. 246-264. In Foreign Relations of the
United States, 1924. Vol. I. Washington: Govt.
Print. Off., 1939. [S1.1:924]

Request by Reed Smoot to negotiate with the countries
of Denmark, Norway, Sweden, Switzerland, Holland, and
South Africa to allow Mormon visas. Apparently polygamy
is still an issue in Mormon missionary activity in 1924.

[1431] U.S. House. 68th Congress. 1st Session. H.J. Res. 114,
"Joint resolution proposing an amendment to the Constitution
of the United States, January 3, 1924." [Washington:
Govt. Print. Off., 1924] 1p.

Referred to the Committee on the Judiciary.

"Polygamy and polygamous cohabitation shall not exist
within the United States..."

DLC, UPB, US1C

1925

"I do not want to detract any credit from the
Oregon Trail, but it followed the south side
of the river while the Mormon Trail follows
the north side of the river. The unfortunate
situation regarding the Oregon Trail folks is
that when the State highway system was built
through Nebraska it was built generally along
the line of the Mormon Trail, and if you now
name the Federal highway system through
Nebraska the `Oregon Trail' as outlined in
this bill with the exception of, possibly,
three points, or not to exceed 25 miles, you

are naming the highway following the Mormon
Trail the 'Old Oregon Trail,' and you will
not have 25 miles of the road anywhere near
the line of the Oregon Trial as it is historically
known to have been located. If you want the
name of the Oregon Trail where it belongs; if
you want the name of the Mormon Trail where
it belongs, and deem that you have power to
name highways, do so, but do not violate history."

[Entry 1432]

[1432] U.S. House. Committee on Roads. The Old Oregon Trail:
Hearings before the Committee on Roads, House of
Representatives, Sixty-eighth Congress, Second Session
on H.J. Res. 232, H.J. Res. 328 and S. 2053. January
23, February 13, 19, and 21, 1925. Washington: Govt.
Print. Off., 1925. [Y4.R53/2:Or3] 205p.

On pages 56, 174, Hon. E. O. Leatherwood of Utah
presents testimony on the Mormon Trail.

Also includes a reprint from the Historical Record,
Vol. 9, January 1890, which includes a list of the
fourteen companies of Ten.

[Flake 9121]
CU, DLC, NjP, UHi, ULA, UPB, USlC

1926

"Missionaries were sent out, prominent among
whom were Oliver Cowdery, Sidney Rigdon, and
Parley and Orson Pratt. Numerous churches
were organized in different States, and in
1831 headquarters were established at Kirtland,
Ohio. From the first the policy of segregating
the converts from the 'gentiles' was followed,
and in 1831 a colony of believers was settled
in Jackson County, Mo. Here they met some
opposition from their neighbors, which grew
violent in the fall of 1833 and culminated in
their being driven from the county by mob
violence."

[Entry 1433]

[1433] "Latter-day Saints," pp. 665-677. In U.S. Bureau of the
Census. Religious bodies: 1926. V. II, Separate
denominations. Washington: Govt. Print. Off., 1929,
[C3.2:926, C3.35:926/vol.2]

Statistics, with a brief history and account of the
doctrine of the church.

[1434] [Vacant]

[1435] "Reorganized Church of Jesus Christ of Latter Day Saints,"
pp. 678-687. In U.S. Bureau of the Census. Religious

bodies: 1926. V. II, Separate denominations. Washington: Govt. Print. Off., 1929. [C3.2:926, C3.35:926/vol.2]

Statistics, with a brief history and account of the doctrines of the RLDS church.

[1436] U.S. National Park Service. Glimpses of our National Monuments. Washington: Govt. Print. Off., 1926. 72p. [I29.21:M76/2/926]

Mormons mentioned at Pipe Springs National Monument, pp. 51-52, and Scotts Bluff National Monument, pp. 53-56.

1927

"This valley has been known to the Mormons since the late fifties, and Brigham Young named it Little Zion Canyon in 1861."

[1437]

[1437] U. S. National Park Service. Glimpses of our National Parks. Washington: Govt. Print. Off., 1927. 62p. [I29.6:N21/2/927]

Brief description of Zion National Park on pp. 57-59, where the Mormons are mentioned, and it is indicated that Brigham Young named it Little Zion Canyon in 1861.

1929

"This same year of 1858 saw the first recorded crossing of the Colorado from the north, by white men, since Escalante. This was accomplished by Jacob Hamblin, a well-known Mormon, a missionary and Indian agent, from Utah to the Hopi towns. An Indian guided him to the Ute ford (Crossing of the Fathers) and he used it thereafter almost yearly. These Mormons for long years were the only persons besides Navajos and Utes to cross the river anywhere. The ford, known to few, was difficult and dangerous at all times and impossible except at low water."

[Entry 1438]

[1438] U.S. National Park Service. Circular of General Information Regarding Grand Canyon National Park, Arizona. [Washington] Govt. Print. Off., 1929. 72p. [I29.6:G76/929]

Mormons, pp. 22, 24, 62. Mentions the first recorded crossing of the Colorado by white men in 1858, accomplished by Jacob Hamblin, a well-known Mormon, p. 22. Page 24 mentions Powell's expedition when the deserters tried to reach the Mormon settlements on the north.   Page 62 mentions emergency services Kaibab Trail and the Mormon Flats.

[1439] U.S. National Park Serivce. Glimpses of our National Monuments. Washington: Govt. Print. Off., 1929.   81p. [I29.21:M76/2/929]

Mormons mentioned at Pipe Springs National Monument, pp. 54-55, and Scotts Bluff National Monument, pp. 57-60.

1930

"Pipe Springs is famous in Utah and Arizona history.   In 1858 Jacob Hamblin was sent by President Brigham Young, of the Mormon Church, to visit the Hopi Indians in northern Arizona.   His party consisted of 10, including a Piute Indian guide, and so the story goes, they camped by a marvelous spring in the midst of the desert.   Hamblin was a noted rifle shot and the conversation turned on the question of marksmanship.   A wager was made that he could not shoot a hole through a handkerchief at 20 yards.   Hamblin fired several shots at the square of silk hung by the upper two corners, but the force of the bullet only swept the handkerchief back without penetrating it.   Stung by his failure and his friend's laughing remark that he could not shoot straight, Hamblin declared that if he would stick his pipe up as a target he would shoot the bottom out without breaking the bowl.   Up went the pipe and crack the rifle.   Hamblin made good his word and from that time on the spring has been called Pipe Springs."

[Entry 1440]

[1440] U.S. National Park Service. Glimpses of our National Monuments. Washington: Govt. Print. Off, 1930.   74p. [I29.21:M76/2/930]

Mormons mentioned at Pipe Springs National Monument, pp. 52-53, and Scotts Bluff National Monument, p. 57.

Author/Subject Index

Adams, George J., 31

Adams, William, 1367

Agriculture, 464, 524, 525

Aiken, Thomas, 246

Aiken party, 246

Allen, Clarence E., 1056, 1098

American Baptist Home Missionary Society, 587

American Home Missionary Society, 871

American River, 63

American Samoa, 1366

Amy, Jennie, 1191-1194, 1205; Oscar A., 1191-1194, 1205; Royal D., 1191-1194, 1205

Anti-Mormon Ring, 966

Arizona Strip, 1351-1352

Arizona Territory, 328, 941, 1002, 1167-1171
  Annexation, 1351-1352

  Mormon settlements, 525, 533

  Statehood, 1167, 1282

Armstrong, Francis, 834, 1148; George W., 76, 88

Army
  Mormon relations, 242, 243, 277

  Need for, 250, 311

Arny, W. F. M., 210

Arthur, Chester A., 529, 530, 548, 549, 559, 632, 633, 654, 655

Ascension, Mexico, 1063

Ashurst, Henry F., 1413

Atwood, R. H., 281

Austria, 498, 656

Avery, Franklin C., 1198; Thomas, 1198

Ayers or Ayres, Edwin B., 1055, 1187–1188

Babbitt, Almon W., 27, 35, 37, 39

Ballif, Serge F., 1344

Bannack Indians, 428

Barlow, James M., 674, 674a

Barnes, A. J., 429

Bartch, G. W., 1421

Baskin, Robert N., 445–446, 463a, 773, 851, 887, 910, 912, 923

Baskin vs. Cannon, 446–447

Bassett, Kate Smith, See Smith, Kate

Bassett, Sarah Ann, 841, 978; Thomas E., 757; William E., 978, 1044–1047

Bassett vs. United States, 978, 1044–1047

Bates, Edward, 159

Beale, Howard K., 159

Bean, C. C., 956, 958, 966

Bear River, 22

Beason, H. G., 949, 950, 962

Beckwith, Edward, 72

Belgium, 499

Belmont, Perry, 550

Bennett, E. J., 300; H. M., 928–929; Risden Tyler, 775, 807–808

Bergen, John, 1198

Berger, Victor L., 1418

Berne, Switzerland, 890

Bernhisel, John M., 43, 45, 48, 55, 92, 126

Berry, James H., 1318

Beveridge, Albert Jeremiah, 1319

Bierbower, V., 602

Biesinger, Thomas, 656

Bingham, John Armor, 114

Bingham County, Idaho, 757

Birney, R. Jr., 461

Black, Jeremiah Sullivan, 634

Blair, Henry W., 737; James Gorrall, 360

Blanchard, Newton C., 551

Blazzard, Caleb D., 1075-1080; James, 1075-1080; John, 1075-1080; John H., 1076, 1078; Mark H., 1076, 1078-1079; Orson D., 1076, 1078, 1079; Thomas, 1075-1080

Blazzard, Mariam, See Steers, Mariam Blazzard

Book of Mormon, 1206

Boutwell, George S., 772, 773

Boyce, William W., 115

Bradley, H., 369

Bramall, William, 504

Brandebury, Lemuel G., 45, 50, 51, 52, 54, 55

Bridger, James, 968, 1101
  Heirs of, 1117

Brigham Young Academy, 438

Brigham Young Memorial Association, 1161

Brigham Young University, 1429

Brimhall, George H., 1320

Broadhead, James Overton, 979

Brocchus, Perry E., 45, 47, 50, 51, 52, 54, 55, 160

Bromley, William H., 794

Brown, Byron W., 964; Cecelia Dibbles, 1225; Clarence T., 1225; Joseph Emerson, 557, 657, 658; Louisa, 1225; Maggie C. Shipp, 1225

Brownlow, Walter P., 1247

Buchanan, James, 90, 96, 116-121, 154, 157, 173, 194, 197, 198

Budge, William, 1019, 1028

Buford, Louis M., 1207

Bunn, William M., 659

Burr, David H., 83

Burrows, Joseph H., 552; Julius C., 553, 1293, 1304-1305, 1320

Butler, John M., 869, 870

C. O. Whittemore v. Thomas H. Cope, 996-997, 1055, 1184-1188

Cache Valley, 452

Cain, Elizabeth, 471, 489, 490; Joseph M., 471, 488-490, 644

Caine, John T., 644, 772, 773, 809, 823, 852-854, 910, 912, 913, 923, 926, 956, 966, 980-983, 1028, 1092, 1114-1115; Thomas, 826, 958

Call, Wilkinson, 557, 810, 847

Camp Douglas, 229, 280, 285
  Cannon, 264

Camp Floyd, 183
  Illiness, 199

Campbell, Allen G., 511, 517, 518, 532, 546, 558, 562, 563, 565, 605; Marius Robinson, 1428

Campbell vs. Cannon, 500, 511, 517, 518, 532, 546, 553, 554, 558, 562, 563, 565, 579, 595a, 596, 604, 605, 607, 629, 630, 644

Cannon, Amanda, 711; Angus M., Jr., 711, 733; Angus M., 708-711, 733, 1147, 1320; Clara, 711; Clara C. Mason, 733; Eliza T., 837; Emily Little, 837; George M., 711; George Q., 400, 417, 440, 446-447, 485, 500, 503, 511, 517, 518, 532, 546, 554, 558, 562, 563, 565, 567, 572, 605, 606, 834, 837, 984, 1014-1015, 1022, 1111, 1151, 1153; Lewis T., 1274; Martha Tolly, 837; Sarah, 711; Sarah Jane, 837

Cannon vs. Pratt, 462

Cannon vs. United States, 708-711

Carleton, A. B., 667, 674-677, 679-680; James H., 200, 205, 1281

Carlin Indians, 481

Carlton, A. B., 1019

Carrington, Albert, 503, 863

Carson Valley, Nevada, 49, 103, 140, 142, 172

Casas Grandes, Mexico, 1063, 1407

Cassidy, George Williams, 591, 595

Catlin, George C., 813

Cedar City, Utah, 71

Celestial marriage, 926, 1030-1032

Chandler, Jeff, 772, 773

Chapin, F. L., 1127

Chapman, Sarah A., 993-995, 1110-1111, 1125, 1136, 1213

Chapman vs. Handley, 993-995, 1110-1011, 1125, 1136, 1213

Chihuahua, Mexico, 1260

Chorpenning, George, 351

Church and State, 359, 398, 415, 417, 564, 576, 634, 641, 642, 1114-1115

Church Farm, 1148

Church property, 161, 917, 979, 1001, 1020, 1036-1037, 1086, 1112-1113, 1133, 1141, 1143, 1147-1150, 1158-1159
   Confiscation, 686, 766, 823, 835, 878, 939

   Restoration of, 1164, 1179, 1210

Civil War, 201-203, 210, 253

Clagett, William Horace, 388

Clark, Frances Carter, 840, 965; Hannah S., 840, 965; John, 870; Joseph, 840, 965; Sarah, 840, 965

Clawson, Ellen C., 667; Hiram B., 667; Rudger, 660-664, 690-695, 813a

Clawson vs. United States, 660-664, 690-695, 813a

Clayton, John Middleton, 65a-65b

Clayton, Nephi W., 748, 749, 753, 755, 932, 942

Clayton vs. Utah Territory, 747-749, 753, 755, 932, 942, 985

Clegg, Dora, 1303

Cleveland, Grover, 713-714, 855, 856, 1162-1163, 1203, 1225

Clinton vs. Englebrect, 393

Clive, J. H., 1080

Coalville, Utah, 336

Collins, Harvey, 1414; Patrick A., 775

Colonia Diaz, Mexico, 1367

Colonia Juarez, Mexico, 832

Colonia Morelos, Mexico, 1419

Colorado, 384, 385

Colorado River, 1351-1352

Comstock, Cyrus Ballou, 282

Congressional Church Women's Missionary Union, 1005

Congressional delegates
  Seating of, 541a, 644, 947, 1225-1231, 1235-1238, 1240, 1246-
  1250, 1253, 1255-1259, 1261-1263, 1270-1273, 1289, 1291-1295,
  1298-1302, 1305-1306, 1311-1316, 1318-1319, 1323-1330

Connor, Patrick Edward, 211-212, 229-244, 258-267, 281, 283-285,
  300

Contested election, 313, 315-316, 400, 417, 446-447, 485, 500,
  511, 517-518, 532, 546, 553-554, 558, 562-563, 565, 579, 595a,
  605, 607, 629-630, 644

Cook, A. L., 635

Cope, George H., 988-990, 1051, 1184-1186, 1188; Jack, 1186;
  Janet, 988-990, 1051; Jeannette, 1185, 1188; Margaret, 1051,
  1185, 1188; Mary Ann, 1186; Thomas, 996-997, 1051; Thomas H.,
  988, 990, 996-997, 1051, 1055, 1184-1188

Cope vs. Cope, 988-990, 1051

Corey, George L. Jr., 1127

Corralitos, Mexico, 1063

Corinne Reporter, 396

Cory, Winifred Graham, 1413, 1415

Cradlebaugh, John, 174, 196, 245, 246, 1218, 1286

Cragin, Aaron Harrison, 329

Craig, James, 213

Cravens, Jordan E., 556

Crismon, Charles, 489-490; Elizabeth T., 489

Critchlow, J. J., 451

Crumpacker, Edgar D., 1249

Cullom, Shelby Moore, 330, 331, 350, 665, 666

Cullom bill, 330-331, 333-335, 342-344, 347-349

Cumming, Alfred A., 121, 122, 123, 152, 161, 175, 176

Cummings, Horace H., 1390, 1401-1402

Curtis, George Ticknor, 501, 738, 750, 764; Samuel Ryan, 124

Cutler, Thomas R., 909

Daines, Franklin D., 1408

Dallin, Cyrus E., 1161

Danites, 4, 397, 552

Davis, Elisha W., 636; Samuel D., 927, 949, 950, 962

Davis vs. Beason, 927, 949-950, 986

Dawes, Henry L., 313

Dawson, John W., 201-202

DeArmond, David A., 1250

Delaware State Assembly, 1227, 1322

Democratic Party, 1116

Denmark, 502, 1215, 1251, 1275

Denominational schools, 919

Denver, J. W., 93, 94

Depew, Chauncey M., 1282

Deseret alphabet, 74, 75, 332

Deseret State, 13-14, 20, 24, 33, 37-38
    Constitution, 21, 36, 150, 224, 308, 361, 362, 373

Destroying angel, 203

Dickson, William H., 747, 753, 755, 1112

Dillingham, William P., 1323

Dinsmore, Hugh Anderson, 1226

Dinwoody, Henry, 870

District Courts, 298, 346, 358, 389, 404, 472

Dodds, P., 640

Dodge, Augustus Caesar, 65c-65d

Dodge, Grenville Mellen, 286-287, 314

Dole, William P., 214

Doty, James Duane, 247

Drake, Thomas J., 231, 235

Drum, Richard Coulter, 266-267

Du Pont, Henry A., 1325

Dubois, Fred T., 882, 887, 892, 910, 912, 923, 1028, 1304, 1306, 1324

Dubrow, H. M., 1127

Duck Valley Reserve, 481

Dwight Peck, et. al., plaintiffs and respondents, vs. Cecelia Rees, 1052-1054

Earle, George, 351

Edmunds Act, 547-548, 550-552, 556-557, 564, 573, 575, 577, 579-580, 588, 591, 594-596, 601, 603, 625, 639, 657, 666, 678, 707
  Amendments, 646, 651, 652, 698

Edmunds-Tucker Act, 735-736, 743-744, 746, 771-772, 775, 799-801, 806-810, 817, 820-826, 830-831, 847
  Amendments, 1024, 1030-1038, 1119

Education, 175, 176, 830a

Elbridge Tufts vs. Eleanore Tufts, 1072-1073

Eldredge, Horace S., 834, 837-838

Ellis, Wilhelmina C., 1320

Emery, George W., 441, 463, 463a, 464

Emigration See Immigration

Enabling Act, 1189, 1225

Endowment House, 1072-1073

Erwin Cotton Mills Co., West Durham, N.C., 1392

Etheridge, Emerson, 177

Ethier, Anthony, 248, 251

Evans, George S., 249, 254

Everett, Emma, 734

Eyring, Henry, 873

Faith healing, 199

Fanaticism, 212

Faulkner, Charles James, 128, 129

Fergus Ferguson, appellant vs. Clarence E. Allen, 1056

Ferguson, Fergus, 1056; Louisa Young, 503

Ferry, E. P., 966

Fiction, Anti-Mormon, 334

Fiftieth Ward, 1279

Finland, 728

Fitch, Thomas, 335, 363, 392

Five Civilized Tribes, 883

Foraker, Joseph B., 1293, 1326

Forney, Jacob, 130, 162

Fort Bridger, 968, 1101, 1117

Fort Douglas, 259

Fort Hall Agency, and Reservation, Idaho, 428, 535, 635

Fosnes, M. C., 1303

Foster, Stephen Clark, 178-179

France, 478

Freer, R. H., 1253, 1271

Freeze, James P., 1149-1150

Frelinghuysen, Frederick Theodore, 390, 391

Fremont, John Charles, 13-14, 18, 69, 71

Fuller, Frank, 365

Gale, Hoyt, S., 1398

Gannett, Henry, 1254

Gardner, J. F., 715

Gardo House, 1149

Garfield, James, 531

Gentiles, 172, 303

Germany, 671, 672, 987, 1220, 1274, 1344

Ghost legislature, 228

Ghost-dance religion, 1000

Gibson, Albert M., 716, 743, 772-773

Godfrey, G. L., 667, 674-677, 679-680

Gold coins, 261

Gooch, Daniel Wheelright, 180

Goodwin, Charles Carroll, 744

Gosiute Indians, 244

Graham, John C., 1246, 1267-1268

Graham, Winifred See Cory, Winifred Graham

Grand Army of the Republic, 665

Grand Canyon National Park, 1436

Grant, Ulysses S., 353, 366, 389, 393-394, 404, 430-433

Grantsville, Utah, 526

Great Basin, 323

Great Britain, 479, 504, 673, 717, 960, 987

Great Salt Lake, 476

Great Salt Lake City See Salt Lake City

Green, Levi A., 434

Green River Coal Basin, 336

Greenwood, A. B., 163

Grill, Philip, 793

Groesbeck, Nicholas H., 793

Grout, William Wallace, 1255

Gurley, Zenos Hovey, 561

Hafen, Lyman, 672; Johann George, 672

Hague, James Duncan, 336

Hale, Susan G., 134

Hall, Benjamin F., 203

Hamblin, Jacob, 223, 1438

Hamburg American Packet Co., 1105, 1108

Hamlin, John Henry, 1320

Hampton, Brigham Y., 756

Handcart pioneers See Mormon pioneers

Handley, Benjamin T., 993, 1011, 1125; Charles T., 1011; Elizabeth, 994-995, 1010-1011, 1136; Emma N., 1011; George, 993-995, 1010,

1213; Harry L., 993; Harvey, 1011; John, 993, 1010-1011; William F., 1011

Hans Nielsen, petitioner, 856a, 857-859, 861

Hansen, William L., 1416

Harding, Stephen S., 215, 231, 235, 250, 257

Harris, B. D., 45, 50-52, 54-55; Emma, 907; John, 907; Thomas F., 908

Harrison, Benjamin F., 991-992, 1057-1058, 1126, 1225

Harvey, Thomas H., 6, 10

Hatch, A. C., 640

Hatton, Charles, 505

Hawn's Mill, 966

Hayden, Fredinand V., 367-369, 452

Hayes, Rutherford B., 480, 506-507

Haymore, M. S., 1368

Hazelton, George Cochrane, 562

Hazen, H. B., 311

Henderson, Hester, 930

Hendrickson, John, 930

Herman, Hoyt, Jr., 1197

Herriman, O. P., 1127

Hewitt, Abram S., 564

Heywood, Joseph L., 298

Hickman, Josiah, 1320

Higbee, Elias, 2

Hill, Mary Jane, 1075-1080

Hintze, F. F., 1221

Historian Office, 1149

Hoge, E. D., 667, 674-677, 679-680

Holeman, John H., 40, 41

Home industry, 56

Homesteading, 68, 447

Hooper, William H., 299, 313, 315-319, 337-340, 343, 384-385, 395-396, 416

Hoover, Herbert, 1412

Hopkins, Albert Jarvis, 1327

Hopt, Frederick, 668-670

Hopt vs. Utah, 668-670

House, John Ford, 563

Houston, Samuel, 76a-76b

How, John, 481

Howe, Richard, 1075-1080

Hughes, John Taylor, 12

Humphreys, A., 181

Hungary, 498, 656

Hurt, Garland, 80, 88, 95

Idaho, 516, 578, 659, 715, 752, 769, 769a, 830a, 865, 874, 882, 888, 892, 927-929, 940, 949, 950, 962, 973, 986, 1007-1008, 1019, 1029a, 1290, 1303
  Election laws, 973

  Legislative assembly, 969

  Mormon settlements, 461

  Mormon teachers, 862, 892, 945-946

  Statehood, 951, 976, 980-983, 1012, 1018, 1021, 1027-1028, 1029a, 1043

  Suffrage, 950

Iliff, T. C., 1225

Illinois, 147, 151
  General Assembly, 1376

Immigration, 206, 268, 317, 425, 477, 682, 818, 1068, 1068a-1068b, 1102, 1105, 1108, 1118, 1122, 1254, 1316a
  Germany, 987

  Great Britain, 64, 479, 504, 832, 960, 987, 1108

  Land tenure, 206

  Mexico, 873

  Netherlands, 484

  Northern Europe, 64

Italy, 482, 508

Ives, Joseph C., 105

J & R. H. Porter, and Co., 166, 604, 608, 623

J. C. Irwin & Co., 166, 647

J. D. Page, respondent, vs. the Utah Commission, 1195-1197

Jack, James, 747-749, 755, 932, 942; Mary Ann, 1055, 1186-1188

Jennings, James E., 672; William, 489-490

Jensen, Jens Jorgen, 1215; Thomas P., 1251

Jenson, Andrew, 1320

Johnston, David Emmons, 1256

Jones, George Washington, 565; Henry, 246

Joseph P. Ledwidge, respondent, vs. George H. Matson, 1127-1128

Juab Stake Academy, 1172

Judicial system, 380, 385, 391, 408, 410, 412-414, 418, 421-423

Kane, Thomas, 317

Kanesville, Iowa, 26, 29, 30

Kearns, Thomas, 1296, 1297

Keitt, L. M., 182

Kelley, E. L., 561

Kempster, Walter, 1105

Kershaw, Andrew, 906; Rose W., 906

Kessler, E. A., 1080; Edward A., 1055, 1187-1188

Kimball, Heber C., 132; James N., 564a; Sarah M., 751

King, Clarence, 336

Kingdom of God, 576, 849

Kinney, John Fitch, 259, 270-273

Knight Woolen Mills Company, 1387

Knox, Philander Chase, 1328-1330

LaMar, Lucius Quintus Cincinnatus, 557

Landis, Charles Beary, 1257

Lanham, Samuel W. T., 1271

Larkin, Elijah A., 1220

Larsen, Andrew, 841; Joseph, 1215

Late Corporation of the Church of Jesus Christ of Latter-day
Saints vs. The United States, 815-816, 835, 844, 867-870, 931,
934-937, 954, 998, 1110-1113, 1120, 1129, 1133, 1137-1138, 1144-
1146, 1156

Leatherwood, E. O., 1432

Ledwidge, Joseph P., 1127-1128

Lee, John D., 454; Willis Thomas, 1398

Leffler, Shepherd, 29, 30

Leggett, William, 1055, 1187-1188

Letcher, Jerrold R., 1195-1197

Lewis, Micajah G., 274, 275

Liberal Party, 628, 1098, 1114-1115

Lillywhite, [Bishop], 1368

Lindsay, John S., 676a, 677

Little, James T., 667

Little Cottonwood Mining district, 521

Little Zion Canyon, 1423

Littlefield, Charles Edgar, 1258, 1271

Liverpool, England, 832

Lloyd, Mary, 930

Lockwood, Daniel W., 357

Logan, Utah, 1246

Logan Temple, 688, 705, 1054

Lord, Eliot, 637

Lund, Anthon H., 1221; C. N., 1215

Lyon, Caleb, 67

McBride, J. R., 966; Thomas, 526, 532

McCall, Samuel W., 1259

McClernand, John A., 938

McCune, H. F., 673

McDonald, Angus, 1000; Joseph E., 816, 869-870, 910, 912, 923

McDowell, Irvin, 276

McGrorty, William, 313, 315-316

McGrorty vs. Hooper, 313, 315-316

McKean, James B., 363

McLeod, Norman, 296

Mail contracts, 351

Manifesto, 977, 984, 991-992, 1009, 1022, 1041, 1067

Marks, William, 31

Marriage, 440
  Licenses, 426, 427

  Registration, 401, 407, 544, 696, 701

Martin, Henry, 204

Massachusetts, 593
  Legislature, 1374

Matson, George H., 1127-1128

Maxwell, George R., 400, 417, 485

Maxwell vs. Cannon, 400, 417, 485

Mayhugh, John S., 638

Mead, Elwood, 1283

Meadow Valley, Nevada, 274, 327

Merrill, Charles E., 1320

Messiah, 1109

Methodist Episcopal Church, 574, 592, 1346

Mexico, 512, 873, 905, 1063, 1367
  Mormon Colonies, 1207, 1260, 1367-1369, 1407, 1419-1422

Michigan, 31
  Legislature, 589, 1377

Miles, John H., 457, 509, 510, 513; Jonathan D., 533

Miles vs. United States, 483, 509-510, 513

Miller, Samuel H., 573

Milo, George, 289

Mining industry, 243, 260, 274, 294-295, 322, 336, 464, 521

Minniss, J. F., 640

Missionary activity, 477
  Austria, 498, 656

  Belgium, 499

  Denmark, 502, 1215, 1251, 1275

  Europe, 1347, 1430

  France, 478

  Germany, 671-672, 1220, 1274, 1344

  Great Britain, 479

  Hungary, 498, 656

  India, 673, 717

  Italy, 482, 508

  Mexico, 512

  Norway, 522, 536, 728

  South Africa, 1430

  Sweden, 522, 536, 728

  Switzerland, 770, 890, 891

  Turkey, 894

Missouri, 147, 151
  Persecutions, 1-4

  Woman's Suffrage Association, 631

Mix, Charles E., 97

Moapa River Reserve Agency, 429

Monaghan Baptist Church, Greenville, S.C., 1391

Monchard, M., 277

Montana Legislation, 1357

Montgomery, Marcus Whitman, 871

Mooney, James, 1000

Morey, Henry L., 575

Morgan, John Tayler, 557

Mormon Battalion, 7-9, 11, 15, 19, 23, 228, 317, 439, 1371

Mormon Bibliography, 1353

Mormon Church
  Business, 1297

  Coal lands, 1147

  Court cases, 1090, 1131

  Disincorporation, 619, 698, 815-816, 844, 866-870, 895-896, 914, 931, 934-937, 954, 998, 1110-1113, 1120, 1133, 1137-1138, 1144-1146, 1156

  History, 591, 772-773, 1293

  Incorporation, 42, 186, 195

  Land policy, 336

  Politics, 1094

  Power of, 531

  Statistics, 193, 999, 1002, 1017, 1025, 1307, 1356, 1403, 1433

  Succession, 300, 1304

  Turkey, 1221

  Vote control, 438, 442

Mormon Control Act, 547, 806

Mormon cooperatives, 520

Mormon cow, 66, 76a-76b, 78, 87

Mormon depredations, 246

Mormon doctrine, 5, 15, 772-773, 827-829
  Apologetics, 772-773

  Second Coming, 1109

Mormon ferry, 22, 169

Mormon hierarchy, 160, 385, 388, 395
  Abuse by, 160

Mormon industry, 369, 372

Mormon pioneers, 167, 1398, 1423

Mormon roads, 357, 375

Mormon schools, 475, 845, 884-886, 919, 958, 1038, 1106, 1152, 1178, 1206, 1366, 1389-1390, 1401-1402
  American Samoa, 1366

Voter rights, 667, 674-677, 679-681, 699, 719, 779, 782, 833, 1195-1197, 1208-1209

Mormons have stepped down and out of Celestial Government - The American Indians have stepped up and into Celestial Government, 1000

Morrill, Justin S., 85, 98-99, 136

Morrill Act, 73, 208-209, 216-220, 225, 306, 539
  Repeal, 443, 447, 497

Morris, William A., 1404

Morrisites, 237

Morse, Elijah Addison, 1132

Moulton, Samuel W., 577

Mountain Meadows Massacre, 162-163, 165, 167, 197-198, 205, 207, 223, 246, 315, 329, 334, 378, 434, 454, 463, 463a, 466, 697, 773, 1281

Muddy settlements, Nevada, 327, 357

Muller, Jacob, 1274

Murphy, Jesse J., 675-677; N. O., 1002

Murphy vs. Ramsey, 667, 674-677, 679-681, 719

Murray, Eli H., 514-515, 537, 641-642, 682-683, 702, 720, 725, 784

Musser, A. Milton, 732; Annie Segmiller McCullough, 732; Belinda Pratt, 732; Joseph B., 1434; May, 732

National Home Missionary Society, 864

National Reform Association, 1392

Nauvoo, Illinois, 317, 552

Navajo Indians, 453, 622

Nebraska Legislature, 1358-1359

Negro, 56

Neil, John B., 516, 578

Nelson, Thomas Amos Rogers, 184-185

Netherlands, 484

Nevada, 168, 299, 327-328
  Mormon settlement, 357, 637

New Mexico statehood, 1167

Newman, Angie F., 795, 803, 913

Newson, Ruth A., 993, 1011

Nielsen, Anna Lavinia, 861; Caroline, 861; Hans, 856a, 857-859, 861

Nilsson, Peter, 536

Noell, Thomas Estes, 304, 305

Non-Mormons see Gentiles

Nord Deutscher Lloyd, 1105

Norrell, Albert G., 1195, 1197

Norris, Moses, 67a-67b

Norway, 522, 536, 728, 987, 1288

Oates, William C., 579

Oatman, Olive, 105

Ohio Legislature, 1360

Oneida Co., Idaho, 1052-1054

Oregon Legislature, 1378

Oscar A. Amy, deceased vs. Royal D. Amy, 1191-1194, 1205

Ottinger, George M., 346

Ouray Indian Agency, Utah, 640, 715, 745

Overland mail, 236, 238-239, 241, 244, 251, 276

Owen, Caroline, 457, 513; Ephraim Jr., 1

Paasch, Hannah, 836

Paddock, A. S., 667, 674-677, 679, 680

Paden, William, 1225

Page, Henry, 1176; J. D., 1195-1197; John E., 5

Paine, Halbert Eleazer, 485, 517, 518

Paiute Indians, 622

Parish, Orine, 246

Parowan, Utah, 71

Patten, James I., 486

Peale, A. C., 369

Peay, George T., 836

Peck, Dwight, 1052-1054

Peelle, Stanton J., 580

Penal institutions, 472

Pendleton, George Hunt, 557

People, etc. respondents, vs. John D. Lee, 454

People of Utah Territory, respondent, vs. B. Y. Hampton, 756

People vs. Hopt, 684

People's Party of Utah, 1040, 1050, 1065, 1067, 1114-1115, 1158-1159

Perpetual Emigrating Fund Company, 44, 74-75, 82, 426-427, 682, 686, 818, 855, 863, 875, 939, 1001

Perris, Fred T., 352, 364

Perris v. Higley, 352, 364, 415

Perry, C. A., & Co., 341

Petitions, 519, 534, 555, 570, 574, 581-584, 685, 689, 721-724, 757-763, 819-822, 876-881, 943-945, 1165

Pettigrew, J. R., 667, 674-677, 679, 680

Philips, John F., 1175

Pipe Springs National Monument, 1436, 1439-1440

Plural marriage, 349, 381-383, 926

Plymouth Church of Portland, Maine, 585

Polygamy, 65c-65d, 67, 67a-67d, 77, 91, 136, 138-139, 159, 174, 257, 300, 304-305, 329, 353, 366, 385, 395, 421-422, 424, 430, 433, 438, 463, 463a, 480, 487, 501, 526, 531, 537, 554, 560, 571, 585-587, 589-590, 592-593, 602a, 624, 627, 655, 686, 688, 696, 702, 725, 776, 804, 805, 819, 871, 885-887, 889, 910, 912, 923, 938, 952-953, 956-957, 959, 966, 977, 1007-1009, 1031-1032, 1041, 1057-1058, 1066-1067, 1094-1096, 1098, 1100, 1142, 1177, 1218, 1234-1236, 1251, 1286, 1293, 1296-1297, 1312-1313, 1337-1341, 1346

 Amnesty, 991, 1071, 1091, 1093, 1124, 1126, 1135, 1139, 1162-1163, 1181-1183, 1190, 1200, 1225

 Arizona, 1314

 Constitutional amendment, 495, 611, 649-650, 767-768, 780-781, 783, 802, 842-843, 897, 899-904, 926a, 963, 969a, 1103, 1232-1233, 1238-1239, 1241-1245, 1265-1266, 1269, 1276-1278, 1280-1281, 1284-1285, 1287, 1309-1310, 1316, 1321-1322, 1331-1336, 1342, 1345, 1348-1350, 1354, 1357-1362, 1370, 1374-1383, 1385-

1386, 1391–1392, 1394–1395, 1397, 1399–1400, 1406, 1409, 1411, 1417, 1424–1426, 1431

Convictions, 855–856, 882, 898, 925, 946, 958, 1014–1015, 1050, 1065

Court cases, 436–437, 439, 441–443, 448, 456, 465, 469, 470, 483, 509–510, 513, 564a, 660–664, 690–695, 708–711, 732–734, 739–742, 750–751, 785–794, 813a, 814, 834, 836–841, 856a, 857–859, 861, 906–909, 927–930, 964–965, 978, 988–990, 993–997, 1010–1011, 1016, 1026, 1044–1047, 1051, 1055, 1059–1061, 1075–1080, 1125, 1136, 1184–1188, 1191–1194, 1198, 1205, 1213, 1219, 1283a, 1312

Courts, 412–414

Disfranchisement, 459, 568, 976, 980–983, 1003–1004, 1062

Divorce, 658, 686, 1072–1073

Home life, 713–714

Homesteading, 68, 73

Idaho, 516, 578, 716, 769–769a, 854, 874, 882, 888, 898, 927–929, 940, 945–946, 949–950, 973, 986, 1029a

Immigration, 477, 484, 1048, 1068, 1068a–1068b, 1102, 1105, 1108, 1118, 1122, 1201, 1316a, 1393

Incidence, 854, 882, 887

Indians, 535, 638, 745

Inheritance, 686, 988–990, 993–997, 1010–1011, 1051, 1055, 1059–1061, 1075–1080, 1125, 1136, 1184–1188, 1191–1194, 1205, 1213
Land tenure, 700, 769, 833

Lawlessness, 98–99

Legalization of, 354, 360, 371

Legislation, 84–85, 96a, 177–180, 184–185, 187–188, 190–192, 194–195, 208–209, 215–221, 225, 290, 324–326, 330–331, 334, 342–345, 347–349, 376–377, 380, 392, 399, 401–403, 406–407, 425, 431–432, 473, 538–545, 547, 550–552, 612–620, 625–627, 646, 651–652, 698–701, 716, 718–719, 735, 744, 746, 763, 776, 778, 799–801, 806, 818a, 926a, 977, 1023–1024, 1029–1031, 1034–1035, 1062, 1089, 1119

Legislation, favorable, 333, 335, 337–340, 356, 736, 743

Pardons, 874

Petitions see Petitions

Prosecution, 399, 402, 410, 418, 726

Public officers, 1234, 1240, 1246, 1267–1268, 1290, 1303

Punishment, 188, 310, 377

Recruitment, 1347, 1413, 1415

States right, 182, 191

Statute of limitation, 493-494, 540, 543, 588

Suppression, 189-190, 290, 294, 324, 376, 391, 394, 506, 507

Test oath, 384, 455, 538-539, 541-542, 598, 600, 609, 612, 617-618, 643, 653, 678, 712, 758-759, 812, 827-829, 830a, 846, 865, 928-929, 962, 1012, 1018-1019, 1023, 1027-1029, 1033, 1040, 1043, 1155

Twin Relics, 86, 329

Woman suffrage, 320, 355, 405, 409, 651, 703, 705, 737, 766, 803

Women, 350, 516

Polygamy laws
Enforcement of, 514-515, 529-530, 725

Mormon endorsement, 872

Repeal, 738

Violations of, 230

Polygamy trials, 687, 706, 739-742, 750
Jury selection, 437, 449, 456-458, 539, 668-670, 684, 793, 1016

Witnesses, 545, 614, 698, 841, 909

Pomeroy, Charles, 344

Pope, John, 291

Porter, James, 166, 312, 387, 604, 608, 623, 704, 731, 774, 796; Richard H., 166, 312, 387, 604, 608, 623, 704, 731, 774, 796

Postal service, 164

Postmasters, 1246, 1267-1268, 1290, 1303

Potter, Duff, 246

Powell, John Wesley, 321

Powers, Horace Henry, 1261

Pratt, Arthur, 675-676, 747-749, 753, 755, 932, 942, 985, 1059-1061; Harmel, 674, 674a, 679-680; Mary Anne M., 676a, 677; Milando, 1059-1061; Nilson, 673; Orson, 1059-1061

Presbyterian Church, 560, 586, 627

Preuss, Charles, 13

Price, George Frederick, 292-296; Walter L., 1080

Priesthood, 472

Probate courts, 352, 364, 386, 389, 395, 404, 410, 412-415, 420, 434-435, 564a, 747-749, 753, 755, 932, 942, 985, 1129

Prostitution, 756, 871

Provo, Utah, 76, 196, 1218, 1246, 1286

Provost guard, 262

Pyramid Lake Reserve, 434

Raft River, Idaho, 275

Ramsden, Mary E., 906

Ramsey, Alexander, 667, 674-677, 679-680

Randall, Alfred, 679-680; Mildred E., 679-680

Ranney, Ambrose A., 596

Rawlins, Joseph L., 1123, 1134, 1234

Raymond, Rossiter Worthington, 322

Red Star Line, 1105, 1108

Reed, Samuel, 278; Thomas Brackett, 826

Rees, Cecilia, 1052-1054

Religious liberty, 215, 764-765

Reorganized Church of Jesus Christ of Latter Day Saints, 281, 561, 594, 1006, 1175, 1304
  Statistics, 1307, 1405, 1435

Republican Party, 1116

Reynolds, George, 436-437, 439, 441-443, 465, 469-470, 491

Reynolds vs. United States, 436-437, 439, 441-443, 465, 469-470, 491

Rice, Norman L., 300

Rich, Ben E., 1303; Henry A., 1344

Richards, Charles, 1220; Franklin S., 564a, 750, 765, 772, 773, 856a, 887, 910, 912, 923, 948, 956, 958, 966, 1098, 1114-1115, 1279; J. T., 1279

Roberts, B. H., 947, 1225-1231, 1235-1238, 1240, 1246-1250, 1253, 1255-1259, 1261-1263, 1270-1273, 1320, 1418; Cecilia Dibbles, 1225; Louisa, 1225

Robinson, J. W., 416

Rogers, Lester T., 1129; William H., 223

Romney, George, 870; Junius, 1422

Ronnow, Charles C., 1251, 1275

Rusling, James F., 309, 375

Salt Creek, 241

Salt Lake City, 17, 61, 262, 309, 372, 648, 1218, 1279, 1286
  Land Tenure, 471, 488-490

Salt Lake Telegraph, 287

Salt Lake Temple, 521

Salt Lake Tribune, 396

Sampson, A. J., 1063

San Bernardino, 62-63, 200, 1414

San Carlos Agency, Arizona, 533

Schisms, 16

Schools, 175-176
  Elections, 727

  Idaho, 752

  Non-Mormon, 528

Schow, Andrew P., 1026

Schurz, Carl, 526

Scotland, 961

Scott, William Lawrence, 830

Scotts Bluff National Monument, 1436, 1439-1440

Second Coming, 1109

Second Manifesto, 1293

"Separatism in Utah, 1847-1870," 1408

Seville, William P., 134

Sheen, Isaac, 16

Sherman, Hoyt Jr., 1195, 1197

Shipp, Maggie C., 1225

Shoshone and Bannack Agency, Wyoming, 486, 505

Shoshone Indians, 83, 130, 638

Shoup, George Laird, 951

Simms, William Emmett, 189, 190

Simpson, Hannah Powell, 734; James Hervey, 167, 323; Thomas, 734

Sinclair, Charles E., 135

Sioux Indians, 1000

Skinner, Charles Rufus, 601

Smith, Christina, 839; David H., 1263; James, 839; John H., 1114-1115, 1320; Joseph F., 570, 1111, 1291, 1293, 1326, 1346; Joseph III, 300, 594; Joseph Jr., 4; Kate, 841, 978, 1044-1047; M. A., 956; Orson, 1246, 1267; Sarah Jane, 839; Truman, 32, 33; William, 16, 20, 28

Smith, Truman, 67c-67d

Smoot, Reed, 1289, 1291-1295, 1298-1302, 1305-1306, 1311-1316, 1318-1320, 1323-1330, 1332-1341, 1368, 1387, 1413, 1415, 1429-1430; William A., Jr., 672

Snow, Adeline, 791; Caroline, 790; Eleanor, 790-791; Eliza R., 467, 491; Harriet, 790-791; Lorenzo, 602, 750, 765, 785-788, 790-792, 814; Mary, 790-791; Minnie, 790-791; Phoebe, 790-791; Sarah, 790; Zerubbabel, 55, 359, 398

Snow vs. United States, 359, 398, 602, 785-788

Sonora, Mexico, 1419

Sorenson, Mary, 836

South Dakota House of Representatives, 1350

Spalding, F. S., 1392

Spencer, Emily, 513

St. George, Utah, 357

Stal, Ola Nilsson, 536

Stansbury, Howard, 17, 53, 61, 317

Steers, Mariam Blazzard, 1075-1080

Steptoe, E. J., 79

Stevenson, Edward A., 769-769a, 830a, 888, 1007-1008, 1028

Stewart, Sarah Jane, 1075-1080

Stone, A. I., 1127; E. A., 535; Ralph W., 1398

Strang, James J., 31

Stringfellow, George, 489-490; Samuel, 488-490

Stringfellow v. Cain, 471, 488-490

Struble, Isaac S., 889, 1012

Sutton, Warner P., 873

Sweden, 522, 536, 728

Switzerland, 492, 523, 729, 770, 813, 890, 891, 961, 1289

Syracuse, New York, 590

Tatlock, Erasmus W., 1195, 1197

Taylor, Adelbert A., 1344; John, 132, 738, 1320; Miles, 191; Robert W., 1237, 1271

Telegraph, 24, 137, 148

Temple Block, 1001

Temple endowments, 300, 1283a

Temple Lot Case, 1175

Temple work
   Inheritance, 1052-1054

Tennessee Legislature, 1362

Territorial officers, 43, 45-47, 70, 100, 135, 196, 231, 298, 301, 358, 730, 1121

Territory vs. Evans, 1013

Thatcher, George W., 1195, 1197; Moses, 512

Thayer, Eli, 192

Theocracy, 52, 64, 65a-65b, 90, 138-139, 160, 212, 374, 466, 526, 683, 697, 720, 769, 819, 826, 849, 851, 871, 910, 912-913, 920-921, 923, 966, 1007-1008, 1023, 1116, 1208-1209, 1296-1297, 1312-1313, 1337-1341

Thomas, Arthur L., 537, 952-953, 1014-1015, 1066-1067, 1093-1094; L., 222

Thompson, Jennie V., 1129; John B., 138-139; Robert B., 2

Thomson, James, 1198

Thomson vs. Avery, 1198

Tithing, 537

Tithing Yard, 1001, 1147, 1150

Tooele Valley, Utah, 244

Tucker, John Randolph, 603, 831; Pomeroy, 823

United States, respondent, vs. Thomas F. Harris, 908

United States, respondent, vs. Thomas R. Cutler, 909

United States, respondent, vs. Thomas Simpson, 734

United States, respondent, vs. Tithing Yard and Offices and James P. Freeze, 1150

United States, respondent, vs. William E. Bassett, 841

United States, respondent, vs. William H. Bromely, 794

United States vs. the Late Corporation of the Church of Jesus Christ of Latter-day Saints, See the Late Corporation of the Church of Jesus Christ of Latter-day Saints

United States vs. Lorenzo Snow, 602, 785-788

United States vs. S. B. Christensen, 1016

United States vs. Tithing Yard, 1147

University of Deseret, 438, 496, 609

Utah
  Boundaries, 318-319

  Constitution, 440, 1202

  Government relations, 1408

  History, 1042, 1428

  Pioneers, 682

  Population, 1264

  Schools, 108-109, 175-176

  Statehood, 272-273, 317, 363, 365, 374, 376, 379, 384-385, 440, 448, 501, 566, 599, 811, 819, 848, 851, 876-881, 887, 893, 910-913, 915, 920-921, 923-924, 926, 943-944, 948, 955-957, 959, 969, 971-972, 1057-1058, 1081-1085, 1087-1089, 1096-1099, 1104, 1116, 1123, 1130, 1132, 1134, 1139, 1142, 1157, 1160, 1166-1171, 1177, 1189, 1199, 1203

Utah Commission, 549, 559, 597, 598, 610, 632, 633, 643, 653, 654, 687, 688, 706, 712, 726, 730, 767, 768, 817, 827-829, 846, 885, 886, 925, 962, 970, 974, 977, 991, 1009, 1049-1050, 1062, 1065, 1070-1071, 1091-1092, 1095, 1124, 1154-1155, 1173-1174, 1190, 1195-1197, 1200, 1204, 1208-1209, 1216

Utah Democratic Territorial Committee, 576

Utah Expedition, 96, 101-102, 104, 106-129, 131-134, 135, 137, 141, 143-145, 147-149, 151-158, 164, 166, 171, 173, 312, 321, 341, 387, 604, 608, 623, 647, 703, 731, 774, 796, 968, 1101, 1117, 1218, 1252, 1286, 1355
  Claims, 166

Veater, S. H., 1420

Vermont Legislature, 1380-1381

Vest, George Graham, 557, 847

Virgin River, 357

Wagon roads, 167, 169-170

Waite, Charles Burlingame, 316; Charles V., 231, 235

Walbridge, Hiram, 73

Wallace, William S., 251

Ward, Artemus, 304-305

Wasatch National Forest, 1429

Washington Legislature, 1361

Washington, Joseph E., 1043, 1157

Washington (state), 1354

Watkins, C. N., 928, 929, 973

Watson, Helen, 1279; James, 870

Watts, Lucy D., 1076-1078

Welling, Milton H., 1412

Wells, Emmeline B., 467, 497

West, Caleb W., 804-805, 848-849, 920-922, 958, 966, 1098, 1114-1115, 1158-1159, 1180-1183, 1202

West, Joseph A., 772, 773, 804

Western College of Women, 1333

Western Shoshone Agency, Nevada, 481, 638

Wheat, 1412

Wheeler, George Montague, 327-328, 357, 476

Whipple, A. W., 62

White, Barnard, 789; Jane Fyfe, 789

Whittemore, C. O., 996-997, 1055, 1184-1188

Widstoe, Osborne J. P., 1389

Williams, Rufus K., 564a; Sarah Ann, 978, 1044-1047; Thomas, 1252; Zina Young, 497

Williamson, R. W., 63

Willis, William, 673

Wilson, Edgar, 1273; Jeremiah M., 910, 912, 923, 957, 971, 1019, 1028; John, 19, 25; John T., 956

Wisconsin Legislature, 1375, 1379, 1382

Woman suffrage, 304-305, 320, 350, 355, 405, 409, 464, 467-468, 621, 631, 766, 803

Woman's Christian Temperance Union of Esceola, Nebraska [i.e. Osceola], 1311

Women's Reading Club, Rutherford, N. J., 1311

Women's Relief Corps, Salt Lake City, 972

Wood, Fernando, 270, 271

Woodruff, Wilford, 977, 984, 992, 1009, 1014-1015, 1022, 1098, 1111, 1172

Woods, George L., 381-383, 426-427

Woolley, H. S., 928-929, 973

Woolley vs. Watkins, 928-929, 973

World War I, 1412, 1416

Worthington, A. S., 1302

Wright, George, 252-255, 280

Wyss, Marie, 523

Young, Adelia, 1191-1194, 1205; B. S., 1186; Dora L., 503; Emeline A., 503; Levi E., 1404; Willard, 461, 476

Young, Brigham, 38, 41, 46, 49, 55-59, 64-65, 67, 74-75, 81, 83, 88-90, 92-93, 102, 108-109, 138-139, 153, 160, 210, 212, 228, 232, 265, 269, 279, 284, 288-289, 297, 302, 322, 375, 462, 471, 488-490, 1161, 1180
   Connor Fued, 232-233, 258-259

   Disloyalty of, 261

   Estate, 503

   Indian Agent, 223, 226

   Power of, 234, 255, 259, 283, 289, 292-294

   Will, 503

Young Ladies' Mutual Improvement Association, 496

Young Men's Mutual Improvement Association, 496

Zion National Park, 1423, 1437

Zions Cooperative Mercantile Institute (ZCMI), 1363-1365, 1372-1373, 1384, 1388, 1396, 1410, 1427

Title Index

amendment to the   Constitution ... prohibiting polygamy, 1265

Hearings before the Committee on Territories in regard to the admission of Utah, 958, 966

Hearings before the Committee on Territories in relation to the exercise of the elective franchise in the Territory of Utah, 1029

Henry Page. Letter from the acting Secretary of the Treasury, 1176

Hester Henderson, ex parte, 930

Home rule for Utah, 1115

Homes of Soldiers, 1416

Immigration Investigation, 1068, 1105

Immigration of Aliens into the United States, 1316a

In equity. The United States of America, plaintiff, vs. The Late Church of Jesus Christ of Latter-day Saints, 931

In Equity. The United States of America, plaintiff vs. The Perpetual Emigrating Fund Company, 863

In opposition to the resolution reported from the Committee on Priviledges and Elections "that Reed Smoot is not entitled to a seat", 1328-1330

In re Reed Smoot, 1316

In re Rudger Clawson, 813a

In re Snow, 814

In re the estate of George Handley, 993

In support of the resolution ... "That Reed Smoot is not entitled to a seat as a senator, 1305

In the matter of Brigham H. Roberts, 1225

In the matter of Senate bill 10, 746

In the matter of the contested election from Utah Territory ... George Q. Cannon, 532

In the Matter of the Estate of George Handley, 994-995, 1213

In the Matter of the Estate of Orson Pratt, 1059-1060

In the Matter of the Estate of Orson Pratt, Milando Pratt, and others, appellants, v. Arthur Pratt, 1061

In the matter of the estate of Oscar A. Amy, 1191-1194, 1205

In the matter of the estate of Thomas Cope, 996-997

On the amendment to the bill to supress polygamy, 810

Pacific wagon roads, 169

Papers in case of C. A. Perry & Co., 341

Papers in the case of Baskin vs. Cannon, 447

Pay and mileage allowed George Q. Cannon, 606

People, etc., respondents, v. John D. Lee, 454

People of the Territory of Utah, ex relations the Board of
    Education vs. Utah Commissioners, 1064

People of the Territory of Utah, on the relation of Wm. H.
    Dickson, 755

People of Utah Territory, respondent, v. B. Y. Hampton, 756

People v. Hopt, 684

Perris v. Higley, 415

Petition of the citizens of Utah Territory praying that the
    elective franchise ... be restricted to those who give
    unqualified allegiance, 1040

Petition of the residents of Utah Territory, 379

Petition of 22,626 women of Utah, 448

Plea for religious liberty and the rights of conscience, 764-765

Polygamous marriages in Utah, 360

Polygamy, 776, 1089

Polygamy [Hearing, February 25, 1902], 1280

Polygamy in the territories of the United States, 194

Polygamy in Utah, 180, 344, 702

Polygamy in Utah - a dead issue, 854

Polygamy in Utah and New England contrasted, 658

Polygamy question, 192

Polygamy. Speech of Hon. Charles R. Skinner, of New York, 601

Polygamy. Speech of Hon. John Randolph Tucker of Virginia, 603,
    831

Polygamy. The work of the Industrial Christian Home Association,
    860

Population of Utah Counties and minor civil divisions, 1264

Postmasters in Idaho living in polygamy, 1303

347

349

351

Speeches of Hon. Risden T. Bennett of North Carolina, 808

State government for Utah, 365

Statistical report on the sickness and morality in the Army, 199

Stringfellow v. Cain, 471

Suffrage in Utah, 405

Suppression of polygamy in Utah, 778

Territory of Nevada, 142

Territory v. Evans, 1013

That brief, 744

To prevent persons living in bigamy or polygamy from holding any
    civil office, 609

To the Senate and House of Representatives in Congress assembled,
    771

True condition of Utah, 1099

Undemocratic–unAmerican–unconstitutional, 847

United States, appellant, v. S. B. Christensen, 1016

United States, appellant, vs. The Late Corporation of the Church
    of Jesus Christ of Latter-day Saints, 1137-1138

United States, complainant, v. Church of Jesus Christ of Latter-
    day Saints, 895-896, 954

United States, ex relations, Thomas McBride, 526

United States of America, appellant, v. The Late Corporation of
    the Church of Jesus Christ of Latter-day Saints, 1110-1111,
    1144-1146

United States of America, plaintiff, vs. Horace S. Eldredge, 834

United States of America, respondent, v. Byron W. Brown, 964

United States of America, respondent, v. Joseph Clark, 965

United States of America, respondent, vs. Lorenzo Snow, 785-788,
    790-792

United States of America vs. The late Corporation of the Church
    of Jesus Christ of Latter-day Saints, 835, 1112

United States, respondent, v. A. Milton Musser, 732

United States, respondent, v. Andrew J. Kershaw, 906

United States, respondent, v. Andrew P. Schow, 1026

353

Series Index

447-448, 473-474, 527, 598, 604-610, 622-624, 642-644, 687, 696-
697, 702-704, 706, 726, 731, 752, 767, 774-776, 778, 784, 796-
798, 803, 827, 849, 885, 892, 897-898, 905, 913-916, 918, 921,
925, 940-941, 953, 959-962, 967-970, 977, 1014, 1020-1022, 1025,
1029a, 1038-1042, 1050, 1067-1068, 1068a-1068b, 1071, 1093, 1102,
1105-1109, 1117-1118, 1124, 1139-1142, 1151-1154, 1174, 1176-
1179, 1183, 1190, 1201-1202, 1208, 1210-1211, 1216, 1218, 1222,
1238, 1266-1267, 1270, 1281, 1286, 1293, 1303, 1316, 1316a, 1371

Special Consular Reports, 987, 1288

Supreme Court Reports (U.S.), 398, 415, 462, 470, 471, 513, 663-
664, 711, 719, 814, 861, 927, 978, 985-986, 998, 1051, 1125, 1156

Territory of Utah Laws, 1089, 1161; See also Acts, Resolutions,
and Memorials, passed at ... Legislative Assembly of the Territory
of Utah.

Territory of Utah [Supreme Court] Reports, 436-437, 454, 457,
503, 684, 732-734, 756, 789-794, 813a, 836-841, 895-896, 906-909,
917, 930, 954, 964-965, 993, 1016, 1026, 1054, 1056, 1061, 1064,
1072, 1113, 1128, 1147-1150, 1184, 1197, 1205

U.S. American Republics Bureau, Monthly Bulletin, 1260

U.S. Army. Engineers School. Occasional Papers, 134

U.S. Attorney General. Annual Report, 818, 875, 939, 1001, 1090

U.S. Attorney General. Opinions, 298, 312, 387, 727, 730, 812,
846, 1131

U. S. Board of Indian Commissioners. Annual Report, 933

U.S. Bureau of American Ethnology. Annual Reports, 1000

U.S. Bureau of the Census. Reports, 193, 521, 524-525, 999,
1006, 1017, 1264, 1307-1308, 1356, 1403, 1405, 1433, 1435

U.S. Commissioner of Education. Report, 332, 438, 450, 528, 752,
845, 862, 884, 892, 918, 1172, 1206, 1366, 1389-1390

U.S. Commissioner of Indian Affairs. Annual Report, 1, 10-11,
25, 40, 59, 65, 76, 81, 89, 93-95, 97, 130, 162, 165, 181, 204,
214, 268-269, 288, 428-429, 434, 451, 453, 481, 486, 505, 533,
535, 635-636, 638, 640, 715, 745, 883

U.S. Congress. Bills, 86a, 149, 156, 195, 225, 325-326, 347a,
348, 356, 376-377, 380, 399, 401-402, 406-407, 418-422, 425, 449,
455-456, 458-459, 493-495, 538-545, 611-621, 625-627, 646-652,
698-701, 705, 735, 779-783, 799-802, 833, 842-843, 899-904, 963,
969a, 1023-1024, 1030-1037, 1103-1104, 1119, 1143, 1212, 1217,
1223-1224, 1239-1245, 1268-1269, 1276-1278, 1284-1285, 1287,
1317, 1342, 1348-1349, 1355, 1363-1365, 1370, 1372, 1383, 1386,
1388, 1394-1397, 1399, 1406, 1409-1411, 1417, 1425-1427, 1429,
1431

U.S. Department of Agriculture. Office of Experiment Stations.
Bulletin, 1283